Lecture Notes in Computer Science 7274

Commenced Publication in 1973
Founding and Former Series Editors:
Gerhard Goos, Juris Hartmanis, and Jan van Leeuwen

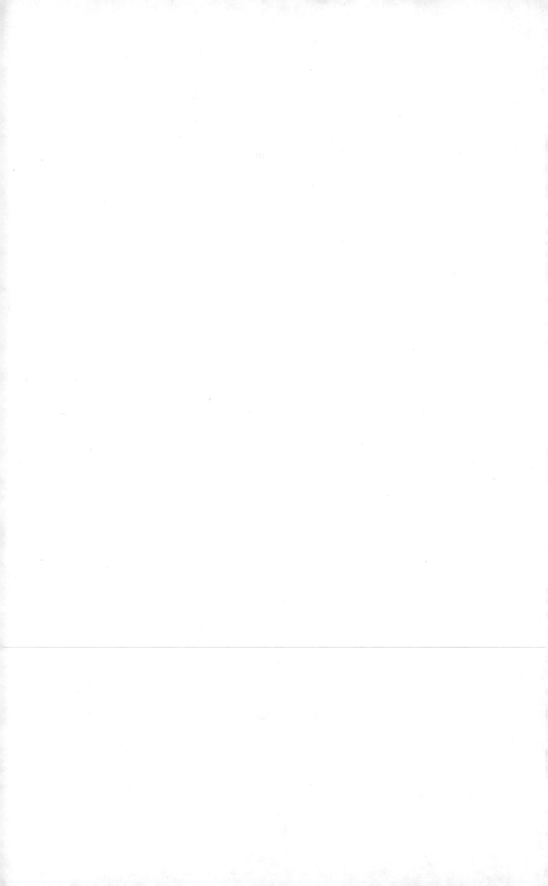

Marjan Sirjani (Ed.)

Coordination Models and Languages

14th International Conference, COORDINATION 2012
Stockholm, Sweden, June 14-15, 2012
Proceedings

 Springer

Volume Editor

Marjan Sirjani
Reykjavik University
School of Computer Science
Menntavegur 1, 101 Reykjavik, Iceland,
E-mail: marjan@ru.is

ISSN 0302-9743   e-ISSN 1611-3349
ISBN 978-3-642-30828-4   e-ISBN 978-3-642-30829-1
DOI 10.1007/978-3-642-30829-1
Springer Heidelberg Dordrecht London New York

Library of Congress Control Number: 2012938864

CR Subject Classification (1998): C.2, D.2, H.4, I.2, F.1, H.3

LNCS Sublibrary: SL 2 – Programming and Software Engineering

Typesetting: Camera-ready by author, data conversion by Scientific Publishing Services, Chennai, India

Printed on acid-free paper

Springer is part of Springer Science+Business Media (www.springer.com)

Foreword

In 2012, the 7th International Federated Conferences on Distributed Computing Techniques (DisCoTec) took place in Stockholm, Sweden, during June 13–16. It was hosted and organized by KTH Royal Institute of Technology. The DisCoTec 2012 federated conference was one of the major events sponsored by the International Federation for Information Processing (IFIP) and it acted as an umbrella event for the folllowing conferences:

- The 14th International Conference on Coordination Models and Languages (Coordination)
- The 12th IFIP International Conference on Distributed Applications and Interoperable Systems (DAIS)
- The 14th Formal Methods for Open Object-Based Distributed Systems and 32nd Formal Techniques for Networked and Distributed Systems (FMOODS/FORTE)

Together, these conferences cover the complete spectrum of distributed computing subjects ranging from theoretical foundations to formal specification techniques to systems research issues.

At a plenary session of the conferences, Schahram Dustdar of Vienna University of Technology and Bengt Jonsson of Uppsala University gave invited talks. There was also a poster session, and a session of invited talks from Swedish companies involved in distributed computing: Spotify, Peerialism, and Severalnines. In addition to this, there were three workshops:

- The Third International Workshop on Interactions Between Computer Science and Biology (CS2BIO) with keynote talks by Jane Hillston (University of Edinburgh, UK) and Gianluigi Zavattaro (University of Bologna, Italy)
- The 5th Workshop on Interaction and Concurrency Experience (ICE) with keynote lectures by Marcello Bonsague (Leiden University, The Netherlands) and Ichiro Hasuo (Tokyo University, Japan)
- The 7th International Workshop on Automated Specification and Verification of Web Systems (WWV) with a keynote talk by José Luiz Fiadeiro (University of Leicester, UK)

I would like to thank the Program Committee Chairs of each conference and workshop for their effort. The organization of DisCoTec 2012 was only possible thanks to the dedicated work of the Publicity Chair Ivana Dusparic (Trinity College Dublin, Ireland), the Workshop Chair Rui Oliveira (Universidade do Minho, Portugal), the Poster Chair Sarunas Girdzijauskas (Swedish Institute of Computer Science, Sweden), the Industry-Track Chair György Dán (KTH Royal College of Technology, Sweden), and the members of the Organizing Committee from KTH Royal Institute of Technology and the Swedish Institute of Computer Science: Amir H. Payberah, Fatemeh Rahimian, Niklas Ekström, Ahmad Al-Shishtawy, Martin Neumann, and Alex Averbuch. To conclude I want to thank the sponsorship of the International Federation for Information Processing (IFIP) and KTH Royal Institute of Technology.

June 2012   Jim Dowling

Preface

This volume contains the papers presented at Coordination 2012: the 14th International Conference on Coordination Models and Languages held during June 13–14, 2012, in Stockholm. The conference focused on the design and implementation of models that allow compositional construction of large-scale concurrent and distributed systems, including both practical and foundational models, runtime systems, and related verification and analysis techniques.

The Program Committee (PC) of Coordination 2012 consisted of 31 top researchers from 14 countries. We received a total of 55 submissions from 23 countries out of which the PC selected 18 papers. Each submission was reviewed by at least three independent referees. After a careful and thorough review process, the PC selected 18 papers for publication, based on their quality, originality, contribution, clarity of presentation, and relevance to the conference topics. The selected papers constituted a program covering a varied range of topics including coordination of social collaboration processes, coordination of mobile systems in peer-to-peer and ad-hoc networks, programming and reasoning about distributed and concurrent software, types, contracts, synchronization, coordination patterns, and families of distributed systems. The program was further enhanced by an inspiring invited talk by Schahram Dustdar from Vienna University of Technology titled "Elastic Coordination—Principles, Models, and Algorithms."

The success of Coordination 2012 was due to the dedication of many people. We thank the authors for submitting high-quality papers, and the Program Committee (and their co-reviewers) for their careful reviews, and lengthy discussions during the final selection process. We thank Gwen Salaun from INRIA who acted as the Publicity Chair of Coordination 2012. With his help we had an increase of 1.6 in the number of submissions compared to last year. We thank the providers of the EasyChair conference management system, which was used to run the review process and to facilitate the preparation of the proceedings. Finally, we thank the Distributed Computing Techniques Organizing Committee (led by Jim Dowling) for their contribution in making the logistic aspects of Coordination 2012 a success.

June 2012   Marjan Sirjani

Organization

Steering Committee

Farhad Arbab	CWI and Leiden University, The Netherlands (Chair)
Gul Agha	University of Illinois at Urbana Champaign, USA
Dave Clarke	Catholic University of Leuven, Belgium
Wolfgang De Meuter	Vrije Universiteit Brussels, Belgium
Rocco De Nicola	University of Florence, Italy
Gruia-Catalin Roman	Washington University in Saint Louis, USA
Carolyn Talcott	SRI, USA
Vasco T. Vasconcelos	University of Lisbon, Portugal
Gianluigi Zavattaro	University of Bologna, Italy

Program Committee

Farhad Arbab	CWI and Leiden University, The Netherlands
Borzoo Bonakdarpour	University of Waterloo, Canada
Marcello Bonsangue	Leiden University, The Netherlands
Roberto Bruni	Università di Pisa, Italy
Carlos Canal	University of Málaga, Spain
Frank De Boer	CWI, The Netherlands
Wolfgang De Meuter	Vrije Universiteit Brussel, Belgium
Rocco De Nicola	University of Florence, Italy
Patrick Eugster	Purdue University, USA
Robert Hirschfeld	Hasso-Plattner-Institut (HPI), Germany
Jean-Marie Jacquet	University of Namur, Belgium
Mohammad Mahdi Jaghoori	CWI, The Netherlands
Christine Julien	University of Texas at Austin, USA
Ramtin Khosravi	University of Tehran, Iran
Natallia Kokash	CWI, The Netherlands
Christian Krause	Hasso Plattner Institute (HPI), Germany
Doug Lea	SUNY Oswego, USA
Jay Mccarthy	Brigham Young University, USA
Shiva Nejati	Simula Research Lab, Norway
Andrea Omicini	Università di Bologna, Italy
Jose Proenca	Katholieke Universiteit Leuven, Belgium
Jan Rutten	CWI, The Netherlands
Gwen Salaün	Grenoble INP - INRIA - LIG, France
Michael Ignaz Schumacher	University of Applied Sciences Western Switzerland (HES-SO)

Manuel Serrano	INRIA, France
Marjan Sirjani	Reykjavik University, Iceland
Meng Sun	Peking University, China
Vasco T. Vasconcelos	University of Lisbon, Portugal
Carolyn Talcott	SRI International, USA
Mirko Viroli	Università di Bologna, Italy
Franco Zambonelli	Università di Modena e Reggio Emilia, Italy

Additional Reviewers

Appeltauer, Malte	Melgratti, Hernan
Bainomugisha, Engineer	Merro, Massimo
Becker, Basil	Mostrous, Dimitris
Bozga, Marius	Neumann, Stefan
Bromuri, Stefano	Nobakht, Behrooz
Costa, David	Ouederni, Meriem
De Koster, Joeri	Padovani, Luca
Ferreira, Carla	Perscheid, Michael
Giachino, Elena	Pianini, Danilo
Grande, Johan	Poll, Erik
Gubian, Michele	Quilbeuf, Jean
Güdemann, Matthias	Ricci, Alessandro
Harnie, Dries	Rot, Jurriaan
Helvensteijn, Michiel	Salaun, Gwen
Jafari, Ali	Santini, Francesco
Jongmans, Sung-Shik T.Q.	Scholliers, Christophe
Kemper, Stephanie	Schumann, René
Kersten, Anne	Steinert, Bastian
Lincke, Jens	Taeumel, Marcel
Lluch Lafuente, Alberto	Tiezzi, Francesco
Lombide Carreton, Andoni	Urovi, Visara
Loreti, Michele	Vallejos, Jorge
Marques, Eduardo R.B.	Vogel, Thomas
Martins, Francisco	Wong, Bernard
Mauro, Jacopo	Zavattaro, Gianluigi

Elastic Coordination
Principles, Models, and Algorithms
Invited Talk

Schahram Dustdar

Vienna University of Technology

Elasticity is seen as one of the main characteristics of Cloud Computing today. Social computing, as one of the most prominent applications deployed on Cloud infrastructures, would gain significantly from elasticity. In this talk I will discuss the main principles of elasticity related to coordination, present a fresh look at this problem, and examine how to integrate people in the form of human-based computing and software services into one composite system, which can be modeled, programmed, and instantiated on a large scale in an elastic way.

Table of Contents

Statelets: Coordination of Social Collaboration Processes

Vitaliy Liptchinsky, Roman Khazankin, Hong-Linh Truong,
and Schahram Dustdar

Distributed Systems Group, Vienna University of Technology
Argentinierstrasse 8/184-1, A-1040 Vienna, Austria
{lastname}@infosys.tuwien.ac.at

Abstract. Today people work together across time, space, cultural and organizational boundaries. To simplify and automate the work, collaboration employs a broad range of tools, such as project management software, groupware, social networking services, or wikis. For a collaboration to be effective, the actions of collaborators need to be properly coordinated, which requires taking into account social, structural, and semantic relations among actors and processes involved. This information is not usually available from a single source, but is spread across collaboration systems and tools. Providing a unified access to this data allows not only to establish a complete picture of the collaboration environment, but also to automate the coordination decision making by specifying formal rules that reflect social and semantic context effects on the ongoing collaboration processes. In this paper we present Statelets, a coordination framework and language for support and coordination of collaboration processes spanning multiple groupware tools and social networking sites, and demonstrate its suitability in several use cases.

Keywords: Coordination Language, Collaboration, Social Context, Groupware Integration.

1   Introduction

Groupware and social software foster collaboration of individuals who work across time, space, cultural and organizational boundaries, i.e., virtual teams [22]. Problem of people coordination in collaborative processes has been already extensively studied in academia, (e.g., in [7,9]), and addressed in industry with ever more groupware products incorporating workflow and orchestration mechanisms (e.g., Microsoft Sharepoint). However, in many cases, people interact and contribute in divergent commercial or non-profit on-line collaboration platforms, such as social networks, open source development platforms, or discussion forums, that remain decoupled, isolated and specific to their domains. The problem of coordination in such a setup gets a new look, where processes that need to be coordinated are decentralized and distributed across different specialized tools and online services.

M. Sirjani (Ed.): COORDINATION 2012, LNCS 7274, pp. 1–16, 2012.

Social network context is an integral part of human coordination. For example, the following context aspects have an impact on the behavior of collaborating individuals: actions taken by neighbors in social network [10], social neighbors' preferences [4], and the social network structure itself [25]. The degree of the impact varies from network context simply 'carrying' the information that can be used in a process to forcing adjustment or even cancellation of ongoing actions. Also, social context can imply mutual dependency between processes, reflected by such common coordination mechanisms in social networks as collective actions [4], i.e., 'I'll go if you go'. Social network context can be used for such advanced activities as expertise location [17], composition of socially coherent collaborative teams [5], discovery of unbiased reviewers, and so on.

Along with the social component of the network context, semantic relations between processes may affect coordination decisions as well. In groupware and wiki-like platforms, processes are reflected as incremental changes of common deliverables (e.g., documentation of an idea, a technical specification, or a source code file) connected into dependency and semantic networks. Relations between these artifacts may influence the collaboration process. For example, actions on a document should not be performed before related documents reach a certain condition, or a change in a related document might force to re-do an activity.

Due to an information-centric nature of both social and semantic contexts, we combine these notions together and define *network context of a collaboration process* as *information about related processes and people, their actions and states*. In our previous work [15] we discussed network context effects on collaboration processes, and presented an approach for modeling them.

In spite of growing interest to social network effects in academia [4,10,25], the problem of network context-based coordination has not been properly addressed by coordination languages and frameworks. As examined in the paper, existing coordination languages lack necessary features to enable efficient programming of coordination based on network effects. We refer here to suitability as an amount of efforts a developer needs to spend to express such coordination rules. Also, supplying the developer with social and semantic network context requires horizontal composition of groupware and social networking sites, which imposes yet additional challenges [6,14], which are not addressed properly by existing frameworks as well.

In this paper we present Statelets, a programming language for coordination of social collaboration processes spanning multiple software systems. A distinguishing characteristic of Statelets is the support for coordination based on social and semantic network effects. Although the primary focus of the paper is the programming language, our contribution also includes a conceptual architecture of the underlying framework that aims at integration of groupware and social networks to extract social and semantic contexts. To evaluate Statelets, we have implemented use cases that show its advantages and suitability to the domain.

The rest of this paper is structured as follows: Section 2 provides a motivating example and identifies the features that are crucial for a network context-based coordination language. In Section 3 we explore the suitability of existing coordination languages for the problem at hand in the perspective of these features. Sections 4 and 5 describe the Statelets coordination language and the conceptual architecture of the underlying framework respectively. Section 6 demonstrates the usage of the language with use cases. The paper is concluded in Section 7.

2   Motivation

As a motivating example, let us consider open source software engineering. Projects in software engineering can be classified into analysis projects and engineering projects (See Fig. 1b). An analysis project represents a non-routine and changeable process, whereas an engineering project represents a rather routine and stable process. Both types of projects produce deliverables, such as source code or technical documentation. Projects get assigned to members of open source communities, who are located via social (professional) networks and online collaboration services, and are then hold responsible for the progress of corresponding activities.

Projects can be related to or depend on each other. For example, two projects are related if they contribute to the same software product, are functionally interdependent, or share components, goals, or resources. Similarly, social and professional relations and technical dependencies exist between project members, e.g., a software engineer depends on engineers who wrote previous versions of the component or worked on the code in the past. Figure 1a depicts various relations between projects and their members.

The key to success of such engineering and analysis projects are advanced activities, such as expertise and resource discovery. Such activities are not possible without integration of professional (e.g., XING, LinkedIn) and private (e.g., Facebook, MySpace) social networks, and online collaboration tools (e.g., Source-Forge). Figure 1a depicts integration and execution environment of processes that correspond to analysis and engineering projects. Engineering projects are more specific to the domain, and, therefore, require more specific groupware, e.g., VersionOne, or Jira. Analysis projects, on the contrary, require more flexible and wide-spread groupware, such as MediaWiki (engine for Wikipedia).

Given the setup described above, let us consider the following possible coordination rules:

1. *If an Analysis project is in* Post-Deliberation *phase, and all its related Analysis projects have transitioned to* Post-Deliberation *phase, then, if any changes have occured among solutions in those projects during the transition, the project should be switched back to* Deliberation *phase and the changes should be communicated to the project's team.* This rule ensures proper communication of new or adjusted solutions between teams of interrelated Analysis projects and allows a collaboration team to produce solutions that are not affected by possibly incorrect solutions produced by other teams. Similar strategies were adopted in agile software engineering methodologies, e.g., in SCRUM estimation game[1].

---

[1] http://scrummethodology.com/scrum-effort-estimation-and-story-points/

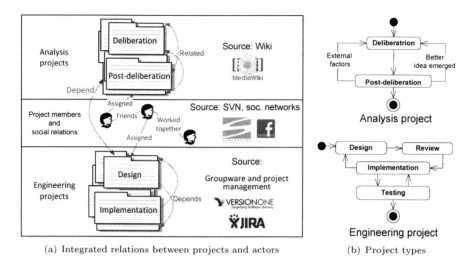

(a) Integrated relations between projects and actors   (b) Project types

Fig. 1. Projects in open source software engineering

2. *An engineering project design should be reviewed by an expert from a functionally dependent project. Moreover, it is preferable to assign an expert socially unrelated to the project team members.* This rule tries to avoid biased reviews by finding socially unrelated experts.

3. *In case of an expertise request, an appropriate expert should be socially connected to one of the project team members, or work on a related project.* This rule ensures faster expert onboarding.

4. *When starting an engineering project, a socially coherent team of qualified experts should be assembled, which has connections to members of related projects.* This rule tries to maximize probability of a project success by ensuring a good social environment in advance.

5. *An engineering project can be started, if at least one project it depends on has passed* `Design phase`. This rule defines a balance between total serialization of dependent projects `Design phases`, which results in a longer time-to-market, and total parallelization of `Design phases`, which results in more iterations.

6. `Design phase` *of a project cannot be finished until all projects it depends on pass* `Design phase`. This rule minimizes chances of potential rework and wasted efforts.

7. *If an engineering project is in* `Implementation phase`, *and any of the projects it depends on has switched back to* `Design phase`, *then the project should switch back to* `Design phase`. This rule covers possible redesign cases and ensures proper handling of late adjustments.

8. *All impediments in a project should be communicated to any engineer in every related project.* This rule ensures timely communication between project teams.

Let us consider the challenges that a developer faces when implementing the aforementioned rules. Based on the challenges, we further draw conclusions and identify the most important features that reflect the effectiveness of a coordination language and its underlying framework.

1. *Optimized horizontal integration of external collaboration projects.* The motivation scenario involves integration of many social networks and groupware products, such as MediaWiki, Subversion, LinkedIn, Facebook, and VersionOne. The developer should concentrate on the coordination logic, and not on how to extract the needed information from external sources. As APIs of collaboration platforms could not provide all the needed information in the right form, the framework needs to decouple the concepts perceived by the developer from representation and transformation issues and take care of the optimizing the data exchange seamlessly for the developer. Different authorization mechanisms and the necessity for identity mapping between entities coming from different sources makes integration even more complex. The coordination language should in turn support the unconditioned access to externally provided data in a manner that enables the optimization, and the language's semantics should reflect the nature of external APIs, i.e., consider distinct behavioral classes of APIs' methods (e.g., methods with and without side-effects).

2. *Condition-Action rules.* Rules 5, 6, and 7 take the declarative *condition-action* form, as opposed to more common *event-condition-action* rules, because the developer is interested in situations or patterns that need to be managed rather than in events that lead to these situations. When a condition depends on external data sources, problems of continuous checking and polling arise. Additionally, when a condition depends on time (e.g., escalation), timers get involved as well. These problems should be abstracted away from the developer and be handled by the framework, while the coordination language should support *condition-action* expressivity.

3. *Network context querying and processing.* Integration of groupware and social software enables social resource discovery and process coordination based on rich network context. Manipulations with network context, as it can be seen from most of the rules above, can be significantly simplified with quantifiers (as in Rules 5, 6, or 8), and disjunctions (as in Rule 3), as they naturally fit for expressing the coordination logic.

4. *Network context synchronization.* As depicted by Rule 1, when multiple related entities fulfill a rule, the action should be taken for all such entities simultaneously to avoid a situation when the action for one entity discards the condition for other related entities. Such synchronization issues should be handled at the framework level and be taken into account by the language design.

3   Related Work

In this section we examine existing coordination and orchestration languages with respect to the features outlined in the previous section. Table 1 summarizes

Table 1. Natively supported features in selected coordination languages

	Seamless integration	Condition-Action	Context queries	Context synchronization
Control-driven languages [1,12,13]	+/−	−	−	−
Linda-based languages [2,3]	−	+	+	−
Reactors [8]	−	+	+	−
CEP languages [20,21,23]	−	+	+	−
BPEL4Data (BEDL) [18]	−	+	−	−

the suitability of considered languages to network context-based coordination. The suitability of a language can be characterized as the amount of efforts a developer needs to spend on a task at hand. We therefore regard the native support of the aforementioned features, i.e., when no additional effort is needed for their realization.

Control-driven coordination and orchestration (workflow) languages based on messages (channels), such as BPEL [1], Orc [13], or Workflow Prolog [12] are specifically designed for integration of services like those in external APIs. They can also simulate network effects via messages or events, i.e., by notifying related processes. However, context querying using point-to-point messages would result in "chatty" communication, and context synchronization would require the implementation of complex protocols similar to two-phase commit. Also, support for integration is limited, as difference between methods w/o side-effects is not considered.

Data-driven (Linda-like [11]) coordination languages (for example, [2]) express coordination as dependencies between removal/reading and insertion of atoms from or into a shared space. However, groupware APIs are often assymetric and do not provide *insert/remove* operations for each *read* operation. It is therefore hard to align API method calls with the removal and insertion of atoms, because the actual changes made by API calls are not explicit and occur rather as side-effects. Basic Linda operators provide only limited expressivity of conditions expressing network context, unlike reactive Linda extensions [3] that introduce additional *notify* operation. Two coordination approaches are used in reactive extensions [3]: parallel (e.g., JavaSpaces, WCL) and prioritized (e.g., MARS, TuCSoN (ReSpecT)). In order to express network context synchronization, parallel reactions require implementing two-phase synchronization protocols, similarly to control-driven languages. Prioritized extensions make the implementation even more difficult by restricting the usage of coordination operators within reactions.

Reactors [8] is a coordination language where networks of reactors can be defined by means of relations. The behavior of reactors in the neighborhood is observed as sequences of their states, which can be queried with Datalog-based language, thus allowing the context querying. Also, Reactors eliminate the distinction between events and conditions. Reactors react to stimuli defined as insertion or removal of relations. This is suitable for integrating RESTful APIs, but is limited to them, as many groupware APIs are coarse-grained and it is not intuitive to map insertion and removal of tuples to API calls. In general, reactors are executed concurrently and independently. Synchronous execution can only be achieved through a composition of reactors, which is not intuitive to implement.

Given that processes can publish their states as events, modern Complex Event Processing languages (e.g., [21]) can express conditions on network context using event correlation and predicates. However, representation of external data retrieved from request-response web APIs in the form of events is not intuitive. Moreover, the recursiveness [16] (See Rule 1) of collaboration processes can significantly complicate the definition of network context queries.

Typically, rules in Rule-based languages fire non-deterministically, thus complicating the network context synchronization. However, two notably different approaches here are: (i) to derive dependencies from postconditions (e.g., [23]), which in scope of external APIs integration might be not known, or not possible to define; and (ii) by explicit operators (e.g., [20]), which do not allow to specify dependencies based on relations between events.

In XML-based language BPEL4Data [18] processes can communicate via shared business entities, resembling thus a shared-space paradigm. Business entities are represented as XML documents. Simple conditions can be expressed as guards on Business entities using XPath/XQuery. However, it is not intuitive to describe network context querying, i.e., conditions on a graph of related XML documents. Synchronization between processes is achieved through additional processes and locks. Similarly to CEP languages, integration with BEDL requires representation of external data changes in the form of CRUDE notifications or invocations, which is not always intuitive.

As it can be seen, existing approaches partially support requirements outlined in the motivating scenario, but none of them provides a full spectrum of features necessary for efficient programming of coordination based on network effects.

4 Statelets Coordination Language

In this section we present Statelets, the coordination language designed for orchestration of activities in groupware and social software systems. The language natively supports all four features outlined in the previous section. However, native support of the 'Seamless integration' feature requires additionally implementation of an extensible framework, conceptual design of which is discussed in the next section. The main building block of Statelets is *statelet* - a construct that corresponds to a state of a process and denotes coordination rules that should be fulfilled when the process resides in this state. Statelets do not completely describe collaboration processes, but rather are complementary reactions to workflows defined in groupware systems and human collaboration activities. A statelet consists of mainly two parts: a condition(s) that formally describes an anticipated situation and an action(s) which have to be undertaken if such a situation is detected. Conditions are given in a form of *context queries* against the data integrated from external collaboration projects, and the actions are given as either *triggers* that correspond to external commands in collaboration software, or *yield* constructs that activate other statelets. All the data integrated from external sources by the framework is accessed as *relations* in the language. This allows the developer to easily design the coordination rules by seamlessly combining the relations originating from diverse platforms into single conditions.

4.1   Context Queries and Commands

Assymetric nature of many collaborative software APIs is reflected in Statelets as segregation of operations[2] to read (side-effect free) operations, i.e., queries, and modify operations, i.e., commands. Such segregation allows a programmer to specify what API methods are side-effect free and what are not, enabling thus the framework to treat them differently.

Queries. Read operations define data models, which in Statelets are represented as a unified hypergraph comprised of overlay networks. Even though the data model is defined by collaboration software adapters, additional relations may be integrated, (e.g., Core Relations Library), denoting side-effect free external computation. For example, querying the *Factorial(X, Factorial)* relation results in computation of a factorial by an integrated component. Also, additional virtual relations can be defined on top of the basic data model. For instance, a SocialRelation virtual relation below is defined by means of relations coming from Facebook and MySpace.

```
relation SocialRelation(User1, User2):
  Facebook.Friends(User1, User2) || MySpace.Friends(User1, User2);
```

Querying a hypergraph relation at runtime creates a *data stream*, i.e., a lazy sequence of records, which is gradually initialized by the framework with each set of vertexes matching the given relation found. Given that relations in hypergraph constitute predicates, data streams can be formed by expressions using the following binary operators based on the First-order logic:

- Operators &&, ||, not, and -> correspond appropriately to $\wedge$, $\vee$, $\neg$, and $\rightarrow$ first-order logic connectives with implicit existential quantification attached to all variables within the expression.
- Operators =>, -!, and -x correspond to conditional ($\rightarrow$) connector with implicit universal quantification over the variables present in the left part of the expression. Variables in the right part of the expression, that are not present in the left part, are quantified as $\exists$, $\exists!$, and $\neg\exists$ appropriately. Clearly, second and third operators can be expressed using the first one.

---

[2] http://martinfowler.com/bliki/CQRS.html

Basically, a query expression describes a pattern (a subgraph) within a hypergraph. Appropriately, a data stream resulted from evaluation of this query contains all occurrences of the pattern.

Queries in Statelets can be evaluated using `define` and `wait` operations:

- `define` operation simply evaluates a query expression and searches shared space hypergraph for pattern instances. Each pattern instance found along the hypergraph search is pushed into the data stream. If no instances are found, then `define` returns an empty data stream.
- `wait` operation continuously evaluates a query expression until at least one pattern instance is found. Therefore, `wait` operation always returns non-empty data stream.

For instance, if it is necessary to wait until all related to the project documents are completed, then we can use the following code snippet:

```
wait Related(Project, Document) => Status(Document, 'Completed');
```

Here a data stream is created that remains uninitialized until the condition is satisfied. However, if it is simply necessary to check if all related documents are completed, then the following code snippet can be used:

```
define Related(Project, Documents) => Status(Document, 'Completed');
```

Here an uninitialized data stream is created, which either is initialized with all related documents if all of them are completed, or is initialized as empty. A statelet can run many queries, getting thus many data streams. If query expressions within a statelet share variables, then resulting streams are joined by those shared variables.

Commands. Commands represent groupware API methods with side effects, for example, send an e-mail, or delete a document. Commands in Statelets are executed using `trigger` keyword:

```
trigger AssignReviewer(Document, Reviewer);
```

Commands in Statelets are used to process or handle records of data streams defined by query evaluations. If a data stream is not yet initialized, then a command is suspended until it is initialized (similar to lists with unbound dataflow tail [24]). However, if a data stream is empty, then the command is not executed at all. A command can be executed for `any` or for `every` record in a data stream, or for the whole collection of records. `Any` quantifier is a default quantifier, which is implicitly attached if no quantifiers are specified. Consider the example below:

```
trigger SendForReview(every Team, any Programmer, all Documents);
```

This reads as follows: send a list of Documents (all Documents) for a review to any Programmer in every Team.

4.2 Programming Coordination

Coordination is managing dependencies between activities. Apart of being able
to express basic dependencies between human activities, Statelets also support
network context-based coordination.

Dependencies between Activities. A statelet by itself describes precedence
dependency: once completion of a human activity is registered in a shared space,
a succeeding activity is triggered by a command. Statelets can be composed using
alternative keyword expressing thus multiple different outcomes of a manual
or automated activity. We exemplify usage of such composition in the use case
scenarios. The statelet in the example below describes dependencies between
design activity, project owner notification activity, and assignment of multiple
experts activity:

```
statelet DesignPhase(Project):
{
  wait DesignDocument(Project, Document) && Status(Document, 'Completed');
  trigger NotifyProjectOwner(Project);
  define ExpertiseKeywords(Document, Keyword) && FindEngineers(Expert, Keyword);
  trigger Assign(every Keyword, any Expert, Project);
};
```

Dependencies between Processes. A process in Statelets is comprised of a
sequence of statelets that produce each other by using **yield new** operation,
i.e., a sequence of states. A process may reside in multiple orthogonal states,
requiring thus presence of many statelets in parallel. Therefore, a statelet is
technically a coroutine: it can produce multiple new statelets along its execution. Statelet by itself complements shared space hypergraph at runtime, sim-
ulating thus a relation. In other words, a statelet can query existence of other
statelets in its neighborhood similarly to how it queries for existence of specific relations and nodes in a shared space hypergraph. A process in Statelets
thus communicates with its neighborhood by changing its own state. In other
words, observable behaviors of Statelets processes are sequences of *states*, rather
then *messages*. This behavior was inspired by Cellular Automata [19], a popular
abstraction for modeling complex behaviors in social and biological networks.
If a statelet queries for the presence of another statelet, then such situation
is treated by the framework as dependency, i.e., the assumption is that any
actions triggered by a statelet can discard conditions of dependent statelets.
Therefore, the framework ensures that actions of a statelet are triggered after
conditions in dependent statelets are checked. Appropriately, if two statelets
are mutually dependent, then the framework executes their actions simultaneously, allowing thus for expressing simultaneity dependencies, i.e., network context synchronization and collective actions (see Sec. 2). Lifetime of a statelet
is bound to the data streams defined within it. A statelet is visible in shared
space hypergraph until all its data streams are initialized. Once the statelet
starts processing data streams by triggering actions, it becomes invisible to
other statelets, i.e., queries being evaluated within **wait** operations of all other
statelets will not consider presence of the relation correspondent to the statelet.

Let us consider an example: an engineering project can be started if design of all projects it depends on is finalized, and if at least one of them is in the implementation phase. The following code snippet implements this rule:

```
statelet DesignFinalizedPhase(Project):
{
  wait Depends(Project, DepProject) => (DesignFinalizedPhase(DepProject)
    || ImplementationPhase(DepProject));
  yield new ImplementationPhase(Project);
};
```

4.3 Feature Support and Prototype Implementation

All four features outlined in Sec. 2 are integral part of and natively supported by Statelets. Data streams and segregation of operations realize the horizontal integration feature. `Wait` operation enables *condition-action* rules. Implicit quantifiers in queries along with explicit quantifiers in commands allow for easy network context querying and processing. Statelet dependency solves the synchronization problem.

Statelets employ accustomed C-based syntax. Prototypes of the Statelets interpretor and the initial version of the language runtime are implemented in the functional programming language F#, and are publicly available for download[3].

The complete abstract syntax tree of the Statelets coordination language is provided below:

```
Quantifier Q ::= any | every | all
Constant C ::= boolean | number | string
 Identifier ID ::= string without spaces
Expression variables EVARS ::= ( ID | C | _ ) list
Command variables EPARS ::= ( Q ID | C ) list
Expression E ::= EVARS | (ID, EVARS) | (E && E) | (E || E) | (not E) | (E -> E)
   | (E => E) | (E -! E) | (E -x E)
VirtualRelation VR ::= (ID, ID list, E)
Statement S ::= define E | wait E | trigger ID EPARS | yield new ID EPARS
Statelet ::= (ID, ID list, S list )
```

5   Statelets Framework

In this section we present the conceptual architecture of the Statelets framework that enables horizontal integration of collaborative software systems. The focus of this paper is on the coordination language, therefore technical details are not provided. Figure 2 shows the high level design of the framework comprised of the following layers:

Connectors. Groupware APIs are diverse by their nature and employ distinct protocols. This requires creation of fine-tuned integration points, i.e., connectors. Connectors define supported relations and commands, and adapt object models of groupware APIs to fit Statelets semantic model. Connectors may support not only initialization of data streams corresponding to atomic relations, but also

---

[3] http://sourceforge.net/p/statelets/

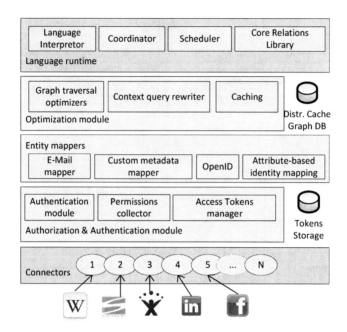

Fig. 2. Statelets framework architecture

interpretation of queries on relations in order to better utilize flexibility of APIs and improve efficiency.

Authentication and Authorization. User-centric APIs are designed for vertical composition [6], and often require authorization and authentication mechanisms with direct user involvement (e.g., OAuth 1.0/2.0). This complicates traversal of social graphs, and imposes needs to store and maintain certificates, application and user tokens, or even credentials. Moreover, a mechanism to update or collect new tokens should be present as well.

Entity Mapping. Many user accounts and entities map to the same entity in the real world. For instance, users usually have different accounts per each collaboration tool they use, and two files in different tools may represent the same research paper. Typical approaches to entity mappings [14] are attribute-based identity, by e-mail address, by custom metadata, or even direct mappings (e.g., based on Facebook Open Graph or OpenID).

Optimizations. Authentication and authorization mechanisms together with identity mappings algorithms may introduce high latency. Additionally, some data in social networks, like a friendship connection, or a user profile, change rarely. This introduces unnecessary overhead for queries with existential quantifiers, i.e., 'find any socially related expert in given area'. In this case, caching and heuristic approaches may bring substantial value.

Language Runtime. The language interpretor is responsible for code parsing and interpretation of the language semantic model. The scheduling component is responsible for polling graphs of artifacts and user profiles. The coordination component is responsible for enforcing dependencies between activities and processes at runtime.

The multi-layer design decouples integration and optimization issues from the coordination logic. The developer therefore only operates with entity abstractions and is not required to comprehend technical details of data access, whereas the other layers are handled by appropriate integration experts.

6 Use cases

This section demonstrates the implementation of two process types considered in Sec. 2, namely Analysis and Engineering projects. The use cases exemplify main language features and implementation of coordination based on network effects. More use-cases can be found online[3].

6.1 Analysis Projects

MediaWiki engine used in Wikipedia is used as an underlying groupware platform. Typically, work on wiki pages is coordinated by non-functional attributes, for example, 'Category:All articles with unsourced statements'. Similarly, we add a special marker category which is used to denote **Post-Deliberation phase** of a project. Two analysis projects are considered to be related, if one of the project wiki pages contains a link to a wiki page from the other project. Synchronization between related projects is achieved in two steps: (i) residing in the Post-Deliberation phase, a process waits until all related processes switch to the Post-Deliberation phase; (ii) all changes made in related projects since last synchronization are communicated to every team member in related projects, and related projects switch back to the Deliberation phase simultaneously.

```
statelet AnalysisProject.Deliberation(WikiPage, Timestamp):
{
 wait Wiki.Categories(WikiPage, "PostDeliberation");
 yield new AnalysisProject.PostDeliberation(WikiPage, Timestamp);
};

statelet AnalysisProject.PostDeliberation(WikiPage, Timestamp):
{
 wait
  ((Wiki.Links(WikiPage, RelatedPage) => AnalysisProject.PostDeliberation(RelatedPage, _))
  -> Wiki.Revisions(RelatedPage, _, RelRevTimestamp))
  && >(RelRevTimestamp, Timestamp) && System.DateTime.Now(now);
 define Wiki.Revisions(WikiPage, Contributor, _);
 trigger Wiki.EmailUser(every Contributor, every RelatedPage, all RelRevTimestamp);
 trigger Wiki.DeleteCategory(WikiPage, "PostDeliberation");
 yield new AnalysisProject.Deliberation(WikiPage, now);
}
alternative
{
 wait WikiPage -x Wiki.Categories(WikiPage, "PostDeliberation");
 yield new AnalysisProject.Deliberation(WikiPage, Timestamp);
};
```

This use case exemplifies simplicity of network context synchronization and collective actions implementation in case of recursive collaboration processes.

6.2   Engineering Projects

To save space, we exemplify only expertise discovery in social neighborhood. The algorithm combines two ideas: (i) try to find a reviewer from a related project, which is not socially related to any of the project team members; (ii) try to find any reviewer who has appropriate expertise. In this example, social context is retrieved from Facebook, LinkedIn, and Subversion (two engineers are socially related if they committed to the same project in subversion). Project data is retrieved from the VersionOne groupware. Subversion and VersionOne are depicted in the code snippet as SVN and V1 respectively.

```
relation SVN.Related(User1, User2):
 SVN.Logs(Path, User1, _, _, _) && SVN.Logs(Path, User2, _, _, _);

relation SocialRelation(User1, User2):
 SVN.Related(User1, User2) || Facebook.Friends(User1, User2);

statelet EngeneeringProject.InProgress(Story):
{
 wait V1.Attribute(Story, "Status", "Completed");
 yield new EngineeringProject.ImplementationFinished(Story);
}
alternative
{
 wait
  V1.Attribute(Story, "Status", "Review") && not V1.Relation(Story, "Reviewer", _)
  && V1.Relation(Story, "Developer", Dev)
  && V1.Relation(Story, "FunctionalRelation", RelStory)
  && V1.Relation(RelStory, "Developer", RelDev)
  && LinkedIn.Profile(RelDev, Profile) && ExpertiseFits(Profile, Story)
  && (not SocialRelation(Dev, RelDev) || RelDev);
 trigger SetRelation(Story, "Reviewer", any RelDev);
 yield new EngineeringProject.InProgress(Story);
};
```

The use case exemplifies implementation of such advanced activities as location of socially connected experts, unbiased reviewers, and so on. The use case also shows benefits arising from horizontal composition of social networking sites.

7   Conclusions and Future Work

This paper proposes a novel coordination language for network context-based coordination, and demonstrates its suitability through use cases. Compared to existing approaches, our contribution provides a full spectrum of features that are crucial for network context furnishing and coordination based on it. We have shown that these features are necessary for an effective coordination of social collaboration processes. However, at present the language is in its inception phase, and does not support advanced features (e.g., hierarchical composition of Statelets) for expressing more complex and large-scale coordination problems than those exemplified in the use cases. Therefore, our future work includes further advancement of the Statelets coordination language, and design and development of various techniques aiming at optimized integration of various groupware and social networking sites APIs. Although Statelets was designed with the focus on collaboration, we do not exclude its applicability in other areas.

References

1. Arkin, A., Askary, S., Bloch, B., Curbera, F., Goland, Y., Kartha, N., Liu, C.K., Thatte, S., Yendluri, P., Yiu, A.E.: Web services business process execution language version 2.0 (May 2005)
2. Banâtre, J.-P., Fradet, P., Le Métayer, D.: Gamma and the Chemical Reaction Model: Fifteen Years After. In: Calude, C.S., Păun, G., Rozenberg, G., Salomaa, A. (eds.) Multiset Processing. LNCS, vol. 2235, pp. 17–44. Springer, Heidelberg (2001)
3. Busi, N., Zavattaro, G.: Prioritized and Parallel Reactions in Shared Data Space Coordination Languages. In: Jacquet, J.-M., Picco, G.P. (eds.) COORDINATION 2005. LNCS, vol. 3454, pp. 204–219. Springer, Heidelberg (2005)
4. Chwe, M.S.Y.: Communication and coordination in social networks. Review of Economic Studies 67(1), 1–16 (2000)
5. Dustdar, S., Bhattacharya, K.: The social compute unit. IEEE Internet Computing 15(3), 64–69 (2011)
6. Dustdar, S., Gaedke, M.: The social routing principle. IEEE Internet Computing 15(4), 80–83 (2011)
7. Dustdar, S.: Caramba a process-aware collaboration system supporting ad hoc and collaborative processes in virtual teams. Distributed and Parallel Databases 15, 45–66 (2004)
8. Field, J., Marinescu, M.C., Stefansen, C.: Reactors: A data-oriented synchronous/asynchronous programming model for distributed applications. Theoretical Computer Science 410(23), 168–201 (2009)
9. Florijn, G., Besamusca, T., Greefhorst, D.: Ariadne and HOPLa: Flexible Coordination of Collaborative Processes. In: Ciancarini, P., Hankin, C. (eds.) COORDINATION 1996. LNCS, vol. 1061, pp. 197–214. Springer, Heidelberg (1996)
10. Galeotti, A., Goyal, S., Jackson, M.O., Vega-Redondo, F., Yariv, L.: Network games. Review of Economic Studies 77(1), 218–244 (2010)
11. Gelernter, D., Carriero, N.: Coordination languages and their significance. Commun. ACM 35, 97–107 (1992)
12. Gregory, S., Paschali, M.: A Prolog-Based Language for Workflow Programming. In: Murphy, A., Vitek, J. (eds.) COORDINATION 2007. LNCS, vol. 4467, pp. 56–75. Springer, Heidelberg (2007)
13. Kitchin, D., Cook, W., Misra, J.: A Language for Task Orchestration and Its Semantic Properties. In: Baier, C., Hermanns, H. (eds.) CONCUR 2006. LNCS, vol. 4137, pp. 477–491. Springer, Heidelberg (2006)
14. Ko, M.N., Cheek, G., Shehab, M., Sandhu, R.: Social-networks connect services. Computer 43(8), 37–43 (2010)
15. Liptchinsky, V., Khazankin, R., Truong, H.L., Dustdar, S.: A novel approach to modeling context-aware and social collaboration processes. In: The 24th International Conference on Advanced Information Systems Engineering (CAiSE 2012) (2012)
16. Martinez-Moyano, I.: Exploring the dynamics of collaboration in interorganizational settings. In: Creating a Culture of Collaboration: The International Association of Facilitators Handbook, vol. 4, p. 69 (2006)
17. McDonald, D.W., Ackerman, M.S.: Just talk to me: a field study of expertise location. In: Proceedings of the 1998 ACM Conference on Computer Supported Cooperative Work, CSCW 1998, pp. 315–324. ACM, New York (1998)

18. Nandi, P., Koenig, D., Moser, S., Hull, R., Klicnik, V., Claussen, S., Kloppmann, M., Vergo, J.: Data4bpm, part 1: Introducing business entities and the business entity definition language (bedl) (April 2010)
19. Neumann, J.V.: Theory of Self-Reproducing Automata. University of Illinois Press, Champaign (1966)
20. Núñez, A., Noyé, J.: An Event-Based Coordination Model for Context-Aware Applications. In: Lea, D., Zavattaro, G. (eds.) COORDINATION 2008. LNCS, vol. 5052, pp. 232–248. Springer, Heidelberg (2008)
21. Plociniczak, H., Eisenbach, S.: JErlang: Erlang with Joins. In: Clarke, D., Agha, G. (eds.) COORDINATION 2010. LNCS, vol. 6116, pp. 61–75. Springer, Heidelberg (2010)
22. Powell, A., Piccoli, G., Ives, B.: Virtual teams: a review of current literature and directions for future research. SIGMIS Database 35, 6–36 (2004)
23. Shankar, C., Campbell, R.: A policy-based management framework for pervasive systems using axiomatized rule-actions. In: Proceedings of the Fourth IEEE International Symposium on Network Computing and Applications, pp. 255–258. IEEE Computer Society Press, Washington, DC (2005)
24. Van Roy, P., Haridi, S.: Concepts, Techniques, and Models of Computer Programming. The MIT Press (February 2004)
25. Zhang, Y., Bolton, G.E.: Social Network Effects on Coordination: A Laboratory Investigation. SSRN eLibrary (2011)

A Social Software-Based Coordination Platform
Tool Paper

Davide Rossi

Computer Science Department - University of Bologna - Italy
rossi@cs.unibo.it

Abstract. Organizational best practices are unstructured, emergent processes that freely coordinate actors engaged in reaching organizations' goals. In recent years we are witnessing the wide adoption of social software (blogs, microblogs, wiki, forums, shared calendars, etc.) as primary technological tools to support organizational best practices, fostering their creation, evolution and sharing, allowing their continuous refinement and alignment with the organization's mission and evolving know-how.

While organizational best practices and social software tools are good candidates to support specific processes within the organization (and among organizations) they also present several issues, when compared to classic BPM tools - those based on structured coordination and well-defined process models: since they have no explicit representation it is hard to analyze them (by analytic techniques or by simulation), to monitor their evolution and to support their execution; moreover it is hard to extract explicit knowledge from them.

In this paper we present a set of tools that complement social software in creating a real coordination platform, mitigating some of the aforementioned issues.

1 Introduction

Coordination can be structured or emergent. By this we mean that coordination can be based on the idea of enforcing/supporting interaction patterns among actors on the basis of a well-defined model or can be the result of independent agents defining (and refining) their interactions in an emergent way.

BPMSs (Business Process Management Systems) and social software are instances of these two models: BPMSs support process monitoring and enactment on the basis of a process model defined by some kind of modeling language or notation whereas social software is an emergent coordination *facilitator*. Social software supports social interaction and social production and raises the level and scope of the interaction facilitated by computer and computer networks [9]. It uses a self-organization and bottom-up approach where interaction is coordinated by the collective intelligence of the individuals; the latter do not necessarily know each other and are not organized a priori in a structured way. By publishing and processing information in blogs, microblogs, wiki, forums; by using tagging

M. Sirjani (Ed.): COORDINATION 2012, LNCS 7274, pp. 17–28, 2012.
© IFIP International Federation for Information Processing 2012

services; by collaboratively editing documents, users reach organizational goals following sequences of activities that have been refined in previous interactions.

A BPMS is a coordination platform; social software, per se, is not. Social software provides a set of basic tools to enable information sharing and exchange but provides no support for automating interaction patterns. In this paper we present a set of tools that, combined with social software, implement a coordination platform. We aim, specifically, at a platform supporting *organizational best practices*: the unstructured, emergent processes that freely coordinate actors engaged in reaching organization's goals by interacting with social software tools.

This paper is structured as follows: in the next section we describe how social software can be augmented to become a coordination platform; in section 3 we describe the tools we designed. Section 4 contains a case study that shows the platform in action. Section 5 introduces the coordination model that underpins the platform. Section 6 discusses our approach. Section 7 concludes the paper by presenting some related work and possible future enhancements.

2   The Platform

Coordination allows actors (persons and software systems) to share information and synchronize their activities. At a very basic level of analysis we can argue that social software is not a coordination platform in which, while offering a way to share information, it lacks the ability to synchronize actors. When social software tools are used in a process in which, for example, user A has to wait for user B to complete a given task before resuming their activities, it is responsibility of user A to realize that user B completed their task (which is typically performed by checking the information shared using the social software tools). In other words, users have to manually extract the relevant state information in order make their processes progress. Moreover social software does not provide any method to automatize sequences of activities, even when they are basic parametric sequences of interaction via a web browser; while automatization is not a basic requirement for a coordination platform in itself, it is evident that this ability is essential in order to provide support for organizational best practices.

These observation lead us to the design of two tools, InFeed and WikiRec-Play, whose role is, respectively, to provide mechanisms to extract/manipulate information from web applications and to record/replay parametric sequences of interactions with web applications. The interplay between these tools allows users to define sequences of parametric activities (performed on social software) that can be synchronized with other actors' activities (monitored by extracting relevant state information from social software).

Our goal is to support organizational best practices and it would have been unreasonable to build a prescriptive coordination system, that is a system that enforces coordination patterns; moreover we wanted to support the sharing of best practices and this can be facilitated by sharing information extractions/manipulations and parametric interaction sequences. To achieve this the two tools are themselves integrated with a social software tool (a wiki that is used as a repository extractions/manipulations and parametric interaction sequences) and can provide recommendations to the users on the basis of the currently visited page and the information stored on the wiki. The user can then decide to adopt a recommendation, add it to their favorites and, eventually, make its firing automatic.

3   The Tools

3.1   WikiRecPlay

WikiRecPlay is a Firefox extension that allow users to record and re-play sequences of web activites (interactions with web sites using a browser). The way users perform such activities has been subject to changes in the recent past: web applications are getting more interactive, ubiquitous and easy to use; the social dimension has become crucial: different users —with different skills and tools— share content easily and complete tasks together, in a new and spontaneous way. From a technical perspective, monolithic server-side applications are being replaced by Ajax-based ones that load and manipulate (pieces of) content client-side. WikiRecPlay has been designed to support users in automating web interactions within this context.

In order to define what we wanted from WikiRecPlay we selected a number of test cases built around known web applications [1]: *GoogleDocs* for its very sophisticated interface and Ajax-based machinery; *MediaWiki* and *WordPress* for their relevance as social software tools; *PizzaBo* and *JQueryUI* for the large amount of highly dynamic client-side code.

WikiRecPlay has been built on an *event-based* model, in order to work on highly dynamic web pages: the application is able to record and re-play the events occurring in the browser (mouse click, form filling, selections, etc.). An alternative approach would have been to capture, store and reply HTTP transactions but such an approach cannot cope with (client-side) dynamic pages, leaving all Ajax-based applications unsupported.

Figure 1 shows the main interface of WikiRecPlay. The sidebar lists all loaded sequences and allows users to edit or replay each of them. A new sequence can be recorded and stored through the same interface.

Figure 2 shows the interface for editing a sequence. Once it has been recorded, in fact, its details appear in the 'Step list' panel. Each step can be configured, moved or deleted separately.

Each step is associated to an event occurring on a page element. The interface shows a screenshot of the page highlighting that element with a red bordered rectangle, and allows users to decide:

– which event needs to be captured

---

[1] http://docs.google.com, http://www.mediawiki.org, http://wordpress.com
http://www.pizzabo.it, http://jqueryui.com

Fig. 1. The sidebar

Fig. 2. Configure sequence steps

Fig. 3. Set parameters before re-playing a sequence

- which information users are expected to provide
- how event-related data (like the content of a text field) will be set when re-playing the same sequence. Three options are available: (i) *default value*, to use the values originally recorded, (ii) *ask at start time*, to make users provide that information before playing the whole sequence, or (iii) *ask during execution* to let the application stop the sequence re-play and ask the user to provide the required data right before they are used.

All these data are automatically collected by WikiRecPlay when recording a sequence; users can update and customize them at any time.

Figure 3 shows a sample interface for inserting data when re-playing a sequence. Such a dialog is dynamically built by WikiRecPlay from the description of [each step of] a registration.

A relevant feature of WikiRecPlay are *synchronization steps*, these are steps that can be suspended until a given event occurs (or a timeout expires). The event does not have to be necessarily triggered on the same page and can be associated to different web applications, like the publication of some content on Twitter, the tagging of a photo on Facebook and so on. This mechanism makes it possible to replay sequences that need to synchronize with activities carried out by different users. In order to support this feature WikiRecPlay can halt a sequence until an XPath predicate on the content of a RSS stream changes from false to true (see Sect. 5 for a discussion on this topic). InFeed, the second tool presented below, has the ability of producing RSS streams as the result of extractions and manipulations of data coming from different sources (other feeds, web applications like social software tools or services like microblogs and e-mails) and is thus the ideal companion to WikiRecPlay. Synchronization steps can be inserted in a sequence after it has been recorded and before storing it. When a synchronization step is inserted as the first step of a sequence we call that a *guarded sequence*. Guarded sequences can be inserted (as any other sequence) among the favorites of a user and the user has the option to mark the sequence so that any time its starting guard is satisfied the sequence is automatically replayed (or *fired*).

WikiRecPlay also allows users to share sequences. Users can store data in two places: in a local XML file or on a wiki (which the sidebar is configured to communicate to). Wikis make it possible not only to easily share sequences but also to edit and improve them collaboratively.

Another relevant feature of WikiRecPlay is the ability, given the current web page the user is visiting and the set of sequences stored in the Wiki to propose to the user the execution of all the sequences that start from the current page (possibly filtering only guarded sequences that would be activated). This becomes a kind of recommendation system that improves the awareness of the user with respect to existing sequences that are (possibly) description of (part of) organizational best practices.

WikiRecPlay: Implementation Details. WikiRecPlay is built on the standard Firefox extension mechanisms and, in particular, the XPCOM framework. The overall application follows the *MVC (Model-View-Controller)* design pattern. An internal XML format —whose details are not relevant here— has been defined to describe sequences and steps and is used throughout the application. The main modules of WikiRecPlay are listed below:

Recorder: captures all the activities (DOM events) performed by the user. **Player**: reads a sequence descriptor and replays it, in case asking input data to the user; the player exploits browser facilities to send HTTP requests and to parse responses. **LocalStorageManager:** saves sequence descriptors in a local repository, by epxloiting the browser storage space. **WikiStorageManager:**

saves sequence descriptors on a wiki. This module is in charge of login to the wiki, posting data, retrieving sequences or updating them. It uses the WikiGateway API [14] —that defines a set of operations exported by multiple wiki clones— so that WikiRecPlay is not bounded to a specific server-side platform. **Validator:** validates sequence descriptors, before saving and exporting them. This module actually communicates with a web-service exporting validation features.

While a detailed description of the inner workings of WikiRecPlay is out the scope of this paper we want to highlight that one of the main problems we had to face is related to dynamic web pages: since most elements can be created/moved/deleted at any time it can be tricky (if at all possible) to associate events and current page elements; in several occasions we had to rely on *smart heuristics* to overcome these kind of problems.

3.2   InFeed

InFeed is a feed aggregator/manipulator with an integrated e-mail gateway. It is implemented as a mixed client and server side mashup making use of Dapper[2] (a web content extractor) and Pipes[3] (a visual, interactive feed aggregator and manipulator), both from Yahoo!. With InFeed it is possible to extract data from web applications (this includes usual social software tools but also services like Google Docs, Google Calendar, Twitter, etc...), process them and render them as a feed. The resulting feed can be very terse and easy to parse. For example it is possible to set up a InFeed process that generates a simple "run, I'm away" item in a feed when a Google calendar alarm e-mail has been received and the user tweeted "#infeed away" (after any eventual previous "#infeed available" tweet). This simple feed can easily be used in a synchronization step in WikiRecPlay and let a sequence being played automatically.

4   A Case Study

Consider the following organizational best practice. A group of bird watchers (that interact by participating to a public forum) decides to set up a photographic context. In order to run the context the forum itself will be used: a new section is created (e.g. "photo contests"); each time a new contest is run, a thread is created in this section (e.g. "photo contest for the month of May"). The user who created this thread is the contest manager. The contest manager, in the first post, details the subject of the contest (e.g. "eagles in the wild"). Participants have to submit their photos by replying on this same thread; their post have to include a link to the image and an embedded Goggle map detailing the place where the photo was taken. Once the submission period is over the manager locks the thread and starts a poll. The poll runs for a period of time after which it is closed and the manager announces the winner by editing the first post of the contest thread.

---

[2] http://open.dapper.net/
[3] http://pipes.yahoo.com/

This is a glaring example of emergent coordination: users defined how to interact with social software tools in order to complete the *photographic contest process*; no formal description of the process exists but all participant are expected to follow a best practice. In case of anomalies (e.g. too few votes received) it is easy to modify the process (e.g. ask the participant to vote for others' submission). Notice that while we are giving a rather detailed description of the workflow, still this is not a well-defined process in which no formal description of it exists, since this is the result of emergent behavior, and it is very well possible that it will be freely subject to refinements and modifications in future iterations of the contest.

Our platform can support users in participating to this organizational best practice: sequences can be recorded and shared with respect to the various actions required: open a new contest, submit a photo, vote, and so on. These sequences can be used to automate some of the more time consuming (and boring) actions, like submitting a photo, by allowing users to replay (in a parametric way) the sequence in which the user first has to submit his photo to a photo hosting site (like Photobucket), retrieve the URL to access it from outside, connect to Google maps, enter the coordinate for the place, retrieve the HTML fragment to embed the map then, at last, connect to the forum, identify the active contest thread and post the submission. WikiRecPlay can also assist new users in which it has the ability, once users enter the contest thread, to suggest them that a "submit photo" sequence is available, thus allowing them to participate to the contest even if they are not aware about the rules that the community decided. Other useful sequences include, for example, close a contest thread and create a poll. By adding a synchronization step at the beginning of the sequence and setting up a InFeed process as explained in section 3 it is possible to let this sequence fire automatically when a Google calendar signals an event (so the manager just has to set up the correct event in its calendar and can forget about closing the contest manually). It is even possible for a user willing to participate to the next context, whose subject has been anticipated, but who is going to be away with limited connectivity in the period when the context is be run, to prepare his submission and let the corresponding sequence fire automatically when he tweets "#photocontest submit".

Users, by creating and sharing these sequences (that are generally created for their own benefit, to automatize repetitive/boring interactions) concur to the spreading of organizational know-how. Several experiments [8] have been conducted on using groupware tools within organizations in order to share how-to knowledge but most failed because users have no immediate gain in publishing their knowledge (to the contrary, they feel they are wasting time); with this respect our platform elicits user participation by giving them immediate benefits.

5   The Coordination Model

Up to this point our description of the platform focused on its usage; this decision postponed a discussion to its underpinning model for the last part of the paper.

While unusual, we believe this decision helps in better assessing its relevance in the context for which the platform has been designed. In this section we present a more formalized view of the adopted coordination model.

First of all we introduce the concept of process state that we previously informally hinted. Please notice that in this section we assume for process the broad definition of a coordinated set of activities leading to a goal (and not, for example, the instance of a process model), a definition that includes organizational best practices. In our context the state of a process is the combination of all the data related to the process, data that can be scattered through the various social software tools (like blog posts, twitter messages, RSS feed items and so on) and emails exchanged by the actors involved in the process.

Actors pursue their goals through sequences of interactions with various web applications; these sequences are composed of steps; each interaction step results in a modification of the process state (of course there are interactions between the actors and the tools that does not result in a state modification, we simply do not take these into account here). We can then represent a sequence through its steps:

$$a_1, a_2, ..., a_n$$

Some of the steps can be freely performed after their preceding ones has been executed; others require that different actions in the process are performed before being activated. A typical example of this behavior is that of a scientific journal editor waiting for three reviews from different reviewers to be received before deciding whether to accept or reject a submitted article (using social software tools we can support this process using a forum and an organizational best practice that suggest that reviews should to be posted as replies in a thread where the submitted article is attached to the first message). We make these synchronization requirements explicit in the sequence by introducing synchronization steps. These steps halt the execution of a sequence until the process reaches a specific state (or, more precisely, until a condition upon a subset of the state is satisfied). In the aforementioned example the synchronization steps that halts the sequence waiting for the three reviews to be posted is satisfied when the number of the posts in the submission thread (that is displayed in the forum web interface) reaches the value 4.

By denoting with s a synchronization step, the sequence becomes:

$$a_1, ..., a_j, s_1, a_{j+1}, ..., a_k, s_2, a_{k+1}, ...$$

We can add a dummy sequence step at the beginning of the sequence and split it at the synchronization steps obtaining sub-sequences of the form:

$$s_1, a'_1, ..., a'_{n'}$$

$$s_2, a''_1, ..., a''_{n''}$$

$$...$$

By adding a causal requirement to each step $s_1, ..., s_n$ (in order to impose the sequential activation of the sub-sequences) we produce $s'_1, ..., s'_n$ that we use to replace the original synchronization steps in our sub-sequences.

The sub-sequences thus obtained are rules in which the first step is a guard and the following ones are actions that change the state of the system. The use of state-based rules to realize coordination belongs to several well-known coordination models, languages and systems: this is the case of Gamma [3] - inspired languages (such as the CHAM [4]), of Interaction Abstract Machine [12] -inspired languages (such as LO [1]), of blackboard-inspired languages (such as (Extended) Shared Prolog [6]) and, to some extent, to Event-Condition-Action-based workflow execution engines too (such as the one described in [5]).

It should be noted, however, that while most of the aforementioned proposals assume a rewriting approach in which the rules (atomically) consume and produce elements of state, in our approach the guards do not consume state elements but simply check a state-based predicate. One of the main consequences of this approach is that, if no countermeasures are applied, once a rule has its guard satisfied that rule can fire an indefinite amount of times until the predicate associated to the guard becomes false. In order to avoid this behavior, as described in Sect. 3, rules are activated only when a predicate associated to a guard changes from false to true which means that, technically, the rules are based on a state-transition event. Another relevant issue to keep in mind with respect to the coordination model and its actual implementation is that our systems realizes a *coordination overlay* on top of social software and, as such, it inherits most of its limitations. This means that there is not a synchronized view of the shared state and locking is not available (since is not provided by the underlying system), thus it is not possible to guarantee transactionality, atomicity and mutual exclusion. Consider also that state changes are not notified by the Web applications and our system has to recur to polling (which amplifies the state-view synchronization problem).

While these limits are significant the reader has to keep in mind that this system has been designed to support (and sometimes replace) the users in their interactions within Web applications and, as such, these are the very same limits human users have to cope with.

The coordination model we just introduced is quite similar to the one proposed in X-Folders [13]. The differences in the platform, however, are noteworthy: X-Folders operates on information stored in document spaces and actions are sequences of Web service calls.

In general we argue that the use of a rule based coordination model in the context of social software is quite natural: the fact that actions depend on a shared state and not on the state of singular actors and the fact that interaction patterns are not imposed from the environment (coordination is endogenous, not exogenous [2]) clearly point to rule-based models as the better candidates. It is interesting to notice that the structured/emergent dichotomy we cited in Sect. 1 is related to the one between exogenous and endogenous coordination languages: exogenous coordination languages (most business process modeling languages and notations fall under this category) are the ideal partners of structured coordination whereas emergent coordination is naturally better addressed by endogenous languages (the astute reader may argue that structured coordination can be addressed with endogenous coordination languages as well; true, but this case in not relevant in the context of this paper).

It is worth to notice that, whereas internally WikiRecPlay is implemented on the basis of the presented model, the rule-based approach is never directly exposed to the end user who can keep thinking in terms of long interaction sequences that are usually easier to understand since users tend to take a personal perspective of the process that ultimately results in the sequence of actions they are in charge of.

6   Discussion and Related Works

Most of the existing coordination systems proposed to complement social software tools are based on a prescriptive approach and usually require the modification of the tools (that, ultimately, means that usual online services cannot be adopted); this is for example the case for [7]. Some research work has also been carried on the idea of sharing interaction sequences for web applications (part of what WikiRecPlay does), CoScripter [10] (and its evolution ActionShot [11]) being notable examples. Just like WikiRecPlay, CoScripter allow users to share recordings into a Wiki to share them. The main differences between WikiRecPlay and CoScripter are: (i) CoScripter encodes user gestures with an easy-to-read scripting language that mimics natural language whereas WikiRecPlay adopts a much more refined user interface; (ii) CoScripter does not support most dynamic pages in which elements are created/modified after the page is loaded in the web browser whereas WikiRecPlay has been designed to support most of these pages; (iii) recordings personalization in CoScripter is implemented by using a *personal database* in which user-dependent data can be stored whereas WikiRecPlay allows the user to personalize recordings by showing dialogs in which instance data can be provided; (iv) CoScripter has only basic support to halt a sequence replay whereas WikiRecPlay can halt an action sequence and resume its execution when a specific event takes place. This last point is possibly the most glaring difference with respect to our approach: CoScripter, in fact, can only be used to replay the interactions of a single user with a web application but cannot be used in the context of multi-user coordinated processes since it lacks support any explicit synchronization support.

7   Conclusions

Social software is an enabling technology for emergent processes. Social software, however, is not a coordination platform in which it offers no support other than making information available. In this paper we presented a coordination platform built on top of social software, that requires no modifications to the existing tools and that plays nicely with the open collaboration idea that is promoted by social software. The platform is implemented by augmenting social software tools with WikiRecPlay and InFeed providing support for defining, sharing, automating interaction sequences and synchronizing users' activities, that is: providing support to share and enact organizational best practices.

Both WikiRecPlay and InFeed, while actual running software, are to be mainly intended as poofs-of-concept, as such they present several limitations. One of the current limits of WikiRecPlay is that it is only available when the user's browser is in execution. This means that automatic guarded sequences are not fired when the browser is not running. While this is a major limit to the actual use of our platform (we acknowledge this, and in fact we are working on a off-line, server-side version of the sequence player) the existing implementation has to be intended as a proof-of-concept and as such it serves its purpose. InFeed does not suffer from the major limitations present in WikiRecPlay, and it is also a much simpler system, since it delegates most of its functionalities to Dapper and Pipes. This also mean, however, that it inherits all the limits of these systems (that are usually restriction with respect to the intended use rather than technical limitations - for example Dapper cannot be used, by design, to extract content from sites that can be accessed only after authentication).

Future versions will enhance the tools and improve their "on-the field usability" but the basic working mechanism are going to be the same of the current proof-of-concept implementations.

References

1. Andreoli, J.-M., Pareschi, R.: Communication as fair distribution of knowledge. In: OOPSLA, pp. 212–229 (1991)
2. Arbab, F.: What do you mean, coordination? Technical report, Bulletin of the Dutch Association for Theoretical Computer Science, NVTI (1998)
3. Banâtre, J.-P., Le Métayer, D.: Programming by multiset transformation. Commun. ACM 36(1), 98–111 (1993)
4. Berry, G., Boudol, G.: The chemical abstract machine. Theor. Comput. Sci. 96(1), 217–248 (1992)
5. Bussler, C., Jablonski, S.: Implementing agent coordination for workflow management systems using active database systems. In: Proceedings Fourth International Workshop on Research Issues in Data Engineering, Active Database Systems, pp. 53–59 (February 1994)
6. Ciancarini, P.: Coordinating rule-based software processes with esp. ACM Trans. Softw. Eng. Methodol. 2(3), 203–227 (1993)
7. Dengler, F., Koschmider, A., Oberweis, A., Zhang, H.: Social Software for Coordination of Collaborative Process Activities. In: zur Muehlen, M., Su, J. (eds.) BPM 2010 Workshops. LNBIP, vol. 66, pp. 396–407. Springer, Heidelberg (2011)
8. Ellis, C.A., Gibbs, S.J., Rein, G.: Groupware: some issues and experiences. Commun. ACM 34(1), 39–58 (1991)
9. Erol, S., Granitzer, M., Happ, S., Jantunen, S., Jennings, B., Johannesson, P., Koschmider, A., Nurcan, S., Rossi, D., Schmidt, R.: Combining BPM and social software: contradiction or chance? Journal of Software Maintenance and Evolution: Research and Practice 22(6-7), 449–476 (2010)

10. Leshed, G., Haber, E.M., Matthews, T., Lau, T.: Coscripter: automating & sharing how-to knowledge in the enterprise. In: Proceeding of the Twenty-Sixth Annual SIGCHI Conference on Human Factors in Computing Systems, CHI 2008, pp. 1719–1728. ACM, New York (2008)
11. Li, I., Nichols, J., Lau, T., Drews, C., Cypher, A.: Here's what i did: sharing and reusing web activity with actionshot. In: Proceedings of the 28th International Conference on Human Factors in Computing Systems, CHI 2010, pp. 723–732. ACM, New York (2010)
12. Andreoli, J.-M., Ciancarini, P., Pareschi, R.: Interaction abstract machines. In: Trends in Object-Based Concurrent Computing, pp. 257–280. MIT Press (1993)
13. Rossi, D.: X-folders: documents on the move. Concurr. Comput.: Pract. Exper. 18(4), 409–425 (2006)
14. Shanks, B.: Wikigateway: a library for interoperability and accelerated wiki development. In: Proceedings of the 2005 International Symposium on Wikis, WikiSym 2005, pp. 53–66. ACM, New York (2005)

Synchronization of Multiple Autonomic Control Loops: Application to Cloud Computing

Frederico Alvares de Oliveira Jr., Remi Sharrock, and Thomas Ledoux

Ascola Research Group (Mines Nantes-INRIA, LINA)
Ecole des Mines de Nantes,
4, rue Alfred Kastler, 44307 Nantes, France
{frederico.alvares,remi.sharrock,thomas.ledoux}@mines-nantes.fr

Abstract. Over the past years, Autonomic Computing has become very popular, especially in scenarios of Cloud Computing, where there might be several autonomic loops aiming at turning each layer of the cloud stack more autonomous, adaptable and aware of the runtime environment. Nevertheless, due to conflicting objectives, non-synchronized autonomic loops may lead to global inconsistent states. For instance, in order to maintain its Quality of Service, an application provider might request more and more resources while the infrastructure provider, due to power shortage may be forced to reduce the resource provisioning. In this paper, we propose a generic model to deal with the synchronization and coordination of autonomic loops and how it can be applied in the context of Cloud Computing. We present some simulation results to show the scalability and feasibility of our proposal.

Keywords: Cloud Computing, Autonomic Computing, Autonomic Loop Synchronization, Coordination.

1   Introduction

The necessity of modern software systems to be more responsive and autonomous to environment changes is one of the main reasons for the popularization of Autonomic Computing [7]. Cloud Computing is one of the most expressive examples of this great adoption. Indeed, the flexibility inherent to cloud services along with the high variability of demand for those services have recently contributed to the large adoption of Autonomic Computing in Cloud-based systems [1].

In point of fact, from the application provider perspective, Autonomic Computing makes application capable of reacting to a highly variable workload by dynamically adjusting the amount of resources needed to be executed while keeping its Quality of Service (QoS) [11]. From the infrastructure provider point of view, it also makes the infrastructure capable of rapidly reacting to environment changes (e.g. increase/decrease of physical resource usage) by optimizing the allocation of resources and thereby reduce the costs related to energy consumption [4].

However, getting several control loops working on common or inter-dependent managed elements is not a trivial task [6]. For example, in order to cope with

M. Sirjani (Ed.): COORDINATION 2012, LNCS 7274, pp. 29–43, 2012.

a high demand, Application Providers may request more and more computing resources to the Infrastructure Provider. At the same time, the Infrastructure Provider may turn off part of its physical infrastructure to meet power constraints. Therefore, dealing with multiple control loops with conflicting objectives (performance *vs* power) may lead to inconsistent global results. Besides, inter-control loop interactions must be synchronised and coordinated for the various phases of adaptations [13].

This paper proposes a generic model for synchronization and coordination of control loops. We have studied a communication model for several control loops and proposed a coordination protocol based on interloop events and actions. To allow safe interactions, we propose a shared knowledge-based synchronization pattern. That way, decisions taken by one control loop may take into consideration some information provided by other control loops. This model is applied to a Cloud Computing scenario in which several self-adaptive applications interact with a common self-adaptive infrastructure. The objective at the application level is to manage the runtime context to minimize costs while maximizing the QoS, whereas at the infrastructure level, the objective is to manage the context to optimize the utilization rate. The feasibility and scalability of this approach is evaluated via simulation-based experiments on the Cloud Computing scenario.

The remainder of this paper is organized as follows: Section 2 presents our contribution by describing a generic model for synchronization and coordination of multiple control loops. In Section 3, this model is instantiated in a scenario of Cloud Computing. Section 4 presents the evaluation of our approach. Section 5 presents a brief discussion about the most relevant works related to this paper. Finally, Section 6 concludes the paper and provides some future research directions.

2   A Multiple Control Loops Architecture Model

Autonomic computing [7] aims at providing self-management capabilities to systems. The managed system is monitored through sensors, and an analysis of this information is used, in combination with knowledge about the system, to plan and execute reconfigurations through actuators. Classically, an autonomic manager internal structure is implemented by a MAPE-K (Monitor-Analyze-Plan-Execute phases over a Knowledge base) control loop [5]. Bottom-up interactions between the managed system and the autonomic manager are realized via *events* whereas top-down interactions via *actions*.

Our approach aims to provide synchronized and coordinated control loops by introducing a synchronization of the shared knowledge and a coordination protocol.

2.1   A Model of Autonomic Behavior

We make a distinction between three kinds of control loops:

- **Independent**: this type of control loop is completely independent from the others. The source of the received events is always the managed system

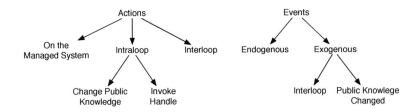

Fig. 1. Actions and Events hierarchy

and the actions are executed only on the considered system. There is no communication between control loops and the knowledge is entirely internal (private to the control loop).

- **Coordinated**: this type of control loop communicates with the others. Events may come from other control loops and actions may notify other control loops. A business-specific protocol defines a way for the control loops to communicate. In this case, we do not consider the sharing of information between control loops but only simple asynchronous communication.
- **Synchronized**: this type of control loop synchronizes with the others in order to share some information for a collective activity. Access to this shared information may lead to concurrency and consistency problems.

In our Cloud Computing scenario, we consider coordinated and synchronized control loops and demonstrate both situations.

A Public and Private Knowledge Model. In the case of synchronized control loops, regarding the sharing of information we separate the knowledge base in two parts: the **private knowledge** that stores the internal information needed by the internal control loop phases and the **public knowledge** shared among other control loops. The public knowledge base may have to be synchronized if the actions executed by the control loops require to modify the information (directly or indirectly). Indeed, the simultaneous actions of multiple control loops may require to change the public knowledge at the same time (concurrency problem) and may lead to non-logical global results (consistency problem). In our approach, we consider that the owner of the public knowledge is the only one able to modify it directly, which limits the concurrency problem.

Actions. In order to clarify the interactions between several control loops, it is important to differentiate actions and events that are part of the managed system and those part of the multi control loop system model. Figure 1 introduces a hierarchy of the different types of events and actions.

Actions can be executed on the considered managed system, can start a phase within the control loop (intraloop) or notify another control loop (interloop).

The actions on the managed system and the interloop actions are always executed by the execution phase of the control loop. The intraloop actions are either executed by the monitoring phase to launch the analysis phase or the execution phase ($M \rightarrow A$ or $M \rightarrow E$), by the analysis phase to launch the planning phase ($A \rightarrow P$) or by the planning phase to launch the execution phase ($P \rightarrow E$).

An interloop action may notify another control loop as if it was asking for a service and waiting for the response. In this case, the planning phase creates a handler that contains all the other actions that have to be executed in response to this interloop action. This interloop action is therefore a notify action that creates an interloop event for the target control loop.

Intraloop actions are either Change Public Knowledge or Invoke Handler actions. In our approach, we consider that these actions do not need analysis or planning phases to be launched, which corresponds to the $M \rightarrow E$ case.

Events. In Figure 1, we differentiate endogenous and exogenous events. The source of endogenous events is always the considered managed system. The source of exogenous events is another control loop. For the exogenous events, we consider the difference between the interloop events - created by the interloop action - and the Public Knowledge Changed - created by the Change Public Knowledge action.

In order for the control loops to send and receive events, we consider that they already implement the publish/subscribe paradigm. The control loops using some public knowledge of other control loops automatically subscribe to the Public Knowledge Changed events.

2.2   Control Loop Synchronization and Coordination

Token Protocol for Synchronizing the Public Knowledge. The public knowledge is divided into one non-critical section and some critical sections. One control loop may access multiple non-critical sections but one and only one critical section at a time in order to avoid deadlocks. To synchronize the public knowledge we introduce a simple token protocol. Each critical section is associated with one token. As for transactions in databases, this synchronization protocol ensures that only one control loop can access a critical section. To access the critical section, a control loop has to get the corresponding token. To get the token, a control loop can either ask explicitly for the token with a TOKEN REQUEST message (active token request) or can receive the token from another control loop with a TOKEN TRANSFER message (passive token reception). Whenever a control loop does not need the token anymore it releases it with a TOKEN RELEASE message. Whenever a token is requested, the requester has to wait for a TOKEN ACQUIRED message. Each control loop having a public knowledge with critical sections implements a token manager which is in charge of managing the token protocol.

Control Loop Coordination Protocol. Considering the coordinated case with multiple control loops, we take into consideration what we call the collaboration problem where two control loops have to communicate in order to accomplish a global activity together. Indeed, the execution phase of one control loop may ask another control loop a service and wait for the result in return. To do this, the first control loop triggers an interloop event that starts the second control loop. As for the "future objects" in distributed concurrency problems [2], the first control loop creates at the same time a handler containing all the actions that need to be executed after the service is terminated. The interloop event is, as always, detected by the monitoring phase of the second control loop. Once the service is terminated, another interloop event is sent back to the caller control loop. Parts of the results may be transferred using the public knowledge base, to do this, the interloop events may be coupled with token transfer messages.

Timing the Control Loops. All the control loops are evolving in a dynamic environment where multiple events may occur simultaneously. The arrival rate of these events may vary from one control loop to another and are usually stored in a waiting queue. In order to manage the arrival of these events, the monitoring phase of each control loop has a scheduling process. This scheduler may implement different policies, some of them may take into account the events priorities. In our approach and for the sake of simplicity, we consider a FIFO (First-In First-Out) scheduling policy without priorities for endogenous events, and consider the interloop events that invoke handlers with the highest priority. Indeed, handlers are containing actions that have to be executed in response to a service request and need to be treated in priority in order for the source event to be considered as treated as soon as possible. Therefore, one event is considered to be treated only if the entire control loop is finished, including the possible handlers.

In order to formalize the timings, we introduce these notations:

$$T_i^j = T_{lock} + \mu_i^j \tag{1}$$
$$\mu_i^j = T_i^{jA} + \rho_i(modif) * (T_i^{jP} + T_i^{jE}) \tag{2}$$
$$T_i^{jE} = T_i^{jE_{actions}} + \rho_i(interloop) * (T_{i'}^{j'} + T_i^{jE_{handler}}) \tag{3}$$

T_i^j : Time to treat event i for control loop j

T_{lock} : Waiting time for the token to be acquired

μ_i^j : service time on control loop j for event i

$\rho_i(modif)$: probability to start a planning and execution phase (modification of the system required)

T_i^{jA} : Analysis phase time for event i and control loop j

T_i^{jP} : Planning phase time for event i and control loop j

T_i^{jE} : Execution phase time for event i and control loop j

$T_i^{jE_{actions}}$: First part of the execution phase time for event i and control loop j

$\rho_i(interloop)$: Probability to ask another control loop a service with an interloop event

$T_{i'}^{j'}$: Time for the other control loop j' to treat the interloop event i'

$T_i^{jE_{handlers}}$: Time to execute the handlers for event i and control loop j

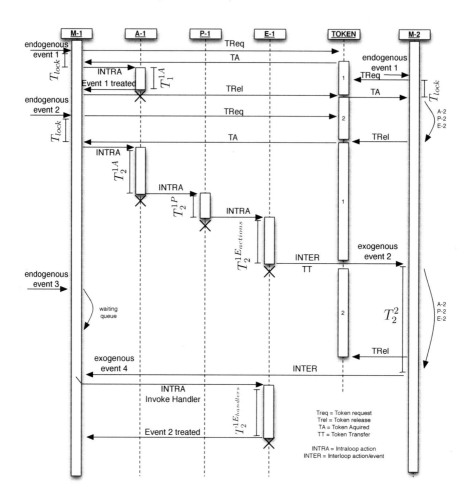

Fig. 2. Control loops coordination and token synchronization protocols and timings

Figure 2 shows how two control loops would use the token synchronization protocol and the coordination protocol with a sequence diagram. The M-1 to E-1 vertical lines are the phases of the first control loop and we show only the monitoring phase of the second control loop M-2. The TOKEN line shows which control loop has the token to access one critical section of the public knowledge of the second control loop.

As we can see the monitoring phases are continuously listening for events. A first endogenous event arrives for control loops 1 and 2. The control loop 1 acquires the token (TReq and TA), launches the analysis (INTRA) and releases the token straight after the event is treated (TRel). The same goes for control loop 2 which acquires the token as soon as it is released by control loop 1.

A second endogenous event is treated by control loop 1 which requires a coordination between control loop 1 and control loop 2. First, the loop 1 acquires the token and launches the analysis A-1, the planning P-1 and the execution phases E-1. As we can see control loop 1 sends an exogenous event to control loop 2 (first INTER, exogenous event 2) along with the token (TT). This allows control loop 2 to eventually modify its knowledge. As soon as control loop 2 finishes to treat this event, it sends back an exogenous event to control loop 1 (second INTER, exogenous event 4), which allows control loop 1 to execute the handler (INTRA invoke handler) and to finish treating the event 2.

3   Cloud Computing Scenario

The objective of this section is to instantiate the generic model presented in Section 2 in the context of Cloud Computing. First, we give some definitions and assumptions for this scenario. Then, we present a multi-control loop architecture along with its possible events, actions and public knowledge.

3.1   Definitions and Assumptions

The Cloud Computing architecture is typically defined as a stack of several inter-dependent systems, in which systems on lower layer are service providers to subsystems on upper layers. Our scenario consists of two types of inter-dependent managed systems: Applications and Infrastructure. An application is defined as a set of components. Each component offers a set of services, which, in turn, might depend on a set of references to services offered by other components. Services are bound to references through bindings. The application can operate in different architectural configurations, which are determined by the subset of components used and how they are linked to each other. In other words, one configuration is composed of a set of bindings. In addition, each configuration has also its QoS defined in terms of performance and an application-specific QoS. The former corresponds to the application responsiveness when dealing with a given number of simultaneous requests λ (requests/sec), whereas the latter is a quality degree specific to the application domain.

The infrastructure consists of a set of Physical Machines (PMs), whose computing resources (CPU and RAM) are made available by means of Virtual Machines (VMs). There might be one or several classes of VM, each one with a different CPU or RAM capacity. Application Providers are charged an amount per hour for using a VM instance. They may deploy the same component on one or more VMs, that is, for each component there might be one or several instances. Finally, the Infrastructure Provider may give a limited number of discounts for each VM classes in order to attract Application Providers so as to occupy portions of resources that are not being utilized and hence improve their utilization rate.

Figure 3 illustrates two cloud applications hosted by the same infrastructure. Application 1 is composed of 4 components and Application 2 is composed of

3 components. The dotted lines express a potential bind between components, whereas the solid lines mean a binding of the current configuration. For application 1, there are two possible configurations ($\{c_1, c_2, c_3\}$ and $\{c_1, c_4, c_3\}$). For application 2, there are also two possible configurations: $\{c_1, c_2\}$ and $\{c_1, c_3\}$.

The infrastructure is composed of 3 PMs and offers computing resources through three different kinds of VMs (small, medium and large). There are 7 VMs instances to host all the components of both applications. It should be noticed that there are two instances for components c_2 (application 1) and c_1 (application 2), that is, there are two VMs allocated to each component. That way, components may scale up and down according to the application demand.

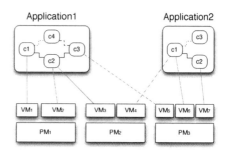

Fig. 3. Cloud Computing Scenario

3.2   Multi-control Loop Architecture

This scenario comprises several coordinated control loops: one at the infrastructure level, namely the infrastructure manager (IM) and one per-application at application level, namely application manager (AM), as shown in Figure 4.

AMs control loops aim at minimizing the amount of VMs needed to keep the level of QoS as high as possible. Furthermore, AMs are able to adapt their application's architectural configuration in order to cope with resource restriction imposed by the IM. More precisely, AMs monitor/listen for events that come either from the application itself or from the IM; analyze whether or not it is necessary to reconfigure the application by considering the execution context (e.g. the workload, the current application configuration, the current mapping of components to VMs, etc.); elaborate a reconfiguration plan; and execute actions corresponding to the reconfiguration plan.

Regarding the IM, apart from dealing with requests sent by AMs, its objective is to optimize the placement of these VMs on PMs so that it is possible to reduce the number of PMs powered on and consequently reduce the energy consumption. To this end, the IM monitors/listens for events that come either from the infrastructure itself (e.g. PMs Utilization) or from the AMs; analyze whether or not it is necessary to replace or to change its current configuration by considering the execution context (e.g. the current mapping VMs to PMs); plan and execute the reconfiguration.

As previously mentioned, multiple control loops might have conflicting objectives. Particularly in this scenario, while the IM looks forward to allocate all VMs in the fewest possible number of PMs (due to energy constraints reasons), some AMs may request more VMs in order to cope with an increase in the demand. In this context, we can apply the coordination and synchronization protocols presented in Section 2. The coordination protocol defines a set of messages

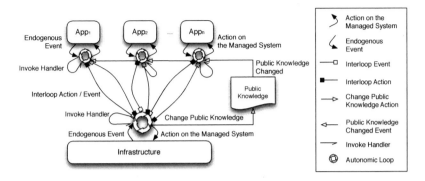

Fig. 4. Multi-control loop Architecture for the Cloud Computing Scenario

exchanged by control loops that transformed into actions and events and used for instance to inform AMs about energy shortage at the infrastructure level. The synchronization protocol defines a set of public knowledge (critical) sections that are used for all control loops. For instance, the IM can change the VMs renting fees by putting some VMs on sale. The shared knowledge is used by AMs to take into consideration those changes in order to take better decisions.

Application Manager Events and Actions. Workload Increased/Decreased are endogenous events corresponding to the percentage of the workload increase/decrease within a pre-defined amount of time. It triggers the analysis phase to determine whether or not it is necessary to request or release resources (VM). The result of this process is translated into a Request VMs interloop action (Figure 5 (a)) or Stop and Unbind Component actions on the application (managed system), followed by a Release VMs interloop (Figure 5 (b)).

It is important to notice that in this scenario the public knowledge resides at infrastructure level and it corresponds to the VMs renting fees. Hence, Renting Fees Changed is a Public Knowledge Changed event that happen when the VM Renting Fees are changed (e.g. new VMs with discount available). This kind of event triggers the analysis phase that may result in a Request VMs action (scale up) (Figure 5 (c)).

Scale Down is an interloop (exogenous) event whose objective is to notify the AM (from the IM) that it should meet some constraints on the number of VMs allocated to the application. Basically, it informs which VMs among those allocated to the application should be immediately destroyed, giving AMs an amount of time to adapt to this constraint. Thus, this event triggers an analysis phase to reallocate the components on a smaller number of VMs. To this end, it might be necessary to change the application architectural configuration (e.g. to replace components that are more resource consuming). As a result, a set of Deploy, Bind/Unbind, Start/Stop Component actions on the application, followed by a Release VMs interloop action are executed (Figure 5 (d)).

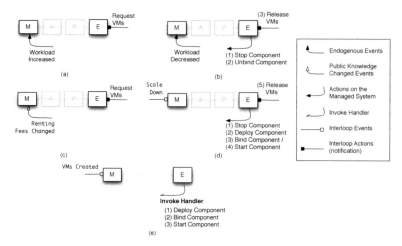

Fig. 5. Application Manager Events and Actions

Finally, VMs Created is also an interloop event which objective is to notify (from the IM) that the VMs Requested are ready for use. It triggers the execution phase that does nothing but invoking the handler (Figure 5 (e)). In this case, the executor deploys the components on the created VMs, bind those components to other (existing or new ones) and start the just deployed components.

Infrastructure Manager Events and Actions. Regarding the IM, VM Requested is an interloop event that happens when some AM performs a Request VMs interloop action. They trigger the analysis phase that evaluates the placement of the requested VMs on PMs so as to minimize the number of PMs needed. The result of this analysis is translated into a set of Power-on PM actions and a set of Create VM actions on the infrastructure. Finally, it notifies the AM that requested the VMs by executing a VMs Created interloop action (Figure 6 (a)).

VMs Released is also an interloop event that happens when some AM performs a Release VMs interloop action. It is directly translated into VM Destroy actions on the infrastructure (Figure 6 (b)).

Energy Shortage is an endogenous event that comes from the infrastructure context data (e.g. power meters or an announcement of energy unavailability). It triggers the analysis phase to determine which VM should be destroyed. As a consequence, which PMs should be powered-off. The result is translated into a Scale Down interloop action to notify the concerned AMs about the constraints. Then, it sets a timeout after which the VMs to be destroyed have actually to be destroyed along with a set of possible Power-off PM actions (if there are unused PMs) may take place on the infrastructure (Figure 6 (c)).

Low PM Utilization is also an infrastructure endogenous event which is detected anytime a PM has been under-utilized during a certain period of time. It triggers the analysis phase to evaluate whether to give a certain number of discount on VMs or not. The result is translated into an Update Renting Fees (Change Public Knowledge) action (Figure 6 (d)).

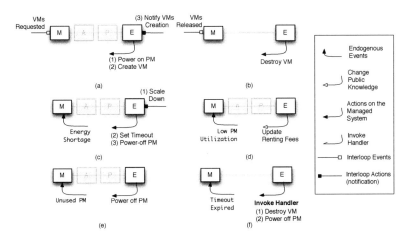

Fig. 6. Infrastructure Manager Events and Actions

Similarly, Unused PM is an infrastructure endogenous event which is detected anytime a PM has not hosted any VM during a certain period of time. It directly triggers the execution phase that runs Power-off PM actions (Figure 6 (e)).

Finally, Timeout Expired is an infrastructure endogenous event which is detected when the timeout set along with the Scale Down interloop action expires. It directly triggers the execution phase that invokes the handler specified before the Scale Down interloop action. This handler simply executes a set of Destroy VM and Power off PM actions on the infrastructure (Figure 6 (f)).

Public Knowledge Management. In our scenario, only one token is used, since the Renting Fees is the only Public Knowledge resource that is accessed by more than one control loop. At the application level, every time an AM triggers the analysis phase that takes into account the discount prices, a TOKEN REQUEST message is sent to the token manager that responds back with a TOKEN ACQUIRED message, once it has the token available. A TOKEN TRANSFER message is sent along with a Request VMs interloop action from the AM to the IM. Once the requested VMs (in discount) are created and the Renting Fees are updated, the IM sends a TOKEN RELEASE message to the token manager.

In the same way, the IM sends a TOKEN REQUEST every time a Low PM Utilization event is detected. Once it receives a TOKEN ACQUIRED message, it analyzes the discount opportunity. If there are discounts to be given, the IM sends a TOKEN RELEASE after having updated the Renting Fees. Otherwise, the TOKEN RELEASE message is sent right after the analysis phase is done.

4   Evaluation

This section aims at presenting some results obtained from experiments on the proposed approach. We applied the proposed model to the cloud computing scenario presented in Section 3 and performed simulation-based evaluations regarding the system stability and scalability when dealing with several control loops. The evaluation regarding the optimization problems (e.g. QoS and energy consumption trade-off improvements) were already addressed in our previous works [11]. We first describe the experiment setup, then we present and discuss the results found.

4.1 Setup

The experiments were performed on a machine with the following configuration: Intel Core 2 Duo processor, 4GB DRAM, Mac OS X Lion operating system. Concerning the simulator, Java 6 was used to implement it. Based on our experience from previous work [1], the execution time for each phase of each control loop j was fixed as follows: $T^{jA} = 2 * T^{jP}$ and $T^{jE} = 3 * T^{jP}$. For sake of simplicity we assigned the same values for each phase execution time to all kinds events. More precisely, for all AMs $T^{amA} = T^{imA} = 200 \pm \epsilon_A, T^{amP} = T^{im^P} = 100 \pm \epsilon_P$ and $T^{amE} = T^{imE} = 300 \pm \epsilon_E$, where ϵ_A, ϵ_P and ϵ_E means a variation of more or less at most 20% of the value.

We generate the arrival rates for the endogenous events based on a Poisson distribution. Table 1 shows two classes of arrival rates used in the experiments: high and low. Furthermore, we perform several runs while varying the number of AM control loops: $10, 20, 30, 50$ and 70. The idea is to observe how the variation of these parameters (arrival rates and number of AMs) can affect the system performance (e.g. the token waiting time and events processing time).

When the AMs detect a Workload Increased event, the probability that the result of the analysis phase requires a Request VMs interloop action was fixed to 0.7 (i.e. $\rho_{wi}(modif) = 0.7$ and $\rho_{wi}(interloop) = 1$). Idem for a Workload Decreased event. When they receive a Renting Fees Changed event, the probability that the result of the analysis phase requires a Request VMs interloop action was fixed in 0.3 (i.e. $\rho_{rfc}(modif) = 0.3$ and $\rho_{rfc}(interloop) = 1$). The others events are treated in a deterministic way, i.e. the probabilities $\rho_i(modif)$ and $\rho_i(interloop)$ are equal either to 0 or 1 [1].

4.2 Results

Table 1. Arrival Rates for Endogenous Events

Class	Workload Increased	Workload Decreased	Low PM Util.	PM Unused	Energy Shortage
High	0.1	0.1	0.1	0.05	0.01
Low	0.05	0.05	0.05	0.025	0.01

Stability. Figure 7 shows the average token waiting time T_{lock} evolution in time. Each line corresponds to one run regarding a different number of AMs in the system. When dealing with low arrival rates

---

[1] Due to space limitations, we omit this information.

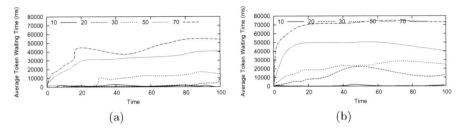

Fig. 7. Average Token Waiting Time for (a) Low and (b) High Arrival Rates

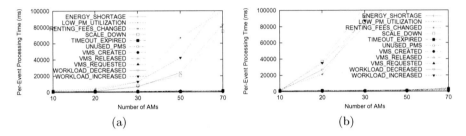

Fig. 8. Per-Event Processing Time for (a) Low and (b) High Arrival Rates

(Figure 7 (a)), for 50 and 70 AMs, T_{lock} increases until it reaches a peak and stabilizes afterwards. For 10, 20 and 30 AMs, T_{lock} remains always under $10000ms$. When dealing with high arrival rates (Figure 7 (b)), we can observe a similar behavior for all the curves. Notice that T_{lock} rapidly increases for the highest numbers of AMs (i.e. 30, 50, 70) and stabilizes afterwards.

Scalability. Figure 8 presents the evolution of the event processing time (T_i^j, for control loop j and event i) when varying the number of AMs in the system. Not surprisingly, Workload Increased, Renting Fees Changed, Scale Down and Workload Decreased trigger the most time consuming processes, since the two first ones might be followed by a token request, which may lead to a sharp increase of the token manager queue. The two last ones may stay stuck waiting until the others have finished.

Discussion. With respect to the stability, there might be high token waiting times as the arrival rates approach the service rate (frequency in which a control loop can process an event). For instance, a high rate of the Workload Increased event along with a high number of concurrent AMs may produce a token arrival rate that might exceed the token manager service, leading to an infinite growth of the token manager queue. However, as long as the arrival and service rates are well managed, the token waiting time will always tend to stabilize.

Conversely, the number of AMs along with high arrival rates may have a negative impact on the system scalability. For instance, for events that depend on a token, a long token waiting time may lead to long event processing time. Thus, the more AMs the longer the token waiting times and consequently the event processing times. Again, by adjusting the arrival rates and the number of AMs in the system properly, the system can be scaled with respect to the number of AMs and the frequency of requests f produced by them (resulting from the coordination). Although the control of exceeding arrival rates has not been tackled in this work, we believe that admission control techniques [14], along with event prioritization / preemption policies, can be effective to implement it.

5   Related Work

The issue of orchestrating autonomic managers has been addressed by IBM since 2005 [5] and the first interesting results have been proposed by J. Kephart and al. in order to achieve specific power-performance trade-offs [6]. The authors developed architectural and algorithmic choices allowing two managers to work together to act in accordance, resulting in power savings.

Coordinating multiple autonomic managers to achieve specific and common goal have been receiving a lot of attention in the last years. [8] identifies five different patterns of interacting control loops in self-adaptive systems where each pattern can be considered as a particular way to orchestrate the control loops. [3] goes further and proposes a collection of architectural design patterns addressing different classes of integration problems focusing on the possibly conflicting goals. [10] proposes a hierarchical model of control loops where a coordination manager orchestrates the other autonomic managers to satisfy properties of consistency. [13] extends control loops with support for two types of coordination: intra-loop and inter-loop coordinations very close to ours; however, the implementation framework is dedicated to a self-healing use case.

In comparison to these works, this paper provides a more focused discussion to the general problem of orchestrating autonomic managers and proposes a generic model to manage the coordination of multiple autonomic loops.

In the context of Cloud Computing, [12] proposed an approach for cloud resources management which objective is to determine the number of VMs necessary and thereafter to pack those VMs into the minimum number of PMs. Our work extends this approach by providing coordination protocols to cope with conflicting objectives. Finally, focusing on the granularity constraints of actuators and sensors, [9] relied on *proportional thresholding* in order to provide a more effective control for coarse-grained actuators. Our work, instead, focuses on minimizing conflicting objectives by providing a shared data-based knowledge along with a set of protocols to help the coordination and synchronization of multiple control loops.

6   Conclusion

The flexible and dynamic nature of modern software systems is one of the main reasons for the popularization of Autonomic Computing. As a consequence, multiple control loops cohabiting in the system is more and more often used. However, managing multiple control loops towards a single goal is not an easy task, since it may pose problems like conflicting objectives and concurrency issues.

In this context, this paper proposed a generic model to manage the synchronization and coordination of multiple control loops. The model was applied to a scenario in the context of Cloud Computing and evaluated under simulation-based experiments. The results suggest the feasibility of our approach by showing that the system scales and stabilizes in time.

Currently, we are working on a more realistic experimentation setup. Firstly, we aim at deploying the Cloud Computing scenario on a large scale physical infrastructure under mainstream cloud solutions (e.g. OpenNebula, Eucalyptus, etc.). After, we plan to evaluate our proposal in other scenarios than Cloud Computing to show the genericity of our approach.

References

1. Alvares De Oliveira Jr., F., Lèbre, A., Ledoux, T., Menaud, J.M.: Self-management of applications and systems to optimize energy in data centers. In: Brandic, I., Villari, M., Tusa, F. (eds.) Achieving Federated and Self-Manageable Cloud Infrastructures: Theory and Practice. IGI Global (May 2012)
2. Eugster, P.T., Felber, P.A., Guerraoui, R., Kermarrec, A.M.: The many faces of publish/subscribe. ACM Computing Surveys 35(2), 114–131 (2003)
3. Frey, S., Diaconescu, A., Demeure, I.: Architectural integration patterns for autonomic management systems. In: Proc. of the 9th IEEE International Conference and Workshops on the Engineering of Autonomic and Autonomous Systems (EASe 2012). IEEE (April 2012)
4. Hermenier, F., Lorca, X., Menaud, J.M., Muller, G., Lawall, L.J.: Entropy: a consolidation manager for clusters. In: Proc. of the International Conference on Virtual Execution Environments, VEE 2009 (2009)
5. IBM: An architectural blueprint for autonomic computing. Tech. Rep. (June 2005)
6. Kephart, J.O., Chan, H., Das, R., Levine, D.W., Tesauro, G., Rawson, F., Lefurgy, C.: Coordinating Multiple Autonomic Managers to Achieve Specified Power-Performance Tradeoffs. In: Proc. of the 4th International Conference on Autonomic Computing (ICAC 2007), pp. 24–24. IEEE (June 2007)
7. Kephart, J., Chess, D.: The vision of autonomic computing. Computer 36(1) (2003)
8. Lemos, R.D., et al.: Software Engineering for Self-Adaptive Systems: A Second Research Roadmap (Draft Version of May 20, 2011). Tech. Rep. (October 2010) (2011)
9. Lim, H.C., Babu, S., Chase, J.S., Parekh, S.S.: Automated control in cloud computing: challenges and opportunities. In: Proceedings of the 1st Workshop on Automated Control for Datacenters and Clouds, ACDC 2009. ACM (2009)
10. Mak-Karé Gueye, S., de Palma, N., Rutten, E.: Coordinating energy-aware administration loops using discrete control. Proc. of the 8th International Conference on Autonomic and Autonomous Systems, ICAS 2012 (March 2012)
11. Alvares de Oliveira, Jr. F., Ledoux, T.: Self-management of applications qos for energy optimization in datacenters. In: Proc. of the 2nd International Workshop on Green Computing Middleware (GCM 2011), pp. 3:1–3:6. ACM (2011)
12. Van, H.N., Tran, F.D., Menaud, J.M.: Sla-aware virtual resource management for cloud infrastructures. In: Proceedings of the 9th IEEE International Conference on Computer and Information Technology, CIT 2009. IEEE Computer Society (2009)
13. Vromant, P., Weyns, D., Malek, S., Andersson, J.: On Interacting Control Loops in Self-Adaptive Systems. In: Proc. of the 6th International Symposium on Software Engineering for Adaptive and Self-Managing Systems, pp. 202–207. ACM (2011)
14. Wu, L., Garg, S.K., Buyya, R.: Sla-based admission control for a software-as-a-service provider in cloud computing environments. Journal of Computer and System Sciences, 195–204 (2011)

Subobject Transactional Memory

Marko van Dooren and Dave Clarke

IBBT-DistriNet, KU Leuven, Leuven, Belgium
{firstname.lastname}@cs.kuleuven.be

Abstract. Concurrent object-oriented programs are hard to write because of the frequent use of state in objects. In a concurrent program, this state must be protected against race-conditions and deadlocks, which costs a lot of effort and is error-prone. Software transactional memory is a mechanism for concurrency control that is similar to mechanisms used in databases. The programmer does not deal with low-level locks, but instead uses transaction demarcation to protect shared memory.

We show that in a statically typed subobject-oriented programming language, a transactional program requires less effort than writing a regular object-oriented programming. In addition, we show how transactionality can be added to existing classes without performing code transformations or using a meta-object protocol.

1 Introduction

With the rise of multi-core processors, there is growing demand for multi-threaded applications. But to ensure proper functioning of the program, data that is shared between threads must be guarded to avoid problems such as lost updates and dirty reads. With lock-based approaches, the programmer must place locks in the appropriate places in the code to prevent race conditions. Placing all locks correctly, however, is very hard and requires a lot of effort. Software transactional memory [17] (STM) is popular mechanism to support transactional behavior of a program that avoids the problems associated with lock-based approaches. A programmer must only demarcate transactions, and the STM ensures that the code in a transaction is executed atomically and isolated.

STM implementations can be divided into two categories: language implementations and library implementations. Language implementations add dedicated language constructs to provide STM functionality and/or modify the language run-time to support transactional semantics [2,5,12,13,16] The advantages of language implementations are that they allow low-level optimizations and impose a minimal syntactic overhead on the programmer. The disadvantages are that using non-standard language implementation is usually not an option in an industrial setting, and that the implementation of a customized transaction mechanism usually is difficult.

Library STM implementations in static languages [6,9,10,11] provide an API to use the STM. The advantage of this approach is that neither the language nor the run-time must be adapted. The disadvantage is that the programmer must use reified memory locations instead of the variables that are normally used, which results in more boilerplate code. In addition, existing classes cannot be made transactional.

M. Sirjani (Ed.): COORDINATION 2012, LNCS 7274, pp. 44–58, 2012.

Library STM implementations in dynamic languages work by dynamically rewriting the program [15], or modifying the language semantics via a meta-object protocol [7]. In these approaches, the language semantics are changed without using modified language run-times or external code generation tools. Therefore, the programming overhead is limited and the standard language run-time can be used. The disadvantage of these approaches is that the required language features are not available in static programming languages.

The contribution of this paper is to show that an STM library in a statically typed subobject-oriented programming language [19,18] can offer the same ease of use as dynamic STM libraries and dedicated language implementations. We show that a transactional subobject-oriented program contains even less boilerplate code than a non-transactional object-oriented program. In addition, transactional behavior can be added to existing non-transactional classes. We present a proof-of-concept implementation of a multi-version concurrency control mechanism.

Overview

Section 2 gives a short introduction to subobject-oriented programming. Section 3 discusses how subobjects can be used to write transactional applications. Section 4 present our proof-of-concept implementation. Section 5 discusses related work, and Section 6 concludes.

2   A Subobject-Oriented Approach

The focus of this paper is on improving the ease of use of an STM library in a static language. Our proof-of-concept implementation is not optimized for performance or memory footprint.

The context of our approach is a development process that uses a statically typed programming language. We do not allow modifications to the compiler or the language run-time for two reasons. First, such modifications are typically not allowed in an industrial setting. Second, such modifications make it harder to use develop transaction mechanisms that are better suited for the read/write pattern of a particular application.

In this paper we use *subobject-oriented programming* to make an application transactional. Subobject-oriented programming, which was developed by the first author [19,18], augments object-oriented programming with a mechanism to compose classes from other classes. While the composition mechanism is relatively recent, and thus not supported in mainstream programming languages, it is important to note that it is a *general purpose* language construct. As such, we treat our prototype language JLo as a standard programming language. The remainder of this section gives an introduction to subobject-oriented programming.

2.1   An Introduction to Subobject-Oriented Programming

Subobject-oriented programming augments object-oriented programming with subobjects. A subobject can be seen as a combination of inheritance and delegation, and allows a developer to easily create classes using other classes as configurable building blocks. Subobjects allow high-level concepts such as associations, bounded values, and graph nodes to be encapsulated in regular classes and reused to build applications. Subobjects avoid the name conflicts of regular multiple inheritance but still allow repeated inheritance, unlike traits and mixins.

Fig. 1 shows how subobjects can be used to create a class of elevators. An elevator is positioned on floor between the ground floor and the highest floor in the building, and carries a load between 0kg and the maximum capacity.

```
class Elevator {
  subobject floor BoundedValue<Int> {
    export getValue() as getFloor,
           setValue(Int) as selectFloor;
  }
  subobject currentLoad BoundedValue<Int> {
    export getValue() as getLoad,
           increaseValue(Int) as load,
           decreaseValue(Int) as unload;
  }
  Elevator(Int nbFloors, Float capacity) {
    subobject.floor(0,0,nbFloors);
    subobject.currentLoad(0,0,capacity);
  }
}
// Client code                    // Equivalent client code
Elevator elevator=...;
elevator.selectFloor(1);          // elevator.floor.setValue(1);
elevator.load(100);               // elevator.currentLoad.add(100);
elevator.selectFloor(0);          // elevator.floor.setValue(0);
```

Fig. 1. A subobject-oriented class of elevators

Instead of duplicating the code to keep a value within certain bounds, the concept of a bounded value is captured in class *BoundedValue*. Class *Elevator* uses subobjects of type *BoundedValue* to model its floor and its current load. By default, the interface of *Elevator* does not contain any methods of the *floor* subobject. To add such methods to the interface of *Elevator*, they are exported in the body of the subobject. This avoids an explosion of name conflicts when a class uses multiple subobjects of the same type, as is the case for class *Elevator*.

An *export* clause creates an *alias* for a subobject member. For example, subobject *floor* exports the getter and setter methods of its value under the respective names *getFloor* and *selectFloor*. A client can therefore change the floor of the elevator by invoking either *elevator.selectFloor(...)* or *elevator.floor.setValue(...)*. The alias relation both methods cannot be broken in any way. If a subclass of *Elevator* overrides *setFloor*, the new definition also overrides the *setValue* method of its *floor* subobject.

Subobject methods that are not exported can still be accessed by clients. A client can access subobject *floor* as a real object of type *BoundedValue<Int>* through the expression *elevator.floor*. She can then use the resulting reference to increase the current floor by invoking *elevator.floor.increaseValue(...)*..

Subobject *currentLoad* models the current load of the elevator, and has the same type as the *floor* subobject. Contrary to the semantics of traditional repeated inheritance, however, both subobjects are completely isolated by default. Invoking *selectFloor* on an elevator will only change the *value* field of the *floor* subobject. Similarly, internal calls in the *floor* subobject are bound within the *floor* subobject. The subobject behaves as if *this* is replaced with *this.floor* in the subobject code in the context of class *Elevator*. A subobject can invoke methods on another subobject, but only if they it is explicitly given a reference to such a subobject, or if its methods are overridden in the composing class to do this. Parts of subobjects can be joined by overriding members of both subobjects in the composed class. In this paper, however, we do not need this functionality.

```
class BoundedValue<T extends Number> {
  subobject max Property<T> {...}
  subobject value Property<T> {
    export getValue, setValue;
    def isValid(T t) =
      outer.min.getValue <= t && t <= outer.max.getValue;
  }
  subobject min Property<T> {...}
  ...
}
```

Fig. 2. Enforcing the bounds of a bounded value

The composed class can override subobject members by redefining them in the body of the subobject. Fig. 2 shows how class *BoundedValue* ensures that its value remains between its bounds. Class *BoundedValue* uses three subobjects of type *Property<T>* for its value and its bounds. The *setValue* method of *Property* invokes *isValid* to verify if the given value can be set. Subobject *value* overrides *isValid* to check if the given value exceeds the bounds. The **outer** expression is used to access the getter methods of the min and max subobjects to obtain the bounds. The value of the *outer* expression is the same as the value of *this* in the directly enclosing context. Similar to the *this* expression, calls on *outer* are bound dynamically.

```
class EventElevator {
  subobject floor EventBoundedValue<Int>;
}
```

Fig. 3. Refining a subobject

A subobject can be *refined* in a subclass, which can customize the subobject by over-riding its methods and changing its super class. The class of the new subobject is a sub-class of the class of the refined subobject and the new superclass. A *rule of dominance* is used to resolve conflicts, similar to C++ and Eiffel. Suppose that *EventBoundedValue* is a subclass of *BoundedValue* that sends events if its value is changed. Fig. 3 shows how subobject refinement is used for elevators that send events when changing floors. The export clauses are not redefined, as they are inherited from *Elevator.floor*. With manual delegation it would not be possible to modify the bounded value unless *Elevator* would have contained additional boilerplate code to change the delegation object.

More details on subobject-oriented programming can be found in earlier work [19], but note that the paper uses the term *component* instead of *subobject*.

3   Subobject Transactional Memory

The key to implementing software transactional memory with subobjects is that subobject-oriented programs use subobjects to store the state of an object instead of fields. The class library of JLo contains a class *Property* that models an encapsulated field. Instead of using fields to store the state of object, a programmer can use subobjects of type *Property*. To maintain backward compatibility with Java, there are additional property classes for encapsulated lists, sets, and maps. After all, if a list of objects of type T is stored in a *Property<List<T>>* subobject, it is impossible to encapsulate the list because the client can directly access list. Fig. 4 shows a part of class *Property*, along with an example of how to use it. In an object-oriented style, the code in class *Property* would have been duplicated for every field in the application.

```
class Property<T> {
  T _value;
  def getValue() = _value;
  def setValue(T t) {
    if(isValid(t)) _value = t
    else throw new IllegalArgumentException();
  }
  def isValid(T t) = true; // can be overridden in subobjects
}

class Person {
  subobject name Property<String> {
    export getValue() as getName, setValue(String) as setName;
  }
  subobject children ListProperty<Person> {
    export add(Person) as addChild, values() as getChildren;
  }
}
```

Fig. 4. Implementing state with subobjects

```
class Person {
  subobject TProperty<String> name {
    export getValue as getName, setValue as setName;
  }
  subobject TListProperty<Person> children {
    export add(Person) as addChild, values as getChildren();
  }
}
```

Fig. 5. A JLo implementation of a transactional person

Using subobjects to store the state of an object provides the opportunity to intercept all read and write operations in an application. Suppose for example that *TProperty*, *TListProperty*, and so forth are subclasses of *Property*, *ListProperty*, and so forth that override all mutators and inspectors to add transactional behavior. We can then use a *TProperty<String>* subobject in *Person* to make the state transactional. The code in Fig. 5 and Fig. 6 show the JLo and Java implementations of a transactional class of persons with a name and a list of children. The Java implementation uses versioned boxes. Two things are noteworthy. First, the transactional JLo implementation is almost identical to the non-transactional JLo implementation. Second, the JLo implementation is not only simpler than the Java implementation, but also simpler than a non-transactional Java implementation. In addition, the more functionality the properties offer, the bigger the difference becomes. For example, methods such as *addAll()* are still accessible in the JLo version as *person.children.addAll()*, whereas the object-oriented implementation version would need an additional delegation method.

```
class Person {
  VBox<String> name;

  String getName() {
    return name.get();
  }
  void setName(String name) {
    name.set(name);
  }
  List<Person> getChildren() {
    return new ArrayList<Person>(children.get());
  }
  void addChild(Person person) {
    children.get().add(person);
  }
}
```

Fig. 6. A Java implementation of a transactional person

3.1   Making Existing Classes Transactional

To be practical, the STM should be able to work with non-transactional third-party code. Remember from Fig. 1 and Fig. 2 that *Elevator* uses *BoundedValue* subobjects, and that *BoundedValue* uses three *Property* subobjects. Suppose that *BoundedValue* is a class from a third-party library, and uses regular *Property* subobjects for its bounds. To create a transactional elevator class, we need to create a class of transactional bounded values without modifying (or reimplementing) *BoundedValue*.

Remember from Sect. 2 that the type of a subobject can be changed in a subclass through subobject refinement. Fig. 7 shows the definition of *TBoundedValue*, which refines the *min*, *max*, and *value* subobjects such that the value and the bounds are store in *TProperty* subobjects. No conflicts resolution is required because *BoundedValue* only overrides the *isValid* methods of its *Property* subobjects while *TProperty* does not override them. The resulting subobjects in *TBoundedValue* uses the validation methods defined in *BoundedValue* and the inspector and mutator methods defined in *TProperty*.

```
class TBoundedValue<T> extends BoundedValue<T> {
  subobject max TProperty<Int>;
  subobject value TProperty<Int>;
  subobject min TProperty<Int>;

  TBoundedValue(T min, T val, T max) {
    super(min, val, max);
    subobject.min(min);
    subobject.value(val);
    subobject.max(max);
  }
}
```

Fig. 7. Creating a transactional bounded value through subobject refinement

The constructors for the subobjects must be called explicitly in *TBoundedValue* because the subobject types have changed. These subobject constructor calls *replace* the corresponding subobject constructor calls in *BoundedValue*, and are executed when the original subobject constructor calls would have been executed. This prevents the construction of a subobject of the wrong type in the constructor of *BoundedValue*, but still guarantees that the subobjects are initialized at the correct time.

Similar to *TBoundedValue*, class *TElevator* can also be implemented as a subclass of *Elevator* that refines the *floor* and *currentLoad* subobjects, as shown in Fig. 8. It is of course also possible to create a transactional elevator from scratch by directly using *TBoundedValue* subobjects instead of *BoundedValue* subobjects.

The application logic of the program is not affected by the STM. Only the types of the subobjects that store data are different. Other than the types of the subobjects that store data, the interfaces of transactional classes such as *TElevator* and *TBoundedValue* are the same as the interfaces of their non-transactional versions. Therefore, code that

```
class TElevator extends Elevator{
  subobject floor TBoundedValue<Int>;
  subobject currentLoad TBoundedValue<Int>;

  TElevator(Int nbFloors, Float capacity) {
    super(nbFloors, capacity);
    subobject.floor(0,0,nbFloors);
    subobject.currentLoad(0,0,capacity);
  }
}
```

Fig. 8. Adding transactional behavior to a non-transactional elevator class

uses a the transactional class looks no different than code that uses the non-transactional class. For example, the *isValid* methods, which are written in *BoundedValue* for non-transactional *Property* subobjects do not have to be modified in *TBoundedValue*, where they work with *TProperty* subobjects.

In an object-oriented style, is not always possible to add transactional behavior to a class by overriding the individual getter and setter methods because fields are often read and modified directly within a class. But even if the data is stored in reified memory locations, anticipation and additional boilerplate code for the initialization is required to be able to replace the delegation objects with transactional objects. Fig. 9 illustrates the problem. Suppose that class *Elevator* uses *Box* objects instead of regular fields to store its state. Without introducing additional boilerplate code to allow a subclass to initialize the boxes, the state cannot be replaced with *VBox* objects to add transactionality.

In a subobject-oriented programming, no anticipation is required because it requires less effort to store state in subobjects than to use fields. JLo still provides support for fields due to backward compatibility with Java, but we plan to remove this feature and use "native" code in the few core library classes that use fields.

3.2 Transaction Demarcation

Transactions are demarcated by writing the transactional code in the body of the *execute* method of a subclass of *Transaction*. The advantage over using separate *start* and *stop* calls is that the *stop* call could accidentally be forgotten. The *execute* method, which is protected, is invoked by the *commit* method of *Transaction*. If the code in *execute* throws an exception or if the transaction manager detects a conflict, the default policy is to abort the transaction and propagate the exception. Custom retry policies can be defined by overriding the *retry* method of *Transaction*. The code in Fig. 10 illustrates how two threads can use the elevator without running the risk of overloading the elevator or trying to load the elevator when it is on the wrong floor.

Adding transaction demarcation to an existing program can be done by overriding the methods that must be executed as a transaction and performing a *super* call in the *execute* method of a *Transaction*. Methods that create new threads may have to be reimplemented to ensure that all threads run in a separate transaction.

```
class Elevator {
  private Box<Int> nbFloors = new Box<Int>(0);
  private Box<Int> floor = new Box<Int>(0);
  private Box<Int> capacity = new Box<Int>(0);
  private Box<Int> load = new Box<Int>(0);

  Int nbFloors() {return nbFloors.get();}
  Int floor() {return floor.get();}
  Int capacity() {return capacity.get();}
  Int load() {return load.get();}

  Elevator(Int nbFloors, Float capacity) {
    this.nBfloors.set(nbFloors);
    this.capacity.set(capacity);
  }
}
class TElevator extends Elevator {
  // Impossible to change Box objects to VBox objects.
}
```

Fig. 9. Object-oriented delegation requires anticipation and additional boilerplate code

```
TElevator elevator = new TElevator(3,150);
new Thread() {
  void run() {for(int i=0;i<100;i++) {
              new Transaction() {
                void execute() {
                  elevator.setFloor(2);
                  elevator.load(100);
                  elevator.setFloor(0);
                }
              }.commit();
            }
}.start();
new Thread() {
  void run() {for(int i=0;i<100;i++) {
              new Transaction() {
                void execute() {
                  elevator.setFloor(1);
                  elevator.load(100);
                  elevator.setFloor(0);
                }
              }.commit();}
            }
}.start();
```

Fig. 10. Demarcating transactions with the Command pattern

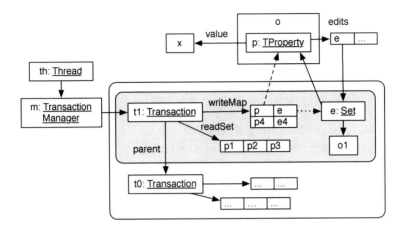

Fig. 11. Thread-local transaction managers provide a unique view per transaction

4   Example Implementation

In this section, we discuss our STM implementation. The current implementation uses multi-version concurrency control [14,3], but other mechanisms can be used as well.

Classes *TProperty*, *TListProperty*, and so forth are subclasses of the regular property classes *Property*, *ListProperty*, and so forth that add transactional behavior. The transactional classes override the mutator and inspector methods to log all reads and writes to provide transactional behavior. Write operations are reified as subclasses of *Edit*. Transactions are modeled by the *Transaction* class.

Figure 11 illustrates the run-time object layout. The solid arrows represent normal object references. The striped arrows represent weak object references, which are implemented with *WeakReference* object in Java. Weak references do not prevent an object from being garbage collected. The heap contains an object o with a transactional single valued property p. Transaction t_1 is nested in transaction t_0, and has modified the value of p to a reference to o_1 via the *Set* object e. Class *Set* is a subclass of *Edit* that represents a write operation to a single valued property. In addition, the transaction has performed read operations on transactional properties p_1, p_2, and p_3.

Class *TransactionManager* has a static thread-local variable *manager* that stores a reference to a *TransactionManager* object. This gives each thread its own transaction manager which it can access via *TransactionManager.manager*. A *TransactionManager* keeps a reference to the transaction in which it is currently running. Nesting of transactions is reflected in the object structure of the *CompositeTransaction* objects, which keep a reference to their parent transaction. In Fig. 11, transaction t_1 is nested in transaction t_0, but it is not running in a separate thread.

To give a transaction its own unique version of the state of an object, it keeps track of all reads and writes that are performed during its execution. The reads are stored as a set of property subobjects that were read. The writes are stored as a map that stores the latest *Edit* that was performed on a property subobject within the transaction. In the example in Fig. 11, single valued property p points to o_1 within transaction t_1, whereas it points to x in every transaction that has not modified p.

Transactions in Action

The diagram in Fig. 12 illustrates the process of setting the value of *p* to *v*. The dotted arrows represent temporary references via local variables. Instead of directly modifying a its field, subobject *p* creates an object *s* of class *Set* that references the new value *v*. Subobject *p* then and passes *s* to the transaction manager, which tells its transaction *t* of the current thread to absorb *s*. Transaction *t* first checks whether its write map already contains an *Edit* for subobject *p*. If that is the case, it tells the current *Edit* for *p* to absorb *s*; otherwise, it registers *s* in its write map and lets *s* register itself in the edit list of *p* to keep it from being garbage collected. For a *Set* object, the *absorb* method simply replaces the referenced value.

The diagram in Fig. 13 illustrates the process of reading the value of a single valued property. Subobject *p* asks the transaction manager to search for an *Edit* object that is associated with *p* in the current transaction. If an *Edit* object *e* is found, it is returned and *p* uses *e* to determine the current value. If no *Edit* object is found, the value that is stored in *p* is returned. In either case, transaction *t* adds *p* to its read set.

The *Edit* objects for the other property classes are similar, but their implementation is more complex because the data structures are more complex. For example, the *Edit* objects for a transactional list property become part of a linked list when being absorbed. In addition, setting the *i-th* item in a list also implies a read operation. Otherwise, there would be no conflict with a concurrent transaction that reduces the size of the list below *i*.

When a transaction is committed, conflict resolution is performed, and the transaction is aborted when a cycle in the waits-for graph is detected. When a nested

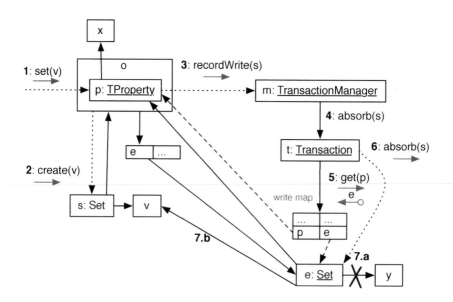

Fig. 12. Setting the value of a transactional property

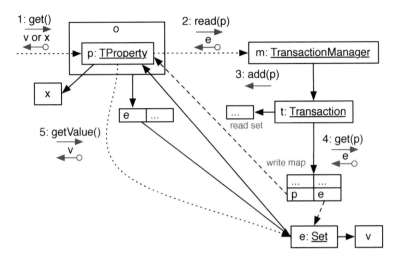

Fig. 13. Getting the value of a transactional property

transactions commits, the read set and write map are merged with those of its parent transaction. When a root transaction commits, the *Edit* objects apply their modifications to the fields of the corresponding property subobjects. Read and write operations that are performed outside of transactions are applied directly to the fields of the property subobjects.

Memory Management

To ensure proper memory management, both the key and value references in the map are weak references, each property subobject stores strong references to all basic transactions that are applied to it. As a result, objects that were created and modified within a transaction can be freed by the garbage collector when they are no longer reachable in the view of any transaction.

Because of the weak references in the write map, however, we must prevent garbage collection of objects that are created within a transaction and are referenced by a reachable object through an *Edit* object. The *Edit* object has a strong reference to the newly created object, but there is no strong reference to the *Edit* object. Therefore, each property subobject keeps a list of strong references (list *edits* in Fig. 11) to the *Edit* objects that have modified it, and are part of living transactions. The *Edit* objects register themselves when they become part of the object structure in the write map.

Suppose for example that object *v* of Fig. 13 was created within the current transaction and is referenced only by the transaction-local version of *p*. In this case, *v* cannot be garbage collected because of the strong reference of *e*, which in turn is referenced by *p* via the *edits* list. But if *p* is set to a new value within the transaction, the strong reference from *e* is replaced with a reference to the new value. Object *v* then becomes unreachable and will be garbage collected.

5   Related Work

Approaches for software transactional memory can be divided into two categories: language approaches and library approaches. Language implementations add dedicated language constructs to provide STM functionality and/or modify the language runtime to support transactional semantics. Library approaches provide STM functionality through an API or by using the metaprogramming facilities of languages. For reasons of space, we only discuss the approaches that are most closely related to our approach.

Language Approaches. Isolation types [4,5] provide a language approach that is similar to versioned boxes. Instead of implementing an STM, isolation types implement a revision control system that is similar to revision control systems used for managing source code. Every asynchronous task runs isolated from the others and has its own revision of the shared state. When tasks are joined, the state revisions are merged. Conflict resolution is defined by the isolation type, is deterministic, and can never fail. The execution of concurrent programs is therefore deterministic, but isolation is not guaranteed. Isolation type require the addition of dedicated language constructs to C#.

Static Library Approaches. TBoost.STM [9], DSTM2 [10], Versioned Boxes [6], and SAW are library approach for static programming languages.

TBoost.STM (formerly known as DracoSTM [9]) is a C++ library for software transactional memory. Memory locations are reified as objects of the *native_trans* class. Fields and local variables are wrapped in *native_trans* objects and reads and writes are performed by invoking methods on the current transaction object. As a result, algorithms must be adapted to work with the transaction mechanism. The authors provide a list class that can be used without knowing about the transaction mechanism.

DSTM2 [10] is a Java STM library with a customizable transaction mechanism. Transactional classes are written as interfaces with getter and setter methods. To construct an object whose class implements that interface, the *Class* object of the interface is given to a transactional factory. The factory dynamically generates code that implements the getters and setters in a transactional manner. The transaction mechanism can be changed by changing the factory. DSTM2 cannot work with existing code since standard Java classes do not use the transactional factories.

Versioned Boxes [6] are reified memory locations that are used to write transactional applications. Mutator and inspector methods for single values, lists, and so forth are implemented by delegating the calls to the versioned box. Existing classes written in an object-oriented style cannot be made transactional because such classes may access their fields directly.

SAW [20] is a Java library that adds synchronization to existing classes through aspect weaving. Classes and transactional methods are marked with *@shared* and *@atomic* annotations. The authors implement both an STM mechanism and a lock-based mechanism. The active mechanism is chosen by selecting a particular aspect. This choice, however, is not transparent because the programmer must manually prevent dead-locks when the lock-based mechanism is used. As a result, SAW is more difficult to use than a pure STM.

Dynamic Library Approaches. SSTM [7] and the Smalltalk library of Renggli and Nierstrasz [15] are library approaches for dynamic programming languages. These approaches provide transactional functionality by using the metaprogramming facilities of the host language.

CSTM [7] is an STM framework based on context-oriented programming. The framework is implemented in ContextL, a context-oriented extension of CLOS. Slots in an object do not store values directly, but instead store a reified memory location object. The default behavior of these memory locations is to get and set the memory value directly. ContextL provides a layered slot access protocol that allows context layers to modify the behavior of slot accesses. A mode layer defines the semantics of regular slot accesses and defines the transaction demarcation. The transaction layer defines the semantics of transactional slot accesses. The transaction mechanism can be change at run-time by enabling a different transactional layer. The enable the STM for a class, the class must be annotated with the *define-transactional-class* function. Transactions are demarcated by wrapping the code in a call to the *atomic* function. The use of memory location objects is similar to the use of property subobjects.

Renggli and Nierstrasz implement a Smalltalk STM library that exploits the dynamic nature of Smalltalk [15]. Their implementation lazily rewrites the Smalltalk program while it runs to insert the transactional behavior. State accesses are rewritten to redirect the control flow to the transaction mechanism. Primitive operations, such as *#at:* and *#put:* are annotated with the name of an equivalent non-primitive method that must be used instead in transactional code. When an object is accessed in a transaction, two copies are made. One object represents the initial object, while the other object represents the transaction-local object. When a transaction is committed, the initial object is compared to the current version of the original object to detect conflicts. A transaction is created by sending the *#atomic* to a block.

6 Conclusion and Future Work

Existing STM libraries for static object-oriented programming languages require additional boilerplate code compared to STM librarires for dynamic languages, or dedicated language extensions.

We have defined an STM library for a static subobject-oriented programming programming language. We have shown that this library not only requires less boilerplate code than static object-oriented STM libraries, but also requires less boilerplate code than a regular object-oriented program. In addition, transactional behavior can be added to existing subobject-oriented classes. We have implemented a multiversion concurrent control mechanism as a proof-of-concept.

We plan to combine subobjects with classboxes [1] or higher-order hierarchies [8], which are generic modularization techniques, to simplify adding transactionality to an application. The transactional property classes can then be placed in a separate classbox or hierarchy. Similarly, a subclass of *Thread* would create a transaction when a new thread is started. To make an application transactional, a programmer would then extend both the original application and the transactional classbox or hierarchy.

References

1. Bergel, A., Ducasse, S., Nierstrasz, O.: Classbox/j: controlling the scope of change in Java. In: OOPSLA, pp. 177–189 (2005)
2. Berger, E.D., Yang, T., Liu, T., Novark, G.: Grace: safe multithreaded programming for C/C++. In: OOPSLA, pp. 81–96 (2009)
3. Bernstein, P.A., Goodman, N.: Concurrency control in distributed database systems. ACM Comput. Surv. 13(2), 185–221 (1981)
4. Burckhardt, S., Baldassin, A., Leijen, D.: Concurrent programming with revisions and isolation types. In: OOPSLA, pp. 691–707 (2010)
5. Burckhardt, S., Leijen, D., Sadowski, C., Yi, J., Ball, T.: Two for the price of one: a model for parallel and incremental computation. In: OOPSLA, pp. 427–444 (2011)
6. Cachopo, J.A., Rito-Silva, A.: Versioned boxes as the basis for memory transactions. Sci. Comput. Program. 63, 172–185 (2006)
7. Costanza, P., Herzeel, C., D'Hondt, T.: Context-oriented software transactional memory in common lisp. In: DLS, pp. 59–68 (2009)
8. Ernst, E.: Higher-Order Hierarchies. In: Cardelli, L. (ed.) ECOOP 2003. LNCS, vol. 2743, pp. 303–328. Springer, Heidelberg (2003)
9. Gottschlich, J.E., Connors, D.A.: DracoSTM: A practical C++ approach to software transactional memroy. In: Proceedings of the 2007 ACM SIGPLAN Symposium on Library-Centric Software Design (LCSD). In conjunction with OOPSLA (October 2007)
10. Herlihy, M., Luchangco, V., Moir, M.: A flexible framework for implementing software transactional memory. In: OOPSLA, pp. 253–262 (2006)
11. Herlihy, M., Luchangco, V., Moir, M., Scherer III, W.N.: Software transactional memory for dynamic-sized data structures. In: PODC, pp. 92–101 (2003)
12. Kulkarni, A., Liu, Y.D., Smith, S.F.: Task types for pervasive atomicity. In: OOPSLA, pp. 671–690 (2010)
13. Lublinerman, R., Zhao, J., Budimlić, Z., Chaudhuri, S., Sarkar, V.: Delegated isolation. In: OOPSLA, pp. 885–902 (2011)
14. Reed, D.P.: Naming and Synchronization in a Decentralized Computer System. PhD thesis, Cambridge, MA, USA (1978)
15. Renggli, L., Nierstrasz, O.: Transactional memory in a dynamic language. Comput. Lang. Syst. Struct. 35, 21–30 (2009)
16. Saha, B., Adl-Tabatabai, A.-R., Hudson, R.L., Minh, C.C., Hertzberg, B.: McRT-STM: a high performance software transactional memory system for a multi-core runtime. In: PPoPP, pp. 187–197 (2006)
17. Shavit, N., Touitou, D.: Software transactional memory. Distributed Computing 10, 99–116 (1997)
18. van Dooren, M., Jacobs, B.: Implementations of subobject-oriented programming (2012), http://people.cs.kuleuven.be/marko.vandooren/subobjects.html
19. van Dooren, M., Steegmans, E.: A Higher Abstraction Level Using First-Class Inheritance Relations. In: Bateni, M. (ed.) ECOOP 2007. LNCS, vol. 4609, pp. 425–449. Springer, Heidelberg (2007)
20. Yamada, Y., Iwasaki, H., Ugawa, T.: SAW: Java synchronization selection from lock or software transactional memory. In: 2011 IEEE 17th International Conference on Parallel and Distributed Systems (ICPADS), pp. 104–111. IEEE (2011)

Partial Connector Colouring[*]

Dave Clarke and José Proença

IBBT-DistriNet, Department of Computer Science,
K.U. Leuven, Belgium
{firstname.lastname}@cs.kuleuven.be

Abstract. Connector colouring provided an intuitive semantics of Reo connectors which lead to effective implementation techniques, first based on computing colouring tables directly, and later on encodings of colouring into constraints. One weakness of the framework is that it operates globally, giving a colouring to all primitives of the connector in lock-step, including those not involved in the interaction. This global approach limits both scalability and the available concurrency. This paper addresses these problems by introducing partiality into the connector colouring model. Partial colourings allow parts of a connector to operate independently and in isolation, increasing scalability and concurrency.

1 Introduction

Reo [1] is a visual language for coordinating components and web services using connectors composed from a small, but open, collection of primitives. A lot of research has gone into semantic models for Reo, with the following (incomplete) goals: to facilitate reasoning about Reo connectors; to provide context-dependent behaviour; and to enable efficient implementations. Connector colouring [8] provided a great leap forward on these three fronts. Firstly, it is an intensional semantic model that also gives a visual representation of what's going on inside a connector. Secondly, connector colouring offered the first context dependent semantics for Reo. Thirdly, the semantics were simple enough to enable a straightforward implementation of Reo [4]. Further improvements in implementation efficiency were obtained by encoding connector colouring as constraints and using SAT and constraint satisfaction techniques [9].

The problem with the resulting implementation approach, and indeed with connector colouring as a semantic model, is that it gives only a *global* description of the behaviour of a connector, with *all* primitives participating *lock-step* to determine what to do next. In the constraints encoding, the constraints of all primitives are conjoined together to compute the next step. This has three negative consequences: the amount of available concurrency is reduced; implementations are inherently unscalable; and the behavioural possibilities offered by connectors are actually reduced—some desirable behaviour becomes impossible.

[*] This research is partly funded by the EU project FP7-231620 HATS: Highly Adaptable and Trustworthy Software using Formal Models (http://www.hats-project.eu) and KULeuven BOF Project STRT1/09/031: DesignerTypeLab.

M. Sirjani (Ed.): COORDINATION 2012, LNCS 7274, pp. 59–73, 2012.

This paper proposes a solution to this problem which overcomes these negative consequences, simply by considering certain partial connector colourings as valid. Rather than giving behaviour to the entire connector, a partial colouring can give behaviour to a part of a connector in a coherent fashion. This enables the local colouring of multiple parts of a connector concurrently and independently. The details of partial connector colouring are worked out for existing colouring schemes and new encodings as constraints are presented. We describe how existing constraint satisfaction engines can be used to implement partial colouring, and provide some benchmarks.

The paper is organised as follows. Section 2 gives a review of Reo and the connector colouring model. Section 3 details the problem being addressed. Section 4 describes one solution, namely, partial connector colouring. Section 5 reviews and adapts the constraint-based encoding of connector colouring. Section 6 discusses the implementation of our approach and gives some benchmarks. Section 7 discusses related work and Section 8 concludes.

2   Background: Reo and Connector Colouring

2.1   Reo Coordination Model

Reo [1] is a coordination model, wherein coordinating *connectors* are constructed by composing more primitive connectors. Reo's primitives, such as channels, offer a variety of behavioural policies regarding synchronisation, buffering, and lossiness. Being able to compose connectors out of smaller primitives is one of the strengths of Reo. It allows, for example, multi-party synchronisation to be expressed simply by plugging simple channels together. In addition, Reo's graphical notation helps bring intuition about the behaviour of a connector.

Communication with a primitive occurs through its ports, called *ends*: primitives consume data through their *source ends*, and produce data through their *sink ends*. (Source and sink ends correspond to the notions of source and sink in directed graphs.) Connectors are formed by plugging the ends of primitives together, without loss of generality, in a 1:1 fashion, connecting a sink end to a source end, to form *nodes*. Data flows through a connector from primitive to primitive through nodes, subject to the constraint that nodes cannot buffer data—the two ends in a node are synchronised. The behaviour of each primitive depends upon its current state and the semantics of a connector can be described *per-state* in a series of *rounds*. *Data flow* on a primitive's end occurs when a single datum is passed through that end. Within any round data flow may occur on some number of ends. This is equated with the notion of *synchrony*. Components attach to the boundary of a connector.

Some Reo primitives are:

Replicator $\left(a \underset{c}{\overset{b}{\longleftarrow}} \right)$ replicates data synchronously from a to b and c.

Merger $\left(\begin{array}{c} a \\ b \end{array} \!\!\! \succ\!\!\!\longrightarrow c \right)$ copies data synchronously either from a to c or b to c, but not from both.

Priority merger $\left(\begin{array}{c} a \\ b \end{array} \!\!\! \succ\!\!\!\longrightarrow c \right)$ behaves like a merger, but prefers to select data from a over b, if both alternatives are possible. The ! marks the higher priority input.

LossySync $\left(a \dashrightarrow b \right)$ has two possible behaviours. Data can either flow synchronously from a to b, when possible, or can flow on a but not on b. The LossySync is context-dependent, in that it prefers to allow data to flow from a to b rather than lose it.

Sync $\left(a \longrightarrow b \right)$ passes data synchronously from a to b

SyncDrain $\left(a \succ\!\!\!\longrightarrow\!\!\!\prec b \right)$ synchronises ends a and b, consuming the data.

AsyncDrain $\left(a \succ\!\!\!+\!\!\!+\!\!\!\prec b \right)$ consumes data either from a or from b, but not from both.

FIFO$_1$ $\left(a \longrightarrow\!\!\Box\!\!\longrightarrow b \right)$ is a stateful channel representing a buffer of size 1. When the buffer is empty it can receive data on a, but not output data on b. It then changes state and becomes full. A full FIFO$_1$ with data d, denoted $\left(a \longrightarrow\!\!\boxed{d}\!\!\longrightarrow b \right)$, can output d through b, but cannot receive data on a. It then changes state and becomes empty again.

Exclusive Router ($\bigotimes$) denotes an exclusive router, which has one input and multiple outputs. The input data is synchronously sent to exactly one output.

Doing nothing—no data flow—is always one of the behavioural possibilities.

In diagrams of connectors, nodes will be denoted ($\bullet$). In general, these can also have multiple source and sink ends, to denote generalised mergers and replicators, but these can be encoded in terms of binary mergers and replicators.

Example 1. The *synchronous merge* connector, presented in Fig. 1, is a common workflow pattern [18]. The connector controls the execution of two components A and B such that either A executes, or B executes, or both execute. The connector then synchronises on the completion of whichever of A and/or B ran.

2.2   Connector Colouring: An Overview

The connector colouring (CC) semantics for Reo [8] is based on colouring the ends of a connector using 2 colours to represent the presence or absence of data flow. A more refined version using 3 colours enabled context-dependent semantics. In each state, each primitive has a set of possible *colourings* that determine its synchronisation constraints. Each colouring is a mapping from the ends of a primitive to a colour, and the set of the colourings of a connector is called its *colouring table*. These tables are composed by considering each entry in one table with every entry in the other and joining compatible ones. Compatibility

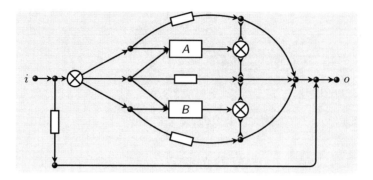

Fig. 1. Synchronous merge connector

Primitives and their colouring tables   Connector and its colouring table

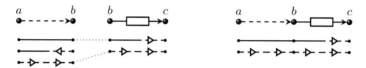

Fig. 2. Connector colouring. The dotted lines indicates compatible colourings.

between colourings is determined by ensuring that they match where two ends are joined to form a node. Fig. 2 illustrates the idea.

2-Colouring. The 2-colouring scheme consists of colours ———•, which denotes the presence of data flow, and - - - -•, which denotes its absence. For orientation, the • indicates the end. When plugging together colouring tables to compute the behaviour of connectors, both colours match only with themselves. That is, ———•——— and - - -•- - - are the only valid combinations.

3-Colouring. The 3-colouring scheme is used to express context-dependent behaviour. A primitive depends on its context if its behaviour changes non-monotonically with increases in possibilities of data flowing on its ends [8,6]. That is, by adding more possibilities of data flow, the primitive actually rules out already valid behaviour possibilities. One colour (———•) marks ends in the connector where data flows, and two colours mark the absence of data flow (- ◁-• and - ▷-•). The arrow indicates the *reason for no flow*, which can be either because no data is being written or because connector or component is not ready to receive the data. The arrow flows from the cause. - ◁-• denotes that the reason for no-flow originates from the context, and we say that the end *requires a reason* for no flow. Dually, - ▷-• indicates that the reason for no-flow originates from the primitive and we say that the end *gives a reason* for no-flow. Two 3-colours match if both represent flow, or if the reason for no-flow comes from at least

Table 1. Colouring tables for some primitives

Channel	Representation	Colouring table
LossySync	a - - - - - $\to$ b	a •———• b a •——◁-• b a •-▷--▷-• b
Priority Merger	a ↘ b ↗ $\to$ c	a ↘ >-▷-• c ; a ↘ >-◁-• c b ↗ ; b ↗ a ↘ ; a ↘ b •——• c ; b ↗ >-• c
FIFOEmpty$_1$	a —▢→ b	a •——▷-• b a •-▷--▷-• b

one of the ends. That is, the valid combinations are: ———•, -◁-•◁-, -▷-•◁-
and -▷-•▷-, but not -◁-•▷-. Table 1 presents the colouring tables for some
primitives. Fig. 2 gives a small example illustrating how 3-colouring works.

2.3 Formalism

Let $\mathcal{X}$ be the global set of node names. Let $\mathcal{X}^{\updownarrow} = \{x^{\downarrow} \mid x \in \mathcal{X}\} \cup \{x^{\uparrow} \mid x \in \mathcal{X}\}$.
Here $x^{\downarrow}$ denotes that x is a source end, and $x^{\uparrow}$ denotes that x is a sink end.
Let 'o' range over the set $\{\uparrow, \downarrow\}$; define $\bar{o}$ as $\bar{\uparrow} = \downarrow$ and $\bar{\downarrow} = \uparrow$. Let $\mathcal{P}$ be the
set of primitives in a connector. Let P range over subsets of $\mathcal{P}$. Function $ends$:
$\mathcal{P} \to \mathbb{P}(\mathcal{X}^{\updownarrow})$ gives the ends of a primitive. $nodes$: $\mathcal{P} \to \mathbb{P}(\mathcal{X})$ gives the set
of nodes (which is the set of ends with the direction marking removed). These
functions can be lifted to operate on $\mathbb{P}(\mathcal{P})$ in the obvious way. Function $internal$:
$\mathbb{P}(\mathcal{P}) \to \mathbb{P}(\mathcal{X})$ gives all the internal nodes and $boundary$: $\mathbb{P}(\mathcal{P}) \to \mathbb{P}(\mathcal{X}^{\updownarrow})$ gives
all the boundary ends for connector with primitives P. These are constrained by
$internal(P) \cap boundary(P)^{\ddagger} = \emptyset$, where $(-)^{\ddagger}$ removes the $\uparrow$ or $\downarrow$. A collection of
primitives $\mathcal{P}$ is a *well-formed connector* whenever $\forall p, p' \in \mathcal{P} \cdot ends(p) \cap ends(p') = \emptyset$. That is, each node in $\mathcal{P}$ appears at most once as a sink and once as a source.

Connector colouring is formalised as follows, adapting the original description [8]. The basis of connector colouring is a *colouring scheme*, a tuple
$(Colour, \frown)$, consisting of a set of colours and a symmetric *match* relation
$\frown \subseteq Colour \times Colour$ that determines when two colours may be plugged together.

Definition 1 (Connector Colouring). *Given colouring scheme* $(Colour, \frown)$,
a colouring for connector P *is a function* $c : X \to Colour$, *where* $X = ends(P) \subseteq \mathcal{X}^{\updownarrow}$, *that maps each end to a colour such that for all* $x \in internal(P)$,
$c(x^{\uparrow}) \frown c(x^{\downarrow})$. *A colouring table over ends* $X \subseteq \mathcal{X}^{\updownarrow}$ *is a set of colourings with domain* X. *Two colouring tables over disjoint sets of ends are compatible, denoted*
$c_1 \frown c_2$, *whenever* $\forall x \in X \cdot x^{\circ} \in dom(c_1) \land x^{\bar{\circ}} \in dom(c_2) \Rightarrow c_1(x^{\circ}) \frown c_2(x^{\bar{\circ}})$. *The*
product of two colouring tables T_1 *and* T_2 *with disjoint domains, denoted* $T_1 \odot T_2$,
is the following colouring table, whose domain is the union of the domains of T_1
and T_2, $T_1 \odot T_2 = \{c_1 \cup c_2 \mid c_1 \in T_1, c_2 \in T_2, c_1 \frown c_2\}$.

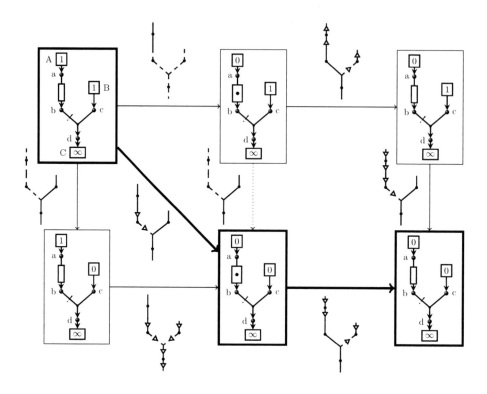

Fig. 3. Evolution of example connector

2-colouring is given by colouring scheme where $\mathcal{C}olour = \{\text{——•}, \text{- - -•}\}$, where binary relation $\frown$ is '='. 3-colouring is given by $\mathcal{C}olour = \{\text{——•}, \text{-▷-•}, \text{-◁-•}\}$ and $\frown = \{\langle\text{——•}, \text{——•}\rangle, \langle\text{-◁-•}, \text{-▷-•}\rangle, \langle\text{-▷-•}, \text{-◁-•}\rangle, \langle\text{-▷-•}, \text{-▷-•}\rangle\}$.

The second colouring from Fig. 2, namely a ——•◁-• b, is formalised as colouring $\{a^\downarrow \mapsto \text{——•}, b^\uparrow \mapsto \text{-◁-•}\}$. It models the scenario where end a has data flow and end b has no data flow but requires a reason for its absence.

A stateful connector with ends X and states Q can be modelled using automata with transition structure $\Delta \subseteq Q \times (X \to \mathcal{C}olour) \times Q$, such that state changes occur only when flow occurs at some end.

3 Problem Statement

The problem with connector colouring semantics (and their encoding into constraints) is that it takes a global view of the connector, that is, all primitives of the connector are considered at every round. This has two negative consequences. Firstly, it eliminates the opportunity to exploit the concurrent, potentially asynchronous, evolution of distinct parts of a connector. Secondly, it means that implementations based on connector colouring will not be scalable.

Consider the connector in the top left-hand corner of Fig. 3. This consists of a $FIFO_1$ connected to priority merger. On the boundary are three components: Both A and B are attempting to write a single message, while C is able to accept as many messages as possible. The different boxes in the figure correspond to different states of this connector. The transitions between these states are labelled with a 3-colouring if one exists, and a 2-colouring if not. (Valid 3-colourings can be converted to valid 2-colourings by forgetting the direction-of-reason arrows.)

Ideally, all transitions except the dotted one should be permitted—the dotted transition violates the preference of the priority merger. However, 2-colouring allows all transitions, which is too lax. On the other end of the spectrum, the only reachable transitions permitted by 3-colouring are those indicated with a thick line. 3-colouring rules out the dotted transition, but it also rules out other possibilities. Consider, for example, the transitions from the start state. These correspond to allowing writers A and B to succeed independently or together. But 3-colouring allows only both succeeding together. The other two behaviours are reasonable, as there is no channel synchronising actions A and B.

4   Partial Connector Colouring

The problems described in the previous section are solved by partial connector colouring. The idea is simple: only part of the connector is coloured to determine the behaviour. The part that is not coloured plays no role in the computation. The challenge is determining which partial colourings are sensible; this comes down determining where the boundary of the coloured part can be draw and what that boundary may look like.

Partial connector colouring is based on partial colouring schemes, which are triples $(\mathcal{C}olour, \frown, \mathsf{valid})$, where $\mathcal{C}olour$ is a set of colours, $\frown \subseteq (\mathcal{C}olour + 1) \times (\mathcal{C}olour + 1)$ is a symmetric matching relation such that $\bot \frown \bot$, and $\mathsf{valid} : \mathcal{C}olour \to 2$ is a predicate that states which colours can appear on the boundary of the coloured part, defined as $\mathsf{valid}(x)$ if and only if $x \frown \bot$.

Definition 2 (Partial Connector Colouring). *Given a partial colouring scheme $(\mathcal{C}olour, \frown, \mathsf{valid})$, a partial colouring $c : X \rightharpoonup \mathcal{C}olour$ for $X \subseteq \mathcal{X}^{\updownarrow}$ is a partial function from ends to colours. The remainder of the definition (partial colouring tables and table composition) follows Definition 1, with partial colourings instead of total colourings.*

A light gray colour will be used to denotes places where no colouring is computed—that is where the colouring table is undefined. Valid partial colourings satisfy two well-formedness conditions on the internal ends and boundary ends.

Definition 3 (Valid Partial Colouring). *A partial colouring $c : X \rightharpoonup \mathcal{C}olour$ for connector P, where $X = \mathrm{ends}(P)$, is valid iff for all $x \in \mathrm{internal}(P)$, $c(x^{\uparrow}) \frown c(x^{\downarrow})$ and $\mathsf{valid}(x^{\circ})$ holds for all $x^{\circ} \in \mathrm{boundary}(P)$.*

Partial 2-colouring is defined as $Colour = \{$——•$, - - -•\}$ and $\frown = \{\langle$——•$,$——•$\rangle$, $\langle - - -•, - - -•\rangle, \langle - - -•, \perp\rangle, \langle\perp, - - -•\rangle, \langle\perp, \perp\rangle\}$. Only valid$(- - -•)$ holds. A valid partial 2-colouring is one where no data flows at the boundaries. *Partial 3-colouring* is defined as $Colour = \{$——•$, -\triangleright-•, -\triangleleft-•\}$ and $\frown = \{\langle$——•$,$——•$\rangle, \langle-\triangleleft-•, -\triangleright-•\rangle$, $\langle-\triangleright-•, -\triangleleft-•\rangle, \langle-\triangleright-•, -\triangleright-•\rangle\langle-\triangleright-•, \perp\rangle, \langle\perp, -\triangleright-•\rangle, \langle\perp, \perp\rangle\}$. Only valid$(-\triangleright-•)$ holds. A valid partial 3-colouring is one where all boundary ends give a reason for no flow.

Partial 2- and 3-colouring schemes are well-behaved with respect to composition; the composition of two valid colourings produces a valid colouring. A partial n-colouring scheme can be seen as an $(n + 1)$-colouring scheme, but the way it is used is different, as the aim is to avoid computing the $(n + 1)$th colour.

The level of granularity expressed thus far is that of whole primitives, but we can go finer. For some primitives, the behaviour of some ends is independent of their other ends. This means that different parts of the primitive can be coloured (or not coloured) independently. This kind of behaviour is called *split colouring*.

We illustrate split colourings using the $FIFO_1$ buffer. Consider the partial colouring of the $FIFO_1$ buffer is it its empty state in Fig. 4(a). It is the case that both ends of this primitive are independent (in the empty state), so the colour tables could be presented as in Fig. 4(b), where the $FIFO_1$ is actually treated as two separate primitives. Based on this, the effective colouring table for the $FIFO_1$ buffer is the one in Fig. 4(c).

The remainder of the figure revisits our example connector. Fig. 4(d) shows an attempt to find a colouring without split colourings for one of the transitions leaving the initial state, but this colouring is not valid due to the node marked x. This corresponds to a writer blocking for no reason. With split colourings, the colouring in Fig. 4(e) can instead be used. This colouring does not even look at the writer; it is not blocked, just not involved in the computation.

Two conditions govern the validity of a split colouring. The first is that when we split the colouring table for the connector and then rejoin it, as in Fig. 4(a–c), no additional data flow behaviour is introduced. The second condition deals with stateful primitives. As each split colouring is derived from some partial colouring, which itself may cause a change in the state, consistency demands that no no-flow colouring can result in a state change *and* that any combination of split colourings do not result in different state changes—there is at most one state

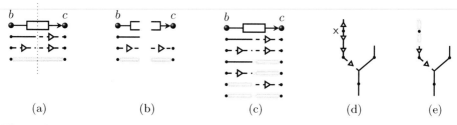

(a)   (b)   (c)   (d)   (e)

Fig. 4. Splitting the colouring table of an empty $FIFO_1$ buffer (a–c). Candidate connector without split colourings (d) and with them (e).

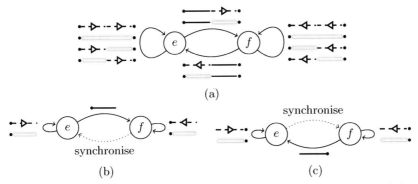

Fig. 5. Splitting the automaton of a FIFO$_1$. The automata for the parts of the split FIFO$_1$ have an *out-of-phase* synchronisation step to keep the same view on the state.

change among the split colourings. Formal conditions capturing the correctness criteria have been explored in Proença's thesis [16].

When only one part causes a change of state, the two parts need to synchronise to ensure that both have the same view on the state. We illustrate with an example. Fig. 5(a) gives an automaton for a FIFO$_1$, where transitions are labelled with the split colourings that cause the respective transitions—each transition has multiple colourings. When the primitive is split it results in the two automata shown in Fig. 5(b–c), one for each end of the FIFO$_1$. Now, if a data flow transition is taken in the first automaton in state e, the second automaton is not aware of the state change, as it has no behaviour to change the state. In order for them to get into the same state, an *out-of-phase* synchronisation step is made between the two ends of the split primitive.

Fig. 6 presents what partial 3-colouring will allow. Split colouring of the FIFO$_1$ primitive is required for the transitions marked **1** and **2**. Not only does partial 3-colouring with split colouring allows all desirable behaviours, but it also reduces the computation required to achieve these, thereby increasing scalability. It allows *mosaic evolution*, whereby different parts of the connector can evolve at different rates, increasing concurrency. Partial and split colourings thus offer more potential concurrency, as the ends can be computed independently, better scalability, as the size of the connector being considered can be smaller, and more behavioural possibilities.

5   Constraint-Based Encoding

In previous work we showed how to encode connector colouring as constraints [9]. The constraints encode three aspects of behaviour: *synchronisation constraints* (SC) describe the presence or absence of data flow at each end—that is, whether or not those ends synchronise; *data flow constraints* (DFC) describe the data flow at the ends that synchronise (which connector colouring does not capture); and *context constraints* (CC) describe the direction of the reasons for no-flow.

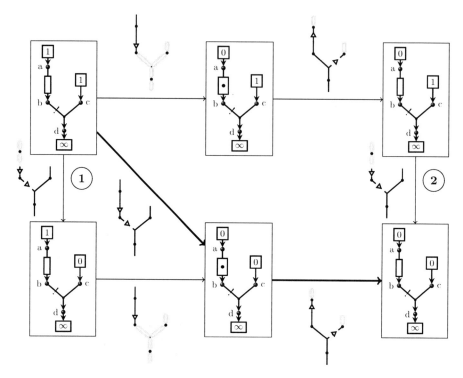

Fig. 6. Evolution of example connector with partial colouring

For encoding 2-colouring, context constraints can be dropped. State and state transitions can also be encoded, but we omit them here for brevity.

Constraints are defined over (1) propositional synchronisation variables $\mathcal{X}$, (2) data flow variables $\widehat{\mathcal{X}} = \{\widehat{x} \mid x \in \mathcal{X}\}$ ranging over $\mathcal{D}ata_{\perp} \stackrel{\frown}{=} \mathcal{D}ata \cup \{\texttt{NO-FLOW}\}$, where $\mathcal{D}ata$ be the domain of data and where $\texttt{NO-FLOW} \notin \mathcal{D}ata$ represents 'no data flow', and (3) propositional context variables $\mathcal{X}^{\updownarrow}$. The encoding of colourings into constraints is given in the following table:

Colouring	Constraint	Colouring	Constraint
$x^{\downarrow} \mapsto \text{———}$	x	$x^{\uparrow} \mapsto \text{———}$	x
$x^{\downarrow} \mapsto \text{-▷-•}$	$\neg x \wedge x^{\downarrow}$	$x^{\uparrow} \mapsto \text{-▷-•}$	$\neg x \wedge x^{\uparrow}$
$x^{\downarrow} \mapsto \text{-◁-•}$	$\neg x \wedge \neg x^{\downarrow}$	$x^{\uparrow} \mapsto \text{-◁-•}$	$\neg x \wedge \neg x^{\uparrow}$

Constraints are expressed as quantifier-free, first-order logical formulas. Table 2 presents the semantics of some commonly used primitives. A *solution* to a formula ψ is an assignment of variables, defined in the usual manner [9].

The following axiom captures the relationship between the different kinds of variables, and it is applicable to all ends in a connector:

$$(\neg x \leftrightarrow \widehat{x} = \texttt{NO-FLOW}) \wedge (\neg x \rightarrow x^{\uparrow} \vee x^{\downarrow}) \qquad \text{(flow axiom)}$$

Table 2. Channel Encodings. SC=synchronisation constraints. DC=data flow constraints. CC=context constraints.

Channel	Representation	SC	DFC	CC
Sync	$a \longrightarrow b$	$a \leftrightarrow b$	$\widehat{a} = \widehat{b}$	$a \vee \neg a^{\downarrow} \vee \neg b^{\uparrow}$
LossySync	$a \dashrightarrow b$	$b \to a$	$b \to (\widehat{a} = \widehat{b})$	$\neg a \to (\neg b \wedge \neg a^{\downarrow} \wedge b^{\uparrow}) \wedge$ $\neg b \to ((a \wedge \neg b^{\uparrow}) \vee \neg a)$
Priority Merger	$\begin{array}{c} a \\ b \end{array} \!\!\!\succ\!\!\!\!\to c$	$(c \leftrightarrow (a \vee b)) \wedge \neg (a \wedge b)$	$a \to (\widehat{c} = \widehat{a}) \wedge$ $b \to (\widehat{c} = \widehat{b})$	$(c \wedge \neg a) \to \neg a^{\downarrow} \wedge$ $(c \wedge \neg b) \to b^{\downarrow} \wedge$ $\neg c \to ((\neg a^{\downarrow} \wedge \neg b^{\downarrow}) \vee \neg c^{\uparrow})$
Replicator	$a \longrightarrow\!\!\!\!\begin{array}{c} b \\ c \end{array}$	$(a \leftrightarrow b) \wedge$ $(a \leftrightarrow c)$	$\widehat{b} = \widehat{a} \wedge \widehat{c} = \widehat{a}$	$a \vee \neg a^{\downarrow} \vee \neg b^{\uparrow} \vee \neg c^{\uparrow}$
FIFO$_1$ (empty)	$a \longrightarrow \square \longrightarrow b$	$\neg b$	$\top$	$(\neg a \to \neg a^{\downarrow}) \wedge b^{\uparrow}$
FIFO$_1$ (full)	$a \longrightarrow \boxed{d} \longrightarrow b$	$\neg a$	$b \to (\widehat{b} = d)$	$a^{\downarrow} \wedge (\neg b \to \neg b^{\uparrow})$

The first clause captures that NO-FLOW is used as the value of a data flow variable when no flow occurs, which is the same as when the corresponding synchronisation variable is $\bot$. The constraint $x^{\uparrow} \vee x^{\downarrow}$ is interpreted as saying that the reason for no data flow either comes from the sink end, from the source end, or from both ends. The second clause is dropped when using 2-colouring. Let $\texttt{Flow}(X)$ denote the conjunction $\bigwedge_{x \in X} (\neg x \leftrightarrow \widehat{x} = \texttt{NO-FLOW}) \wedge (\neg x \to x^{\uparrow} \vee x^{\downarrow})$.

The constraints for an entire connector are obtained by taking the conjunction of the constraints of the primitives making up the connector and adding in the flow axiom for the ends present. For example, the connector in Fig. 2 is encoded in constraints as follows:

$$\begin{aligned} \Psi_{SC} &= b \to a \wedge \neg c & \Psi_{DFC} &= b \to (\widehat{a} = \widehat{b}) \wedge \top \\ \Psi_{CC} &= \neg a \to (\neg b \wedge \neg a^{\downarrow} \wedge b^{\uparrow}) \wedge \neg b \to ((a \wedge \neg b^{\uparrow}) \vee \neg a) \wedge (\neg b \to \neg b^{\downarrow}) \wedge c^{\uparrow} \\ \Psi &= \Psi_{SC} \wedge \Psi_{DFC} \wedge \Psi_{CC} \wedge \texttt{Flow}(\{a, b, c\}). \end{aligned}$$

5.1 Partial 2- and 3-Constraints

Now we can modify the constraints generated to handle partial colouring. The first difference is that the constraints will be applied not to all primitives, but to a subset of the primitives—split primitives treated as separate primitives. First, let $constraints_p$ denote the constraints for connector p, and define $constraints_P = \bigwedge_{p \in P} constraints_p$. Two kinds of additional are constraints generated. The first ensures that the solution to the constraints corresponds to a valid partial colouring by constraining the boundary:

$$\bigwedge_{x^{\circ} \in boundary(P)} \neg x \wedge x^{\circ} \qquad \text{(boundary)}$$

The 2-colouring variant is obtained by dropping the '$\wedge x^{\circ}$' part. It is straight-forward to show that the collection of constraints faithfully encodes partial 2/3-colouring. An additional kind of constraint is added to check whether there is any flow within a connector, as ultimately we are only interested in partial colourings where something happens:

$$\bigvee_{x \in internal(P)} x \qquad\qquad \text{(internal-flow)}$$

6   Implementation and Benchmarks

Partial connector colouring is implemented using constraint satisfaction in a fashion similar to our constraint-based implementation of Reo [9]. The previous implementation collected all the constraints for a connector and solved them. The resulting solution described the behaviour in the connector.

To exploit partiality, a different approach is required. This involves trying to solve the constraints for a part of the total connector; if no solution is found, a larger part is tried. More specifically, each thread operating on a connector performs the following steps. The thread is initially given a number of primitives, which it is said to *own*. It collects the constraints for those primitives, including the boundary and internal flow constraints, and solves the resulting constraint satisfaction problem. A solution corresponds to flow within that part of the connector, so the thread ensures that the corresponding data is moved to where it belongs and the states of stateful primitives change. If, however, there is no solution, then the part of the connector the thread is operating on is expanded and the algorithm repeats. When two threads attempt to *own* the same part of the connector, one claims both parts of the connector and the other thread is returned to the thread pool to be reassigned work.

Due to the nature of this approach, we cannot expect that it will always be better—implementations will need to be tuned to specific connectors. Nevertheless, a number of preliminary benchmarks do show that partial connector colouring can produced a faster implementation. The benchmarks consist of two parametric connectors, depicted in Fig. 7. These connector each have a part that can be repeated a given number of times. We ran four versions of our implementation on these connectors on a 8-core 2.4 GHz Intel Xeon desktop with 16 GB RAM running Ubuntu Linux. As a baseline, the first version implemented the original connector colouring model. The other versions implement partial connector colouring, using one, two and four threads. These results show that partial colouring can lead to a faster, more concurrent, and scalable implementation.

There are however a number of dimensions where heuristics can be applied to improve the performance of the implementation, such as choosing the number of threads, choosing where they start computing, and choosing how the set of primitives considered grows. These will be investigated in future work.

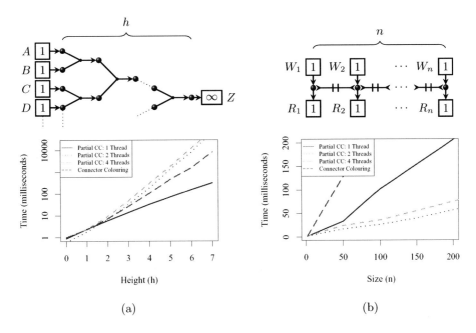

Fig. 7. Benchmarks: Multiple Merger (a) demonstrates that partial connector colouring offers an order of magnitude improvement for one thread, though multiple threads create too much contention. Pairwise Asynchronous (b) demonstrates significant advantages of partial colouring, which scales well as more threads (cores) are added.

7   Related Work

Many semantic models exist for Reo. Clarke et al. [6] outline the difference between various models. Only connector colouring [8], Reo automata [6], intentional automata [10], and the tile model [3] capture context dependent behaviour. Connector colouring was the first to do so, and the others refine it in one way or another. The models are all distinct—and the relationship between them has not been investigated—but for our purposes, we do not consider automata-based models as these do not lead to scalable implementations. The constraint-based encoding of Reo [9] offers orders of magnitude improvement in performance and scalability of Reo implementations.

Wegner describes coordination as constrained interaction [19] and Montanari and Rossi express coordination as a constraint satisfaction problem [15]. They describe how to solve synchronisation problems using constraint solving techniques, but they do not encode context dependency or identify the benefits of partiality. Lazovik et al. [13] utilise constraints to provide a choreography framework for web services. The choreography, the business processes, and the requests are modelled as a set of constraints. Their setting, however, cannot express the same kinds of coordination patterns as Reo. The analogy between

Reo and constraint satisfaction has already been made [2], and indeed Klüppelholz and Baier encode the constraint automata model for Reo in terms of binary decision diagrams in order to model check Reo connectors [12]. Constraint automata are represented by binary decision diagrams, encoded as propositional formulæ. Their encoding is similar to ours, though they use exclusively boolean variables, whilst our constraint encoding is phrased in terms of a richer data domain.

Minsky and Ungureanu introduce the Law-Governed Interaction (LGI) mechanism [14], implemented by the Moses toolkit, where in laws are constraints specified in a Prolog-like language, enforced on regulated events of the agents, such as sending or receiving messages. This mechanism targets distributed coordination of heterogenous agents using a policy that enforces extensible laws. However, laws are local, in the sense that can only refer to the agent being regulated. While this allows LGI to achieve good performance, it limits expressiveness.

Bruni et al.'s stateless algebra of connectors [7] and Sobociński's [17] stateful extension resemble the core of Reo, though they lack context dependency and data. The semantics is similar to 2-colouring in this limited setting. Bliduze and Sifakis [5] present a semantics for their BIP coordination model in terms of boolean propositions. Although similar, BIP is not as expressive as Reo as it lacks the ability to filter data passing through connectors. Jongmans et al. [11] present an encoding of 3-colouring in terms of 2-colouring that resembles our encoding into propositional constraints. Their approach adds fictitious nodes into the Reo level, whereas ours is completely under the surface.

8   Conclusion

This paper presented partial connector colouring which improves on the existing connector colouring semantics for Reo and their subsequent encoding as constraints in three respects. Firstly, the semantics enable a more scalable implementation by avoiding the lock-step evaluation of an entire connector. Secondly, the amount of concurrency is increased by enabling different parts of a connector to evolve independently at different rates. Finally, partial 3-colouring retains the context dependent behaviour of 3-colouring but regains some of the behavioural possibilities lost due to the lock-step computation. Benchmarks have also been presented to confirm the possible performance improvements.

An interesting direction for future work is a more in depth empirical exploration of the heuristics alluded to in Section 6.

References

1. Arbab, F.: Reo: a channel-based coordination model for component composition. Mathematical Structures in Computer Science 14(3), 329–366 (2004)
2. Arbab, F.: Composition of interacting computations. In: Goldin, D., Smolka, S., Wegner, P. (eds.) Interactive Computation: The New Paradigm, pp. 277–321. Springer-Verlag New York, Inc., Secaucus (2006)

3. Arbab, F., Bruni, R., Clarke, D., Lanese, I., Montanari, U.: Tiles for Reo. In: Corradini, A., Montanari, U. (eds.) WADT 2008. LNCS, vol. 5486, pp. 37–55. Springer, Heidelberg (2009)
4. Arbab, F., Koehler, C., Maraikar, Z., Moon, Y., Proença, J.: Modeling, testing and executing Reo connectors with the Eclipse Coordination Tools. In: International Workshop on Formal Aspects of Component Software (FACS), Malaga. ENTCS (2008)
5. Bliudze, S., Sifakis, J.: Synthesizing Glue Operators from Glue Constraints for the Construction of Component-Based Systems. In: Apel, S., Jackson, E. (eds.) SC 2011. LNCS, vol. 6708, pp. 51–67. Springer, Heidelberg (2011)
6. Bonsangue, M.M., Clarke, D., Silva, A.: Automata for Context-Dependent Connectors. In: Field, J., Vasconcelos, V.T. (eds.) COORDINATION 2009. LNCS, vol. 5521, pp. 184–203. Springer, Heidelberg (2009)
7. Bruni, R., Lanese, I., Montanari, U.: A basic algebra of stateless connectors. Theor. Comput. Sci. 366(1-2), 98–120 (2006)
8. Clarke, D., Costa, D., Arbab, F.: Connector colouring I: Synchronisation and context dependency. Science of Computer Programming 66(3), 205–225 (2007)
9. Clarke, D., Proença, J., Lazovik, A., Arbab, F.: Channel-based coordination via constraint satisfaction. Sci. Comput. Program. 76(8), 681–710 (2011)
10. Costa, D.: Formal Models for Component Connectors. PhD thesis, Vrij Universiteit Amsterdam (2010)
11. Jongmans, S.-S.T.Q., Krause, C., Arbab, F.: Encoding Context-Sensitivity in Reo into Non-Context-Sensitive Semantic Models. In: De Meuter, W., Roman, G.-C. (eds.) COORDINATION 2011. LNCS, vol. 6721, pp. 31–48. Springer, Heidelberg (2011)
12. Klüppelholz, S., Baier, C.: Symbolic model checking for channel-based component connectors. ENTCS 175(2), 19–37 (2007)
13. Lazovik, A., Aiello, M., Gennari, R.: Choreographies: Using constraints to satisfy service requests. In: Proc. of the Advanced International Conference on Telecommunications and International Conference on Internet and Web Applications and Services, p. 150. IEEE Computer Society, Washington, DC (2006)
14. Minsky, N.H., Ungureanu, V.: Law-governed interaction: a coordination and control mechanism for heterogeneous distributed systems. ACM Transactions on Software Engineering and Methodology 9(3), 273–305 (2000)
15. Montanari, U., Rossi, F.: Modeling process coordination via tiles, graphs, and constraints. In: 3rd Biennial World Conference on Integrated Design and Process Technology, vol. 4, pp. 1–8 (1998)
16. Proença, J.: Synchronous coordination of distributed components. PhD thesis, LIACS, Leiden University (May 2011)
17. Sobociński, P.: Representations of Petri Net Interactions. In: Gastin, P., Laroussinie, F. (eds.) CONCUR 2010. LNCS, vol. 6269, pp. 554–568. Springer, Heidelberg (2010)
18. van der Aalst, W.M.P., ter Hofstede, A.H.M., Kiepuszewski, B., Barros, A.P.: Workflow patterns. Distributed and Parallel Databases 14(1), 5–51 (2003)
19. Wegner, P.: Coordination as Constrained Interaction (Extended Abstract). In: Hankin, C., Ciancarini, P. (eds.) COORDINATION 1996. LNCS, vol. 1061, pp. 28–33. Springer, Heidelberg (1996)

Using Coordinated Actors to Model Families of Distributed Systems[*]

Ramtin Khosravi[1,2] and Hamideh Sabouri[1]

[1] School of ECE, University of Tehran, Iran
[2] School of CS, Institute for Studies in Fundamental Sciences (IPM), Tehran, Iran

Abstract. Software product line engineering enables strategic reuse in development of families of related products. In a component-based approach to product line development, components capture functionalities appearing in one or more products in the family and different assemblies of components yield to various products or configurations. In this approach, an interaction model which effectively factors out the logic handling variability from the functionality of the system greatly enhances the reusability of components. We study the problem of variability modeling for a family of distributed systems expressed in actor model. We define a special type of actors called coordinators whose behavior is described as Reo circuits with the aim of encapsulating the variability logic. We have the benefits of Reo language for expressing coordination logic, while modeling the entire system as an actor-based distributed model. We have applied this model to a case study extracted from an industrial software family in the domain of interactive TV.

1 Introduction

Software Product Line Engineering (SPLE) focuses on proactive reuse to reduce the cost of developing families of related systems. The goal is to promote reuse from source code to other project artifacts as well, including models, documents, etc. [1]. A key factor to achieve this is the explicit modeling and management of commonalities and variabilities among the products in the family. Based on the domain and characteristics of the software family, suitable ways to manage variabilities in relevant models must be devised. In this paper, we deal with the class of distributed software systems that are modeled as actor systems, which is a well-known model for distributed and concurrent systems [2] (Sect. 2.1).

There are various approaches to variability modeling. Some use annotative techniques in which parts of the model are annotated with specific features and are present in the configurations that include those features. This technique is more effective for smaller variations. When two variants differ in more than a few lines of code, using annotations clutters the code and reduces maintainability. On the other hand, compositional variability management uses components to handle variability [3]. Each variant may be implemented by a separate component

---

[*] This research was in part supported by a grant from IPM. (No. CS1390-4-02).

M. Sirjani (Ed.): COORDINATION 2012, LNCS 7274, pp. 74–88, 2012.

and alternatives for a variation point implement a common interface, through which other components have a uniform access to the variants. This method is more modular and is more flexible in the sense that the binding time for variation points can be deferred easily to runtime. This makes the compositional approach suitable for reconfigurable software, where decision about the variants is made at runtime and can be changed dynamically [4]. This is specifically useful for distributed systems in which failures or topology changes may require more flexibility in configuration.

As the actor model can be treated as a component-based approach to engineer a distributed system, compositional variability management seems a good match for engineering families of actor systems. In [5], handling variability in an actor-based modeling language Rebeca [6] is studied where both annotative and compositional methods are used. However, expressing variability logic in actors has the risk of making the core functionality of the actors messy.

Taking a compositional variability management approach for an actor system makes the variability handling logic more about wiring of actors and routing messages to appropriate actors. Having a way to model the variability logic in a modular way and separate from the functionality will make the actors more reusable and variability logic more manageable. This is almost the same as the objective of coordination language Reo [7] that aims to capture the glue code between components in a compositional and modular way (Sect. 2.2).

Hence, we define a special type of actors called *coordinators* and define their behavior using Reo circuits. Externally, coordinators can be treated as ordinary actors communicating with other actors/coordinators via asynchronous message passing. This is essential to keep message passing as the basic communication means in a distributed environment. Coordinators will be discussed in more detail in Sect. 3. To express the way we integrate Reo circuits in an actor system precisely, we present a formal operational semantics for the model in Sect. 4. Our approach to variability management is dynamic in the sense that the configuration parameters are modeled as inputs to the coordinators. This enables dynamic changes in the configuration, making our method closer to re-configurable architectures as opposed to statically generating coordinators from a given configuration (which has the benefit of less runtime overhead).

We use coordinated actors to model a part of a real-world distributed system in the domain of interactive TV systems (Sect. 5). We show how coordinators can capture variability logic among a set of components in a distributed environment, keeping the components free from the variability handling code.

To the best of our knowledge, little work has been done addressing product lines of distributed systems based on asynchronous message passing. In [8], a methodology is presented for design, implementation and verification of highly configurable systems, such as software product lines. This methodology is centered around the ABS language, which is a class-based language built on top of the active object concurrency model of Creol [9], using asynchronous method calls. The full ABS modeling framework extends ABS by delta modeling language (DML) that is based on delta-oriented programming [10] to describe code-level variability. The implementation of a product family contains a core module and a set of delta modules specifying the changes that should be applied to the core module to obtain a new product. In [11] a method is presented for verification of families of services which is based on modal transition systems. Although the service-based computing is inherently distributed, the authors have used a synchronous model leaving support for asynchronous interactions to future work.

2   Preliminaries

2.1   Actor Model for Distributed Computing

Actor model is a well-known model for concurrent and distributed computing. The basic units of concurrency are called actors which communicate solely through asynchronous message passing. Each actor has a unique identifier and an unbounded message queue. An actor may know the identifier of a number of other actors to which it can send messages. An actor takes messages from its input queue one at a time. Processing each message will result in (a) a set of newly created actors, (b) a set of messages sent to other actors, and (c) the new behavior of the recipient actor. As soon as the new behavior is specified, it can take the next message from the input queue to process. The behavior replacement essentially makes the behavior of the actors history-sensitive. Hence the actor model is known as a concurrent object-based computation model.

In practice, it is possible to describe the behavior of the actors using functional or imperative paradigms. The way we treat actors in this paper is independent of the implementation paradigm.

2.2   Reo Coordination Language

Reo is a channel-based coordination language in which complex entities, called connectors, are constructed out of simpler ones. The behavior of each connector in Reo defines a specific coordination pattern, through which the system components perform I/O operations. The simplest connector types are called channels which are basic means of communication with exactly two ends. Channel ends are of two types: the source end through which data enters the channel, and the sink end through which data exits the channel. Reo does not impose any constraint on the channel behavior, so that each type can have its own policy for synchronization, buffering, sequencing, computation and data management. A number of channel types are commonly used in the literature. We use the following set of channels in this paper which are defined briefly in the following (Fig. 1).

Synchronous channel (Sync) Read and write operations are performed only if there is a data item on the source end and the sink end is ready to read. If one of the ends is not ready, the other end will be blocked.

Synchronous Drain channel (SyncDrain) The write operation is performed in this channel only if both ends are ready to write. If one of the ends is not ready, the other end will be blocked.

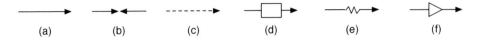

Fig. 1. Common channel notations: (a) Synchronous (b) Synchronous Drain (c) Lossy Synchronous (d) FIFO-1 (e) Filter (f) Transform

Lossy Synchronous channel (LossySync) A LossySynch channel is similar to a Sync channel, except that it always accepts all data items through its source end. If it is possible for it to simultaneously dispense the data item through its sink, the channel transfers the data item; otherwise the data item is lost.

One-place FIFO channel (FIFO1) In a one-place FIFO channel, the source end may put a data item on the channel if the buffer is empty. In this case, the sink end will be blocked. Furthermore, the sink end can perform the read operation if the buffer is full. In this case, the source end will be blocked.

Filter channel The read/write operation is synchronously performed (like Sync channel) with the condition that the data on the source end must satisfy a filter condition associated with the channel.

Transform channel The read/write operation is synchronously performed (like Sync channel) and a transformation function associated with the channel is applied to the input data to produce the output.

A connector is then constructed out of a number of channels organized in a graph of nodes and edges. A node consists of one or more channel ends. When all channel ends are of type source (resp. sink), the node is called a source node (resp. sink node), otherwise, it is called a mixed node. There are several ways to combine a set of channel ends of both types into a single node (Fig. 2).

The data items simply flow through a *flow through* node. A write on a *replication node* succeeds only if all outgoing channels are capable of consuming the written data. A *merge node* delivers a value out of one of the incoming channels non-deterministically. In our method, we usually face with the issue of prioritization over two or more inputs. In such cases, we use a special type of connector named *priority merger* which behaves like a merge node but one of its source ends has higher priority than the other (indicated by the exclamation mark). Whenever data is present on both its source ends, the data from the preferred input is passed to the sink end.

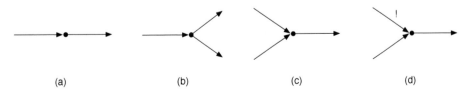

Fig. 2. Three types of mixed nodes: (a) flow through, (b) replication, (c) non-deterministic merge, and (d) a priority merger depicted as a node

3   Handling Variability through Coordination

We assume there are a number of special kind of actors named *coordinators* with their behavior specified as a Reo circuit (Fig. 3). The coordination logic, expressed as a Reo circuit, has one special input port for reading incoming messages from other actors, and a number of input ports specifying product configuration parameters. On the other side, there are a number of output message ports through which the coordinator sends messages to other actors, each port corresponding to a separate destination actor.

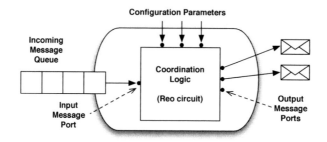

Fig. 3. A coordinator actor

Informally, the coordinator fetches one input message from the input queue and makes the message data ready on the input port of the Reo circuit. The Reo circuit then computes the output messages and provide them on the output ports. Whenever an output message appears on an output port, the coordinator takes the message and sends it to the corresponding actor. It is assumed that the coordinator is always ready to take the output messages, so the Reo circuit never blocks on the output ports.

An important assumption is made about the Reo circuit that is the circuit terminates after a finite number of steps when responding to a single input message. This assumption is made to make the behavior of the coordinators consistent with the semantics of the actor system given above. So, like other actors, a coordinator takes one message from its input queue, processes the message, generates a number of new messages, and possibly changes its own state. Note that the internal state of the Reo circuit (i.e., the contents of its buffer channels) may change when responding to a message, and to respond to the next input message, the Reo circuit continues from its last state.

3.1   Example: Handling Optional Features

As an illustrative example, consider a coffee machine that has an optional feature of adding milk to a coffee. To keep it simple, assume that if this feature is included

```
actor CoffeeMachine {
    def coffeeRequest() {
        CoffeeMaker ! makeCoffee();
    }
    def serveCoffee() { // serve coffee }
}
actor CoffeeMaker {
    def makeCoffee() {
        // make coffee
        AdditivesCoord ! coffeeReady();
    }
}
actor Additives {
    def addMilk() {
        // add milk
        CoffeeMachine ! serveCoffee();
    }
}
```

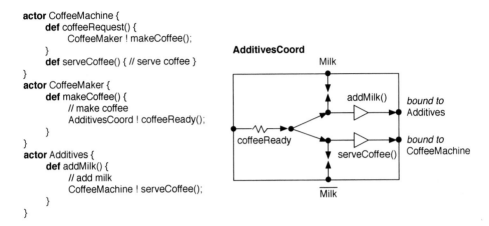

Fig. 4. Handling optional 'Milk' feature

in a product, then coffee is always served with milk. To handle this variability, we consider three functional actors and one coordinator actor as depicted in Fig. 4. The CoffeeMachine actor tells CoffeeMaker to make coffee. When it is done, CoffeeMaker informs a coordinator AdditvesCoord that the coffee is ready. The behavior of AdditivesCoord is described by a simple Reo circuit. To make it simple, we have provided both Milk and $\overline{\text{Milk}}$ configuration inputs to the circuit. The circuit first filters the incoming messages to process 'coffeeReady' only (to be complete, a mechanism must be added to discard irrelevant messages). Based on the presence of 'Milk' feature, the coordinator decides to tell Additives to add milk or just inform CoffeeMachine that the drink is ready.

Note that for this very simple example, the variability could be handled much more easily in the actors itself. As the interactions become more complex however, the benefits of using Reo as a compositional coordination model becomes more evident.

4   Formal Modeling of Coordinated Actor Systems

In this section, we formally demonstrate how the coordinators with their behavior described as Reo circuits are integrated into an actor system. The core material is presented in Sect. 4.3 and 4.4, but to make our description complete, we first give an operational semantics for actor systems in Sect. 4.1 and 4.2.

We use the following notations for working with sequences. Given a set A, the set A^* is the set of all finite sequences over elements of A. We write sequences as $[a_1, a_2, \ldots, a_n]$, where $a_i \in A$. The empty sequence is represented by $[\,]$, and $[h|T]$ denotes a sequence whose first elements is $h \in A$ and $T \in A^*$ is the sequence comprising the elements in the rest of the sequence. For two sequences σ_1 and σ_2 over A, $\sigma_1 \oplus \sigma_2$ is the sequence obtained by appending σ_2 to the end of σ_1.

We assume the following sets are given:

- *Id*: The set of all actor identifiers
- *Data*: The set of all data items that can be communicated in messages. We abstract from the details of this set, but note that it can contain actor identifiers, allowing a dynamic topology for the actor system.
- *State*: The set of all local states of the actors. We also abstract from the details of how actors keep track of their states. This can be a mapping from the actor's variables to values, or a function describing the actor's current behavior.

We also define $Msg = Id \times Data$ as the set of all messages. Each message is a pair (α, m) where α is the receiver and m is the message data. We usually write $\alpha.m$ as an alternative to (α, m).

4.1 Actor Systems

We define an actor as a tuple (α, q, s, b) where:

- $\alpha : Id$ is the unique identifier of the actor,
- $q : Msg^*$ is the unbounded FIFO message queue of the actor,
- $s : State$ is the local state of the actor,
- $b : Msg \times State \leftrightarrow 2^{Actor} \times Msg^* \times State$ is the behavior of the actor. Having $(A, \sigma, s') \in b(\alpha.m, s)$ means that the actor may respond to the incoming message $\alpha.m$ by creating a set of actors A, sending the sequence of messages σ, and changing its local state to s'.

Note that since the behavior of an actor may be modeled non-deterministically, in responding to an incoming message several outcomes may happen, hence b is defined as a relation, not a function. The uniqueness and freshness of identifiers of the actors in A are assumed (expressed later). For a message sequence $\sigma = [\alpha_1.m_1, \alpha_2.m_2, \ldots \alpha_k.m_k]$, we define recipients$(\sigma) = \{\alpha_1, \alpha_2, \ldots, \alpha_k\}$. If α is an actor identifier, then $\sigma_{[\beta]}$ denotes the sequence of messages in σ restricted to β as the recipient, i.e., it is obtained by removing the elements of σ whose recipients are not β.

If *Actor* denotes the set of all actors, then we define a configuration of actors as a set of actors. Since the actors in a configuration has unique identifiers, we define a configuration as a mapping from identifiers to actors: $C : Id \to Actor$. If no actor with identifier α exists in a configuration C, we write $C(\alpha) = \bot$. We use the notation ids(C) to denote the domain of the mapping C, i.e., the set of all actor identifiers in C. We define *Conf* as the set of all configurations.

4.2 Transition System Semantics

For an actor system with initial configuration C_0, we define the transition system $TS = (Conf, Msg, \to, C_0)$, with *Conf* as the set of states, *Msg* as the set of actions (transition labels), C_0 as the initial state, and $\to \subseteq Conf \times Msg \times Conf$ as the transition relation defined as the smallest relation satisfying the following condition.

We have $(C, \alpha.m, C') \in \rightarrow$, (written alternatively as $C \xrightarrow{\alpha.m} C'$) if the following conditions hold:

1. $\alpha \in \mathrm{ids}(C)$ and $C(\alpha) = (\alpha, [\alpha.m | q_\alpha], s_\alpha, b_\alpha)$
2. There exists $(A, \sigma, s'_\alpha) \in b_\alpha(\alpha.m, s_\alpha)$ such that
   (a) $\mathrm{ids}(C') = \mathrm{ids}(C) \cup \mathrm{ids}(A)$
   (b) $C'(\alpha) = (\alpha, q_\alpha \oplus \sigma_{[\alpha]}, s'_\alpha, b_\alpha)$
   (c) $\forall \beta \in \mathrm{ids}(C), \beta \neq \alpha \cdot C(\beta) = (q, s_\beta, b_\beta) \iff C'(\beta) = (q \oplus \sigma_{[\beta]}, s_\beta, b_\beta)$
   (d) $\forall (\gamma, q_\gamma, s_\gamma, b_\gamma) \in A \cdot C'(\gamma) = (\gamma, q_\gamma \oplus \sigma_{[\gamma]}, s_\gamma, b_\gamma)$
   (e) $\mathrm{recipients}(\sigma) \subseteq \mathrm{ids}(C')$

Condition 1 states that the recipient of the message $\alpha.m$ must exist in the configuration C and the $\alpha.m$ must be the first message in the actor's queue. The set of actors in the configuration must remain the same, except for the set of newly created actors (cond. 2a). After processing the message, the actor α changes its local state and possibly sends messages to itself (cond. 2b). All other actors possibly have new messages in their queues, but their state remains unchanged (cond. 2c). A number of new actors are created, and they may have messages in their queues initially (cond. 2d). Note that the recipients of the sent messages σ must exist at the time the messages are sent (cond. 2e).

To ensure uniqueness of identifiers in an actor system we make the following assumption on the behavior of every actor in the system. In every configuration C and an actor $(\alpha, [\alpha.m | q], s, b)$ in C, the behavior function b is defined such that if $(A, \sigma, s') \in b(\alpha.m, s)$, then we have $\mathrm{ids}(A) \cap \mathrm{ids}(C) = \emptyset$ and $|\mathrm{ids}(A)| = |A|$.

4.3 Coordinator Actors

To describe the semantics of a coordinator, we assume the behavior of the Reo circuit is described using a Constraint Automaton [12], which is a well-known semantic model for Reo connectors. The notation we use in this paper is based on [13], as it includes finite runs of constraint automata too. An important point is that when handling variability using Reo circuits, we usually need priority merger which is an example of a context-dependent connector. The original constraint automata semantics for Reo does not handle context dependency (the situation where the behavior of a connector depends on other connectors). This issue is addressed in other automata-based semantics for Reo such as the one based on Reo automata [14]. Despite our use of context-dependent channels, we still express our semantics using constraint automata, as it is much simpler to explain. Furthermore, it is not hard to lift our semantic description to other types of automata-based semantics for Reo, supporting context dependency.

Since each coordinator is regarded as an actor, it will have a unique identifier. Let the set $CId \subset Id$ be the set of identifiers of coordinators. Suppose that the behavior of a coordinator with identifier ρ is defined by the constraint automaton $\mathcal{A} = (\mathcal{Q}, \mathcal{N}, \rightarrow, \mathcal{Q}_0)$. The set of states $\mathcal{Q}$, the set of initial states $\mathcal{Q}_0$, and the transition relation $\rightarrow$ are defined according to the standard semantics of Reo circuits in constraint automata. Assuming the usual partitioning of the node set

$\mathcal{N} = \mathcal{N}^{src} \uplus \mathcal{N}^{snk} \uplus \mathcal{N}^{mix}$ into source nodes, sink nodes, and mix nodes, we have $\mathcal{N}^{src} = \{in, cfg_{\rho_1}, cfg_{\rho_2}, \dots cfg_{\rho_k}\}$, where in is the input node, and cfg_{ρ_i} is the ith configuration port, $\mathcal{N}^{snk} = \{out_{\rho_1}, out_{\rho_2}, \dots, out_{\rho_n}\}$, the set of output ports, and $\mathcal{N}^{mix}$ is determined by the internal structure of the Reo circuit.

To specify the behavior of the coordinator when responding to the incoming message $\rho.m$, we must specify the messages it will create and the change in its local state. The local state of the coordinator is the current state of its behavior constraint automaton. So, suppose the coordinator is in state q and it receives the incoming message $\rho.m$. According to the constraint automata semantics for Reo circuits, and assuming that the behavior of the circuit terminates in finite steps, we will have maximal finite runs of the following form, where N_i is the set of nodes performing I/O operation and δ_i is a function giving data items on nodes.

$$q = q_0 \xrightarrow{N_1,\delta_1} \dots \xrightarrow{N_k,\delta_k} q_k \xrightarrow{\checkmark} q_k$$

Since the message m is put initially on the input node of the coordinator, we must have $in_\rho \in N_1$ and $\delta_1(in_\rho) = m$.

The set of output messages are obtained by taking the data on each output port and putting them as a sequence (to preserve the FIFO semantics of actors). More formally, let $\mu : \mathcal{N}^{snk} \to Id$ specify the binding of the output ports to the identifiers of the destination actors. For each I/O operation (N, δ), we define $\varsigma(N, \delta)$ as the sequence of messages sent during the I/O operation. The sequence is ordered (arbitrarily) based on the output port numbers of the Reo circuit:

$$\varsigma_i(N, \delta) = \begin{cases} [\,] & \text{if } out_{\rho_i} \notin N \\ [\mu(out_{\rho_i}).\delta(out_{\rho_i})] & \text{otherwise} \end{cases}$$

$$\varsigma(N, \delta) = \varsigma_1(N, \delta) \oplus \varsigma_2(N, \delta) \oplus \dots \oplus \varsigma_n(N, \delta)$$

Now, for the I/O-stream $IOS = (N_1, \delta_1) \dots (N_k, \delta_k)\checkmark$, we define the set of output messages as the sequence of $\varsigma(N_i, \delta_i)$, ordered by $i = 1, 2, \dots, k$, as follows:

$$outmsg_\rho(IOS) = \varsigma(N_1, \delta_1) \oplus \varsigma(N_2, \delta_2) \oplus \dots \oplus \varsigma(N_k, \delta_k)$$

It is important to note that initially (i.e., before processing the first message), the automaton is in one of the states in $\mathcal{Q}_0$. After processing of the first message, we assume the automaton saves its current state for processing the next message (hence, the coordination may be history-sensitive).

To integrate our coordination model into actor systems, we consider a coordinator as an actor in our semantic model, hence modeled as a tuple (ρ, q, s, b) as defined in Sect. 4.1. We assume the coordination logic of the coordinator with identifier ρ is defined by a Reo circuit specified by the constraint automaton $\mathcal{A}_\rho = (\mathcal{Q}_\rho, \mathcal{N}_\rho, \to_\rho, \mathcal{Q}_{0_\rho})$ with the set of port names $\mathcal{N}_\rho$ partitioned into $\mathcal{N}_\rho^{src}$, $\mathcal{N}_\rho^{snk}$, and $\mathcal{N}_\rho^{mix}$ as described previously. Also, we assume μ_ρ is the mapping of output ports into actor identifiers.

As said before, the state of a coordinator is the last state of the maximal finite run it has taken to respond to the last message, or one of the initial states of $\mathcal{A}_\rho$

if it has not responded to any message yet. So, we have $s \in \mathcal{Q}_\rho$ and to make it consistent with the definition of ordinary actors, we assume the following:

$$\biguplus_{\rho \in CId} \mathcal{Q}_\rho \subset State$$

The behavior of the coordinator ρ, expressed as the relation $b_\rho : Msg \times State \leftrightarrow 2^{Actor} \times Msg^* \times State$ is the smallest relation satisfying the condition $(A, \sigma, s') \in b_\rho(\rho.m, s)$ if

1. $A = \emptyset$
2. There exists a maximal finite run $s = q_0 \xrightarrow{N_1, \delta_1}_\rho \ldots \xrightarrow{N_k, \delta_k}_\rho q_k \xrightarrow{\checkmark}_\rho q_k = s'$, such that
   (a) $in_\rho \in N_1$ and $\delta_1(in_\rho) = m$
   (b) $\sigma = outmsg_\rho((N_1, \delta_1) \ldots (N_k, \delta_k)\checkmark)$

4.4 Initial Configurations

Initially, we have a set of (non-coordinator) actors of the form $(\alpha, q_{0_\alpha}, s_{0_\alpha}, b_\alpha)$. We assume the initial local states and message queues are unique. We also have a set of coordinators with the identifier set R. A coordinator with identifier $\rho \in R$, can start in one of the possible initial states $(\rho, [\ ], q_0, b_\rho)$ for some $q_0 \in \mathcal{Q}_{0_\rho}$.

5   Case Study

The case presented here is part of a larger project that is currently in progress in the domain of an interactive TV product line at Soroush company[1]. The project has a big feature model, as the product line ranges over various types of product in the subdomains of IPTV, Hospitality, Digital Signage, etc.

The external variabilities that correspond to different usages of the system lead to a relatively large number of internal variabilities too. For example, an IPTV with a large number of subscribers scattered through a vast geographical extent is different from a hotel offering hospitality services through its local TV network in terms of performance and availability requirements. In this section, we present a simplified view of the solution applied to handle an internal variability concerning load balancing of the offered services aiming to improve performance and availability.

5.1   The Video-On-Demand Use Case

In this example, an IPTV network is considered offering various services from which we focus on Video-On-Demand (VOD) service. The subscribers of this service can choose from a set of video contents, and receive the video via a streaming protocol.

---

[1] http://www.soroush.net

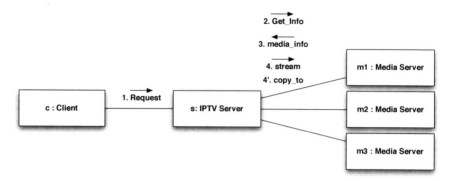

Fig. 5. Interaction diagram showing the basic scenario of VOD

To start the scenario, a client sends a request to the IPTV server. The server maps the requested video to a media resource description. The corresponding media may reside on a number of different media servers. Not every media server contains the specified media resource. If it does, it is possible that it is currently streaming media in its full capacity. So, the IPTV server first asks every media server about the requested media resource and if the server has free streaming capacity. If the IPTV server receives a reply from a media server which says it has the media resource and it has free capacity, then the media server is asked to stream the media to the client.

A variation point is defined for the case that no free server contains the requested media resource. In the simpler variant, a message is returned to the client to inform it that the requested media is not available at this time. In the other variant however, one of the servers that has the media is asked to copy the media into one of the servers that has free capacity. After the media is copied, the free server is asked to stream the media. This scenario is depicted in Fig. 5.

5.2   Modeling Video-On-Demand with Coordinated Actors

We now show how to model VOD interactions using coordinated actors. Due to space limitation, we focus only on the part that the IPTV server receives and processes the media information (messages 3, 4, and 4' in Fig. 5). The IPTV server is supposed to receive one media_info message from each media server. The message format is assumed to be of the form media_info(m, s, h, f) where m denotes the requested media identifier, s is the identifier of the media server that is the sender of the message, h is a boolean value indicating the server s contains the media resource for m, and f is a boolean value showing that the server s has free capacity for streaming.

In the coordinated model, the media servers are supposed to send the media_info message to a coordinator actor, instead of the IPTV directly. The coordinator then decides how to continue based on the values received and the configuration parameter replicate_media which shows if the copying feature is enabled in the product configuration. (To keep the model simpler, we give the

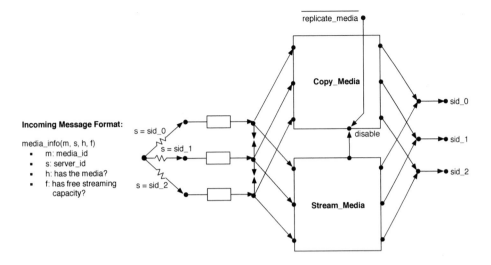

Fig. 6. The behavior of the coordinator for handling media_info messages

negation of this flag as the input to the coordinator.) The behavior of the coordinator for three media servers is depicted as a Reo circuit in Fig. 6.

Upon receiving a message media_info(m, s, h, f), the circuit first routes the message on one of the three channels corresponding to the server with identifier s. It is assumed that the identifiers of the media servers are sid_0, sid_1, and sid_2. The messages are buffered in FIFO1 channels, so that they are processed synchronously. When all buffers are full, the messages are replicated synchronously into two separate circuits Stream_Media and Copy_Media. The former decides if one of the media servers can be chosen to stream the media (i.e., both has the media resource and has free streaming capacity). In this case, a stream message is put on the corresponding output node. The circuit Copy_Media decides if one of the media servers must copy the media resource to another one, and puts the copy_to message on the corresponding output port. The output ports of the two circuits are then merged into single output ports of the coordinator.

The Copy_Media circuit has an input that disables its operation. We merge two values into this input. The first is replicate_media configuration parameter which is enabled if the media replication (copying media files) is not included in the product configuration. The second one is an output from Stream_Media which indicates a suitable server has been found and is sent stream message, hence no copying is necessary.

Figure 7 shows the internals of Stream_Media and Copy_Media circuits. The inputs to Stream_Media circuit are the media_info(m, sid_i, h, f) messages. The filter channels select those media servers that both have the media and have free streaming capacity. The merge node a is to activate at most one of these servers. Note that there are two outgoing channels from a. The SyncDrain is used to keep the passage of data synchronized with the input to the circuit (the choice of the first input is arbitrary, as they are all synchronized from outside of the circuit).

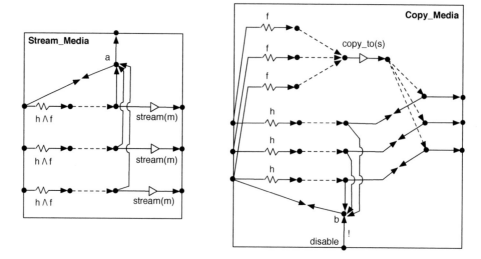

Fig. 7. The internal structure of the Stream_Media (left) and Copy_Media (right) circuits

The Sync channel ending at the circuit port is used to disable Copy_Media in case one of the servers is chosen to stream. The selected server is sent a stream message generated by the corresponding Transform channel.

The input to Copy_Media is the same. The upper set of filters pass the messages from those servers that has free capacity, from which one is chosen as the destination of the copy (hence the server identifier s is passed as the parameter of copy_to). The lower set of filters and subsequent channels choose a server that has the media resource to which the generated copy_to message is sent. The purpose of the merge node b is similar to the node a in Stream_Media, with the additional disable input that has higher priority over all other inputs. Hence, if the disable input is enabled, the data flow from all other inputs will be disabled and no output is sent by copy_to.

The circuits presented above only model the interactions needed to process media_info messages. There are other coordinators to handle other messages that are not discussed here.

We have implemented a simulator of VOD in Erlang language. The choice of the language was made due to its support of actor model, simplicity of the language, and support for distributed execution. A preliminary prototype of Reo simulator specifically designed to be used in our case study is implemented in Erlang. It still needs more work to fully cover Reo features in general case.

6   Discussion and Conclusion

In this paper, we defined a special type of actors named coordinators with their behavior defined by Reo circuits. We used coordinators to handle variabilities in a product line of actor systems. This keeps the variability handling logic separate from the functionality of the components. An important point is that coordinators are still actors, so we can use them in a distributed setting.

Using Reo to describe the behavior of actors has a number of consequences. First, we benefit from the compositional characteristic of the model to reuse parts of the variability handling mechanism. Another advantage of Reo is its support for synchronized interactions. In actor modeling, we usually face with the problem of synchronizing a number of activities. Even thought there exist patterns for this, it still needs to be coded by the modeler and will clutter the main functionality of the system, especially in the absence of language-level abstractions for synchronization. However, as there are a several types of synchronized channels in Reo, various patterns for synchronization can be coded easily in the coordinators.

The BIP model [15] is another way to factor out interaction logic from a set of heterogenous components, by introducing connectors supporting rendezvous and broadcast synchronization patterns. BIP can be compared to our coordinated actors model as a whole. We think Reo is a better choice for our model, as it enables us to create and use various types of connectors in a rich, compositional method covering BIP interaction patterns too.

An issue that may limit the applicability of our model is the fact that the nature of Reo is not dynamic in the sense that channels can be added or re-moved dynamically. This will make a problem when the actor system changes its topology dynamically. The problem of reconfiguring a Reo circuit is studied in [16] and [17] based on graph transformations and coloring semantics. Still, we need proper language-level abstraction and parameterization mechanisms to easily describe reconfiguration in response to a message. Extending the model to support dynamic topology with an integrated precise formal model is a direction in which our work can be improved.

Another related work is the Dreams framework [18] which offers a distributed implementation of Reo using Scala actors. Although this work is not specifially designed to address software product lines, the fact that the coordination can be expressed in a single global Reo circuit, while executed in a distributed manner enables compositional description of the coordination logic. This is currently a weakness in our work, since having a number of different coordinators commu-nicating through message passing we cannot benefit from the compositionality of Reo in reasoning about the coordination logic.

References

1. Pohl, K., Böckle, G., van der Linden, F.J.: Software Product Line Engineering: Foundations, Principles and Techniques. Springer-Verlag New York, Inc. (2005)
2. Agha, G.: Actors: a model of concurrent computation in distributed systems. MIT Press, Cambridge (1986)
3. Kästner, C., Apel, S.: Integrating compositional and annotative approaches for product line engineering. In: Proc. Modularization, Composition and Generative Techniques for Product Line Engineering (McGPLE). University of Passau (2008)

4. Lee, J., Kang, K.C.: A feature-oriented approach to developing dynamically reconfigurable products in product line engineering. In: Proc. of the 10th International on Software Product Line Conference, pp. 131–140. IEEE Computer Society (2006)
5. Sabouri, H., Khosravi, R.: Reducing the model checking cost of product lines using static analysis techniques. In: FACS (to appear, 2012)
6. Sirjani, M., Movaghar, A., Shali, A., de Boer, F.: Modeling and verification of reactive systems using Rebeca. Fundamenta Informaticae 63(4), 385–410 (2004)
7. Arbab, F.: Reo: a channel-based coordination model for component composition. Mathematical Structures in Comp. Sci. 14, 329–366 (2004)
8. Clarke, D., Muschevici, R., Proença, J., Schaefer, I., Schlatte, R.: Variability Modelling in the ABS Language. In: Aichernig, B.K., de Boer, F.S., Bonsangue, M.M. (eds.) FMCO 2010. LNCS, vol. 6957, pp. 204–224. Springer, Heidelberg (2011)
9. Johnsen, E.B., Owe, O., Yu, I.C.: Creol: A type-safe object-oriented model for distributed concurrent systems. Theor. Comput. Sci. 365(1-2), 23–66 (2006)
10. Schaefer, I., Bettini, L., Bono, V., Damiani, F., Tanzarella, N.: Delta-Oriented Programming of Software Product Lines. In: Bosch, J., Lee, J. (eds.) SPLC 2010. LNCS, vol. 6287, pp. 77–91. Springer, Heidelberg (2010)
11. Asirelli, P., ter Beek, M.H., Fantechi, A., Gnesi, S.: A Model-Checking Tool for Families of Services. In: Bruni, R., Dingel, J. (eds.) FMOODS/FORTE 2011. LNCS, vol. 6722, pp. 44–58. Springer, Heidelberg (2011)
12. Baier, C., Sirjani, M., Arbab, F., Rutten, J.J.M.M.: Modeling component connectors in reo by constraint automata. Sci. Comput. Program. 61(2), 75–113 (2006)
13. Klüppelholz, S., Baier, C.: Symbolic model checking for channel-based component connectors. Sci. Comput. Program. 74(9), 688–701 (2009)
14. Bonsangue, M., Clarke, D., Silva, A.: Automata for Context-Dependent Connectors. In: Field, J., Vasconcelos, V.T. (eds.) COORDINATION 2009. LNCS, vol. 5521, pp. 184–203. Springer, Heidelberg (2009)
15. Basu, A., Bozga, M., Sifakis, J.: Modeling heterogeneous real-time components in bip. In: Proc. of the Fourth IEEE Int. Conf. on Software Engineering and Formal Methods, pp. 3–12. IEEE Computer Society (2006)
16. Krause, C., Maraikar, Z., Lazovik, A., Arbab, F.: Modeling dynamic reconfigurations in Reo using high-level replacement systems. Sci. Comput. Program., 23–36 (January 2011)
17. Koehler, C., Costa, D., Proença, J., Arbab, F.: Reconfiguration of reo connectors triggered by dataflow. ECEASST 10 (2008)
18. Proenca, J.: Synchronous Coordination of Distributed Components. PhD thesis, Leiden University (2011)

Scoped Synchronization Constraints for Large Scale Actor Systems

Peter Dinges and Gul Agha

Department of Computer Science
University of Illinois at Urbana–Champaign, USA
pdinges@acm.org, agha@illinois.edu

Abstract. Very large scale systems of autonomous concurrent objects (Actors) require coordination models to meet two competing goals. On the one hand, the coordination models must allow Actors to dynamically modify protocols in order to adapt to requirement changes over the, likely extensive, lifetime of the system. On the other hand, the coordination models must enforce protocols on potentially uncooperative Actors, while preventing deadlocks caused by malicious or faulty Actors. To meet these competing requirements, we introduce a novel, scoped semantics for *Synchronizers* [7,6]—a coordination model based on declarative synchronization constraints. The mechanism used to limit the scope of the synchronization constraints is based on capabilities and works without central authority. We show that the mechanism closes an attack vector in the original Synchronizer approach which allowed malicious Actors to intentionally deadlock other Actors.

1 Introduction

A well-understood lesson from the design of the Internet helps to build scalable software systems: having autonomous, loosely coupled components avoids central bottlenecks that limit system growth. However, another lesson taught by the Internet is often neglected: *every* component in a large system cannot be trusted. The principle that components cannot be trusted not only holds in systems that execute other users' code. Even if all components are under a central trusted regimen, the probability of having a faulty or compromised component increases with the system size.

Coordination models for large systems must therefore take into account that components may be uncooperative or even malicious [14,12]. Consequently, coordination protocols must be enforced to fulfill their guarantees. For example, ignoring a replication protocol can result in inconsistent state of the participating databases. Furthermore, coordination models for large systems must support dynamic adaptation. Restarting is rarely an option for large systems and the specification of a system is likely to change over its lifetime. Naively addressing these two requirements severely hampers the system's stability: allowing faulty components to impose protocols on all other components can easily result in a deadlock.

M. Sirjani (Ed.): COORDINATION 2012, LNCS 7274, pp. 89–103, 2012.
© IFIP International Federation for Information Processing 2012

The contribution of this article is a novel, scoped semantics for *Synchronizers* [7,6] that is better adapted to the requirements of large scale systems. Synchronizers are declarative synchronization constraints that model coordination by enforcing restrictions on the interaction patterns between components. Following the capability approach to security—but with a twist— we propose to limit the scope of synchronization constraints. The central idea behind our approach is that synchronization constraints restrict not the *targets*, but the *sources* of interactions. Thus, every component may install constraints on other components, but the constraints will affect only interactions originating from components for which the installing component holds the required capabilities.

Without these capabilities, malicious components cannot intentionally deadlock their acquaintances by imposing impossible constraints. Consequently, our scoped semantics close this attack vector. Scoping also mitigates accidental deadlocks of a component from interfering constraints because the scoping requires the interfering constraints to hold overlapping capabilities. However, as we explain later, scoping cannot completely prevent accidental deadlocks.

The questions of constraint inheritance and implementation performance are not addressed in this article. In both cases, however, we believe the new semantics to maintain the characteristics of the conventional Synchronizer semantics, meaning that it does not impose an extra burden.

In the remainder of this article, we briefly introduce Synchronizers (section 2), discuss the challenges of coordination in large systems (section 3), and—from this motivation—develop a scoping mechanism for Synchronizers to adapt them to the requirements of large systems (section 4). Next, we provide the exact semantics of our solution (section 5). The conclusion (section 7) follows after a discussion of related work (section 6).

2   Synchronization Constraints

This section gives a brief overview of *Synchronizers* and their conventional semantics [7,6]. The examples are taken from Frølund and Agha's ECOOP'93 article [7]. The term *Actor* takes the place of the generic *system component* because Actors are precisely defined in their properties [2]: they are concurrently executing mobile objects with perfectly encapsulated state that communicate via asynchronous messages. Actors are autonomous by design; the scalability of the Actor model to large systems is well established [10,15].

Synchronizers are declarative synchronization constraints that can be imposed on groups of Actors. The constraints express under which conditions an Actor is able to handle a message. Until the conditions are met, the message stays in the Actor's message queue. The constraints have a global effect and affect all messages an Actor receives. Conceptually, a Synchronizer can be seen as a special kind of Meta-Actor [11,21] that observes and limits the message dispatch of other Actors. The conventional form of Synchronizers supports disabling and atomicity constraints:

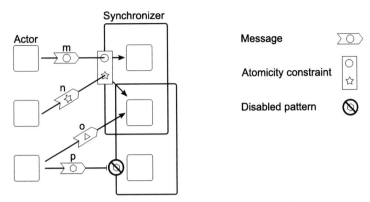

Fig. 1. *Constraints Enforced by Conventional Synchronizers.* Synchronizers support (combinations of) atomicity and disabling constraints. Atomicity constraints ensure that a set of messages is dispatched as a whole and without temporal (happened before [9]) ordering. Messages m and n satisfy the atomicity constraint together and are therefore dispatched at their target Actors. Message p matches a disabling pattern in the lower Synchronizer and therefore cannot be dispatched. Synchronizers can overlap. If message n matched the same disabling pattern as message p, then the atomicity constraint would have to remain unsatisfied, preventing the delivery of message m. Message o matches no pattern and thus is unconstrained.

Under the conventional semantics, Sychronizers observe and control all messages an Actor receives. The synchronization constraints therefore form a conceptual *membrane* around every Actor in a constrained group. Despite Synchronizers being drawn as a single membrane around the whole group, messages sent between two Actors coordinated by the same Synchronizer still have to satisfy the synchronization constraints.

Disabling constraints prevent the constrained Actor from handling messages that match a given pattern. For example, by disabling the handlers for all but the initialization message, a disabling constraint ensures that an Actor dispatches (starts to process) the initialization message before it dispatches any other message.

Atomicity constraints coordinate groups of Actors by bundling messages into indivisible sets. A constraint enforces that either all the messages in a set are dispatched, or none of them are (there is no partial delivery). The constraint provides *spatial* atomicity. An atomicity constraint can, for example, implement a simple online music payment scheme by fusing the *deduct money from credit card* message with the *enable download* message.

Programmers declare Synchronizers as templates. Similar to classes or Actor behaviors, these templates are dynamically instantiated at run-time with concrete values filled in for the parameters. Thus, Synchronizers can adapt the system to meet new specifications during execution. Actors may install Synchronizers at any of their acquaintances. Synchronizers can have local state that changes with the observed messages. They may also overlap, that is, multiple Synchronizers can constrain the same Actor. Figure 1 shows example effects of Synchronizers. In this article, we employ the abstract syntax of Frølund and Agha [7] for Synchronizer declarations given in Figure 2.

$\langle$Synchronizer$\rangle$ ::= $\langle$Id$\rangle$ ($\langle$List$\{$Id$\}\rangle$) { [**init** $\langle$Binding$\rangle$] $\langle$Relation$\rangle$ }
$\langle$Relation$\rangle$ ::= $\langle$Pattern$\rangle$ **updates** $\langle$Binding$\rangle$
          | $\langle$BExp$\rangle$ **disables** $\langle$Pattern$\rangle$
          | **atomic** ($\langle$List$\{$Pattern$\}\rangle$)
          | $\langle$Pattern$\rangle$ **stops**
          | $\langle$Relation$\rangle$, $\langle$Relation$\rangle$
$\langle$Pattern$\rangle$ ::= $\langle$Id$\rangle$. $\langle$Id$\rangle$
          | $\langle$Id$\rangle$. $\langle$Id$\rangle$ ($\langle$List$\{$Id$\}\rangle$)
          | $\langle$Pattern$\rangle$ **or** $\langle$Pattern$\rangle$
          | $\langle$Pattern$\rangle$ **where** $\langle$BExp$\rangle$
$\langle$Binding$\rangle$ ::= $\langle$Id$\rangle$:= $\langle$Exp$\rangle$
          | $\langle$Binding$\rangle$; $\langle$Binding$\rangle$

Fig. 2. *Abstract Syntax for Synchronizer Declarations.* Names in angle brackets denote syntactic categories; $\langle$List$\{\cdot\}\rangle$ stands for a comma-separated list of elements in the given category. We assume the category of identifiers, $\langle$Id$\rangle$, to range over alpha-numeric strings. The categories $\langle$Exp$\rangle$ and $\langle$BExp$\rangle$ denote expressions and Boolean expressions respectively.

Relations define the constraints that a Synchronizer enforces. The patterns are matched against observed messages: using the customary dot-syntax, the identifier before a dot specifies the name of the target Actor (a variable holding an Actor address), and the identifier after the dot specifies the message type. The list of identifiers in parentheses is a list of variable names that get bound to the message arguments.

Variables have a unique binding for every observed message. Thus, using the same variable in two different places means that the same value must appear in these places for the pattern to match. All expressions are free of side-effects.

2.1 Example: Cooperating Resource Administrators

Consider a system that provides two kinds of resources for its users, for example disk drives and optical drives. There are multiple instances of both drive types and each of these resource kinds is governed by an administrating Actor that limits the number of instances that can be used at the same time. Suppose that the disks and optical drives are accessed over the same network connection. To ensure that drive accesses stay within the bandwidth limit, the administrating Actors have to restrict the *total* allocations made of both drive types.

The Synchronizer below implements the necessary coordination pattern using disabling constraints. It stores the total number of allocated drives in the system in an internal counter alloc. Observing requests and releases at the resource administrators updates the counter (lines 5 and 6). When the maximum number of drives has been requested, the Synchronizer disables the request handlers of both administrators (line 4). Thus, neither administrator can process further allocation requests. These pending requests can be processed only after one of them releases a drive.

```
1   AllocationPolicy(adm1, adm2, max) {
2       init alloc := 0
3
4       alloc >= max disables (adm1.request or adm2.request)
5       (adm1.request or adm2.request) updates alloc := alloc + 1,
6       (adm1.release or adm2.release) updates alloc := alloc − 1
7   }
```

2.2   Example: Dining Philosophers

In the classic problem of the dining philosophers, a group of philosophers (processes) must coordinate their behavior to access a number of chopsticks (resources). Typically, five philosophers sit at a round table and a chopstick is placed between each of them. Thus, there as many chopsticks as there are philosophers. To eat (make progress), every philosopher must pick up both, the left and right neighboring chopstick. Without coordination, for instance if every philosopher starts picking up the left chopstick, the system can deadlock and philosophers can starve.

Suppose philosophers and chopsticks are modeled as Actors, and chopsticks implement an allocation policy such that pick messages can be dispatched only if the chopstick is currently lying on the table (free). Philosophers can then use atomicity constraints to prevent deadlocks. By ensuring that every philosopher's two pick requests are either dispatched together, or not at all, every philosopher is guaranteed to always pick up both neighboring chopsticks—given that the constraints are installed following the neighborhood relation. Under certain fairness assumptions about the implementation, this prevents the system from deadlocking. A Synchronizer implementing this approach could look as follows:

```
1   PickUpConstraint(c1, c2, phil) {
2       atomic( (c1.pick(sender) where sender = phil),
3               (c2.pick(sender) where sender = phil) )
4   }
```

3   Coordination in Large Scale Systems

This section discusses the challenges of coordination in large scale Actor systems and demonstrates the semantic problems of Synchronizers in this context.

3.1   Properties of Large Systems

Scalable coordination models must not only use additional resources efficiently, but also address the inherent requirements of large systems:

Support of dynamic reconfiguration and adaptation. Large systems, for instance a cloud computing service, are expensive to reboot. Nevertheless, the environment and specifications of the system are likely to change over the system lifetime, for example when new services are introduced. A scalable coordination model must therefore support dynamic adaptation.

Robustness against misbehaving Actors. The chance of having a faulty, compromised, or malicious Actor in a system increases with the system size. A scalable coordination model must therefore be able to cope with uncooperative Actors and gracefully degrade in the presence of failures. It must also guard its reconfiguration mechanisms against abuse.

The second requirement implies that, in general, Actors in large systems cannot rely on the good intentions of other Actors. We therefore think of Actors as being mutually suspicious, that is, they do not trust each other. Consequently, Actors try to give others as little control over themselves as possible and follow the principle of least authority [12]. In particular, Actors try to avoid making their—eventual—progress in computation dependent on others.

3.2 Problems of Globally Scoped Constraints

Mutual suspicion conflicts with the global scope of synchronization constraints defined in the conventional Synchronizer semantics [6]. Under these semantics, Synchronizers observe and affect all messages a constrained Actor receives. Any Actor may install Synchronizers on acquaintances, which opens the door to malicious Actors causing intentional deadlocks on other Actors, effectively resulting in a denial of service at the target.

For example, suppose that an Actor A can handle messages of type message1, message2, and so on, up to messageN. A malicious Actor M can prevent A from receiving any further messages by installing a Synchronizer that disables all message handlers in A:

```
1   DisablingAttack(a) {
2       true disables (a.message1 or a.message2 or ... or a.messageN)
3   }
```

Similar problems arise from atomicity constraints. If M forces A to only dispatch messages in unison with an anonymous Actor that never receives any messages, then A will deny all service. A Synchronizer achieving this effect could look as follows:

```
1   AtomicityAttack(a, anonymous) {
2       atomic( (a.message1 or a.message2 or ... or a.messageN),
3               anonymous.message )
4   }
```

Malice is not the only source of problems. Even if the access to Synchronizer installation is limited and only legitimate Actors may install Synchronizers, incompatible constraints may cause deadlocks. Consider the case where two independent Actors, originating in different libraries and unaware of each other, impose the BigEndianConstraint and LittleEndianConstraint on a common acquaintance G. The argument of any enjoyEgg message sent to G is either *big* or *little*, which prevents G from enjoying any of them.

```
1  BigEndianConstraint(a) {
2    endianness(e) != "big" disables a.enjoyEgg(e)
3  }
4
5  LittleEndianConstraint(a) {
6    endianness(e) != "little" disables a.enjoyEgg(e)
7  }
```

4   Scoped Constraints

The previous section demonstrated that allowing Synchronizers to constrain *all* messages an Actor receives is problematic in large systems. In this section, we introduce a scoping mechanism for synchronization constraints that restricts their effects to a subset of messages. The exact semantics of this approach are the topic of the next section.

The central idea behind our approach is that synchronization constraints restrict not the receivers, but the sources of messages. Consequently, a constraint installed on Actor A by Actor I should not apply to all messages that A receives. Instead, the constraints should only apply to messages received by A if they were sent by Actors that are under control of I. Thus, the constraints should only apply if the installing Actor I has the capability to impose constraints on the sending Actors.

4.1   Synchronization-Capabilities

Synchronization constraints, and thus Synchronizers, therefore work in the opposite direction of object-capabilities [12]. Object-capability security is the natural security model of Actor systems. Its defining notion is that once an Actor address—the capability for this Actor—is known, any message may be sent to it. Access to services hence depends on the knowledge of Actor addresses; security can be implemented through their careful distribution. The underlying assumptions are that addresses are unique across the system and cannot be guessed. For Actors, the only ways of obtaining knowledge of other Actors' addresses are (1) *initialization*: the system starts with this knowledge distribution; (2) *parenthood*: creating a new Actor yields an address; and (3) *introduction*: addresses are values and can be propagated inside messages.

In addition to object-capabilities, we introduce *synchronization-capabilities* that determine the scope of synchronization constraints. Synchronizers can constrain messages only if they hold the synchronization-capability to the message source. They receive their synchronization-capabilities from the installing Actor. Figure 3 shows the scoping effects of synchronization-capabilities.

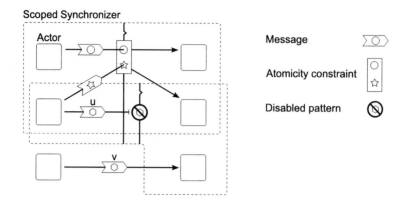

Fig. 3. *Constraints Enforced by Scoped Synchronizers.* Scoped Sychronizers (dashed frames) constrain only messages sent by Actors for which they hold the synchronization-capability. These Actors are placed in the left part of the Synchronizer. Their sent messages must satisfy the constraints before they can be dispatched at the recipients (placed right). Since message u matches a disabling pattern of the lower Synchronizer, it cannot be dispatched. However, the respective Synchronizer lacks control over the sender of message v, so v can be dispatched despite having the same shape as u.

As with object-capabilities, we assume that synchronization-capabilities are unique across the system and cannot be guessed. Their distribution follows similar rules. Actors can obtain synchronization-capabilities through *initialization* and *introduction*. However, the *parenthood* rule is transitive: creating a new Actor yields a synchronization-capability *for this Actor and all its children.* The transitivity of synchronization-capabilities prevents Actors from escaping synchronization constraints by transferring their behavior to a new Actor, thereby changing their identity. Synchronization-constraints hence grant control over families of Actors, including future members whose identities are yet unknown.

The two types of capabilities are separate; a capability of one type cannot be used in places that require the other. This separation allows Actors to send messages to other, potentially untrusted Actors, without submitting to the synchronization constraints of the recipient Actors. In contrast to the conventional Synchronizer semantics, the semantics of scoped Synchronizers ensures that the reply address contained inside a message can be used solely for communication.

4.2   Scoped Synchronization Constraints

With Synchronizers only constraining messages for which they hold the synchronization-capabilities, it becomes unnecessary to restrict access to the Synchronizer installation primitive. Any Actor may therefore install Synchronizers on all its acquaintances. The imposed constraints will simply stay without effect for most messages.

Synchronization-capabilities thus prevent the intentional deadlock scenarios discussed in section 3. Revisiting the DisablingAttack and AtomicityAttack

Synchronizer examples, we see that with scoping the situation is similar to that of the lower right Actor in Figure 3: unless the Synchronizers hold some relevant synchronization-capability, all messages will remain unaffected—as is the case for message v in the figure. Hence, the malicious installing Actor poses no threat if none of the other Actor in the system supplies it with a synchronization-capability. However, even in this case, the deadlock concerns only parts of the system.

Synchronization-capabilities cannot completely prevent deadlocks that arise from incompatible constraints as in the endian example. However, the scoping of constraints mitigates the problem. If the Actors imposing the BigEndianConstraint and LittleEndianConstraint on G possess disjoint synchronization-capabilities, then each Actor's constraints have no effects on messages from the *other* parts of the system. Thus, accidental interference of constraints becomes less likely.

5   Semantics

This section describes in detail the semantics of the synchronization-capabilities introduced in section 4. The semantics are defined in the context of a toy programming language called IMPACT-S. While IMPACT-S embodies some design choices, the general principles behind the design of scoped Synchronizers can be easily extracted from its description.

IMPACT-S adds Actor primitives—message sending and Actor creation—to IMP, a pedagogical example of an imperative language [22]. Furthermore, it adds Synchronizers and synchronization-capabilities. We limit the discussion of IMPACT-S's semantics to the parts relevant to synchronization-capabilities without the distracting bookkeeping and infrastructure necessary for complete semantics. A technical report that is currently being prepared defines the formal semantics of IMPACT-S in the $\mathbb{K}$ rewriting logic framework [18].

5.1   Synchronization-Capabilities

In section 4, we introduced synchronization-capabilities as scoping mechanism for synchronization constraints: the idea is to let Synchronizers control only those messages for whose sender they hold the synchronization-capability. Unlike object-capabilities, synchronization-capabilities are transitive; granting control over the messages sent by an Actor and all its children prevents Actors from escaping their constraints by transferring their behavior and state to a new Actor. Thus, the set of synchronization-constraints $\mathcal{S}$ is partially ordered by this hierarchy of control. For $S_1, S_2 \in \mathcal{S}$, write

$$\text{controls}(S_1, S_2) \quad \text{iff} \quad S_1 = S_2 \text{ or actor}(S_1) \text{ is an ancestor of actor}(S_2),$$

where actor(S_i) denotes the Actor to which the capability S_i belongs. An Actor A is an ancestor of another Actor B if either A created B, or A created an ancestor of B.

5.2   Actor Creation

IMPACT-S implements the controls$(\cdot, \cdot)$ relation through prefix comparison. Internally, synchronization-capabilities are lists of integers. The list for a new Actor is derived by extending the creating Actor's list with the count of child Actors created thus far. Assuming that all lists are distinct when the system starts, this method yields a unique list for every new Actor. Furthermore, the derivation of new lists is distributed and works without communication.

To avoid the redundancy of having every Actor store its own synchronization-capability, IMPACT-S gives Actor addresses—that is, object-capabilities—the same integer-list representation. This way, every Actor has to store only one list of integers that doubles as its address and synchronization-capability. When used as values, the system keeps the two kinds of capabilities separate by tagging the lists with `addr` and `syncap` labels.

Suppose an Actor with address $\mathtt{addr}(i_1; \ldots; i_n)$ creates an Actor with behavior B by executing

$$\text{new } B(a_1, \ldots, a_l),$$

$a_1, \ldots a_l$ being the arguments to the behavior's constructor. Let the new Actor be the k-th child. Then the new Actor's address is $\mathtt{addr}(i_1; \ldots; i_n; k)$, its synchronization-capability is $\mathtt{syncap}(i_1; \ldots; i_n; k)$. Using prefix comparison, we clearly have

$$\text{controls}\big(\mathtt{syncap}(i_1; \ldots; i_n), \mathtt{syncap}(i_1; \ldots; i_n; k)\big).$$

Since the capabilities are separate, both are returned to the creating Actor. Thus, creating an Actor in IMPACT-S yields not only the address of the new Actor, but a pair of capabilities.

5.3   Message Sending and Dispatching

Synchronization constraints determine whether a message can be dispatched (processed) at the receiving Actor. Because communication is asynchronous, the sending Actor cannot answer this question as the state of the recipient Actor may change while the message is in transit. Synchronizers therefore reside at the receiving Actors; they can be regarded as *constraint servers* that are queried by the message dispatch mechanism. This remains true despite the scoping mechanism's focus on message senders. The only change is that Synchronizers now have to possess the right synchronization-capability to control a message.

An Actor's scheduler can dispatch a message only if the message is not disabled by a Synchronizer. The scheduler identifies applicable Synchronizers by matching the message against the patterns declared by installed Synchronizers. The scoped semantics requires not only that the pattern matches (as in conventional Synchronizer semantics), but also that the Synchronizer's synchronization-capability $S_{\text{Sync}} \in \mathcal{S}$ gives it control over the message. Thus, for a message sent by an Actor with synchronization-capability $S_{\text{Act}} \in \mathcal{S}$, the scheduler checks whether

$$\text{controls}(S_{\text{Sync}}, S_{\text{Act}}).$$

To have all matching information available, messages in IMPACT-S are therefore stamped with the sender's synchronization-capability. Thus, the command

$$\texttt{send } m(a_1,\ldots,a_l) \texttt{ to } r$$

executed at an Actor with address $\texttt{addr}(i_1;\ldots;i_n)$ creates a message

$$\texttt{msg}\big(r; \texttt{syncap}(i_1;\ldots;i_n); m; a_1;\ldots;a_n\big).$$

For applicable Synchronizers, the dispatcher then queries whether the constraint is active. This happens *synchronously*; if communication with other dispatchers is necessary, as is the case with atomicity constraints, the dispatcher employs a suitable protocol such as atomic two-phase commitment. The message can be dispatched if

1. *all* disabling patterns allow dispatching the message;
2. *any* of the matching atomic patterns allows dispatching.

For both, disabling and atomic patterns, no match means that the message is enabled.

5.4 Synchronizer State Updates

When a message is dispatched, all Synchronizers belonging to matching update patterns receive a notice. This includes Synchronizers that lack the required synchronization-capability. Making the dispatch of messages public guarantees a consistent view on the system; it allows Synchronizers to take into account the actions of the *uncontrolled* part of the environment.

For example, consider the cooperating resource administrators of subsection 2.1. If the AllocationPolicy Synchronizer was blind to the requests and release messages of some users, then it could not enforce the intended limit on the total number of drive allocations on the users it controls.

However, a globally visible message dispatch is a trade-off. While it allows a consistent view on the system, it enables malicious Actors to spy on other Actors; see Figure 4.

6 Related Work

Actor-Based Coordination. Much of the prior work on Actor-based coordination models ignores the question of trust between Actors. The models either assume cooperative behavior, trustworthy protocols, or—if dynamic reconfiguration is supported—do not clearly specify who has access to coordination primitives and how they are installed. These factors make them less suited for large scale systems.

Like Synchronizers, regulated coordination policies [14] are declarative coordination constraints for autonomous agents. However, the policies have a purely local effect so that agents can be subject to multiple policies without interference. Policies are enforced by trusted agents, which directly translate to proxy

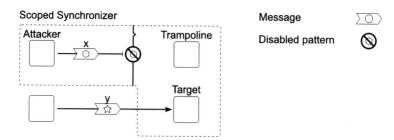

Fig. 4. *Information Leak through Updates.* Scoping only limits the constraining power of Synchronizers. To guarantee a consistent view on the system, Synchronizers can observe all messages that an Actor dispatches—regardless of the synchronization-capabilities the Synchronizer holds. The Attacker Actor exploits this fact to gather information about the Target Actor: First, the Attacker creates a Trampoline Actor and installs a Synchronizer on the Target and the Trampoline. The Synchronizer disables the dispatch of message x at the Trampoline until it observes message y at the Target. Then, the Attacker sends message x to the Trampoline. Once the Trampoline dispatches x, it bounces a message back to the Attacker, providing the Attacker with the knowledge that the Target dispatched message y.

Actors. The strict separation between policies prevents the modular composition supported by (scoped) Synchronizers, which allows, for instance, combining allocation policies (subsection 2.1) for single chopsticks with the philosophers' coordination policies (subsection 2.2).

The *Directors* coordination model [20] organizes Actors into trees. Messages sent between two Actors are delivered to the closest common ancestor and have to be forwarded by all Actors along the branch leading to the recipient. Actors higher in the tree can therefore determine what messages Actors in their sub-tree receive. Unlike Synchronizers, Directors do not support arbitrarily overlapping constraints. Furthermore, the model does not provide semantics for dynamic reconfiguration: Actors are inserted into the tree when they are constructed.

The middleware architectures proposed by Astley [3] and Sturman [19] display problems similar to conventional Synchronizers. Using Meta-Actors [11,21] as foundation, protocols in these frameworks have global effects, which leads to the problems described in section 3.

In the *Actor-Role-Coordinator* (ARC) model [17], coordination is transparent to base-level Actors; coordination tasks are divided into intra-role and inter-role communication. While this hierarchical design provides load-balancing for highly dynamic systems, the coordination structure itself is static. ARC systems therefore avoid security issues through reconfiguration, but require a restart to adapt to changing specifications.

Transactors [5] extend the Actor model with distributed checkpointing as a method for coordination. The goals are fault-tolerance and consistency. In contrast to the assumptions made in this article, Transactors rely on cooperation.

Tuple-Spaces. The anonymous communication provided by tuple-spaces [8] has been proposed as a good fit for open agent systems: writing information tuples on a conceptual global blackboard, agents can coordinate their behavior without knowing each other. This raises robustness concerns in the presence of faulty agents because any agent may remove any tuple from the space. Several mixed static–dynamic [16,23] and dynamic solutions [13] mitigate the problem by limiting the access to tuples. (See these articles for references to many more approaches.)

A recurring goal of security policies in tuple-spaces is secure message passing. The Actor model provides this primitive without the overhead of first sharing, and then enforcing limits on tuples. A tuple-space can be implemented as an Actor, or the Actor model can be extended to include group messaging [1]; if global access to the space is desired, the name of the space can always be provided to any Actor joining the system. The contributions of policy enforcement in tuple-spaces directly apply to the implementation of these tuple-space Actors. We therefore think that tuple-spaces are a valuable communication concept, but are subsumed by the Actor model.

7   Conclusion

We proposed a novel, scoped semantics for Synchronizers that better meets the requirements of coordination in large scale systems. We started with a brief overview of Synchronizers, then demonstrated that the global scope of their constraints allow malicious Actors to intentionally deadlock other Actors, and resolved this challenge by introducing synchronization-capabilities—informally and formally—as a scoping mechanism. While scoping cannot completely prevent accidental deadlocks as sketched at the end of section 3, it still mitigates the problem. The central idea behind our approach was that synchronization constraints should only affect messages originating from Actors to which the constraint-installing Actor holds the capabilities.

Future Work. Declarative synchronization constraints offer a powerful method for describing coordination patterns. However, in their current form, Synchronizers are limited in their expressiveness through their choice to offer but a functional core consisting of two constraint types. An interesting opportunity for future research is extending the selection of available constraints. For instance, syntactic sugar like ordering constraints allows programmers to express their intentions more naturally, and thus make less mistakes. Other concepts like non-interleaving of message sequences cannot be expressed at all.

Another opportunity concerns the robustness of Synchronizers against network partitions and crash failures. Augmenting the semantics with failure detectors [4] appears to be a promising approach. A further interesting direction are methods for handling the information leak discussed in subsection 5.4.

Finally, implementing Synchronizers in a modern Actor framework and conducting a large case study would give interesting insights into the (programmer and computational) performance of Synchronizers.

Acknowledgments. The authors wish to thank Minas Charalambides, Juan Fernando Mancilla Caceres, and the anonymous reviewers for their insightful comments on earlier versions of this article.

This material is based on research sponsored by the Air Force Research Laboratory and the Air Force Office of Scientific Research, under agreement number FA8750-11-2-0084. The U.S. Government is authorized to reproduce and distribute reprints for Governmental purposes notwithstanding any copyright notation thereon.

References

1. Agha, G., Callsen, C.J.: ActorSpaces: An open distributed programming paradigm. In: Proceedings of the 8th ACM SIGPLAN Symposium on Principles and Practice of Parallel Programming, PPOPP 1993, pp. 23–32 (1993)
2. Agha, G.A.: ACTORS — A Model of Concurrent Computation in Distributed Systems. MIT Press series in artificial intelligence. MIT Press (1986)
3. Astley, M., Agha, G.: Customizaton and compositon of distributed objects: Middleware abstractions for policy management. In: SIGSOFT FSE, pp. 1–9 (1998)
4. Chandra, T.D., Toueg, S.: Unreliable failure detectors for reliable distributed systems. J. ACM 43, 225–267 (1996)
5. Field, J., Varela, C.A.: Transactors: a programming model for maintaining globally consistent distributed state in unreliable environments. In: Proceedings of the 32nd ACM SIGPLAN-SIGACT Symposium on Principles of Programming Languages, POPL 2005, pp. 195–208. ACM (2005)
6. Frølund, S.: Coordinating distributed objects - an actor-based approach to synchronization. MIT Press (1996)
7. Frølund, S., Agha, G.: A Language Framework for Multi-Object Coordination. In: Wang, J. (ed.) ECOOP 1993. LNCS, vol. 707, pp. 346–360. Springer, Heidelberg (1993)
8. Gelernter, D.: Generative communication in linda. ACM Trans. Program. Lang. Syst. 7(1), 80–112 (1985)
9. Lamport, L.: Time, clocks, and the ordering of events in a distributed system. Commun. ACM 21(7), 558–565 (1978)
10. Letuchy, E.: Facebook chat. Blog entry (May 2008), http://www.facebook.com/note.php?note_id=14218138919&id=9445547199&index=9 (retrieved on September 25, 2011)
11. Meseguer, J., Talcott, C.: Semantic Models for Distributed Object Reflection. In: Magnusson, B. (ed.) ECOOP 2002. LNCS, vol. 2374, pp. 1–36. Springer, Heidelberg (2002)
12. Miller, M.S.: Robust Composition: Towards a Unified Approach to Access Control and Concurrency Control. PhD thesis, Johns Hopkins University (2006)
13. Minsky, N.H., Minsky, Y., Ungureanu, V.: Safe tuplespace-based coordination in multiagent systems. Applied Artificial Intelligence 15(1), 11–33 (2001)
14. Minsky, N.H., Ungureanu, V.: Regulated Coordination in Open Distributed Systems. In: Garlan, D., Le Métayer, D. (eds.) COORDINATION 1997. LNCS, vol. 1282, pp. 81–97. Springer, Heidelberg (1997)
15. Mok, W.: How twitter is scaling. Blog entry (June 2009), https://waimingmok.wordpress.com/2009/06/27/how-twitter-is-scaling/ (retrieved on September 25, 2011)

16. De Nicola, R., Gorla, D., Hansen, R.R., Nielson, F., Nielson, H.R., Probst, C.W., Pugliese, R.: From Flow Logic to Static Type Systems for Coordination Languages. In: Lea, D., Zavattaro, G. (eds.) COORDINATION 2008. LNCS, vol. 5052, pp. 100–116. Springer, Heidelberg (2008)

17. Ren, S., Yu, Y., Chen, N., Marth, K., Poirot, P.-E., Shen, L.: Actors, Roles and Co-ordinators — A Coordination Model for Open Distributed and Embedded Systems. In: Ciancarini, P., Wiklicky, H. (eds.) COORDINATION 2006. LNCS, vol. 4038, pp. 247–265. Springer, Heidelberg (2006)

18. Rosu, G., Serbanuta, T.-F.: An overview of the K semantic framework. J. Log. Algebr. Program. 79(6), 397–434 (2010)

19. Sturman, D.: Modular Specification of Interaction Policies in Distributed Computing. PhD thesis, University of Illinois at Urbana-Champaign (1996)

20. Varela, C.A., Agha, G.: A Hierarchical Model for Coordination of Concurrent Activities. In: Ciancarini, P., Wolf, A.L. (eds.) COORDINATION 1999. LNCS, vol. 1594, pp. 166–182. Springer, Heidelberg (1999)

21. Venkatasubramanian, N., Talcott, C.L.: Reasoning about meta level activities in open distributed systems. In: PODC, pp. 144–152 (1995)

22. Winskel, G.: The Formal Semantics of Programming Languages. MIT Press, Cambridge (1993)

23. Yang, F., Aotani, T., Masuhara, H., Nielson, F., Nielson, H.R.: Combining Static Analysis and Runtime Checking in Security Aspects for Distributed Tuple Spaces. In: De Meuter, W., Roman, G.-C. (eds.) COORDINATION 2011. LNCS, vol. 6721, pp. 202–218. Springer, Heidelberg (2011)

First-Order Dynamic Logic for Compensable Processes[*]

Roberto Bruni[1], Carla Ferreira[2], and Anne Kersten Kauer[3]

[1] Department of Computer Science, University of Pisa, Italy
[2] CITI / Departamento de Informática, Faculdade de Ciências e Tecnologia,
Universidade Nova de Lisboa, Portugal
[3] IMT Institute for Advanced Studies, Lucca, Italy

Abstract. Compensable programs offer a convenient paradigm to deal with long-running transactions, because they offer a structured and modular approach to the composition of distributed transactional activities, like services. The basic idea is that each activity has its own compensation and that the compensable program fixes the order of execution of such activities. The main problem is how to guarantee that if one or even many faults occur then the compensations are properly executed so to reach a consistent configuration of the system. We propose a formal model for such problems based on a concurrent extension of dynamic logic that allows us to distill the hypothesis under which the correctness of compensable programs can be ensured. The main result establishes that if basic activities have a correct compensation we can show the correctness of any compound compensable program. Moreover, we can use dynamic logic to reason about behavioural and transactional properties of programs.

1 Introduction

Recent years have witnessed a massive distribution of data and computation, especially in the case of emerging paradigms like service-oriented computing and cloud computing. This has led to a breakthrough in the design of modern distributed applications, which need to integrate heterogeneous and loosely coupled components or services. When passing from coarse grain design to fine grain implementation, it is often the case that certain groups of activities must be performed in a transactional (all-or-nothing) fashion. However, many such transactions are long-lasting (weeks or even months), which prevents classical lock mechanisms from ACID transactions to be applicable in this setting. Instead, *compensable long-running transactions* seem to offer a more convenient approach, that deals well with distribution and heterogeneity: each activity is assigned a compensation; if the activity succeeds, then the compensation is installed; if the transaction ends successfully, then the installed compensations are discarded; if a fault occurs within the run of the transaction, then the installed compensations are executed (in the reverse order of installation) to compensate the fault and restore the system to a consistent state. While traditional perfect roll-back mechanisms guarantee that the initial state is exactly restored after a fault occurs, in compensable long-running transactions this is not realistic: if a message has been sent it cannot just be held back and

---

[*] Research supported by the EU Integrated Project 257414 ASCENS, the Italian MIUR Project IPODS (PRIN 2008).

M. Sirjani (Ed.): COORDINATION 2012, LNCS 7274, pp. 104–121, 2012.

maybe another message has to be sent for compensation. For example, late canceling of a booking may require some fees to be paid.

Compensable workflows enjoy an intuitive and expressive graphical representation that has become widely popular in areas such as business process modeling and service orchestration. However, analysis and verification techniques require more work to be done in the area of formal foundation and modeling of programs-with-compensations.

Starting from StAC [7] a number of other formalisms emerged, especially in the area of process calculi, and some of them have been applied as semantic frameworks of widely adopted standard technologies [21,18,13]. Such formalisms often employ basic activities abstract in nature [6,8,2] (i.e. taken over an alphabet of labels) or are based on message passing approaches for interaction [26,19,5,12]. Other approaches focus only on a basic notion of reversibility [11,17]. Moreover, although some recent proposals addressed the problem of compensation correctness [25,9], they miss a well-established logic counterpart, to be used by analysts, designers and programmers to prove some basic consistency properties of faulty systems after a compensation.

In this paper, we improve over existing literature on compensable workflows by proposing a rigorously formalised concurrent programming language with compensations and developing a logical framework based on dynamic logic to investigate program properties. The choice of extending dynamic logic is not incidental: we have been inspired by the interesting literature using deontic logic for error handling [4,10]. The main novelties with respect to previous approaches is that we study concurrent programs based on compensation pairs. At the semantic level, instead of interpreting programs over pairs of states (initial and final), we take traces and make explicit the presence of possible faults. A more detailed discussion of related work is given in Sections 2.1 and 2.2. The main result establishes some sufficient conditions under which a compensable program is guaranteed to always restore a correct state after a fault.

Structure of the paper. In Section 2 we overview some background on logical formalisms for error handling, and more specifically about first-order dynamic logic that we shall extend twice: in Section 3 to deal with concurrent programs and in Section 4 to deal with compensable (concurrent) programs. Our framework is detailed over a toy running example. Some concluding remarks are discussed in Section 5 together with related work and future directions of research.

2   First Order Dynamic Logic

In this section we recap the basic concepts of first order dynamic logic [14]. It was introduced to reason directly about programs, using classical first order predicate logic and modal logics combined with the algebra of regular events. In the second part we shall briefly overview related work on the two main concepts for our extension of dynamic logic, namely deontic formalisms for error handling and concurrency.

Let $\Sigma = \{f, g, \ldots, p, q \ldots\}$ be a finite first-order vocabulary where f, g range over Σ-function symbols and p, q over Σ-predicates. Each element of Σ has a fixed arity, and we denote by Σ_n the subset of symbols with arity $n > 0$. Moreover let $V = \{x_0, x_1, \ldots\}$ be a countable set of variables. Let $Trm(V) = \{t_1, \ldots, t_n, \ldots\}$ be the set of terms over the signature Σ with variables in V.

Definition 1 (Activities). *Let $x_1, \cdots, x_n \in V$ and $t_1, \cdots, t_n \in Trm(V)$. A basic activity $a \in Act(V)$ is a multiple assignment $x_1, \cdots, x_n := t_1, \cdots, t_n$.*

As special cases, we write a single assignment as $x := t \in Act(V)$ (with $x \in V$ and $t \in Trm(V)$) and the empty assignment for the inaction *skip*.

Example 1. We take an e-Store as our first example (see Fig. 1 for the complete presentation). Activity $acceptOrder \in Act(V)$ is defined as a multiple assignment to variables *stock* and *card* such that $acceptOrder \triangleq stock, card := stock - 1, unknown$. This activity decreases the items in stock by one (the item being sold is no longer available), and resets the current state of the credit card to unknown.

Basic activities can be combined in different ways. While it is possible to consider while programs (with sequential composition, conditional statements and while loops), we rely on the more common approach based on the so-called regular programs.

Definition 2 (Programs). *A program α is any term generated by the grammar:*

$$\alpha, \beta ::= a \mid \alpha ; \beta \mid \alpha \Box \beta \mid \alpha^*$$

A program is either: a basic activity $a \in Act(V)$; the sequential composition $\alpha ; \beta$; the nondeterministic choice $\alpha \Box \beta$; or the iteration α^* for programs α and β.

To define the semantics of programs we introduce a computational domain.

Definition 3 (Computational Domain). *Let Σ be a first-order vocabulary. A first-order structure $\mathcal{D} = (D, I)$ is called the domain of computation such that: D is a non-empty set, called the carrier, and I is a mapping assigning:*

- *to every n-ary function symbol $f \in \Sigma$ a function $f^I : D^n \to D$;*
- *to every n-ary predicate $p \in \Sigma$ a predicate $p^I : D^n \to Bool$.*

A state is a function $s : V \to D$ that assigns to each variable an element of D. The set of all states is denoted by $State(V)$. As usual, we denote by $s[x \mapsto v]$ the state s' such that $s'(x) = v$ and $s'(y) = s(y)$ for $y \neq x$. Now we can extend the interpretation to terms in a given state.

Definition 4 (Term Valuation). *The valuation val of a term $t \in Trm(V)$ in a state $s \in State(V)$ is defined by:*

$$val(s, x) \triangleq s(x) \text{ if } x \in V; \quad val(s, f(t_1, \ldots, t_n)) \triangleq f^I(val(s, t_1), \ldots, val(s, t_n)).$$

Basic activities (and thus programs) are interpreted as relations on states. For basic activities this means evaluating the assignments in the current state replacing the old values of the variables.

Definition 5 (Interpretation of Activities). *The valuation $\rho \in 2^{State(V) \times State(V)}$ of an activity $a \in Act(V)$ is defined by:*

$$\rho(a) \triangleq \{(s, s') \mid s' = s[x_1 \mapsto val(s, t_1), \cdots, x_n \mapsto val(s, t_n)]\}$$

if activity a is defined by a multiple assignment $x_1, \cdots, x_n := t_1, \cdots, t_n$.

Definition 6 (Interpretation of Programs). *We extend the interpretation ρ of basic activities to programs in the following manner:*

$$\rho(\alpha\,;\beta) \triangleq \{(s,r) \mid (s,w) \in \rho(\alpha) \wedge (w,r) \in \rho(\beta)\}$$
$$\rho(\alpha \square \beta) \triangleq \rho(\alpha) \cup \rho(\beta)$$
$$\rho(\alpha^*) \triangleq \rho(\alpha)^*$$

Sequential composition is defined using the composition of relations. The union is used for nondeterministic choice. The iteration is defined as the choice of executing a program zero or more times.

To reason about program correctness, first order dynamic logic relies on the following syntax for logical formulas.

Definition 7 (Formulas). *The set of formulas $Fml(V)$ is defined by the following grammar:*

$$\varphi, \psi ::= p(t_1, \cdots, t_n) \mid \top \mid \bot \mid \neg\varphi \mid \varphi \wedge \psi \mid \varphi \vee \psi \mid \varphi \rightarrow \psi \mid$$
$$\forall x.\varphi \mid \exists x.\varphi \mid \langle\alpha\rangle\varphi \mid [\alpha]\varphi$$

for $p \in \Sigma_n$ a predicate, $t_1, \cdots t_n \in Trm(V)$, $x \in V$ and $\alpha \in Prog(V)$.

The notion of satisfaction for logic formulas is straightforward for first order operators. The program possibility $\langle\alpha\rangle\varphi$ states that *it is possible that after executing program α, φ is true.* The necessity operator is dual to the possibility. It is defined as $[\alpha]\varphi \triangleq \neg\langle\alpha\rangle\neg\varphi$ stating that *it is necessary that after executing program α, φ is true.*

Definition 8 (Formula Validity). *The satisfiability of a formula φ in a state $s \in State(V)$ of a computational domain $\mathcal{D} = (D, I)$ is defined by:*

$$
\begin{array}{lll}
s \models p(t_1, \ldots, t_n) & \text{iff} & p^I(val(s, t_1), \ldots, val(s, t_n)) \\
s \models \top & & \text{for all } s \in S \\
s \models \neg\varphi & \text{iff} & \text{not } s \models \varphi \\
s \models \varphi \wedge \psi & \text{iff} & s \models \varphi \text{ and } s \models \psi \\
s \models \forall x.\varphi & \text{iff} & s[x \mapsto d] \models \varphi \text{ for all } d \in D \\
s \models \langle\alpha\rangle\varphi & \text{iff} & \text{there is a state } r \text{ such that } (s, r) \in \rho(\alpha) \text{ and } r \models \varphi
\end{array}
$$

A formula is valid in a domain $\mathcal{D}$ if it is satisfiable in all states over $\mathcal{D}$, it is valid if it is valid in all domains.

A valid formula for Ex. 1 would be $stock > 0 \rightarrow [acceptOrder]stock \geq 0$ (assuming that the computational domain are the natural numbers).

Below we show how in previous approaches dynamic logic is either extended with deontic formalisms or concurrency. Most of these approaches use propositional dynamic logic [15]. It is more abstract than first order dynamic logic. The interpretation of basic activities is an abstract relation on states, often Kripke frames are used. Thus there is no need for the valuation of terms and the computational domain. However it does not allow for quantification in formulas.

2.1   Deontic Formalisms for Error Handling

In this section we overview previous approaches that combine dynamic logic with deontic logic [27] by introducing operators for permission, obligation and prohibition. While the original deontic logic reasons on predicates, in combination with dynamic logic these operators are applied to actions.

Meyer [20] proposed the use of a violation condition V that describes an undesirable situation, so that the violation condition corresponds to validity of proposition V. The prohibition operator is defined such that $s \models F\alpha$ iff $s \models [\alpha]V$, *i.e.*, it is forbidden to do α in s iff all executions of α terminate in a violation. Obligation and permission are defined based on prohibition. The main problem with Meyer's work is that dependency between permission and prohibition raises paradoxes. Paradoxes of deontic logics are valid logical formulas that go against common sense, *e.g.*, Ross' paradox states if a letter ought *to be sent*, then a letter ought *to be sent or burnt*.

While Meyer focused on permission of states, Meyden [24] defined permission on the possible executions of an action. He extended models for dynamic logic with a relation P on states. An execution of an action α is permitted if every (internal) state transition of α is in P. This implies that if an execution of an action is permitted also each of its subactions must be permitted. This avoids, for example, Ross' paradox. Meyden's definition of violation is however not very different from Meyer's. As shown in [3] there is a correspondence between the two definitions.

In [4] Broersen *et al.* define permission of an action as a proposition over states and actions. Each model contains a valuation function that maps permission propositions over atomic actions to sets of states. Contrary to the previous approaches permission is in fact based on the action itself. For compound actions permission is defined in terms of possible traces and its subactions. Broersen extends this approach in [3] including also concurrency.

Castro and Maibaum [10] refine Broersen's approach. Their definition of violation is very similar, however actions can be combined differently. While previous approaches focused on free choice and sequence for the combination of atomic actions, the authors define the domain of actions as an atomic boolean algebra. Actions can be combined using choice, intersection (*i.e.* concurrency) and a locally restricted form of complement. This allows them to show not only that their logic is sound and complete, but moreover it is decidable and compact.

2.2   Concurrency

There are only a few approaches adding concurrency to dynamic logic. The first, concurrent dynamic logic [23], interprets programs as a collection of reachability pairs, such that for each initial state it assigns a set of final states. In case of parallel composition the sets of final states are joined, while for choice the reachability pairs are joined. In this approach the formula $\langle \alpha \rangle \varphi$ holds in states s such that a reachability pair (s, U) for the interpretation of α exists and each state $s' \in U$ satisfies φ. In particular, the axiom $\langle \alpha \cap \beta \rangle \varphi \leftrightarrow \langle \alpha \rangle \varphi \wedge \langle \beta \rangle \varphi$ is valid, *i.e.*, actions are independent of each other.

For Broersen [3] this is an undesirable property. He considers only true concurrency, *i.e.* executing actions in parallel has a different effect than interleaving them. The interpretation uses the intersection for concurrency. Moreover he considers an open concurrency interpretation, which is not applicable to first order dynamic logic (that follows a closed action interpretation).

In [1] the authors define a dynamic logic for CCS where the interpretation of concurrency is based on the labelled transition system of CCS. Thus concurrency is either interpreted as interleaving or the so-called handshake of CCS. This is the first article applying dynamic logic to a process calculus.

As we have seen, concurrency in dynamic logic is often interpreted as a simultaneous execution. This interpretation is not suited for the kind of systems we want to model, where concurrent programs describe activities that can be executed concurrently, or even in parallel, but do not have to happen simultaneously. A possible approach would be to only allow parallel composition of independent processes, *i.e.*, processes that do not interfere with each other. This requirement is quite strong and excludes most long running transactional systems. In the area of transactional concurrency control, extensive work has been done on the correctness criterion for the execution of parallel transactions. Proposed criteria include, linearizability [16], serializability [22], etc. These criteria are more realistic, since they allow some interference between concurrent transactions. Therefore, for our interpretation of concurrency we used a notion of serializability (less restrictive than linearizability), stating that: the only acceptable interleaved executions of activities from different transactions, are those that are equivalent to some sequential execution. Serializability is presented formally in Def. 17.

3   Concurrent Programs

We will consider an extension of first-order dynamic logic. We keep the definitions for the term algebra and variables from Section 2. Our definition of basic activities is extended to take into account a validity formula.

Definition 9 (Basic Activities). *A basic activity $a \in Act(V)$ is a multiple assignment together with a quantifier and program-free formula $E(a) \in Fml(V)$ that specifies the conditions under which activity a leads to an error state.*

Formula (not) $E(a)$ can be seen as a precondition of activity a: if formula $E(a)$ holds on state s, executing a will cause an error. We exploit $E(a)$ to classify state transitions as successful or failed, depending on whether the precondition holds or not on a given state. We could use instead for each activity a an explicit set of error transitions or error states, but those sets (either of error transitions or states) can be obtained from formula $E(a)$. Another point worth discussing is the use of $E(a)$ as a precondition or postcondition for activity a. Using $E(a)$ as a precondition of a ensures erroneous state transitions do not occur, leaving the system in a correct state (the last correct state before the error). Whereas using $E(a)$ as a postcondition of a, the state transition has to occur to determine if $E(a)$ holds. Note that the empty assignment *skip* is always successful. Consider once more activity *acceptOrder* from Ex. 1. A possible error condition could be $E(acceptOrder) \triangleq stock \leq 0$, that checks if there are any items in stock.

The definition of concurrent programs uses standard dynamic operators, including parallel composition and a test operator for a quantifier-free formula φ.

Definition 10 (Concurrent Programs). *The set $Prog(V)$ of programs is defined by the following grammar:*

$$\alpha, \beta ::= a \mid \varphi? \mid \alpha;\beta \mid \alpha \Box \beta \mid \alpha \parallel \beta \mid \alpha^*$$

Let the computational domain be as in Def. 3, as well as the valuation of terms as in Def. 4. The interpretation of basic activities (and thus programs) differs from the usual interpretation of dynamic logic. First we distinguish between activities that succeed or fail. Second we use traces instead of the relation on states. This is due to the combination of possible failing executions and nondeterminism. We will explain this further when introducing the interpretation of concurrent programs.

Definition 11 (Traces). *A trace τ is defined as a sequence of sets of triples $[\![\ell]\!]$ where $\ell \in \{a, -a, \varphi?\}$ ($a \in Act(V)$ a multiple assignment $x_1, \cdots, x_n := t_1, \cdots, t_n$, $\varphi \in Fml(V)$ a quantifier-free formula) and*

$$
\begin{aligned}
[\![a]\!] &\triangleq \{s\,a\,s' \mid s' = s[x_1 \mapsto val(s,t_1), \cdots, x_n \mapsto val(s,t_n)] \wedge s \models \neg E(a)\} \\
[\![-a]\!] &\triangleq \{s\,a\,s \mid s \models E(a)\} \\
[\![\varphi?]\!] &\triangleq \{s\,\varphi?\,s \mid s \models \varphi\}.
\end{aligned}
$$

We will use $[\![]$ for the singleton containing the empty (but defined) trace; when combined with another trace it acts like the identity. Moreover we use the notation $[\![\ell.\tau]\!] = [\![\ell]\!][\![\tau]\!]$ for traces with length ≥ 1. Note that if $[\![\ell]\!] = \emptyset$ the trace is not defined. When composing traces there is no restriction whether adjoining states have to match or not. The system is in general considered to be open, *i.e.*, even within one trace between two actions there might be something happening in parallel changing the state. When we build the closure of the system traces that do not match are discarded.

A closed trace is a trace where adjoining states match. We define a predicate *closed* on traces such that $closed(s\,\ell\,s') = \top$ and $closed(s\,\ell\,s'.\tau) = closed(\tau) \wedge (s' = first(\tau))$. For closed traces we can define functions *first* and *last* that return the first and the last state of the trace.

Definition 12 (Interpretation of Basic Activities). *The valuation ρ of an activity $a \in Act(V)$ is defined by:*

$$\rho(a) \triangleq [\![a]\!] \cup [\![-a]\!]$$

With this semantic model an activity a may have "good" (committed) or "bad" (failed) traces, depending on whether the initial state satisfies $E(a)$ or not. As it is clear from the interpretation of basic activities, a precondition violation forbids the execution of an activity. Therefore failed transitions do not cause a state change.

Example 2. Take activity *acceptOrder* from Ex. 1 and its error formula $E(acceptOrder)$. In this setting, we have that

$$
\begin{aligned}
[\![acceptOrder]\!] &\triangleq \{s\,acceptOrder\,s' \mid s' = s[stock \mapsto s(stock)-1, card \mapsto unknown] \wedge \\
&\qquad\qquad s \models stock > 0\} \\
[\![-acceptOrder]\!] &\triangleq \{s\,acceptOrder\,s \mid s \models stock \leq 0\}
\end{aligned}
$$

As we mentioned for basic activities, we use traces instead of a state relation for the interpretation of programs. To illustrate this decision consider the behaviour of a compensable program. If it is successful the complete program will be executed. If it fails the program is aborted and the installed compensations will be executed. Thus we need to distinguish between successful and failing executions. Hence we need to extend the error formula E. But extending E to programs does not suffice as programs introduce nondeterminism, *i.e.*, a program with choice may both succeed and fail in the same state. Using E for programs would however only tell us that the program might fail, not which execution actually does fail. For a trace we can state whether this execution fails or not.

Definition 13 (Error Formulas of Traces). *We lift error formulas from activities to traces τ by letting $E(\tau)$ being inductively defined as:*

$$E([]) \triangleq \bot \qquad E([a]\tau) \triangleq E(\tau) \qquad E([\varphi?]\tau) \triangleq E(\tau) \qquad E([-a]\tau) \triangleq \top$$

We exploit error formulas for defining the sequential composition $\circ$ of traces. If the first trace raises an error, the execution is aborted and thus not combined with the second trace. If the first trace succeeds sequential composition is defined as usual, *i.e.* we append the second trace to the first trace.

$$\tau_\alpha \circ \tau_\beta \triangleq \begin{cases} \tau_\alpha & \text{if } E(\tau_\alpha) \\ \tau_\alpha\,\tau_\beta & \text{if } \neg E(\tau_\alpha) \end{cases}$$

Abusing the notation we use the same symbol $\circ$ to compose sets of traces.

Next, to build the trace for parallel composition of two basic programs we would consider the interleaving of any combination of traces:

$$[] \parallel \tau_2 \triangleq \{\tau_2\} \qquad [\ell_1]\tau_1 \parallel [\ell_2]\tau_2 \triangleq \{[\ell_1]\tau \mid \tau \in (\tau_1 \parallel [\ell_2]\tau_2)\}$$
$$\tau_1 \parallel [] \triangleq \{\tau_1\} \qquad \qquad \cup \{[\ell_2]\tau \mid \tau \in ([\ell_1]\tau_1 \parallel \tau_2)\}$$

Now we can define the interpretation of concurrent programs:

Definition 14 (Interpretation of Concurrent Programs). *We extend the interpretation ρ from basic activities to concurrent programs in the following manner:*

$$\rho(\varphi?) \triangleq [\varphi?]$$
$$\rho(\alpha\,;\beta) \triangleq \{\tau_\alpha \circ \tau_\beta \mid \tau_\alpha \in \rho(\alpha) \wedge \tau_\beta \in \rho(\beta)\}$$
$$\rho(\alpha \,\square\, \beta) \triangleq \rho(\alpha) \cup \rho(\beta)$$
$$\rho(\alpha \parallel \beta) \triangleq \{\tau \mid \tau_\alpha \in \rho(\alpha) \wedge \tau_\beta \in \rho(\beta) \wedge \tau \in \tau_\alpha \parallel \tau_\beta\}$$
$$\rho(\alpha^*) \triangleq [] \cup \rho(\alpha) \circ \rho(\alpha^*)$$

Test $\varphi?$ is interpreted as the identity trace for the states that satisfy formula φ. The interpretation of sequential programs is the sequential composition of traces. Failed transitions are preserved in the resulting set as executions of α that have reached an erroneous state and cannot evolve. Choice is interpreted as the union of trace sets of programs α and β. The interpretation of parallel composition is the set of all possible interleavings of the traces for both branches. Iteration is defined recursively (by taking the least fixpoint).

$$eStore \triangleq acceptOrder \; ; ((acceptCard \;\square\; rejectCard \; ; \; throw) \; \| \; bookCourier)$$

$$
\begin{array}{llll}
aO & \triangleq stock, card := stock - 1, unknown & E(aO) & \triangleq stock \le 0 \\
aC & \triangleq card := accepted & E(aC) & \triangleq false \\
rC & \triangleq card := rejected & E(rC) & \triangleq false \\
bC & \triangleq courier := booked & E(bC) & \triangleq card = rejected \\
throw & \triangleq skip & E(throw) & \triangleq true
\end{array}
$$

$\rho(aO \; ; ((aC \;\square\; rC \; ; \; throw) \; \| \; bC)) =$

$$
\begin{array}{lll}
[\![aO.aC.bC]\!] & \cup\; [\![aO.bC.aC]\!] & \cup \\
[\![aO.aC. - bC]\!] & \cup\; [\![aO. - bC.aC]\!] & \cup \\
[\![aO.rC. - throw.bC]\!] & \cup\; [\![aO.bC.rC. - throw]\!] & \cup\; [\![aO.rC.bC. - throw]\!] \quad \cup \\
[\![aO.rC. - throw. - bC]\!] & \cup\; [\![aO. - bC.rC. - throw]\!] \cup\; [\![aO.rC. - bC. - throw]\!] \cup\; [\![-aO]\!]
\end{array}
$$

Fig. 1. *eStore* example

To build the closure of the system, *i.e.*, a program α, we define the set of all closed traces for α such that $closure(\alpha) \triangleq \{\tau \mid \tau \in \rho(\alpha) \wedge closed(\tau)\}$.

Next we show in an example the application of Definition 14. Take program *eStore* defined as in Fig. 1. Note that we abbreviate activities using initials, *e.g.*, we write aO for *acceptOrder*. This program describes a simple online shop and it starts with an activity that removes from the stock the ordered items. Since for most orders the credit cards are not rejected, and to decrease the delivery time, the client's card processing and courier booking can be done in parallel. In this example, the activities running in parallel may interfere with each other as *bookCourier* will fail once the card is rejected. As the order of the execution for the parallel composition is not fixed after rejecting the credit card we issue a throw (defined as the empty assignment that always fails). In the interpretation of program *eStore* we can first distinguish the traces where *acceptOrder* succeeds and where it fails. In the latter case no other action is executable. In the successful case the parallel composition is executed where both branches may succeed or fail and we include any possible interleaving. Note that the traces $[\![-aC]\!]$, $[\![-rC]\!]$ and $[\![throw]\!]$ are not defined, as their condition is not satisfied by any possible state. Building the closure for these traces we can rule out some possibilities, namely $[\![aO.aC. - bC]\!]$, $[\![aO. - bC.aC]\!]$, $[\![aO.rC. - throw.bC]\!]$ and $[\![aO.rC.bC. - throw]\!]$ and $[\![aO. - bC.rC. - throw]\!]$ would be excluded. A possible closed trace would be

$$
closed(\; s \; aO \; s' \, . \, s' aC \; r \, . \, rbC \; s'' \\
\mid s' = s[stock \mapsto s(stock) - 1, card \mapsto unknown] \wedge r = s'[card \mapsto accepted] \\
\wedge s'' = r[courier \mapsto booked] \wedge s \models stock > 0 \wedge r \models \neg card = rejected)
$$

For formulas we include two modal operators related to program success where success of a program is interpreted as not reaching an erroneous state. The modal operator success $S(\alpha)$ states that *every way of executing α is successful*, so program α must never reach an erroneous state. The modal operator weak success $S_W(\alpha)$ states that *some way of executing α is successful*. The failure modal operator $F(\alpha)$ is a derived operator, $F(\alpha) = \neg S_W(\alpha)$, and states that *every way of executing α fails*. Notice that both weak success and program possibility ensure program termination, while success and program necessity do not.

Definition 15 (Formulas). *The set of formulas $Fml(V)$ is defined by the grammar:*

$$\varphi, \psi ::= p(t_1, \cdots, t_n) \mid \top \mid \bot \mid \neg\varphi \mid \varphi \wedge \psi \mid \varphi \vee \psi \mid \varphi \rightarrow \psi \mid$$
$$\forall x.\varphi \mid \exists x.\varphi \mid \langle \alpha \rangle \varphi \mid [\alpha]\varphi \mid \mathsf{S}(\alpha) \mid \mathsf{S_W}(\alpha) \mid \mathsf{F}(\alpha)$$

for $p \in \Sigma_n$ a predicate, $t_1, \cdots t_n \in Trm(V)$, $x \in V$ and $\alpha \in Prog(V)$.

Definition 16 (Formula Validity). *The validity of a formula φ in a state $s \in State(V)$ of a computational domain $\mathcal{D} = (D, I)$ is defined by:*

$s \models p(t_1, \ldots, t_n)$	*iff*	$p^I(val(s, t_1), \ldots, val(s, t_n))$
$s \models \top$		*for all $s \in S$*
$s \models \neg\varphi$	*iff*	*not $s \models \varphi$*
$s \models \varphi \wedge \psi$	*iff*	$s \models \varphi$ *and* $s \models \psi$
$s \models \forall x.\varphi$	*iff*	$s[x \mapsto d] \models \varphi$ *for all $d \in D$*
$s \models \langle \alpha \rangle \varphi$	*iff*	$\exists \tau \in closure(\alpha)$ *such that* $first(\tau) = s \wedge last(\tau) \models \varphi$
$s \models \mathsf{S}(\alpha)$	*iff*	*for all $\tau \in closure(\alpha)$, $first(\tau) = s$ implies $\neg E(\tau)$*
$s \models \mathsf{S_W}(\alpha)$	*iff*	$\exists \tau \in closure(\alpha)$ *such that* $first(\tau) = s$ *and* $\neg E(\tau)$
$s \models \mathsf{F}(\alpha)$	*iff*	$s \models \neg\mathsf{S_W}(\alpha)$

The new modal operators for success and failure are defined according to the description given above. Considering Fig. 1 a possible formula would be $\mathsf{F}(acceptOrder)$, that is only satisfiable in some states. However $stock \leq 0 \rightarrow \mathsf{F}(acceptOrder)$ is a valid formula for any state.

As it was discussed in Section 2, we want an interpretation of concurrency where concurrent activities do not have to happen simultaneously. For example, packing the items in a client's order and booking a courier to deliver that same order are independent activities that can be run in parallel. If, contrary to the example just mentioned, parallel activities are not independent then concurrency becomes more complex: as activities may interfere with each other, this may lead to unexpected results. In this work parallel composition is not restricted to independent programs (such that the set of variables updated and read by those programs is disjoint), however without any restriction the logic is too liberal to state any properties. Instead we use a notion of serializability (Def. 17). We will use the abbreviation $\tau \bowtie \tau'$ for traces τ and τ' denoting

$$\tau \bowtie \tau' \triangleq closed(\tau) \wedge closed(\tau') \wedge first(\tau) = first(\tau') \wedge last(\tau) = last(\tau')$$

Definition 17 (Serializable Concurrent Programs). *Processes α and β are serializable if for every trace $\tau \in closure(\alpha \parallel \beta)$ there exist $\nu \in \rho(\alpha)$ and $\mu \in \rho(\beta)$ such that either $\tau \bowtie (\nu\mu)$ or $\tau \bowtie (\mu\nu)$.*

Note that serializability is defined as an implication, as the equivalence cannot be ensured. The fact that activities may be executed independently does not ensure, in the presence of interference, that those activities may be executed concurrently.

We show some useful logical equivalences involving the novel modal operators. We are particularly considering their interplay with parallel composition.

Proposition 1. *Let α, β be two serializable programs. The following are valid formulas in the presented dynamic logic:*

$$\langle\alpha\rangle\langle\beta\rangle\varphi \vee \langle\beta\rangle\langle\alpha\rangle\varphi \quad \leftrightarrow \langle\alpha \parallel \beta\rangle\varphi \qquad \mathsf{S}(\alpha;\beta \square \beta;\alpha) \qquad \leftrightarrow \mathsf{S}(\alpha \parallel \beta)$$
$$\mathsf{S_W}(\alpha;\beta) \vee \mathsf{S_W}(\beta;\alpha) \leftrightarrow \mathsf{S_W}(\alpha \parallel \beta) \quad \mathsf{F}(\alpha;\beta) \wedge \mathsf{F}(\beta;\alpha) \leftrightarrow \mathsf{F}(\alpha \parallel \beta)$$

4 Compensable Programs

This section defines compensable programs, where the basic building block is the compensation pair. A compensation pair $a \div \bar{a}$ is composed by two activities, such that if the execution of the first activity is successful, compensation $\bar{a}$ is stored. Otherwise, if activity a fails, no compensation is stored. Compensation pairs can be composed using similar operators as for basic programs. The transaction operator $\{[\cdot]\}$ converts a compensable program into a basic program by discarding stored compensations for successful executions and running compensations for failed executions.

Definition 18 (Compensable Programs). *The set $Cmp(V)$ of compensable programs is defined by the following grammar (for $a, \bar{a} \in Act(V)$):*

$$\alpha \quad ::= \ldots \mid \{[\delta]\}$$
$$\delta, \gamma ::= a \div \bar{a} \mid \delta ; \gamma \mid \delta \square \gamma \mid \delta \parallel \gamma \mid \delta^*$$

In order to ensure the overall correctness of a compensable program, the backward program of a compensation pair $a \div \bar{a}$ must satisfy a condition: $\bar{a}$ must successfully revert all forward actions of activity a. In the following we do not require that $\bar{a}$ exactly undoes all assignments of a and thus revert the state to the exact initial state of a. Instead, we require that it performs some compensation actions that lead to a "sufficiently" similar state. The way to determine if two states are similar depends on the system under modeling, so we do not enforce any rigid definition. Still, we propose a concrete notion that may characterize a widely applicable criterion of correctness (but other proposals may be valid as well).

The notion we give is parametric w.r.t. a set of variables whose content we wish to monitor.

Definition 19. *Let X be a set of integer variables. We call $s\backslash_X s'$ the distance over X between two states, i.e., the set of changes occurred over the variables in X, when moving from s to s'. Formally, we define $(s\backslash_X s')(x) = s'(x) - s(x)$ for any $x \in X$ (and let $(s\backslash_X s')(x) = 0$ otherwise).*

For an empty trace the distance is null, the same holds for $s\backslash_X s$.

Definition 20 (Correct Compensation Pair). *Let X be a set of integer variables. Activity $\bar{a} \in Act(V)$ is a correct compensation over X of a iff for all traces $s \, a \, s' \in \rho(a)$ with $s \models \neg E(a)$, then for all $t' \, \bar{a} \, t \in \rho(\bar{a})$ we have $t' \models \neg E(\bar{a})$ and $s\backslash_X s' = t\backslash_X t'$.*

Example 3. For most hotels the cancellation of a booking requires the payment of a cancellation fee. This can be modeled by a compensation pair $bookHotel \div cancelHotel$, where forward activity $bookHotel$ books a room and sets the amount to be paid, while the compensation $cancelHotel$ cancels the reservation and charges the cancellation fee.

$$bookHotel \triangleq rooms, price, fee := rooms - 1, 140\$, 20\$$$
$$cancelHotel \triangleq rooms, price, fee := rooms + 1, fee, 0\$$$

In this example $cancelHotel$ does not completely revert all of $bookHotel$ actions, and in fact it is likely that room cancelation imposes some fees. However, if we are only interested in the consistency of the overall number of available rooms, we can take $X = \{rooms\}$ and consider $s\backslash_X s'$ as a measure of distance. The idea is that a correct compensation should restore as available the rooms that were booked but later canceled.

In Definition 21 each compensable program is interpreted as a set of pairs of traces, where the first element is a trace of the forward program, while the second element is a trace that compensates the actions of its forward program. Compensation pairs are interpreted as the union of two sets. The first set represents the successful traces of forward activity a, paired with the traces of compensation activity $\bar{a}$. The second set represents the failed traces, paired with the empty trace as its compensation. Sequential composition of compensable programs $\delta \, ; \gamma$ is interpreted by two sets, one where the successful termination of δ allows the execution of γ, the other where δ fails and therefore γ cannot be executed. As for the compensations of a sequential program, their traces are composed in the reverse order of their forward programs.

The interpretation of a transaction includes two sets: the first set discards compensable traces for all successful traces; while the second set deals with failed traces by composing the correspondent compensation trace with each failed trace. Notice that for this trace composition to be defined, it is necessary to clear any faulty activities in the failed forward trace. Therefore, in defining the interpretation of a transaction $\{[\delta]\}$, we exploit a function cl that clears failing activities from a run:

$$cl(\llbracket\rrbracket) \triangleq \llbracket\rrbracket \qquad cl(\llbracket\ell\rrbracket\tau) \triangleq \begin{cases} \llbracket E(a)?\rrbracket \, cl(\tau) & \text{if } \ell = -a \\ \llbracket\ell\rrbracket \, cl(\tau) & \text{otherwise} \end{cases}$$

where $E(a)?$ is the test for the error formula of activity a. It is always defined in s as activity a only aborts if $s \models E(a)$, thus it is in general like a skip. In fact, if τ is faulty but successfully compensated by $\bar{\tau}$, then we want to exhibit an overall non faulty run, so that we cannot just take $\tau \circ \bar{\tau}$ (if $E(\tau)$ then obviously $E(\tau \circ \bar{\tau})$). The following lemma states that cl does not alter the first nor the last state of a trace:

Lemma 1. *For any* τ: $\neg E(cl(\tau))$, *first*$(\tau) = $ *first*$(cl(\tau))$ *and* *last*$(\tau) = $ *last*$(cl(\tau))$.

Definition 21 (Interpretation of Compensable Programs). *Now we can define the interpretation* ρ_c *of compensable programs in the following manner:*

$$\rho_c(a \div \bar{a}) \triangleq \{(\tau, \bar{\tau}) \mid \tau \in \rho(a) \wedge \bar{\tau} \in \rho(\bar{a}) \wedge \neg E(\tau)\} \cup$$
$$\qquad\qquad \{(\tau, \llbracket\rrbracket) \mid \tau \in \rho(a) \wedge E(\tau)\}$$
$$\rho_c(\delta \,\square\, \gamma) \triangleq \rho_c(\delta) \cup \rho_c(\gamma)$$
$$\rho_c(\delta \,;\gamma) \triangleq \{(\tau \circ \nu, \bar{\nu} \circ \bar{\tau}) \mid (\tau, \bar{\tau}) \in \rho_c(\delta) \wedge (\nu, \bar{\nu}) \in \rho_c(\gamma) \wedge \neg E(\tau)\} \cup$$
$$\qquad\qquad \{(\tau, \bar{\tau}) \mid (\tau, \bar{\tau}) \in \rho_c(\delta) \wedge E(\tau)\}$$
$$\rho_c(\delta \,\|\, \gamma) \triangleq \{(\tau, \bar{\tau}) \mid (\nu, \bar{\nu}) \in \rho_c(\delta) \wedge (\mu, \bar{\mu}) \in \rho_c(\gamma) \wedge \tau \in \nu \,\|\, \mu \wedge \bar{\tau} \in \bar{\nu} \,\|\, \bar{\mu}\}$$
$$\rho_c(\delta^*) \triangleq \{(\llbracket\rrbracket, \llbracket\rrbracket)\} \cup \rho_c(\delta \,;\delta^*)$$
$$\rho(\{[\delta]\}) \triangleq \{\tau \mid (\tau, \bar{\tau}) \in \rho_c(\delta) \wedge \neg E(\tau)\} \cup$$
$$\qquad\qquad \{cl(\tau) \circ \bar{\tau} \mid (\tau, \bar{\tau}) \in \rho_c(\delta) \wedge E(\tau)\}$$

In Fig. 2 we present a compensable program that specifies a hotel booking system. In this example the activity *bookHotel* updates several variables: it decreases the rooms

$$HotelBooking \triangleq bookHotel \div cancelHotel ;$$
$$(acceptBooking \div skip \ \Box \ cancelBooking \div skip ; throw \div skip))$$

$$\begin{aligned}
&\mathsf{bH} \triangleq rooms, status, price, fee := rooms - 1, booked, 140\$, 20\$ &&E(\mathsf{bH}) \triangleq rooms \leq 0 \\
&\mathsf{cH} \triangleq rooms, price, fee := rooms + 1, fee, 0\$ &&E(\mathsf{cH}) \triangleq false \\
&\mathsf{aB} \triangleq status := confirmed &&E(\mathsf{aB}) \triangleq false \\
&\mathsf{cB} \triangleq status := cancelled &&E(\mathsf{cB}) \triangleq false
\end{aligned}$$

$$\rho_c(\mathsf{bH} \div \mathsf{cH} ; (\mathsf{aB} \div skip \ \Box \ \mathsf{cB} \div skip ; throw \div skip))$$
$$= ([\![\mathsf{bH.aB}]\!], [\![skip.\mathsf{cH}]\!]) \cup ([\![\mathsf{bH.cB.} - throw]\!], [\![skip.\mathsf{cH}]\!]) \cup ([\![-\mathsf{bH}]\!], [\![]\!])$$

Fig. 2. *HotelBooking* example

$$HotelTransactions \triangleq \{[\![HotelBooking_1]\!]\} \parallel \{[\![HotelBooking_2]\!]\}$$

$$\rho(\{[\![HotelBooking]\!]\}) = [\![\mathsf{bH.aB}]\!] \cup [\![\mathsf{bH.cB.}E(throw)?.skip.\mathsf{cH}]\!] \cup [\![E(\mathsf{bH})?]\!]$$

$$\rho(HotelTransactions)$$
$$= [\![\mathsf{bH_1.aB_1}]\!] \parallel [\![\mathsf{bH_2.aB_2}]\!] \quad \cup \quad [\![E(\mathsf{bH_1})?]\!] \parallel [\![E(\mathsf{bH_2})?]\!]$$
$$\cup \ [\![\mathsf{bH_1.cB_1.}E(throw_1)?.skip_1.\mathsf{cH_1}]\!] \parallel [\![\mathsf{bH_2.cB_2.}E(throw_2)?.skip_2.\mathsf{cH_2}]\!]$$
$$\cup \ [\![\mathsf{bH_1.aB_1}]\!] \parallel [\![\mathsf{bH_2.cB_2.}E(throw_2)?.skip_2.\mathsf{cH_2}]\!]$$
$$\cup \ [\![\mathsf{bH_1.cB_1.}E(throw_1)?.skip_1.\mathsf{cH_1}]\!] \parallel [\![\mathsf{bH_2.aB_2}]\!]$$
$$\cup \ [\![E(\mathsf{bH_1})?]\!] \parallel [\![\mathsf{bH_2.cB_2.}E(throw_2)?.skip_2.\mathsf{cH_2}]\!]$$
$$\cup \ [\![\mathsf{bH_1.cB_1.}E(throw_1)?.skip_1.\mathsf{cH_1}]\!] \parallel [\![E(\mathsf{bH_2})?]\!]$$
$$\cup \ [\![\mathsf{bH_1.aB_1}]\!] \parallel [\![E(\mathsf{bH_2})?]\!] \quad \cup \quad [\![E(\mathsf{bH_1})?]\!] \parallel [\![\mathsf{bH_2.aB_2}]\!]$$

Fig. 3. *HotelTransactions* example

available, sets the booking status to *booked*, while the price and cancellation fee are set to predefined values. Next, there is a choice between confirming or canceling the booking. These last two activities do not have a compensation, represented by defining compensation as *skip*. After *cancelBooking* the process is aborted by executing *throw*. Regarding the interpretation of *HotelBooking*, each forward run is paired with a compensation trace that reverts all its successfully terminated activities. For example, the first pair of traces represents a successful execution, where after booking a room the client accepts that reservation. In this case the stored compensation reverts both the acceptance of the booking and the booking it self. Note that as in Example 3, the compensation activity *cancelHotel* does not revert completely its main activity: it reverts the room booking, charges the cancellation fee, and it leaves the booking status unchanged.

Fig. 3 shows the parallel composition of two *HotelBooking* transactions (the subscripts are used only to distinguish activities from different transactions). The set of all possible interleaving is quite large, even after discarding traces that are not satisfied by any possible state. An example of a trace to be discarded is $[\![E(\mathsf{bH_1})?.\mathsf{bH_2.aB_2}]\!]$, as $E(\mathsf{bH_1})$ is true in a state s such that $s \models rooms \leq 0$ and in that case $[\![\mathsf{bH_2.aB_2}]\!]$ could not be executed.

The program of Fig. 3 shows how the interleaved execution of processes may lead to interferences. Consider $\theta_1 = [\![bH_1.cB_1.E(throw_1)?.skip_1.cH_1]\!]$ that describes traces where the booking succeeds and is later canceled by the client, and $\theta_2 = [\![E(bH_2)?]\!]$ that describes traces where no rooms are available and therefore no activity can be executed. Take the interleaving of traces of θ_1 and θ_2 on an initial state s such that $s \models rooms = 1$. In this setting, θ_1 has to be executed first and consequently activity bH_1 books the last room available. There is no serial execution of θ_1 and θ_2 (these sets of traces cannot be sequentially composed), since after the execution of a trace of θ_1 activity bH_2 should succeed (the last room becomes available again after the execution of cB_1). However, the following interleaved execution is possible $[\![bH_1.E(bH_2)?.cB_1.E(throw_1)?.skip_1.cH_1]\!]$, because when bH_2 is executed there are no rooms available. This shows that *HotelTransactions* is not serializable, since some interleaved traces do not correspond to a serial execution.

The aim of compensable programs is that the overall recoverability of a system can be achieved through the definition of local recovery actions. As the system evolves, those local compensation actions are dynamically composed into a program that reverts all actions performed until then. Therefore, it is uttermost important that the dynamically built compensation trace does indeed revert the current state to the initial state. Next, we define the notion of a correct compensable program, where any failed forward trace can be compensated to a state equivalent to the initial state.

Definition 22 (Correct Compensable Program). *Let X be a set of integer variables. A compensable program δ has a correct compensation over X if for all pairs of traces $(\tau, \overline{\tau}) \in \rho_c(\delta)$, if closed$(\tau)$ and closed$(\overline{\tau})$ then first$(\tau)\backslash_X$last$(\tau) = $last$(\overline{\tau})\backslash_X$first$(\overline{\tau})$.*

Serializability is extended from basic programs to compensable programs:

Definition 23 (Serializable compensable parallel programs). *Compensable programs δ and γ are serializable if for all $(\tau, \overline{\tau}) \in \rho_c(\delta \parallel \gamma)$ with closed(τ) and closed$(\overline{\tau})$ there exist $(\nu, \overline{\nu}) \in \rho_c(\delta)$ and $(\mu, \overline{\mu}) \in \rho_c(\gamma)$ such that the following holds: Either $\tau \bowtie (\nu\mu)$ or $\tau \bowtie (\mu\nu)$ and either $\overline{\tau} \bowtie (\overline{\nu}\,\overline{\mu})$ or $\overline{\tau} \bowtie (\overline{\mu}\,\overline{\nu})$.*

The following theorem shows the soundness of our language, since it proves that compensation correctness is ensured by construction: the composition of correct compensable programs results in a correct compensable program.

Theorem 1. *Let X be a set of integer variables and δ a serializable compensable program where every compensation pair is correct over X, then δ is correct over X.*

As in general serializability is hard to prove we suggest the simpler definition of apartness. If the set of variables updated and consulted by two programs are disjoint, those programs can be concurrently executed since they do not interfere with each other (a similar approach was taken in [9]). Two compensable programs δ and γ are apart if they do not update or read overlapping variables, then δ and γ can be executed concurrently and their resulting traces can be merged. The final state of a concurrent execution of apart programs can be understood as a join of the resulting states of each program.

Formulas for basic programs can be easily extended to compensable programs as they can be applied to the forward program and stored compensations can be ignored.

The modal operator $C(\delta)$ states that every failure of δ is compensable. A weak compensable operator $C_W(\delta)$ states that some failures of δ are compensable.

We extend the notion of closed traces from basic to compensable programs as

$$closure(\delta) \triangleq \{(\tau, \overline{\tau}) \mid (\tau, \overline{\tau}) \in \rho_c(\delta) \land closed(\tau) \land closed(\overline{\tau})\}.$$

Definition 24 (Formula Validity). *We extend Definition 16 with the new modal operators for compensable programs.*

$s \models \langle \delta \rangle \varphi$	*iff*	$\exists (\tau, \overline{\tau}) \in closure(\delta)$ *such that* $first(\tau) = s \land last(\tau) \models \varphi$
$s \models S(\delta)$	*iff*	*for all traces* $(\tau, \overline{\tau}) \in closure(\delta)$ *if* $first(\tau) = s$ *then* $\neg E(\tau)$
$s \models S_W(\delta)$	*iff*	$\exists (\tau, \overline{\tau}) \in closure(\delta)$ *such that* $first(\tau) = s$ *and* $\neg E(\tau)$
$s \models F(\delta)$	*iff*	$s \models \neg S_W(\delta)$
$s \models C(\delta, X)$	*iff*	*for all traces* $(\tau, \overline{\tau}) \in closure(\delta)$ *if* $E(\tau)$ *and* $first(\tau) = s$ *then* $first(\tau) \backslash_X last(\tau) = last(\overline{\tau}) \backslash_X first(\overline{\tau})$
$s \models C_W(\delta, X)$	*iff*	$\exists (\tau, \overline{\tau}) \in closure(\delta)$ *such that* $E(\tau)$ *and* $first(\tau) = s$ *and* $first(\tau) \backslash_X last(\tau) = last(\overline{\tau}) \backslash_X first(\overline{\tau})$

Considering Fig. 2 a possible formula is $\langle HotelBooking \rangle status = confirmed$. Moreover we can prove $C(HotelBooking, \{rooms\})$ for any state.

Proposition 2. *Let δ, γ be two compensable programs that are apart. The following are valid formulas in the presented dynamic logic:*

$$C(\delta \parallel \gamma, X) \leftrightarrow C(\delta, X) \land C(\gamma, X) \qquad C_W(\delta \parallel \gamma, X) \to C_W(\delta, X) \lor C_W(\gamma, X)$$

5   Conclusion

In this paper we have introduced a rigorous language of compensable concurrent programs together with a dynamic logic for reasoning about compensation correctness and verification of behavioral properties of compensable programs. In this sense we go one step further of the approach in [25,9], where the formulas were mainly concerned with the temporal order of execution of actions in a message-passing calculus with dynamic installation of compensation, by allowing to express properties about the adequacy of the state restored by the compensation after a fault occurred. As detailed in Sections 2.1 and 2.2, our dynamic logic differs from previous proposal for the way in which concurrency is handled and for dealing with compensations. The works presented in [8,9] study the soundness of a compensating calculus by formalizing a notion of compensation correctness, which we also address in Theorem 1, but do not tackle the subject of verification of behavioral properties for compensable programs. Furthermore, even though compensation correctness is ensured by construction, our logic allows the verification of strong and weak correctness (through a formula) for compensable programs that contain some compensation pairs that are not correct.

Our research programme leaves as ongoing work the development of a suitable computational model and corresponding logic for allowing a quantitative measure of correctness, so that different kinds of compensations can be distinguished (and the best can be selected) depending on their ability to restore a more satisfactory state than the others can do. Moreover, we would like to develop suitable equivalences over states that can reduce the complexity of the analysis, and facilitate the development of automatic reasoning tools.

References

1. Benevides, M.R.F., Schechter, L.M.: A Propositional Dynamic Logic for CCS Programs. In: Hodges, W., de Queiroz, R. (eds.) WOLLIC 2008. LNCS (LNAI), vol. 5110, pp. 83–97. Springer, Heidelberg (2008)
2. Bravetti, M., Zavattaro, G.: On the expressive power of process interruption and compensation. Math. Struct. in Comput. Sci. 19(3), 565–599 (2009)
3. Broersen, J.: Modal Action Logics for Reasoning about Reactive Systems. PhD thesis, Faculteit der Exacte Wetenschappen, Vrije Universiteit Amsterdam (2003)
4. Broersen, J., Wieringa, R., Meyer, J.-J.: A fixed-point characterization of a deontic logic of regular action. Fundamenta Informaticae 48(2-3), 107–128 (2001)
5. Bruni, R., Melgratti, H., Montanari, U.: Nested Commits for Mobile Calculi: Extending Join. In: Levy, J.-J., Mayr, E.W., Mitchell, J.C. (eds.) TCS 2004. IFIP AICT, vol. 155, pp. 563–576. Kluwer Academics (2004)
6. Bruni, R., Melgratti, H., Montanari, U.: Theoretical foundations for compensations in flow composition languages. In: Palsberg, J., Abadi, M. (eds.) POPL 2005, pp. 209–220. ACM (2005)
7. Butler, M., Ferreira, C.: A Process Compensation Language. In: Grieskamp, W., Santen, T., Stoddart, B. (eds.) IFM 2000. LNCS, vol. 1945, pp. 61–76. Springer, Heidelberg (2000)
8. Butler, M., Hoare, C., Ferreira, C.: A Trace Semantics for Long-Running Transactions. In: Abdallah, A.E., Jones, C.B., Sanders, J.W. (eds.) Communicating Sequential Processes. The First 25 Years. LNCS, vol. 3525, pp. 133–150. Springer, Heidelberg (2005)
9. Caires, L., Ferreira, C., Vieira, H.: A Process Calculus Analysis of Compensations. In: Kaklamanis, C., Nielson, F. (eds.) TGC 2008. LNCS, vol. 5474, pp. 87–103. Springer, Heidelberg (2009)
10. Castro, P., Maibaum, T.S.E.: Deontic action logic, atomic boolean algebras and fault-tolerance. Journal of Applied Logic 7(4), 441–466 (2009)
11. Danos, V., Krivine, J.: Reversible Communicating Systems. In: Gardner, P., Yoshida, N. (eds.) CONCUR 2004. LNCS, vol. 3170, pp. 292–307. Springer, Heidelberg (2004)
12. de Vries, E., Koutavas, V., Hennessy, M.: Communicating Transactions - (Extended Abstract). In: Gastin, P., Laroussinie, F. (eds.) CONCUR 2010. LNCS, vol. 6269, pp. 569–583. Springer, Heidelberg (2010)
13. Eisentraut, C., Spieler, D.: Fault, Compensation and Termination in WS-BPEL 2.0 — A Comparative Analysis. In: Bruni, R., Wolf, K. (eds.) WS-FM 2008. LNCS, vol. 5387, pp. 107–126. Springer, Heidelberg (2009)
14. Harel, D.: First-Order Dynamic Logic. LNCS, vol. 68. Springer, Heidelberg (1979)
15. Harel, D., Kozen, D., Tiuryn, J.: Dynamic logic. In: Handbook of Philosophical Logic, pp. 497–604. MIT Press (1984)
16. Herlihy, M.P., Wing, J.M.: Linearizability: a correctness condition for concurrent objects. ACM Trans. Program. Lang. Syst. 12(3), 463–492 (1990)
17. Lanese, I., Mezzina, C.A., Stefani, J.-B.: Reversing Higher-Order Pi. In: Gastin, P., Laroussinie, F. (eds.) CONCUR 2010. LNCS, vol. 6269, pp. 478–493. Springer, Heidelberg (2010)
18. Lucchi, R., Mazzara, M.: A pi-calculus based semantics for WS-BPEL. J. Log. Algebr. Program. 70(1), 96–118 (2007)
19. Mazzara, M., Lanese, I.: Towards a Unifying Theory for Web Services Composition. In: Bravetti, M., Núñez, M., Zavattaro, G. (eds.) WS-FM 2006. LNCS, vol. 4184, pp. 257–272. Springer, Heidelberg (2006)
20. Meyer, J.-J.: A different approach to deontic logic: Deontic logic viewed as a variant of dynamic logic. Notre Dame Journal of Formal Logic 29, 109–136 (1988)

21. OASIS. WSBPEL (2007),
    http://docs.oasis-open.org/wsbpel/2.0/wsbpel-v2.0.html
22. Papadimitriou, C.H.: The serializability of concurrent database updates. J. ACM 26(4), 631–653 (1979)
23. Peleg, D.: Concurrent dynamic logic. J. ACM 34, 450–479 (1987)
24. Van Der Meyden, R.: The dynamic logic of permission. Journal of Logic and Computation 6, 465–479 (1996)
25. Vaz, C., Ferreira, C.: Towards Compensation Correctness in Interactive Systems. In: Laneve, C., Su, J. (eds.) WS-FM 2009. LNCS, vol. 6194, pp. 161–177. Springer, Heidelberg (2010)
26. Vaz, C., Ferreira, C., Ravara, A.: Dynamic Recovering of Long Running Transactions. In: Kaklamanis, C., Nielson, F. (eds.) TGC 2008. LNCS, vol. 5474, pp. 201–215. Springer, Heidelberg (2009)
27. Von Wright, G.: I. deontic logic. Mind LX(237), 1–15 (1951)

A   Proof Theorem 1

We use $\Delta_X(\tau)$ to denote $first(\tau)\backslash_X last(\tau)$ and $\nabla_X(\tau)$ for $last(\tau)\backslash_X first(\tau)$. In the following operation $\oplus$ denotes the union of two distances of two states.

Lemma A. *Let $s, s', s'' \in State(V)$. The following equality holds:*

$$s\backslash_X s' \oplus s'\backslash_X s'' = s\backslash_X s''$$

Theorem 1. *Let X be a set of integer variables and δ a serializable compensable program where every compensation pair is correct over X, then δ is correct over X.*

Proof. We proceed by induction on the structure of compensable δ.

1. $\delta = a \div \bar{a}$. For any $(\tau, \bar{\tau}) \in \rho_c(a \div \bar{a})$ with $\neg E(\tau)$ we conclude by applying the hypothesis that the compensation pair $a \div \bar{a}$ is correct over X. For any failed trace $(\tau, \bar{\tau}) \in \rho_c(a \div \bar{a})$ with $E(\tau)$, we have that $\tau = s\, a\, s$ for some state s such that $s \models E(a)$. Furthermore, the compensation trace for a failed basic activity is empty. It is easy to see that $\Delta_X(\tau) = null$, which concludes the proof for this case.
2. $\delta = \delta_1 \,\square\, \delta_2$. By induction on δ_1 and δ_2.
3. $\delta = \delta_1 \,;\, \delta_2$. We need to distinguish two cases, by the definition of $\rho_c(\delta_1\,;\,\delta_2)$.
   - For any pair $(\tau \circ \nu, \bar{\nu} \circ \bar{\tau}) \in \rho_c(\delta_1\,;\,\delta_2)$ such that $(\tau, \bar{\tau}) \in \rho_c(\delta_1)$, $(\nu, \bar{\nu}) \in \rho_c(\delta_2)$, and $\neg E(\tau)$, then we want to prove that if $closed(\tau \circ \nu)$ and $closed(\bar{\nu} \circ \bar{\tau})$ then $\Delta_X(\tau \circ \nu) = \nabla_X(\bar{\nu} \circ \bar{\tau})$.
     As we consider closed traces we can conclude that also $closed(\tau)$ and $closed(\nu)$ with $last(\tau) = first(\nu)$ and the same holds for the compensation. Thus we can apply the induction hypothesis getting $\Delta_X(\tau) = \nabla_X(\bar{\tau})$ and $\Delta_X(\nu) = \nabla_X(\bar{\nu})$. We build the union of these two sets, *i.e.*, $\Delta_X(\tau)\oplus\Delta_X(\nu) = \nabla_X(\bar{\nu})\oplus \nabla_X(\bar{\tau})$. As $last(\tau) = first(\nu)$ and $last(\bar{\nu}) = first(\bar{\tau})$ we can conclude with Lemma A that $first(\tau)\backslash_X last(\nu) = last(\bar{\tau})\backslash_X first(\bar{\nu})$ which is equivalent to $\Delta_X(\tau \circ \nu) = \nabla_X(\bar{\nu} \circ \bar{\tau})$.
   - For any $(\tau, \bar{\tau}) \in \rho_c(\delta_1\,;\,\delta_2)$ such that $(\tau, \bar{\tau}) \in \rho(\delta_1)$ and $E(\tau)$, then the result follows immediately from the induction hypotheses on δ_1.

4. $\delta = \delta_1 \parallel \delta_2$. With δ_1, δ_2 serializable. For any $(\tau, \overline{\tau}) \in \rho_c(\delta_1 \parallel \delta_2)$ with $(\nu, \overline{\nu}) \in \rho_c(\delta_1)$, $(\mu, \overline{\mu}) \in \rho_c(\delta_2)$ $\tau \in \nu \parallel \mu$, $\overline{\tau} \in \overline{\nu} \parallel \overline{\mu}$, we need to show that if $closed(\tau)$ and $closed(\overline{\tau})$ then $\Delta_X(\tau) = \nabla_X(\overline{\tau})$.

Note that in general neither $closed(\nu)$ and $closed(\overline{\nu})$ nor $closed(\mu)$ and $closed(\overline{\nu})$ holds, because the interleaving is defined independently of this.

According to serializability there exist traces $(\nu', \overline{\nu}') \in \rho_c(\delta_1)$ and $(\mu', \overline{\mu}') \in \rho_c(\delta_2)$ with several different possibilities for a sequential representation (though at least one holds). Without loss of generality we assume that $\tau \bowtie (\nu'\mu')$ and $\overline{\tau} \bowtie (\overline{\nu}'\,\overline{\mu}')$. (The other representations can be treated similarly.)

From $closed(\nu'\,\mu')$ we know that $closed(\nu')$, $closed(\mu')$ and $last(\nu') = first(\mu')$. The same holds for $closed(\overline{\nu}'\,\overline{\mu}')$. Thus we can apply the induction hypothesis. We obtain $\Delta_X(\nu') = \nabla_X(\overline{\nu}')$ and $\Delta_X(\mu') = \nabla_X(\overline{\mu}')$. As for the sequential case we build the union of the two sets $\Delta_X(\nu') \oplus \Delta_X(\mu') = \nabla_X(\overline{\mu}') \oplus \nabla_X(\overline{\nu}')$. From the equivalences and Lemma A we obtain $first(\nu')\backslash_X last(\mu') = last(\overline{\mu}')\backslash_X first(\overline{\nu}')$ which is equivalent to $\Delta_X(\nu'\,\mu') = \nabla_X(\overline{\nu}'\,\overline{\mu}')$. From the equivalences for serializability we can conclude $\Delta_X(\tau) = \nabla_X(\overline{\tau})$.

5. $\delta = \delta_1^*$ (by induction on the depth of recursion).

■

Coordinating Parallel Mobile Ambients to Solve SAT Problem in Polynomial Number of Steps

Bogdan Aman and Gabriel Ciobanu

Romanian Academy, Institute of Computer Science, Iaşi, Romania
"A.I.Cuza" University, Blvd. Carol I no.11, 700506 Iaşi, Romania
gabriel@info.uaic.ro, bogdan.aman@gmail.com

Abstract. In this paper we present a version of mobile ambients, called parMA, having a weak form of replication and a parallel semantics. We investigate how parMA can solve intractable problems in a polynomial number of computational steps. We use parMA to give a semiuniform solution to a well-known strong NP-complete problem, namely to the Boolean satisfiability problem (SAT).

1   Introduction

Ambient calculus is a formalism for describing distributed and mobile computing [11]. In contrast with the π-calculus [19] where mobility is expressed by communication, the ambient calculus uses an explicit notion of *movement* given by moving actions (*in* and *out*) together with an "opening" action and (local) communication. An ambient is a named location, and it represents the unit of movement. The authors of [11] introduce the mobile ambients as "a paradigm of mobility where computational ambients are hierarchically structured, where agents are confined to ambients and where ambients move under the control of agents". Their initial goal was "to make mobile computation scale-up to widely distributed, intermittently connected and well administered computational environments". The resulting ambient model is elegant and powerful, well suited for expressing issues of mobile computations as working environment, allowing access to information or resources [2,16]. Many variants have been proposed; among them, we mention mobile safe ambients [17], push and pull ambient calculus [16] and boxed ambients [7]. Despite the fact that the initial motivation of mobile ambients assumes a high degree of parallelism in their evolution, the usual semantics of the proposed variants is the interleaving semantics.

Some results show that mobile ambients have the computational power of Turing machines by encoding into ambient calculus (or fragments of it) some formalisms known to be Turing complete: asynchronous π-calculus [11,12], counter machines [9] and Turing machines [11,18]. A link between mobile ambients and π-calculus is established in [13], where it is proven that pure mobile ambients can be embedded into a fragment of the π-calculus, namely in the localized sum-free synchronous monadic π-calculus with matching and mismatching. Other authors relate ambients to security issues and to system biology. Some simulators were

M. Sirjani (Ed.): COORDINATION 2012, LNCS 7274, pp. 122–136, 2012.

also developed [14] in which the evolution of mobile ambients can be observed easily (see http://www-sop.inria.fr/mimosa/ambicobjs/).

Many formal machine models (e.g., Turing machines) have an infinite number of memory locations. Mobile ambients are computing devices of finite size having a finite description with a fixed amount of initial resources (ambients and processes), that can evolve to a possibly infinite family of mobile ambients obtained by replication in order to solve a (decision) problem. A decision problem X is a pair (I_X, θ_X) such that I_X is a language over a finite alphabet (whose elements are called instances) and θ_X is a total boolean function (that is, a predicate) over I_X. Its solvability is defined through the recognition of the language associated with it. Let M be a Turing machine with the working alphabet Γ, L a language over Γ, and the result of any halting computation is *yes* or *no*. If M is a deterministic device, it recognizes or decides L whenever, for any string u over Γ, if $u \in L$, then M accepts u (the result on input u is *yes*), or M rejects u (the result on input u is *no*). If M is a non-deterministic device, it recognizes or decides L whenever, if for any string u over Γ, $u \in L$, and only if there exists a computation of M with input u such that the answer is *yes*.

According to [15], the NP-complete problems are divided into weak (e.g., Knapsack) and strong (e.g., SAT) depending on the size of the input. We show how a parallel version of mobile ambients with a weak form of replication can solve NP-complete problems in a polynomial number of steps. We provide a semiuniform solution to the best known strong NP-complete problem (SAT) in a polynomial number of steps [22]. To give such a solution, we treat mobile ambients as "deciding devices" that respect the following conditions: (1) all computations halt, (2) two special names *yes* and *no* are used, and (3) in a halting configuration a channel *ans* is ready to output one of the names *yes* and *no*; the computation is *accepting* if *yes* is present in the halting configuration, and *rejecting* if *no* is present in the halting configuration on channel *ans*. Mobile ambients respect these conditions if we impose some constraints:

- We use a true concurrent semantics allowing processes to run in parallel. The key rule is
  $$P \to P' \text{ and } Q \to Q' \text{ implies } P \mid Q \to P' \mid Q'.$$
  This parallel semantics is natural if we recall that in [11] a process is described as "running even when the surrounding ambient is moving", aspect which the interleaving semantics does not reflect properly. Other reasons to consider a parallel semantics are presented in [14] where the authors present a distributed implementation of mobile ambients.
- A restricted form of replication is used by considering a weaker *duplication* operator which only doubles a process; this means that a reduction rule $!P \to P \mid P$ is used instead of the congruence rule $!P \equiv P \mid !P$ or instead of the reduction rule $!P \to P \mid !P$. This duplication rule is also used by R. Milner in [20]. It helps in controlling all the computations to halt (and so fulfilling condition 1. of deciding devices).
- We use a special symbol ⓢ that helps in delimiting the computational steps. ⓢ is a purely technical device that is used in the subsequent

formalization of the structural operational semantics of parMA; intuitively, ⑤P specifies a process P which is temporarily stalled and so cannot execute any action.

- We use two kinds of action rules: $\rightarrow$ and $\overset{\phi}{\Rightarrow}$. The former is an execution of a set of actions, and the latter is used to remove all occurrences of ⑤ (using a tree parsing algorithm) in order to start a new round of parallel actions.

The differences between parallel and interleaving semantics is underlined also in [5]: "The parallel construct is interpreted in terms of interleaving, as usual in many (timed) process algebras .... Alternatively one could adopt maximal parallelism, which means that at each moment every enabled process of the system is activated". In defining a parallel semantics, we follow the solution used also in [8] where such a semantic is defined in brane calculi [10], a process algebra related to BioAmbients [23].

The paper is organised as follow. Section 2 defines the syntax and semantics of parallel mobile ambients (parMA). In Section 3 we give some notions of complexity, and show how to solve SAT problem in a polynomial number of steps. Section 4 illustrates how mobile ambients compute effectively by considering a SAT instance with three clauses and three variables as an example. Conclusion and references end the paper.

2   Parallel Mobile Ambients

In this section we present a variant of mobile ambients having a parallel semantics. Initially, mobility in ambient calculus involved the authorization to enter or exit certain domains in order to access information; the access to information is controlled at many levels: local computer, local area network, regional area network, wide-area intranet and internet. We consider a framework given by mobile ambients hierarchically structured inside a well-defined environment, where ambients move under the control of agents running inside them.

2.1   Syntax

Table 1 describes the syntax of parMA.

Table 1. Parallel Mobile Ambients Syntax

c	channel name	P, Q	::=	processes
a, b, Env	ambient names		**0**	inactivity
x, y	variables		$M.P$	movement
M ::=	capabilities		$a[P]$	ambient
in a	can enter a		$P \mid Q$	composition
out a	can exit a		$c\langle a\rangle.P$	output action
open a	can open a		$c(x).P$	input action
			$!P$	duplication
			⑤P	stalled

The name Env represents the environment in which the mobile ambients reside, and can appear only once, at the top of the hierarchical structure. Process **0** is an inactive process (it does nothing). A movement $M.P$ is provided by the capability M, followed by the execution of process P. An ambient $a[P]$ represents a bounded place labelled by a in which a process P is executed. $P \mid Q$ is a parallel composition of processes P and Q. An output action $c\langle a \rangle.P$ releases a name a on channel c, and then behaves as process P. An input action $c(x).P$ captures a name from channel c, and binds it to a variable x within the scope of process P. A weak form of replication, namely the duplication of a process P (producing two parallel copies of process P) is denoted by $!P$. The process $\circledS P$ is used to state that process P is temporarily "stalled".

2.2 Operational Semantics

The first component of the operational semantics of parMA is the *structural congruence* $\equiv$. It is the smallest congruence such that the equalities from Table 2 hold. Its role is to rearrange a process in order to apply the action rules given in Table 3. The axioms from Table 2 describe the commutativity and associativity of the parallel composition.

Table 2. Structural Congruence

$P \equiv P$	$P \mid Q \equiv Q \mid P$
$(P \mid Q) \mid R \equiv P \mid (Q \mid R)$	$P \mid 0 \equiv P$
$!0 \equiv 0$	

The set $fn(P)$ of free names of a process P is defined as:

$$fn(P)=\begin{cases} \emptyset & \text{if } P = 0 \\ fn(R) \cup \{a\} & \text{if } P = in\ a.R \text{ or } P = out\ a.R \\ & \text{or } P = open\ a.R \text{ or } P = a[R] \\ fn(R) \cup \{a,c\} & \text{if } P = c\langle a \rangle.R \\ fn(R) \cup \{c\} & \text{if } P = c(x).R \\ fn(R) \cup fn(Q) & \text{if } P = R \mid Q \\ fn(R) & \text{if } P = !R \end{cases}$$

Table 3 introduces two kinds of action rules: $P \to P'$ and $P \overset{\phi}{\Rightarrow} P'$. The former is an execution of a set of actions, and the latter is used to remove all occurrences of $\circledS$ in order to start a new round of parallel actions. The first five rules of Table 3 are one-step reductions for *in, out, open, communication* and *duplication*. In rule **(Com)**, by $P'\{a/x\}$ we denote the substitution by a of each free occurrence of variable x in process P'. The next three rules propagate reductions across ambient nesting and parallel composition. In rule **(Par2)**, by $R \nrightarrow$ is denoted a process R that cannot evolve. Rule **(Struct)** allows the use of structural congruence during reduction. When no rule can be applied in Env, rule **(Step)** is used to delete all occurrences of $\circledS$ in order to start a new round of transitions. It can be noticed that in rules **(Par2)** and **(Step)** we use negative premises: an activity is performed based on the absence of actions. This is due to the fact that sequencing the evolution can only be defined using negative premises, as done for sequencing processes [4,21].

Table 3. Reduction Rules

(In)	$\dfrac{a \neq Env \quad b \neq Env}{a[in\ b.\ P\ |\ Q]\ |\ b[R] \rightarrow b[a[\text{\textcircled{S}}P\ |\ Q]\ |\ R]}$
(Out)	$\dfrac{a \neq Env \quad b \neq Env}{a[b[out\ a.\ P\ |\ Q]\ |\ R] \rightarrow b[\text{\textcircled{S}}P\ |\ Q]\ |\ a[R]}$
(Open)	$\dfrac{a \neq Env}{open\ a.\ P\ |\ a[Q] \rightarrow \text{\textcircled{S}}P\ |\ Q}$
(Com)	$c\langle a \rangle.\ P\ |\ c(x).\ P' \rightarrow \text{\textcircled{S}}P\ |\ \text{\textcircled{S}}P'\{a/x\}$
(Dupl)	$!P \rightarrow \text{\textcircled{S}}P\ |\ \text{\textcircled{S}}P$
(Amb)	$\dfrac{P \rightarrow Q}{a[P] \rightarrow a[Q]}$
(Par1)	$\dfrac{P \rightarrow P' \quad Q \rightarrow Q'}{P\ |\ Q \rightarrow P'\ |\ Q'}$
(Par2)	$\dfrac{P \rightarrow Q \quad R \nrightarrow}{P\ |\ R \rightarrow Q\ |\ R}$
(Struct)	$\dfrac{P' \equiv P,\ P \rightarrow Q,\quad Q \equiv Q'}{P' \rightarrow Q'}$
(Step)	$\dfrac{Env[P] \nrightarrow}{P \overset{\phi}{\Rightarrow} \phi(P)}$

The rules of Table 3 define execution of processes. A complete computational step in mobile ambients is captured by a derivation of the form

$$Env[P] \rightarrow \overset{\phi}{\Rightarrow} Env[P'].$$

This means that a derivation is a compressed representation of a sequence of individual actions followed by a reinitialization step (removing of all $\text{\textcircled{S}}$ symbols).

2.3   Example

To illustrate the basic components of parMA, we use an example in which several students wish to move from the campus to the university and back, having the possibility to use either a tram or a bus. The scenario involves eight ambients and four processes.

$$Env[campus[student[P_1\ |\ P_4]\ |\ student[P_1\ |\ P_4]$$
$$|\ tram[P_2\ |\ P_4]\ |\ bus[P_3\ |\ P_4]]\ |\ univ[student[P_1\ |\ P_4]]]$$

The role of the ambients is suggested by their names. The processes are:

- $P_1 = Q_1\ |\ Q_2$
  $Q_1 = in\ tram.c(x).c(x).c(x).out\ tram.Q_1$
  $Q_2 = in\ bus.c(x).c(x).c(x).c(x).out\ bus.Q_2$

- $P_2 = c(x).out\ campus.c(x).in\ univ.P_2'$
  $P_2' = c(x).out\ univ.c(x).in\ campus.P_2$
- $P_3 = c(x).out\ campus.c(x).c(x).in\ univ.P_3'$
  $P_3' = c(x).out\ univ.c(x).c(x).in\ campus.P_3$
- $P_4 = c\langle a \rangle.P_4$

The communication on channel c, that takes place inside ambients, is used to model the fact that the *tram, bus* and *students* perform the following actions:

- the first $c(x)$ from P_2, P_2', P_3 and P_3' represents the fact that the *bus* and *tram*, once inside the *campus* or *univ*, are willing to wait for *students* that intend to travel between *campus* and *univ*.
- the others $c(x)$ from P_2, P_2', P_3 and P_3' are used to model the fact that the movement of the *tram* and *bus* between *campus* and *univ* takes a number of steps (equal with the number of input actions on channel c).
- all $c(x)$ from Q_1 and Q_2 are used to prevent the *students* from getting out of the *tram* or *bus* before reaching the desired location.

It can be noticed that both *students* from *campus* can enter either the *bus* or the *tram*. Suppose both choose the *tram*. Then the mobile ambient
$$Env[campus[student[P_1 \mid P_4] \mid student[P_1 \mid P_4]$$
$$\mid tram[P_2 \mid P_4] \mid bus[P_3 \mid P_4]] \mid univ[student[P_1 \mid P_4]]]$$
evolves to
$$Env[campus[tram[\text{⑤}out\ campus.c(x).in\ univ.P_2' \mid \text{⑤}P_4$$
$$\mid student[\text{⑤}c(x).c(x).c(x).out\ tram.Q_1 \mid Q_2 \mid \text{⑤}P_4]$$
$$\mid student[\text{⑤}c(x).c(x).c(x).out\ tram.Q_1 \mid Q_2 \mid \text{⑤}P_4]]$$
$$\mid bus[\text{⑤}out\ campus.c(x).c(x).in\ univ.P_3' \mid \text{⑤}P_4]] \mid univ[student[P_1]]]$$
The *tram* and the *bus* are still inside *campus* since they communicated on channel c in order to permit the willing *students* to get inside them. At this moment it can be noticed that only rule **(Step)** can be applied in order to eliminate the symbols ⑤, obtaining the mobile membrane
$$Env[campus[tram[out\ campus.c(x).in\ univ.P_2' \mid P_4$$
$$\mid student[c(x).c(x).c(x).out\ tram.Q_1 \mid Q_2 \mid P_4]$$
$$\mid student[c(x).c(x).c(x).out\ tram.Q_1 \mid Q_2 \mid P_4]]$$
$$\mid bus[out\ campus.c(x).c(x).in\ univ.P_3' \mid P_4]] \mid univ[student[P_1]]]$$
After three steps, the *tram* is inside *univ* where it waits for the students to exit/enter it, while the *bus* is still between the two *campus* and *univ*, being ready to enter *univ* in the next step. Thus the next mobile ambient is obtained
$$Env[campus[\ ] \mid bus[in\ univ.P_3' \mid P_4] \mid univ[tram[P_2' \mid P_4$$
$$\mid student[out\ tram.Q_1 \mid Q_2 \mid P_4]$$
$$\mid student[out\ tram.Q_1 \mid Q_2 \mid P_4]] \mid student[P_1]]]$$
In the next step the two *students* from the *tram* get out inside *univ*, while the *student* that was waiting enters the *tram* in order to reach *campus*. The obtained mobile ambients is
$$Env[campus[\ ] \mid univ[bus[P_3' \mid P_4] \mid tram[out\ univ.c(x).in\ campus.P_2 \mid P_4$$
$$\mid student[c(x).c(x).c(x).out\ tram.Q_1 \mid Q_2 \mid P_4]]$$
$$\mid student[P_1] \mid student[P_1]]]$$

The mobile ambient continues to change, but we stop here since we have illustrated the expressive power of the proposed formalism.

3 Solving NP-Complete Problems in Polynomial Steps

As stated in the introduction, we use mobile ambients as deciding devices, in which all computation starting from the initial ambient agree on the result. A family **MA**, a collection of ambients, solves a decision problem if for each instance of the problem there is a member of the family able to decide on the instance. In order to define the notions of (semi)uniformity, we denote:

- for a suitable alphabet O, each instance of the decision problem is encoded as a string v over O;
- $V = \{v_1, \ldots\}$ - the language of encoded instances of the given problem;
- $\mathbf{MA}(v)$ - the member of **MA** which solves the instance v;
- $\mathbf{MA}_n$ - the member of **MA** which solves all instances of length n.

Definition 1. *The family* **MA**

(i) *decides V if for any string $v \in O^*$, the mobile ambient $\mathbf{MA}(v)$ (or $\mathbf{MA}_n$ for all instances v, $|v| = n$) generates an yes answer whenever $v \in V$ and a no answer otherwise;*

(ii) *is* sound *with respect to V when, for any string $v \in O^*$, if there exists an accepting computation of $\mathbf{MA}(v)$ ($\mathbf{MA}_n$), then $v \in V$;*

(iii) *is* complete *with respect to V when, for any string $v \in O^*$, if $v \in V$, then every computation of $\mathbf{MA}(v)$ ($\mathbf{MA}_n$) is accepting.*

Inspired by the uniformity conditions applied to families of Boolean circuits [6], we imposed similar ones on families of processes. By imposing certain resource restrictions (on number of steps and space) to the function that constructs each member of the family **MA**, it can be ensured that the set of problems decided by the family does not increase. The function is called an

- *uniformity condition* if an instance size is mapped to a mobile ambient that decides all instances of that length;
- *semiuniformity condition* if a single instance is mapped to a mobile ambient that decides that instance.

Definition 2. *If we consider a set of problem instances $V = \{v_1, v_2, \ldots\}$, two classes of functions E, F and a total function $t : \mathbb{N} \to \mathbb{N}$, such that:*

1. *there exist a F-uniform family of mobile ambients $\mathbf{MA} = \{\mathbf{MA}_1, \ldots\}$; this means that there exist a function $f \in F$, $f : \{1\}^* \to \mathbf{MA}$ such that $f(1^n) = \mathbf{MA}_n$, namely all instances v_k of length n are solved by $\mathbf{MA}_n$, where $\mathbf{MA}_n$ can be constructed by a function $f \in F$;*

2. *there exists an encoding function* $e \in E$ *such that* $e(v)$ *is the input process of* $\mathbf{MA}_n$, *for* $|v| = n$;
3. $\mathbf{MA}$ *is t-efficient:* $\mathbf{MA}_n$ *halts in* $t(n)$ *steps (e.g.,* $\mathbf{MA}$ *is polynomial efficient if* $t(n)$ *is polynomial in* n *for all* n*);*
4. $\mathbf{MA}$ *is sound and complete with respect to* V,

then we say that the class of problems V *is solved by an* (E, F)-*uniform family of mobile ambients* $\mathbf{MA}$, *and denote the family by* (E,F)-$\mathbf{MA}(t)$. *The set of languages decided by a uniform family of mobile ambients in a polynomial number of steps is defined as* (E,F)-$\mathbf{PMA} = \bigcup_{k \in \mathbb{N}} (E,F)$-$\mathbf{MA}(n^k)$.

Semiuniformity is a generalization of uniformity, namely

Definition 3. *If we consider a set of problem instances* $V = \{v_1, v_2, \ldots\}$, *a class of functions* H *and a total function* $t : \mathbb{N} \to \mathbb{N}$, *such that:*

1. *there exist a* H-*semiuniform family of mobile ambients* $\mathbf{MA} = \{\mathbf{MA}_{v_1}, \mathbf{MA}_{v_2}, \ldots\}$; *namely, there exist a function* $h \in H$, $h : V \to \mathbf{MA}$ *such that* $h(v_i) = \mathbf{MA}_{v_i}$;
2. $\mathbf{MA}$ *is t-efficient:* $\mathbf{MA}_n$ *halts in* $t(|v_n|)$ *steps;*
3. $\mathbf{MA}$ *is sound and complete with respect to* V,

then we say that the class of problems V *is solved by an* (H)-*semiuniform family of mobile ambients* $\mathbf{MA}$, *and denote the family by* (H)-$\mathbf{MA}(t)$. *The set of languages decided by a semiuniform family of mobile ambients in a polynomial number of steps is defined as* (H)-$\mathbf{PMA} = \bigcup_{k \in \mathbb{N}} (H)$-$\mathbf{MA}(n^k)$.

3.1 Boolean Satisfiability Problem

The SAT problem checks the satisfiability of a propositional logic formula in conjunctive normal form (CNF). Let $\{x_1, x_2, \ldots, x_n\}$ be a set of Boolean variables. A formula in CNF is of the form
$$\varphi = C_1 \wedge C_2 \wedge \cdots \wedge C_m$$
where each $C_i, 1 \le i \le m$ is a disjunction of the form
$$C_i = y_1 \vee y_2 \vee \cdots \vee y_r \ (r \le n),$$
where each y_j is either a variable x_k or its negation $\neg x_k$. In this section we show how, starting from a formula φ, to construct a process P that provides a semiuniform solution to the SAT problem by using mobile ambients with parallel semantics and duplication (for an instance of SAT we construct a mobile ambient which decides it). We start with the process
$$P = P_1 \mid Q_1$$
in which P_1 is used to provide the answer to the problem when placed in parallel with Q_1, a process that generates all possible assignments over the set $\{x_1, x_2, \ldots, x_n\}$ of Boolean variables. In what follows we describe how each of these two processes are constructed starting from the φ formula.

– process Q_1 is defined recursively using the processes Q_i $(1 \le i < n)$ and Q_n. For each variable x_i from the set $\{x_1, x_2, \ldots, x_n\}$ of Boolean variables, we construct a process Q_i defined as follows:

$$Q_i = x_i \langle t_i \rangle . x \langle z \rangle . x \langle z \rangle \mid x_i \langle f_i \rangle . x \langle z \rangle . x \langle z \rangle \mid$$
$$\mid !x_i(y_i).(x(y).x(y).open\ k_i \mid k_i[Q_{i+1}]),\ for\ 1 \le i < n$$
$$Q_n = x_n \langle t_n \rangle \mid x_n \langle f_n \rangle \mid !x_n(y_n).A[x_1 \langle y_1 \rangle \mid \ldots \mid x_n \langle y_n \rangle$$
$$\mid y_1 \langle a \rangle \mid \ldots \mid y_1 \langle a \rangle \mid \ldots \mid y_n \langle a \rangle \mid \ldots \mid y_n \langle a \rangle \mid Q].$$

where:

- process Q contains terms of the form $t_k(b).in\ C_j$ (if x_k appears in C_j) or $f_k(b).in\ C_j$ (if $\neg x_k$ appears in C_j). For example if we consider a 3CNF satisfiability problem with $\varphi = C_1 \wedge C_2 \wedge C_3$ and $X = \{x_1, x_2, x_3\}$, $C_1 = x_1 \vee \neg x_3$, $C_2 = \neg x_1 \vee \neg x_2$ and $C_3 = x_2$ we have
  $$Q = t_1(b).in\ C_1 \mid f_3(b).in\ C_1 \mid f_1(b).in\ C_2 \mid f_2(b).in\ C_2 \mid t_2(b).in\ C_3$$
- each ambient A will contain a different assignment over the set $\{x_1, x_2, \ldots, x_n\}$ of Boolean variables; after Q_n is executed, there will be 2^n ambients A, obtained by using the duplication operator ! that proceeds the processes that generate an A ambient.
- $y_j \langle a \rangle \mid \ldots \mid y_j \langle a \rangle$ stands for m parallel processes $y_j \langle a \rangle$, one for each disjunction, and, after all y_j are instantiated, are used to communicate with the processes from Q.
- $x \langle z \rangle . x \langle z \rangle$ are used to introduce a delay that prevents that an ambient k_i containing a Q_{i+1} is not opened to soon and cause unwanted evolutions.
– process P_1 has the form:
$$P_1 = C_1[\ldots [C_m[J[x(y) \ldots x(y) \mid x \langle z \rangle \ldots x \langle z \rangle . K[out\ J]]$$
$$\mid L[in\ A.ans \langle yes \rangle \mid in\ K.ans \langle no \rangle]]]]$$

where:

- to each disjunction C_i, $1 \le i \le m$ we associate an ambient C_i;
- the ambients C_i, $1 \le i \le m$ are placed one inside the other, forming an ambient structure of depth m. The order in which these ambients are placed is not important (thus the construction is not unique), but for simplicity we consider the ambient
  $$C_1[\ldots [C_m[\ldots]]\ldots]$$
- the previous ambient is used to check if there exists an assignments over the set $\{x_1, x_2, \ldots, x_n\}$ of Boolean variables that respects all these disjunctions. If such an assignment exists, this means that an ambient A containing this assignment, will eventually reach inside ambient C_m (an ambient A enters an ambient C_i if the assignment placed inside A respect the disjunction C_i)
- $x(y) \ldots x(y)$ stands for a $2n + m + 1$ sequence of capabilities $x(y)$, and together with $x \langle z \rangle \ldots x \langle z \rangle$ that stands for a $2n + m + 1$ sequence of capabilities $x \langle z \rangle$, introduces a delay equal with the number of steps needed by an ambient A to get inside ambient C_m, before the ambient K exits ambient J. It can be noticed that if an ambient A gets near the ambient L (inside ambient C_m), this ambient enters the ambient A, generates the yes answer and prevents K to generate the negative answer (the ambient K cannot interact with the ambient L inside the ambient A).

In what follows we explain how these two processes (P_1 and Q_1) once constructed from the φ formula, can generate an answer to the problem.

Starting from P_1 the evolution in the first $2n + 1$ steps is given by the rule $P_i \xrightarrow{\phi} P_{i+1}$, where P_{i+1} is obtained from P_i by performing a communication on channel x. In parallel, starting from the process Q_1, are generated 2^n ambients A that contain all possible assignments over the variables $\{x_1, \ldots, x_n\}$, namely each assignment is contained inside an ambient A.

Next we describe in detail the evolution of Q_1. We have two cases.

Case 1: For $1 \leq i \leq n - 1$, the evolution of each
$$Q_i = x_i\langle t_i\rangle.x\langle z\rangle.x\langle z\rangle \mid x_i\langle f_i\rangle.x\langle z\rangle.x\langle z\rangle$$
$$\mid !x_i(y_i).(x(y).x(y).open\ k_i \mid k_i[Q_{i+1}])$$
from the 2^{i-1} processes Q_i running in parallel, starts with a duplication, because any other reduction is not possible. The process that duplicates is in fact the process containing the ambient labelled by k_i in which the process Q_{i+1} is placed. This is done because the variables $y_1, \ldots, y_{i-1}$, $i \geq 2$ are already instantiated in the process Q_{i+1}, and we want to create two new copies: one in which y_i is replaced by t_i, and one in which y_i is replaced by f_i, keeping also the already instantiated variables. We obtain the process:
$$Q_i^1 = \mathbf{x_i}\langle \mathbf{t_i}\rangle.x\langle z\rangle.x\langle z\rangle \mid \mathbf{x_i}\langle \mathbf{f_i}\rangle.x\langle z\rangle.x\langle z\rangle$$
$$\mid \mathbf{x_i(y_i)}.(x(y).x(y).open\ k_i \mid k_i[Q_{i+1}])$$
$$\mid \mathbf{x_i(y_i)}.(x(y).x(y).open\ k_i \mid k_i[Q_{i+1}])$$
At this moment Q_i^1 has two input actions on channel x_i, and two output actions on channel x_i that are ready to communicate the values of t_i and f_i. This means that two **(Comm)** rules are applied in parallel, leading to:
$$Q_i^2 = \mathbf{x}\langle \mathbf{z}\rangle.x\langle z\rangle \mid \mathbf{x}\langle \mathbf{z}\rangle.x\langle z\rangle$$
$$\mid \mathbf{x(y)}.x(y).open\ k_i \mid k_i[Q_{i+1}\{t_i/y_i\}]$$
$$\mid \mathbf{x(y)}.x(y).open\ k_i \mid k_i[Q_{i+1}\{f_i/y_i\}]$$
After the communications on channels x_i are performed, the communication of t_{i+1} and f_{i+1} inside Q_{i+1} on channels x_{i+1} takes place in two steps. This motivates a delay in opening the ambients k_i, such that the communication from all k_i running in parallel does not get mixed up on channels x_{i+1}, leading to some unwanted assignments. The obtained process is:
$$Q_i^3 = \mathbf{x}\langle \mathbf{z}\rangle \mid \mathbf{x}\langle \mathbf{z}\rangle \mid \mathbf{x(y)}.open\ k_i \mid k_i[Q_{i+1}^1\{t_i/y_i\}]$$
$$\mid \mathbf{x(y)}.open\ k_i \mid k_i[Q_{i+1}^1\{f_i/y_i\}]$$
The channels x_{i+1} are ready to communicate inside the processes Q_{i+1}, and so the capabilities $open\ k_i$ are released in the next step.
$$Q_i^4 = \mathbf{open\ k_i} \mid k_i[Q_{i+1}^2\{t_i/y_i\}] \mid \mathbf{open\ k_i} \mid k_i[Q_{i+1}^2\{f_i/y_i\}]$$
Once the communication inside ambients k_i on channels x_{i+1} has finished, these ambients are opened, thus obtaining

$$Q_i^5 = Q_{i+1}^3\{t_i/y_i\} \mid Q_{i+1}^3\{f_i/y_i\}$$

Since the process Q_i^5 does not contain any capabilities or replication operators, except the ones from Q_{i+1}^3, it means that each Q_i evolves for 5 steps, from which 3 steps are in parallel with the ones from Q_{i+1}.
Case 2: for $i = n$ the evolution of each

$$Q_n = x_n\langle t_n\rangle \mid x_n\langle f_n\rangle$$
$$\mid !x_n(y_n).A[x_1\langle y_1\rangle \mid \ldots x_n\langle y_n\rangle \mid y_1\langle a\rangle \mid \ldots y_1\langle a\rangle \mid \ldots y_n\langle a\rangle \mid \ldots \mid y_n\langle a\rangle \mid Q]$$

from the 2^{n-1} processes Q_n running in parallel, starts with a duplication rule, obtaining

$$Q_n^1 = \mathbf{x_n}\langle \mathbf{t_n}\rangle \mid \mathbf{x_n}\langle \mathbf{f_n}\rangle$$
$$\mid \mathbf{x_n}(\mathbf{y_n}).A[x_1\langle y_1\rangle \mid \ldots x_n\langle y_n\rangle \mid y_1\langle a\rangle \mid \ldots y_1\langle a\rangle \mid \ldots y_n\langle a\rangle \mid \ldots \mid y_n\langle a\rangle \mid Q]$$
$$\mid \mathbf{x_n}(\mathbf{y_n}).A[x_1\langle y_1\rangle \mid \ldots x_n\langle y_n\rangle \mid y_1\langle a\rangle \mid \ldots y_1\langle a\rangle \mid \ldots y_n\langle a\rangle \mid \ldots \mid y_n\langle a\rangle \mid Q]$$

and after communications of t_n or f_n on channels x_n:

$$Q_n^2 = A[x_1\langle y_1\rangle \mid \ldots x_n\langle y_n\rangle \mid y_1\langle a\rangle \mid \ldots y_1\langle a\rangle \mid \ldots y_n\langle a\rangle \mid \ldots \mid y_n\langle a\rangle \mid Q]\{t_n/y_n\}$$
$$\mid A[x_1\langle y_1\rangle \mid \ldots x_n\langle y_n\rangle \mid y_1\langle a\rangle \mid \ldots y_1\langle a\rangle \mid \ldots y_n\langle a\rangle \mid \ldots \mid y_n\langle a\rangle \mid Q]\{f_n/y_n\}$$

Since there are only ambients labelled by A and no *open* capabilities, the process Q_n^2 cannot evolve any more. However, in order to cope with the fact that $Q_i^5 = Q_{i+1}^3\{t_i/y_i\} \mid Q_{i+1}^3\{f_i/y_i\}$, for $1 \le i \le n - 1$, we consider Q_n^2 to be equal with Q_n^3.

Starting from $P_1 \mid Q_1$, after $2n + 1$ steps we obtain $P_{2n+2} \mid Q''$, where:
$$Q'' = A[x_1\langle t_1\rangle \mid \ldots \mid x_n\langle t_n\rangle \mid t_1\langle a\rangle \mid \ldots \mid t_1\langle a\rangle \mid \ldots \mid t_n\langle a\rangle \mid \ldots \mid t_n\langle a\rangle \mid Q]$$
$$\mid \ldots \mid A[x_1\langle f_1\rangle \mid \ldots \mid x_n\langle f_n\rangle \mid f_1\langle a\rangle \mid \ldots \mid f_1\langle a\rangle \mid \ldots \mid f_n\langle a\rangle \mid \ldots \mid f_n\langle a\rangle \mid Q]$$

To illustrate how such a process Q'' looks, we give a small example in which $n = m = 2$, we have $2^2 = 4$ ambients generated by Q_1, and process Q'' is:

$$Q'' = A[x_1\langle t_1\rangle \mid x_2\langle t_2\rangle \mid t_1\langle a\rangle \mid t_1\langle a\rangle \mid t_2\langle a\rangle \mid t_2\langle a\rangle \mid Q]$$
$$\mid A[x_1\langle t_1\rangle \mid x_2\langle f_2\rangle \mid t_1\langle a\rangle \mid t_1\langle a\rangle \mid f_2\langle a\rangle \mid f_2\langle a\rangle \mid Q]$$
$$\mid A[x_1\langle f_1\rangle \mid x_2\langle t_2\rangle \mid f_1\langle a\rangle \mid f_1\langle a\rangle \mid t_2\langle a\rangle \mid t_2\langle a\rangle \mid Q]$$
$$\mid A[x_1\langle f_1\rangle \mid x_2\langle f_2\rangle \mid f_1\langle a\rangle \mid f_1\langle a\rangle \mid f_2\langle a\rangle \mid f_2\langle a\rangle \mid Q]$$

As it can be noticed, the four ambients A contain all the Boolean assignments over the variables $\{x_1, x_2\}$, namely $\{t_1, t_2\}$, $\{t_1, f_2\}$, $\{f_1, t_2\}$, $\{f_1, f_2\}$, and each possible assignment t_i and f_i is kept as an output value on channel x_i.

After obtaining all possible assignments, we need to check which one satisfies all the clauses C_j. To do this, we use the processes Q that contain either terms of the form $t_k(b).in\ C_j$ meaning that x_k appears in C_j, or of the form $f_k(b).in\ C_j$ meaning that $\neg x_k$ appears in C_j. To be able to use the capability $in\ C_j$, there should be a $t_k\langle a\rangle$, respectively a $f_k\langle a\rangle$ inside the ambient A, both resulting from the instantiation of y_k. All ambients that satisfy the clause C_j enter in parallel the ambient C_j. If there exist at least one ambient A that contains $in\ C_1 \mid \ldots \mid in\ C_m$, it means that this ambient can go inside ambient C_m, and contains a solution to the SAT problem; in this case the ambient L enters the ambient A placed inside membrane C_m, releasing the *yes* answer on channel ans (1 step). Otherwise, ambient K exits ambient J, and so ambient L enters K; thus the *no* answer is send on channel ans (2 steps).

We have a deterministic evolution of the mobile ambients, and so no interference (redex overlapping) exists in our solution of SAT problem. This motivates the use of mobile ambients rather than safe mobile ambients [17].

3.2 Analysis

If n is the number of variables $(x_1, \ldots, x_n)$, and m is the number of clauses $(C_1, \ldots, C_m)$, then the number of ambients, capabilities and duplication operators in the initial process is given by the sum of:

- 3 ambients and $4n + 2m + 7$ capabilities in process P_1;
- 10 capabilities, 1 ambient and 1 replication operator in each Q_i, $1 \leq i < n$;
- $n + 3 + mn$ capabilities, 1 ambient and 1 replication operator in Q_n;
- maximum $4m$ capabilities in Q.

Thus, the total size of the initial process is $\mathcal{O}(mn)$. The maximum number of computational steps performed in an execution is equal with $2n+m+3$, a number determined by:

- $2n + 1$ steps to generate all the possible Boolean assignments over a set of variable $\{x_1, \ldots, x_n\}$;
- m steps required by a solution to move inside ambient C_m;
- either 1 step to generate a *yes* answer on channel ans, or 2 steps to generate a *no* answer on channel ans.

It is straightforward to show that:

- the construction of $P_1 \mid Q_1$ is semiuniform;
- sound and complete: $P_1 \mid Q_1$ says *yes* iff the given SAT instance is satisfiable;
- function H required for the above construction is in **P**.

Proposition 1. *Using* parMA, *NP-complete problems can be solved in a polynomial number of steps.*

4 An Example of How Mobile Ambients Solve 3CNF-SAT

To illustrate how mobility can "compute" and solve hard problems, we consider a 3CNF satisfiability problem with $\varphi = C_1 \wedge C_2 \wedge C_3$ and $X = \{x_1, x_2, x_3\}$, $C_1 = x_1 \vee \neg x_3$, $C_2 = \neg x_1 \vee \neg x_2$ and $C_3 = x_2$. In this case $n = 3$ and $m = 3$. We start with the mobile ambient:

$$P = P_1 \mid Q_1$$

where

$$P_1 = C_1[\ldots [C_3[J[x(y) \ldots x(y) \mid x\langle z\rangle \ldots x\langle z\rangle.K[out\ J]] \\ \mid L[in\ A.ans\langle yes\rangle \mid in\ K.ans\langle no\rangle]]]]$$

with Q_i $(1 \leq i < n)$ and Q_n defined as follows

$$Q_i = x_i\langle t_i\rangle.x\langle z\rangle.x\langle z\rangle \mid x_i\langle f_i\rangle.x\langle z\rangle.x\langle z\rangle \mid$$

$$|!x_i(y_i).(x(y).x(y).open\ k_i\ |\ k_i[Q_{i+1}]),\ for\ 1 \le i < 3$$
$$Q_3 = x_3\langle t_3\rangle\ |\ x_3\langle f_3\rangle\ |!x_3(y_3).A[x_1\langle y_1\rangle\ |\ x_2\langle y_2\rangle\ |\ x_3\langle y_3\rangle$$
$$|\ y_1\langle a\rangle\ |\ y_1\langle a\rangle\ |\ y_1\langle a\rangle\ |\ y_2\langle a\rangle\ |\ y_2\langle a\rangle\ |\ y_2\langle a\rangle\ |\ y_3\langle a\rangle\ |\ y_3\langle a\rangle\ |\ y_3\langle a\rangle$$
$$|\ t_1(b).in\ C_1\ |\ f_3(b).in\ C_1\ |\ f_1(b).in\ C_2\ |\ f_2(b).in\ C_2\ |\ t_2(b).in\ C_3]$$

The evolution of this term (by applying duplication and communication rules) leads in the first $2n + 1 = 2*3 + 1 = 7$ steps to the generation of all the possible truth assignments over a set of variables $\{x_1, x_2, x_3\}$. Since we have described in the previous section how Q_1 evolves to Q_1^5, here we just enumerate the first five obtained ambients. In what follows we bold the capabilities and ambients involved actively in an evolution step.

$$P_1\ |\ Q_1 \xrightarrow{\phi} \dots \xrightarrow{\phi} P_6\ |\ Q_1^5$$

We replace Q_1^5 with $Q_2^3\{t_1/y_1\}\ |\ Q_2^3\{f_1/y_1\}$ obtaining

$$P_6\ |\ Q_2^3\{t_1/y_1\}\ |\ Q_2^3\{f_1/y_1\}$$

and then we substitute Q_2^3 processes for obtaining

$$P_6\ |\ \mathbf{x}\langle\mathbf{z}\rangle\ |\ \mathbf{x}\langle\mathbf{z}\rangle\ |\ \mathbf{x}\langle\mathbf{z}\rangle\ |\ \mathbf{x}\langle\mathbf{z}\rangle$$
$$|\ \mathbf{x(y)}.open\ k_2\ |\ k_2[Q_3^1\{t_1/y_1, t_2/y_2\}]\ |\ \mathbf{x(y)}.open\ k_2\ |\ k_2[Q_3^1\{t_1/y_1, f_2/y_2\}])$$
$$|\ \mathbf{x(y)}.open\ k_2\ |\ k_2[Q_3^1\{f_1/y_1, t_2/y_2\}]\ |\ \mathbf{x(y)}.open\ k_2\ |\ k_2[Q_3^1\{f_1/y_1, f_2/y_2\}])$$

In the next step the communication on all channels x takes place in parallel, leading to all the possible assignments placed inside ambients A.

$$\xrightarrow{\phi} P_7\ |\ open\ k_2\ |\ k_2[Q_3^2\{t_1/y_1, t_2/y_2\}]\ |\ open\ k_2\ |\ k_2[Q_3^2\{t_1/y_1, f_2/y_2\}]$$
$$|\ open\ k_2\ |\ k_2[Q_3^2\{f_1/y_1, t_2/y_2\}]\ |\ open\ k_2\ |\ k_2[Q_3^2\{f_1/y_1, f_2/y_2\}]$$

We replace Q_3^2 processes in order to see how the assignments look.

$$P_7\ |\ \mathbf{open\ k_2}\ |\ \mathbf{k_2}[A\{t_1/y_1, t_2/y_2, t_3/y_3\}\ |\ A\{t_1/y_1, t_2/y_2, f_3/y_3\}]$$
$$|\ \mathbf{open\ k_2}\ |\ \mathbf{k_2}[A\{t_1/y_1, f_2/y_2, t_3/y_3\}\ |\ A\{t_1/y_1, f_2/y_2, f_3/y_3\}]$$
$$|\ \mathbf{open\ k_2}\ |\ \mathbf{k_2}[A\{f_1/y_1, t_2/y_2, t_3/y_3\}\ |\ A\{f_1/y_1, t_2/y_2, f_3/y_3\}]$$
$$|\ \mathbf{open\ k_2}\ |\ \mathbf{k_2}[A\{f_1/y_1, f_2/y_2, t_3/y_3\}\ |\ A\{f_1/y_1, f_2/y_2, f_3/y_3\}]$$

where $A = A[x_1\langle y_1\rangle\ |\ x_2\langle y_2\rangle\ |\ x_3\langle y_3\rangle$
$$|\ y_1\langle a\rangle\ |\ y_1\langle a\rangle\ |\ y_1\langle a\rangle\ |\ y_2\langle a\rangle\ |\ y_2\langle a\rangle\ |\ y_2\langle a\rangle\ |\ y_3\langle a\rangle\ |\ y_3\langle a\rangle\ |\ y_3\langle a\rangle$$
$$|\ t_1(b).in\ C_1\ |\ f_3(b).in\ C_1\ |\ f_1(b).in\ C_2\ |\ f_2(b).in\ C_2\ |\ t_2(b).in\ C_3].$$

From this point forward, the performed steps are:

- Since all the possible assignments are generated, we open in parallel all ambients k_2 such that all ambients A become siblings with the ambient C_1, ready to start the checking stage. Also all possible communications inside ambients A are performed, thus launching the $in\ C_j$ capabilities corresponding to the clauses C_j.
- In the next $m = 3$ steps, the solutions of φ should go inside ambient C_3. First, the solutions of C_1 go inside ambient C_1 in parallel.
- Next, from the solutions of C_1 are selected the solutions of C_2, namely the solutions are all moved inside ambient C_2 in parallel.
- Finally, the solutions of C_3 are selected among the solutions of C_1 and C_2, namely the solutions which move in parallel inside ambient C_3.

- Since we have an ambient A inside ambient C_3, an *yes* answer is released on channel *ans* in the next step. In parallel, ambient K comes out of ambient J, but since ambient L is not present, the *no* answer cannot be sent on channel *ans*.
- Alternatively, if after $2n + m + 1$ steps there is no ambient A inside ambient C_3, then ambient K exits ambient J, and so allowing the ambient L to enter ambient K and to release a *no* answer on channel *ans*.

5   Conclusion

There are a large number of process calculi used to model complex systems in which interactions and mobility are essential (e.g., [3]). Following this research line, we have previously extended mobile ambients with timers [2] and types [1] in order to study their ability of modelling complex systems in distributed networks. In this paper we use mobile ambients with a parallel semantic (parMA) in order to study their complexity aspects. Thus we provide a semiuniform solution of the SAT problem in a polynomial number of steps by using mobile ambients with a weak form of replication which work according to a parallel semantics.

As far as we know, this is a first attempt to use mobile ambients with parallelism (as they were introduced initially) to create an algorithm that solves an NP-complete problem in a polynomial number of steps. In this way, we show how the mobile ambients can be coordinated to solve problems. There are several topics that could be investigated as further work, including finding other hard problems and complexity classes that can be solved using mobile ambients or related formalisms (process calculi).

Acknowledgements. The work of Bogdan Aman and Gabriel Ciobanu was supported by a grant of the Romanian National Authority for Scientific Research, CNCS-UEFISCDI, project number PN-II-ID-PCE-2011-3-0919.

References

1. Aman, B., Ciobanu, G.: Mobile Ambients with Timers and Types. In: Jones, C.B., Liu, Z., Woodcock, J. (eds.) ICTAC 2007. LNCS, vol. 4711, pp. 50–63. Springer, Heidelberg (2007)
2. Aman, B., Ciobanu, G.: Timed Mobile Ambients for Network Protocols. In: Suzuki, K., Higashino, T., Yasumoto, K., El-Fakih, K. (eds.) FORTE 2008. LNCS, vol. 5048, pp. 234–250. Springer, Heidelberg (2008)
3. Aman, B., Ciobanu, G.: Mobility in Process Calculi and Natural Computation. Springer (2011)
4. Bloom, B., Istrail, S., Meyer, A.R.: Bisimulation Can't Be Traced: Preliminary Report. In: 15th ACM Symposium on Principles of Programming Languages, pp. 229–239 (1988)
5. Boer, F., Gabbrielli, M., Meo, M.: A Timed Linda Language and its Denotational Semantics. Fundamenta Informaticae 63 (2004)

6. Borodin, A.: On Relating Time and Space to Size and Depth. SIAM Journal of Computing 6, 733–744 (1977)
7. Bugliesi, M., Castagna, G., Crafa, S.: Access Control for Mobile Agents: the Calculus of Boxed Ambients. ACM Transactions on Programming and Systems 26, 57–124 (2004)
8. Busi, N.: On the Computational Power of the Mate/Bud/Drip Brane Calculus: Interleaving vs. Maximal Parallelism. In: Freund, R., Păun, G., Rozenberg, G., Salomaa, A. (eds.) WMC 2005. LNCS, vol. 3850, pp. 144–158. Springer, Heidelberg (2006)
9. Busi, N., Zavattaro, G.: On the Expressive Power of Movement and Restriction in Pure Mobile Ambients. Theoretical Computer Science 322, 477–515 (2004)
10. Cardelli, L.: Brane Calculi - Interactions of Biological Membranes. In: Danos, V., Schachter, V. (eds.) CMSB 2004. LNCS (LNBI), vol. 3082, pp. 257–278. Springer, Heidelberg (2005)
11. Cardelli, L., Gordon, A.: Mobile Ambients. Theoretical Computer Science 240, 177–213 (2000)
12. Charatonik, W., Gordon, A.D., Talbot, J.-M.: Finite-Control Mobile Ambients. In: Le Métayer, D. (ed.) ESOP 2002. LNCS, vol. 2305, pp. 295–313. Springer, Heidelberg (2002)
13. Ciobanu, G., Zakharov, V.A.: Encoding Mobile Ambients into the π-Calculus. In: Virbitskaite, I., Voronkov, A. (eds.) PSI 2006. LNCS, vol. 4378, pp. 148–165. Springer, Heidelberg (2007)
14. Fournet, C., Lévy, J.-J., Schmitt, A.: An Asynchronous, Distributed Implementation of Mobile Ambients. In: Watanabe, O., Hagiya, M., Ito, T., van Leeuwen, J., Mosses, P.D. (eds.) TCS 2000. LNCS, vol. 1872, pp. 348–364. Springer, Heidelberg (2000)
15. Garey, M., Johnson, D.: Computers and Intractability. A Guide to the Theory of NP-Completeness. Freeman (1979)
16. Teller, D., Zimmer, P., Hirschkoff, D.: Using Ambients to Control Resources. In: Brim, L., Jančar, P., Křetínský, M., Kučera, A. (eds.) CONCUR 2002. LNCS, vol. 2421, pp. 288–303. Springer, Heidelberg (2002)
17. Levi, F., Sangiorgi, D.: Mobile Safe Ambients. ACM Transactions on Programming and Systems 25, 1–69 (2003)
18. Maffeis, S., Phillips, I.: On the Computational Strength of Pure Ambient Calculi. Theoretical Computer Science 330, 501–551 (2005)
19. Milner, R.: Communicating and Mobile Systems: the π-Calculus. Cambridge University Press (1999)
20. Milner, R.: The Space and Motion of Communicating Agents. Cambridge University Press (2009)
21. Moller, F.: Axioms for Concurrency. PhD Thesis, Department of Computer Science, University of Edinburgh (1989)
22. Papadimitriou, C.H.: Computational Complexity. Addison-Wesley (1995)
23. Regev, A., Panina, E.M., Silverman, W., Cardelli, L., Shapiro, E.: BioAmbients: An Abstraction for Biological Compartments. Theoretical Computer Science 325, 141–167 (2004)

Recursive Advice for Coordination*

Michał Terepeta, Hanne Riis Nielson, and Flemming Nielson

Technical University of Denmark
{mtte,riis,nielson}@imm.dtu.dk

Abstract. *Aspect-oriented programming* is a programming paradigm that is often praised for the ability to create modular software and separate cross-cutting concerns. Recently aspects have been also considered in the context of coordination languages, offering similar advantages. However, introducing aspects makes analyzing such languages more difficult due to the fact that aspects can be recursive — *advice* from an aspect must itself be analyzed by aspects — as well as being simultaneously applicable in concurrent threads. Therefore the problem of reachability of various states of a system becomes much more challenging. This is important since ensuring that a system does not contain errors is often equivalent to proving that some states are not reachable.

In this paper we show how to solve these challenges by applying a successful technique from the area of software model checking, namely *communicating pushdown systems*. Even though primarily used for analysis of recursive programs, we are able to adapt them to fit this new context.

1   Introduction

Motivation. Aspect-oriented programming [1,2] is a successful programming paradigm that is used in many environments and supported by all major programming languages. Its biggest advantage is the ability to separate cross-cutting concerns and thus make it possible to create very modular software. The classical example is of course logging — in order to be useful it should be performed in many different and unrelated parts of the code. Aspects allow to separate the code for logging from the code implementing the program logic.

Usually an aspect consists of a pointcut and an advice. A pointcut is basically a pattern that specifies when some join point (e.g. location in a program, some action, etc.) matches the aspect. An advice consists of some additional code or actions that should be executed if the pointcut matches. Often an advice might specify actions that should be performed after, before or instead of the matched one. All of this allows one to easily separate the code for the actual functionality from the code for e.g. logging, which could be specified using aspects.

Aspects have also been used in the context of process calculi — [3] introduced a language called AspectK, which is an extension of the coordination

* The research presented in this paper has been supported by MT-LAB, a VKR Centre of Excellence for the Modelling of Information Technology.

M. Sirjani (Ed.): COORDINATION 2012, LNCS 7274, pp. 137–151, 2012.

language KLAIM with aspect-oriented features. However, the introduction of aspects makes the analysis of such languages much more challenging. When one allows the advice to contain before and/or after actions, the code can suddenly "grow" due to advice. Moreover the actions from the advice must itself be subject to other aspects as they have a recursive structure. Therefore it is possible that a process could grow arbitrarily large. In this paper we focus on solving these challenges.

Contributions. We define a process calculi allowing concurrent threads communicating via message-passing. The definition of aspects is quite similar to the one in [3] and allows both before and after actions. Our main contribution is the use of a technique from software model checking field, namely pushdown systems, which have been used for software model checking [4] and static analysis [5,6,7] of recursive programs. We show that they can be adapted to our context and give us the ability to model arbitrarily large processes as well as to summarize the actions they execute. Furthermore, we present how to go a step further and reason about concurrent systems with aspects. We focus on proving unreachability of certain states of such systems since the problem of reachability is often of highest importance — many desired properties of various systems (not only concurrent) can be reduced to the question of reachability of the error states.

Related work. In [8] static analysis techniques have been used to analyze AspectKE (and a programming language AspectKE*), which are based on AspectK. However, these languages do not allow the advice to contain before or after actions, which practically avoids the above mentioned challenges. In this paper we focus on techniques that allow lifting this restriction. In [9,10] the authors use communicating pushdown systems to analyze concurrent programs with recursive procedures and synchronization-based communication. This approach has been also applied to C programs in [11]. Our approach is based on this work, it does however, have some crucial differences. Clearly the context is quite different as we do not deal with procedural programming languages but process calculi. In particular the source of recursion are the aspects and not the procedures. Consequently we shall use the stack in a completely different way. In [9,10,11] the stack is used for storing locations of the programs, whereas we do not even have the concept of location and use the stack to represent the actual process itself (i.e. the action to be executed). In [12] pushdown systems are used to analyze concurrent software, but in a setting of shared memory concurrency. Moreover this approach is under-approximating with respect to control flow, since it performs the analysis under a context bound. That is, it limits the number of possible context switches that the threads can make.

Structure of the paper. The paper is organized as follows. First in Sect. 2 we introduce the language that is used for examples and analysis. Then in Sect. 3 we present the basic theory behind pushdown systems and our adaptation to the context of process calculi with aspects. Furthermore in Sect. 4 we illustrate our approach on an example. Finally we conclude in Sect. 5.

2   Language

Let us introduce the language that we will be working with. It allows multiple threads running concurrently and communication via synchronous message passing.

$$
\begin{array}{lll}
\textit{nets} & N ::= N_1 || N_2 \mid c :: P \mid c :: \mathbf{Rec\,X} . P \\
\textit{processes} & P ::= \sum_i a_i . Q_i \\
& Q ::= P \mid \mathsf{X} \\
\textit{actions} & a ::= \mathbf{receive}(\bar{p})@c \mid \mathbf{send}(\bar{t})@c \mid \\
& \quad\quad \mathbf{if}(e)\, a \mid \mathbf{break} \mid \mathbf{skip} \\
\textit{tests} & e ::= t_1 = t_2 \mid t_1 \neq t_2 \mid \mathbf{true} \\
\textit{terms} & t ::= c \mid x \\
\textit{patterns} & p ::= t \mid !x
\end{array}
$$

For readability we write constants with an uppercase first letter and variables with a lowercase one. One subtlety about **receive** is that the two actions: **receive**$(!x)$@N and **receive**(x)@N are quite different — the former will evaluate to itself when ready to execute and will accept any value from the process N and bind it to x. Whereas in the latter case x is an already bound variable, so assuming that it is bound to C the action will evaluate to **receive**(C)@N and thus only accept C from N. Finally the communication is performed in CSP style [13] where the **send** and **receive** actions specify the recipient and sender respectively.

As already mentioned, one of the main features of our language is the presence of aspects. They can be defined as follows.

$$
\begin{array}{lll}
\textit{aspects} & asp ::= A[cut;\ e] \triangleq adv \\
\textit{advice} & adv ::= as\ \mathbf{break} \mid as\ \mathbf{proceed}\ as \\
\textit{action sequence} & as ::= a\, .\, as \mid \epsilon \\
\textit{pointcut} & cut ::= c :: a
\end{array}
$$

Informally the semantics of the aspects says that before executing an action we need to check what aspects apply to it and then combine the advice from them. Checking if an aspect applies to an action amounts to pattern matching against the *cut* and evaluating the applicability condition e associated with the aspect. Note that in case of **receive** action with input, e.g. **receive**$(!x)$@N, the condition cannot refer to x — the aspect needs to evaluate before executing the action (it must be able to disallow it). But using x in a condition would require executing the action first, thus we do not allow using x in such situations. One of the important things to emphasize here is that we use the order in which aspects are defined and trap actions based on that order. We will use this fact in our analysis. This also means that changing the order can change the behavior of the system. Furthermore the advice from an aspect (i.e. the right-hand side) is also analyzed by all aspects except for the **proceed**, which corresponds to the original trapped action and should be only analyzed by the aspect next in the order. Therefore a single action can be trapped by many aspects.

Example 1. Consider the following process with an aspect (for simplicity we skip here the processes Q and Log and assume that sending anything to them will always succeed).

$$P :: \mathbf{send}(\mathsf{Test})@Q$$

$$A_1[P :: \mathbf{send}(a)@q; \ \mathbf{true}] \triangleq \mathbf{send}(a)@\mathsf{Log}.\mathbf{proceed}$$

The aspect will trap any **send** action of P. However, since the advice will also be analyzed by the aspect it will also trap the **send** action directed to Log. So this example actually demonstrates the possibility of non-termination and a process that can grow infinitely large. Clearly the aspect as defined above is not providing the desired behavior. The correct way to specify it is to restrict what actions should be trapped.

$$A_1[P :: \mathbf{send}(a)@q; \ q \neq \mathsf{Log}] \triangleq \mathbf{send}(a)@\mathsf{Log}.\mathbf{proceed}$$

With this small refinement the aspect will only trap the **send** actions that are not sent to the Log. Thus the system will successfully terminate.

We will now present some more involved example that will be used throughout the paper to demonstrate our approach. Imagine an ATM[1] session — it first receives some credentials from the user and checks the credentials against the information stored on the card. If everything matches it dispenses the cash and informs the bank to deduct the given amount from the account. The following definition models this behavior

$$ATM :: \mathbf{receive}(!credentials, !amount)@\mathsf{User}.$$
$$\mathbf{check}(credentials).$$
$$\mathbf{send}(amount)@\mathsf{User}.$$
$$\mathbf{send}(credentials, amount)@\mathsf{Bank}$$

where **check** is an internal action that does not involve any communication or synchronization and either executes successfully if the credentials are valid or otherwise terminates the session. This process seems reasonable but we can imagine that in order to increase the security of this solution one could add aspects that actually confirmed the credentials with the bank.

$$A_1[ATM :: \mathbf{check}(c); \ \mathbf{true}] \triangleq \mathbf{proceed}.\mathbf{send}(c)@\mathsf{Bank}.$$
$$\mathbf{receive}(!a)@\mathsf{Bank}$$

$$A_2[ATM :: \mathbf{receive}(!a)@\mathsf{Bank}; \ \mathbf{true}] \triangleq \mathbf{proceed}.$$
$$\mathbf{if}(a = \mathsf{Abort}) \ \mathbf{send}(\mathsf{ErrorMessage})@\mathsf{User}.$$
$$\mathbf{if}(a = \mathsf{Abort}) \ \mathbf{break}.$$

The above two aspects make the additional check of credentials with the bank (after checking locally) to improve the security. Obviously we want the ATM session to terminate (with an error message) when this check fails.

---

[1] Automated Teller Machine.

Apart from that we need to define the process modelling the Bank

$$\text{Bank} :: (\textbf{receive}(!credentials)@\text{ATM}.\textbf{send}(\text{Ok})@\text{ATM}.$$
$$\textbf{receive}(credentials, !amount)@\text{ATM})$$
$$+(\textbf{receive}(!credentials)@\text{ATM}.\textbf{send}(\text{Abort})@\text{ATM})$$

We do not define the process for User since it does not actually bring anything interesting to the example.

Now having such a system, one of the things that we would like to guarantee is that whenever the bank aborts a transaction, the ATM will not dispense the cash. In other words we want to ensure that both the bank and the ATM have a consistent view on the transaction. To achieve that we will use communicating pushdown systems that are introduced in the following section.

3   Pushdown Systems

3.1   Basic Concepts of Pushdown Systems

Pushdown systems are a formalism very close to pushdown automata. The main difference is that pushdown automata define languages, i.e. they have some input alphabet and use a stack to decide whether a word is accepted or not. Pushdown systems do not have an input alphabet and thus have a flavor of a description of a system that executes with an unbounded stack[2]. As such they are very useful for analyzing recursive programs — the stack is used to determine the location in the program along with the return locations of the procedures that were called. Below we give the formal definition of a pushdown system.

Definition 1. *A pushdown system is a four-tuple* $\mathcal{P} = (Q, \text{Act}, \Gamma, \Delta)$*, where* Q *is a finite set of control locations (in other words states),* Act *is a finite set of actions,* Γ *is a finite stack alphabet and* Δ *is a finite set of pushdown rules of the form* $\langle p, \gamma \rangle \overset{a}{\hookrightarrow} \langle p', w \rangle$ *where* $p, p' \in Q$*,* $\gamma \in \Gamma$*,* $w \in \Gamma^*$ *and* $a \in$ Act.

Most definitions of pushdown systems require that $|w| \leq 2$. This is useful especially when discussing some algorithms that take advantage of this property. Moreover this is not a restriction — we can easily transform any set of rules that does not satisfy this assumption into one that does by adding new rules and some fresh control locations. Therefore, for convenience and clarity of presentation we will not impose this requirement.

One of the reasons behind the success of pushdown systems and why the rules are presented in this way is that they correspond quite closely to how a procedural program executes. For this we need just three kinds of rules that correspond to calling a procedure, returning from a procedure and simply progressing to the next statement:

$$\langle p, \gamma \rangle \overset{a}{\hookrightarrow} \langle p', \gamma'\gamma'' \rangle \qquad \langle p, \gamma \rangle \overset{a}{\hookrightarrow} \langle p', \epsilon \rangle \qquad \langle p, \gamma \rangle \overset{a}{\hookrightarrow} \langle p', \gamma' \rangle$$

---

[2] Although if the pushdown rules are annotated with actions, as in this paper, then one could say that they constitute the input alphabet.

Moreover it is worth mentioning that $p, p' \in Q$ are often used to store the global state of a program and $\gamma, \gamma', \gamma'' \in \Gamma$ can be used to track the location of the current statement along all the return locations of the various procedures as well as the local state of procedures.

Apart from that, following [9,10], we also need the concept of a configuration of a pushdown system $\mathcal{P}$, which is a pair $\langle q, w \rangle$ such that $q \in Q$ and $w \in \Gamma^*$. Moreover we say that a set of configurations C is regular if for each $q \in Q$ the language $\{w \in \Gamma^* \mid \langle q, w \rangle \in C\}$ is regular. Having the definition of a configuration we can define the transition relation $\overset{a}{\Longrightarrow}$ between configurations — if $\langle p, \gamma \rangle \overset{a}{\hookrightarrow} \langle p', w \rangle$ then $\langle p, \gamma s \rangle \overset{a}{\Longrightarrow} \langle p', ws \rangle$ for all $s \in \Gamma^*$. Moreover, we also define $\overset{a_1 \ldots a_n}{\Longrightarrow}$ to be the reflexive, transitive closure of the above relation. Now we can define the concept of successor configuration. We say that c_s is an immediate successor of c if there exists a such that $c \overset{a}{\Longrightarrow} c_s$ and is a successor of c' if there exist $a_1 \ldots a_n$ such that $c' \overset{a_1 \ldots a_n}{\Longrightarrow} c_s$. Finally the set of all successors of some set of configurations C is defined by:

$$Post^*(C) = \{c' \mid \exists c \in C : c' \text{ is a successor of } c\}$$

The concepts of immediate predecessor, predecessor and set of predecessors are defined analogously.

Clearly a set of pushdown rules gives rise to a possibly infinite transition system and thus a possibly infinite set of reachable configurations. The reason for this is the fact that the stack is unbounded. However, one of the crucial results in this area is that the set of successors (or predecessors) of a regular set of configurations is itself regular. This is essential because even though the number of configuration can be infinite, we can still represent them symbolically using finite automata. In [14,4] efficient algorithms for computing both $Post^*$ and Pre^* were presented. They work by saturating an initial automaton $\mathcal{A}$ (representing some regular set of configurations) by adding new transitions and states to arrive at $\mathcal{A}_{post^*}$ (or $\mathcal{A}_{pre^*}$) automaton that represents the regular set of all its successor (or predecessor) configurations.

3.2   Representing Processes and Aspects

One of the challenges of using pushdown systems in our setting is the fact that there are no procedures and we do not have the concept of program locations. However, the behavior of aspects does remind of a stack. As an example, consider a process $A \cdot B$, if the first action A is trapped by an aspect that gives advice $C \cdot D \cdot \mathbf{proceed}$ then we suddenly have a process $C \cdot D \cdot A \cdot B$ (where A should not be considered by this aspect again). But this can be thought of as a stack — we push two additional actions on it and then want to continue with the remaining ones. In other words we want the stack to characterize the process itself (i.e. the actions to be executed). The only remaining problem is how to ensure that the aspect will not trap action A again. Fortunately there is a solution for that — we can embed some additional information in the stack to indicate what aspect should consider the given action next. Apart from that, since the stack is used for control flow, we can often improve the precision of our analyses by embedding in the stack some information about the communication that takes place. The most natural choices are the sender and receiver as well as the contents of the tuples that are sent or received. However, we usually do not want to consider all possible constants and all possible tuples that can arise at runtime — often just a subset of them along with some abstraction of the remaining ones will be enough. We will call them abstract constants and abstract tuples — since they abstract away from some of the possible runtime values. For instance in our example of an ATM and bank we are probably interested in when Ok and Abort can be sent and received, but the rest of the information (such as the amount of money to be withdrawn) is not that important, because it does not influence the control flow of the processes.

Therefore we define the stack alphabet Γ in the following way

$$\Gamma = ((\text{Proc} \times \text{Proc} \times \text{Tuples}) \cup \text{Internal}) \times (\text{Asp} \cup \{\checkmark\})$$

where Proc is the set of processes, Asp is the set of aspects and $\checkmark$ is a special symbol indicating that all aspects have already analyzed the given action, Tuples is the set of all possible abstract tuples that are sent over the channels in the given system and Internal are internal actions of the process. Note that the definition of pushdown systems requires that these sets are finite. But this is not really a big restriction since we are already using abstract tuples and concrete processes are always finite. Furthermore, we need to define the set of actions. In our case this is actually quite similar to the stack elements. We define them as follows

$$\text{Act} = (\text{Proc} \times \text{Proc} \times \text{Tuples}) \cup \{\tau\}$$

The intuition here is that we do want to know the sender (first component of the tuple), the receiver (the second component) and what is communicated (the third component). This information will be essential in the subsequent section on communicating pushdown systems. Apart from that we also need to accommodate internal actions that are not important from the point of view of synchronization with other processes — thus the inclusion of τ that has the property that $a\tau = \tau a = a$.

Notice that in some cases we do not actually know what is sent/received in a given action (e.g. in **receive**(!x)@N we do not know what x might be). In such cases we can simply generate rules for all the possibilities. However, in many situations we could be quite a bit more clever about this — for instance it should be possible to generate such possibilities lazily, i.e. if some action is never pushed on a stack, we do not really need to add rules to pop it. Another example would be if we can determine that some constant is sent only between two processes, then we do not have to consider it when generating rules for actions of other processes.

Now let us get back to our example. Since we are only interested in Ok and Abort constants and the maximum arity of a tuple send by any process is equal to two, our set of abstract tuples will be:

$$\text{Tuples} = \{(c) \mid c \in \text{C}\} \cup \{(c_1, c_2) \mid c_1 \in \text{C}, \ c_2 \in \text{C}\}$$

where $C = \{Ok, Abort, *\}$ and $*$ stands for any constant other than Ok or Abort.

Rules for creating processes. To create a process the first thing that we do is to push all its actions on the stack. So if we have a process P :: $a_1 . a_2 . a_3$ then we create a rule

$$\langle P, \Box \rangle \xrightarrow{\tau} \langle P, a_1 \ a_2 \ a_3 \rangle$$

where $\Box$ is a "start" symbol that can be used for creating the initial set of configurations (we will explain that later on). Furthermore this idea can be used to express recursion. Consider the following process: Q :: $\mathbf{RecX} . a_1 . a_2 . X$ By pushing X on the stack and treating it as a start symbol of the process we can easily model this recursion — the moment all actions are executed and X is on top of the stack, the rule is used to "recreate" the process:

$$\langle Q, X \rangle \xrightarrow{\tau} \langle Q, a_1 \ a_2 \ X \rangle$$

Apart from that we need to be able to handle choice. This can be achieved by creating all possible linear shapes of the process. For instance when generating the initial rules for process P :: $a_1 . (a_2 + a_3)$ we would create:

$$\langle P, \Box \rangle \xrightarrow{\tau} \langle P, a_1 \ a_2 \rangle \qquad \langle P, \Box \rangle \xrightarrow{\tau} \langle P, a_1 \ a_3 \rangle$$

For the ATM in our example we can generate a set of rules for all choices of $x \in C$ and $y \in C$:

$$\left\{ \begin{array}{l} \langle ATM, \Box \rangle \xrightarrow{\tau} \langle ATM, \ (User, ATM, (x, y), \checkmark) \\ \qquad\qquad\qquad\quad (\mathbf{check}(x), A_1) \\ \qquad\qquad\qquad\quad (ATM, User, (y), \checkmark) \\ \qquad\qquad\qquad\quad (ATM, Bank, (x, y), \checkmark))\rangle \end{array} \ \middle| \ \begin{array}{l} x \in C \\ y \in C \end{array} \right\}$$

As already mentioned, we can often be much smarter about generating the rules and create only a subset of the above (for instance Abort is never sent between User and Bank).

Rules for aspects. When generating the rules for the aspects we often have sufficient information in the stack element of the pointcut to be able to decide whether the aspect traps it or not. In the example above we could easily tell that some of the actions could never be trapped by any of our aspects (the aspects in the example trap only actions of the ATM). However, if we do not know whether the aspect will trap the action, we simply over-approximate and generate rules for both possibilities. One of the essential parts of generating the rules is to update the component of the stack that tracks what aspect should analyze the action next. In other words, if an action a is trapped by aspect A_1 then the **proceed** of the aspect should be the same action a but annotated with the next aspect. To make that clear, let us consider the internal **check** action of our ATM:

$$\left\{ \begin{array}{l} \langle ATM, (\mathbf{check}, (x), A_1) \rangle \xrightarrow{\tau} \langle ATM, \ (\mathbf{check}, (x), \checkmark) \\ \qquad\qquad\qquad\qquad\qquad\qquad\quad (ATM, Bank, (x), \checkmark) \\ \qquad\qquad\qquad\qquad\qquad\qquad\quad (Bank, ATM, (y), A_2) \rangle \end{array} \ \middle| \ \begin{array}{l} x \in C \\ y \in C \end{array} \right\}$$

As can be seen above, we have the internal action **check** with aspect A_1 on the left-hand side of the pushdown rule, but on the right-hand side we annotate it with ✓ as there are no more aspects that can match. This ensures that **check** will not be trapped by this aspect again.

Moreover, we must also handle the **if** conditions. Since we generate rules for various combinations of constants, we can often determine whether a condition is true at the stage of generating the rules. And if so, we can generate rules just for the right branch. However, in general this is not always possible. In such situations we can simply generate the rules for both cases, i.e. one if the condition is true and one if it is false. This corresponds to over-approximating the control flow. Therefore, from the point of view of precision, it might be beneficial to include in the set of abstract constants the ones that are used for comparisons.

Rules for executing actions. All of the above rules do not model the execution of any actions (and thus are considered as internal actions and labeled with τ). Execution in our context is nothing else than simply popping a stack element. So in general we simply create rules of the form $\langle p, a \rangle \overset{l}{\hookrightarrow} \langle p, \epsilon \rangle$ for all possible actions a that are annotated with ✓, where l is either τ if a is an internal action or a otherwise. An example from ATM is as follows:

$$\left\{ \langle \mathsf{ATM}, \ (\mathsf{User}, \mathsf{ATM}, (x, y), \checkmark) \rangle \xrightarrow{(\mathsf{User}, \mathsf{ATM}, (x, y))} \langle \mathsf{ATM}, \ \epsilon \rangle \middle| x \in \mathsf{C} \ y \in \mathsf{C} \right\}$$

which corresponds to execution of all actions where ATM receives a two-tuple from the user. Note that we require that the actions are annotated with ✓, which indicates that all aspects have been considered and the action can be executed.

Finally, we need to define the initial set of configurations whose successors we are interested in. This should clearly be the singleton with the name of the process (control location) and the start symbol (a single element stack). In case of ATM it is $\{\langle \mathsf{ATM}, \square \rangle\}$. Running the *Post** algorithm on it will yield an automaton that represents all the possible future configurations of the thread. In this case it will describe what the process can be in the future (i.e. grow due to advice, shrink due to executing the actions, etc.).

3.3   Communicating Pushdown Systems

For now we have considered only a single thread at a time and we can create pushdown systems for each of them. However, since this construction does not take into account that communication takes place, it is quite an over-approximation of the behavior of the system. In this section we will remedy this and cover both the basic theory behind communicating pushdown systems, as well as how we can use them in our context.

Communicating pushdown systems have been introduced in [9,10] and subsequently used in [11]. We define them here with just slight modifications to accommodate for the fact that we handle message passing and not only synchronization as in [9,10].

Definition 2. *Communicating pushdown system (CPDS) is a tuple* $(\mathcal{P}_1, \ldots, \mathcal{P}_n)$ *of pushdown systems over the same set of actions* Act.

A global configuration of CPDS is a tuple $g = (c_1, \ldots, c_n)$ of configurations of $\mathcal{P}_1, \ldots, \mathcal{P}_n$. We extend the relation $\overset{a}{\Longrightarrow}$ to global configurations in the following way:

- $g \overset{\tau}{\Longrightarrow} g'$ if there is $1 \le i \le n$ such that $c_i \overset{\tau}{\Longrightarrow} c_i'$ and $c_j' = c_j$ for all $j \ne i$
- $g \overset{(s,r,t)}{\Longrightarrow} g'$ if there are $i \ne j$ such that $c_i \overset{(s,r,t)}{\Longrightarrow} c_i'$ and $c_j \overset{(s,r,t)}{\Longrightarrow} c_j'$ ("s" stands for sender, "r" for receiver and "t" for tuple). Finally for all $k \ne i \wedge k \ne j$ we have that $c_k' = c_k$.

Using the pushdown systems we have the ability to characterize the set of all possible successors of some initial regular set of configurations. Moreover we want to annotate the result with the summarization of what happens on the paths to those successor configurations. Note that the pushdown rules are associated with actions, so each path in the transition system of a PDS has a corresponding sequence of actions, which is an element of the language generated by the set of actions. More formally it is a subset of the free monoid Act* generated by the set of actions Act. Moreover, it is important to note that in general the paths of a process correspond to a context-free language [9,10].

Now let us consider a CPDS $(\mathcal{P}_1, \ldots \mathcal{P}_n)$ and assume that we are interested in the question whether a configuration from $C_1' \times \cdots \times C_n'$ is reachable from some configuration from $C_1 \times \cdots \times C_n$. In the following we will use $L_i = L(C_i, C_i')$ to denote the language summarizing all paths of the process i that go from any configuration of C_i to any configuration of C_i'. If we restrict ourselves, just for a moment, to the case where $n = 2$ then this problem is really nothing else than testing for emptiness of the intersection of the languages L_1 and L_2. The intuition behind this is that the intersection is empty only if there are no communication traces of the two processes that would match. However, the problem for reachability for arbitrary n is a bit more demanding. Consider a simple scenario with three process where process 1 first communicates with process 2, then with process 3 and then with 2 again. With the above "recipe" we could get that the $L_1 \cap L_2$ is empty. The problem is that the above does not account for the fact that process 1 communicates with process 3 and that this is not important from the point of view of synchronizing with process 2. Therefore in order to generalize this technique for arbitrary number of processes one has to accommodate for the interleaving of communication between different processes. Therefore we define $\widehat{L_i}$ to be an inverse homomorphic image of L_i

$$\widehat{L_i} = h_i^{-1} L_i$$

where h_i is defined as

$$h_i\,(s, r, t) = \begin{cases} (s, r, t) & \text{if } r = i \vee s = i \\ \epsilon & \text{otherwise} \end{cases}$$

The idea behind this is that process i allows for any communication that does not involve it, to take place between any of its actions. Intuitively when thinking about the pushdown system $\mathcal{P}_i$ we want to extend it with self-loops, which correspond to all possible communication actions of some other processes, on all its control locations. In [9,10] this problem is solved by introduction of interleaving (shuffle) operator. Also note that in case $n = 2$ we simply have $\widehat{L_i} = L_i$.

With the above we can finally reason about the reachability in a system of arbitrary many processes. More formally, if we have sets of global configurations $G = C_1 \times \ldots \times C_n$ and $G' = C'_1 \times \ldots \times C'_n$ and if

$$\widehat{L_1} \cap \ldots \cap \widehat{L_n} = \emptyset$$

then we can conclude that no configuration of G' is reachable from any configuration of G. However, there is still a minor problem with this approach — as already mentioned the generated languages are in general context-free and checking the emptiness of the intersection of context-free languages is undecidable. Therefore the next section will consider abstractions that can be used for over-approximation.

4   Analysis

4.1   Basic Concepts

The $Post^*$ and Pre^* algorithms can annotate the transitions of the $\mathcal{A}_{post*}$ and $\mathcal{A}_{pre*}$ automata with "weights", i.e. some abstraction of the language generated by the set of actions. Our approach is based on [9,10] with some changes to accommodate for our slightly different context.

First of all we recall the definition of a semiring.

Definition 3. *A semiring is a tuple* $(D, \oplus, \otimes, \bar{0}, \bar{1})$ *such that*

- $(D, \oplus, \bar{0})$ *is a commutative monoid (hence* $\bar{0}$ *is a neutral element for* $\oplus$*)*
- $(D, \otimes, \bar{1})$ *is a monoid (hence* $\bar{1}$ *is a neutral element for* $\otimes$*)*
- $\otimes$ *distributes over* $\oplus$*, that is* $a \otimes (b \oplus c) = (a \otimes b) \oplus (a \otimes c)$ *and* $(a \oplus b) \otimes c = (a \otimes c) \oplus (b \otimes c)$
- $\bar{0}$ *is an annihilator for* $\otimes$*, that is* $a \otimes \bar{0} = \bar{0} \otimes a = \bar{0}$

We consider an idempotent[3] semiring $(D, \oplus, \otimes, \bar{0}, \bar{1})$ with an associated abstract lattice $(D, \sqsubseteq, \sqcup, \bot)$ such that $a \sqsubseteq b$ iff $a \oplus b = b$, $\sqcup = \oplus$, $\bot = \bar{0}$. Furthermore we require that the lattice satisfies the ascending chain condition [15].

Moreover we also need to establish a *Galois connection* between the language generated by the transition system of the communicating pushdown system and our abstraction. Below we recall the definition of a Galois connection.

Definition 4. *A Galois connection is a tuple* (L, α, γ, M) *such that* L *and* M *are complete lattices and* α*,* γ *are monotone functions (called abstraction and concretization functions) that satisfy* $\alpha \circ \gamma \sqsubseteq \lambda m.m$ *and* $\gamma \circ \alpha \sqsupseteq \lambda l.l$*.*

---

[3] The operator $\oplus$ is additionally idempotent.

Intuitively a Galois connection specifies a semantically correct way to move our analysis from a precise lattice L (for which certain problems might be very hard or even undecidable) to a more abstract one M which has some desired computational properties. In our case we want to go from possibly infinite $\mathcal{P}(\mathsf{Act}^*)$ to one that allows $Post^*$ to terminate and gives us a decidable way of intersecting languages of various processes. We define the α and γ functions in the following way:

$$\alpha : \mathcal{P}(\mathsf{Act}^*) \to D$$

$$\alpha(L) = \bigoplus_{a_1 \cdots a_n \in L} v_{a_1} \otimes \ldots \otimes v_{a_n}$$

$$\gamma : D \to \mathcal{P}(\mathsf{Act}^*)$$

$$\gamma(x) = \{a_1 \cdots a_n \mid v_{a_1} \otimes \ldots \otimes v_{a_n} \sqsubseteq x\}$$

where v_a is an abstract value of a (which will be defined by a particular abstraction). Note that $\alpha(\emptyset) = \bot$. Furthermore we also require that $\gamma(\bot) = \emptyset$. This gives us the desired property:

$$\forall L_1, \ldots, L_n : \alpha(L_1) \sqcap \ldots \sqcap \alpha(L_n) = \bot \implies L_1 \cap \ldots \cap L_n = \emptyset$$

Therefore, if these languages correspond to some paths between initial and target configurations, we know that there are no paths of those processes that are feasible when the communication is taken into account. This gives us the ability to prove that certain configurations of our system are not reachable.

Finally the only remaining thing to do is to actually compute the abstractions for each of the processes. Let C and C' be two regular sets of configurations and $\mathcal{A}_C$ and $\mathcal{A}_{C'}$ be the automata representing them. We consider the problem of computing $\alpha(L(C, C'))$. Assuming that we have used the $Post^*$ algorithm to compute the $\mathcal{A}_{post^*}$ weighted automaton. In the following we will use $\lambda(t)$ to denote the weight of the transition t. Since our automaton represents all the possible successors of C and we are only interested in some of them (only those in C'), we need to restrict the accepted configurations. In simple cases this can be achieved by querying the automaton for the weight of certain successors. But in general we can construct $\mathcal{A}_{post^*}^{C'}$ that is a restriction of $\mathcal{A}_{post^*}$ to the configurations in C'. To do that we can simply intersect $\mathcal{A}_{post^*}$ with $\mathcal{A}_{C'}$ automaton, that is create an automaton induced by the smallest set of transitions such that if $q_1 \xrightarrow{a} q_1'$ is in $\mathcal{A}_{post^*}$ and $q_2 \xrightarrow{a} q_2'$ is in $\mathcal{A}_{C'}$ then we have a transition $(q_1, q_2) \xrightarrow{a} (q_1', q_2')$ in $\mathcal{A}_{post^*}^{C'}$ and its weight is $\lambda(q_1 \xrightarrow{a} q_1')$. The result is exactly what we want — those successors of C that are in C'. And the weights represent the summarization of what happens along the paths between configurations in C and C'. The final step is to compute (using for instance a slightly modified algorithm presented in [7]):

$$\bigoplus \left\{ \lambda(w) \mid p \xrightarrow{w} q \in \mathcal{A}_{post^*}^{C'} \text{ where } p \text{ is an initial state and } q \text{ a final one} \right\}$$

where we extend λ to work over paths by using $\otimes$.

4.2   Abstraction

There are many possibile abstractions that can be used for these problems, for instance [9,10] presents a few options. Since in our problems we usually do not expect the stack to grow very large, we will use the ith-prefix abstraction as introduced in [11]. The intuition behind it is that we simply impose a maximum length i that a word can have, i.e. we consider prefixes of words. The definition is as follows. Let W_i be the set of words of length less than ore equal to i. Then we define the semiring as follows: $D = \mathcal{P}(W_i)$, $\bar{0} = \emptyset$, $\bar{1} = \{\epsilon\}$, $\oplus = \cup$ and $U \otimes V = \{(uv)_i \mid u \in U, \ v \in V\}$ where $(w)_i$ is the prefix of w whose length is at most i. Moreover for every $a \in \mathsf{Act}$ we take $v_a = a$. Note that this automatically establishes a Galois connection where α and γ are defined as above.

4.3   Experiments

We have implemented this abstraction and used an off-the-shelf library WALi [16] for computing the $Post^*$ weighted automaton. Currently our implementation can be seen as a small library on top of WALi that offers higher level API capable of generating all pushdown rules (and their weights) for a given set of abstract constants. Since the resulting graphs are simply too large to include here, we have simplified the rules (without compromising the results) and present some of the more interesting parts in Fig. 1 and Fig. 2. The annotations on the edges are pairs of stack element (first component; * denotes an ϵ transition) and the weight of the transition (second component). Moreover EA stands for ✓ and LabelAbort() is an additional internal action that we inserted just after the action sending Abort to make it easier to see in the summarization of bank's actions at this point, which is:

```
ATMBank(*)BankATM(Abort)
```

Fig. 1. Part of the simplified graph for the ATM

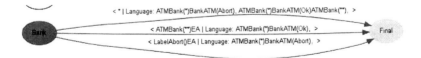

Fig. 2. Part of the simplified graph for the bank

Turning to the ATM, we can see that the process successfully dispenses the money and is about to inform the bank about the withdrawal with the following summarization of its communication:

$$\texttt{UserATM(**)ATMBank(*)BankATM(Ok)ATMUser(*)}$$

Now it should be clear that the intersection of the communication of the bank when it sends the abort message and the ATM when it dispenses the cash is empty — `BankATM(Ok)` and `BankATM(Abort)` do not match. This means that it is impossible for the bank and the ATM to reach this error configuration. In other words the cash will never be dispensed in a situation where the bank aborts the transaction.

5   Conclusions

In this paper we have considered a concurrent language equipped with message-passing primitives and support for the aspect-oriented paradigm. We believe that it also has a lot to offer in the context of coordination languages. In particular it gives us the ability to create very modular systems and separate unrelated functionality, which should make it easier to model complex systems.

However, the addition of aspects with advice allowing before or after actions leads to some interesting challenges. Those additional actions make it possible for a process to "grow" — one action trapped by an aspect can result in advice consisting of two or more actions. Furthermore, since the advice itself is analyzed by aspects, the processes can suddenly become arbitrarily large. Obviously this makes it much more difficult to analyze such systems. Our main contribution is to present an approach that is capable of solving analysis problems is such a context. To achieve this we used a technique from software model checking, namely communicating pushdown systems. Even though it is used mainly for analysis of recursive programs, we managed to adapt it to our setting. It proved to be a very useful and quite flexible tool, able to provide us with description of a process that can be arbitrarily large. Moreover, with the right abstraction, we can compute the summarization of its communication actions, allowing us to reason about the reachability in systems of concurrent threads. Since many safety problems can be reduced to reachability of error states, our approach can be used for verification purposes of such systems.

We believe that this approach can be adapted to various process calculi that use aspect-oriented paradigm. However, application to programming languages might pose additional challenges. Apart from already mentioned differences, we would also have to deal with two sources of recursion (procedures and aspects).

Finally, there are still some interesting future challenges. For instance, the question of how far can we extend the language and still be able to model it using pushdown systems. Moreover, from the point of view of efficiency we would prefer to generate only a small number of rules. On the other hand, to achieve better precision we would like to include as much information in the rules as possible. There is clearly a lot of room for experiments with various approaches and compromises depending on the situation.

References

1. Kiczales, G., Lamping, J., Mendhekar, A., Maeda, C., Lopes, C.V., Loingtier, J.M., Irwin, J.: Aspect-Oriented Programming. In: Aksit, M., Auletta, V. (eds.) ECOOP 1997. LNCS, vol. 1241, pp. 220–242. Springer, Heidelberg (1997)
2. Kiczales, G., Hilsdale, E., Hugunin, J., Kersten, M., Palm, J., Griswold, W.G.: An Overview of AspectJ. In: Knudsen, J.L. (ed.) ECOOP 2001. LNCS, vol. 2072, pp. 327–353. Springer, Heidelberg (2001)
3. Hankin, C., Nielson, F., Nielson, H.R., Yang, F.: Advice for Coordination. In: Lea, D., Zavattaro, G. (eds.) COORDINATION 2008. LNCS, vol. 5052, pp. 153–168. Springer, Heidelberg (2008)
4. Schwoon, S.: Model-Checking Pushdown Systmes. PhD thesis, Technical University Munich (2002)
5. Esparza, J., Knoop, J.: An Automata-Theoretic Approach to Interprocedural Data-Flow Analysis. In: Thomas, W. (ed.) FOSSACS 1999. LNCS, vol. 1578, pp. 14–30. Springer, Heidelberg (1999)
6. Reps, T.W., Schwoon, S., Jha, S.: Weighted Pushdown Systems and their Application to Interprocedural Dataflow Analysis. In: Cousot, R. (ed.) SAS 2003. LNCS, vol. 2694, pp. 189–213. Springer, Heidelberg (2003)
7. Reps, T.W., Schwoon, S., Jha, S., Melski, D.: Weighted pushdown systems and their application to interprocedural dataflow analysis. Sci. Comput. Program. 58(1-2), 206–263 (2005)
8. Yang, F.: Aspects with Program Analysis for Security Policies. PhD thesis, Technical University of Denmark (2010)
9. Bouajjani, A., Esparza, J., Touili, T.: A generic approach to the static analysis of concurrent programs with procedures. In: POPL, pp. 62–73 (2003)
10. Bouajjani, A., Esparza, J., Touili, T.: A generic approach to the static analysis of concurrent programs with procedures. Int. J. Found. Comput. Sci. 14(4), 551–582 (2003)
11. Chaki, S., Clarke, E., Kidd, N., Reps, T., Touili, T.: Verifying Concurrent Message-Passing C Programs with Recursive Calls. In: Hermanns, H., Palsberg, J. (eds.) TACAS 2006. LNCS, vol. 3920, pp. 334–349. Springer, Heidelberg (2006)
12. Lal, A., Touili, T., Kidd, N., Reps, T.: Interprocedural Analysis of Concurrent Programs Under a Context Bound. In: Ramakrishnan, C.R., Rehof, J. (eds.) TACAS 2008. LNCS, vol. 4963, pp. 282–298. Springer, Heidelberg (2008)
13. Hoare, C.A.R.: Communicating sequential processes. Commun. ACM 21(8), 666–677 (1978)
14. Esparza, J., Hansel, D., Rossmanith, P., Schwoon, S.: Efficient Algorithms for Model Checking Pushdown Systems. In: Emerson, E.A., Sistla, A.P. (eds.) CAV 2000. LNCS, vol. 1855, pp. 232–247. Springer, Heidelberg (2000)
15. Nielson, F., Nielson, H.R., Hankin, C.: Principles of program analysis (2. corr. print). Springer (2005)
16. Kidd, N., Lal, A., Reps, T.W.: Wali: The weighted automaton library (December 2007)

Fluid Analysis of Foraging Ants

Mieke Massink and Diego Latella

Istituto di Scienza e Tecnologie dell'Informazione 'A. Faedo', CNR, Italy

Abstract. Workers of the Argentine ant, Iridomyrmex humilis, are known to be capable to find efficiently the shortest route from their nest to a food source. Their approach is based on a simple pheromone trail-laying and following behaviour accessing only local information. In this note we explore the modelling and analysis of foraging ants in Bio-PEPA [8,6]. The simple case study concerns ants that need to cross a bridge with two branches of different length to reach food and carry the food home and is based on empirical data described by Goss and Deneubourg et al. [13,10]. We explore the conditions for which the shortest path emerges as the preferred one by the ants. The analysis is based on stochastic simulation and fluid flow analysis. The behaviour of ant colonies has inspired the development of an interesting class of optimisation algorithms ranging from alternative shortest path algorithms to new scheduling and routing algorithms, algorithms to solve set partition problems and for distributed information retrieval. Process algebraic fluid flow analysis may be an important additional technique to the analysis of such algorithms in a computationally efficient way.

Keywords: Fluid flow, process algebra, collective dynamics, self-organisation, emergence.

1 Introduction

The behaviour of ant colonies has inspired the development of an interesting class of optimisation algorithms ranging from alternative shortest path algorithms to new scheduling and routing algorithms, algorithms to solve set partition problems and for distributed information retrieval, see for example work by Dorigo et al. [11]. The formal specification and scalable analysis of such systems, that in general consist of a large number of autonomous entities, is still a challenging problem. Such analysis is however essential to assure functional and non-functional properties of such systems, especially when they are employed in safety critical applications. Algorithms based on ant colony behaviour are also inspiring the development of techniques to contribute to the solution of difficult problems of self-organisation, self-awareness, autonomous and collective behaviour, and resource optimisation in a complex system setting such as those that can be found in collaborative swarms of robots, see for example the AS-CENS project [1]. In this preliminary work we address the formal modelling and analysis of a colony of foraging ants in Bio-PEPA and in particular we study the emergent behaviour of this model using a process algebra based fluid flow approach.

M. Sirjani (Ed.): COORDINATION 2012, LNCS 7274, pp. 152–165, 2012.

2   The Problem of Foraging Ants

To study the problem of foraging ants the following experimental set up is considered from the literature [13,10]. A nest of ants is situated at site nest and some food is situated at site food. Ants can reach the food from the nest through two alternative branches of a bridge, a long branch passing by locations L1 and L2, and a short branch, passing by locations S1 and S2. The ants choose a branch based on the relative quantity of *pheromone* present at the start of the two branches, i.e. in L1 and S1 for ants leaving choice point A moving towards site food, and L2 and S2 for ants leaving choice point B and going towards site nest. Pheromone is a chemical substance that is released by the ants as they move. It is assumed that once a branch is chosen the ant's decision is not reverted, i.e. the ant eventually arrives at destination once it starts moving along a particular branch. After the ant has found the food it returns to the nest following the same procedure. Pheromone is assumed *not* to be subject to decay in the present set up since the behaviour is studied over a time interval of ca. 40 minutes, which is compatible with the lifetime of pheromone. However, such a feature could be easily added when longer time intervals are of interest. The aim of this modelling exercise is to find a high-level, process algebraic, agent based model that can be used to determine under which conditions which of the two branches is emerging as the preferred one when ants apply the above described local, pheromone based, algorithm. The site nest and choice point A are represented as two different locations. Similarly for site food and choice point B. A constant flow of ants leaving the nest is assumed, with, on average, one ant leaving the nest every two seconds. The choice behaviour of the ants depends on the relative amounts of pheromone present at the beginning of each branch. In [10] a simple general choice function is used, which quantifies the way in which a higher concentration of pheromone on one branch gives a higher probability of choosing that branch, depending on the absolute and relative amounts on the beginning of these branches. The particular choice function suggested for the probability to choose the short branch at a choice point is of the form:

$$prob_S = (k + P\_S_i)^d / ((k + P\_S_i)^d + (k + P\_L_i)^d)$$

where P_S_i represents the amount of pheromone in location S_i and P_L_i the amount of pheromone in location L_i, for $i \in \{1, 2\}$. In a similar way $prob_L$ can be defined. The parameter k quantifies the degree to which ants are sensitive to the difference in amounts of pheromone marking at the two branches when there is still relatively little pheromone present. For example, for $k = 1$ the probability for the first ant passing choice point A to choose one of the branches is $k/2k = 1/2$ because there is no pheromone on either branch yet. Suppose this ant chooses the long branch, then it lays a unit of pheromone at site L1. So, the next ant that passes choice point A in the same direction (assuming that no other ants have passed) has now a probability of $1/3$ to choose the short branch and $2/3$ to choose the long branch. For larger values of k the initial amounts of pheromones laid by the first ants produce a less accentuated difference in the probabilities.

For example, for $k = 20$ and $d = 1$ the probability that the second ant chooses
the short branch reduces to $21/41 = 0.51$. Empirical results described in [10] have
shown that $k = 20$ provides a realistic value. The parameter d in the formula
determines the degree of non-linearity of the choice. A higher value of d amplifies
the effect of the difference between the amounts of pheromone present on the
two branches at a choice point. Empirical results showed that $n = 2$ provides a
good fit between empirical data and the function modelling the choice. Note that
$prob_S + prob_L = 1$. This simple mechanism, in which each ant that passes a choice
point during exploratory recruitment modifies the following ant's probability to
choose a particular branch by adding pheromone on the chosen branch, forms
a positive feedback system in which, after some initial fluctuation, one branch
emerges as being "selected", which is usually the shortest branch.

3   Bio-PEPA Briefly Recalled

Bio-PEPA [8,6,7], is a process algebraic language that originally was developed
for the stochastic modelling and analysis of biochemical systems. Bio-PEPA
models consist of two main kinds of components. The first kind is called the
"species" component, describing the behaviour of individual entities. The second
kind is the *model component*, describing the interactions between the various
species. In the context of the paper, the individual entities are the robots, and
the model component defines how they interact.

The syntax of Bio-PEPA components is defined as:

$$S ::= (\alpha, \kappa) \text{ op } S \mid S + S \mid C \quad \text{with op} = \downarrow \mid \uparrow \mid \oplus \mid \ominus \mid \odot \quad \text{and} \quad P ::= P \bowtie_{\mathcal{L}} P \mid S(x)$$

where S is a *species component* and P is a *model component*.

The *prefix combinator* "op" in the prefix term $(\alpha, \kappa) \text{ op } S$ represents the impact that action α has on species S. Specifically, $\downarrow$ indicates that the number of
entities of species S reduces when α occurs, and $\uparrow$ indicates that this number
increases. The amount of the change is defined by the *stoichiometry* coefficient
κ. This coefficient captures the multiples of an entity involved in an occurring
action. We will see an example of its use in the next section. The default value
of κ is 1 in which case we simply write α instead of (α, κ). Action durations are
assumed to be random variables (RVs) with negative exponential distributions,
characterised by their *rates*. The rate of action α is defined by a so called functional rate or kinetics rate. Action rates are defined in the context section of a
Bio-PEPA specification. The symbol $\oplus$ denotes an *activator*, $\ominus$ an *inhibitor* and
$\odot$ a generic *modifier*, all of which play a role in an action without being produced or consumed and have a defined meaning in the biochemical context. The
operator "+" expresses the choice between possible actions, and the constant
C is defined by an equation $C=S$. The process $P \bowtie_{\mathcal{L}} Q$ denotes synchronisation
between components P and Q, the set $\mathcal{L}$ determines those actions on which the
components P and Q are forced to synchronise. The shorthand $P \bowtie Q$ denotes
synchronisation on all actions that P and Q have in common. In $\hat{S}(x)$, the parameter $x \in \mathbb{R}$ represents the initial amount of the species. A Bio-PEPA *system*

with *locations* consists of a set of species components, a model component, and a context containing definitions of locations, functional/kinetics rates, parameters, etc.. The prefix term (α, κ) op $S@l$ is used to specify that the action is performed by S in location l.

Bio-PEPA is given a formal operational semantics [8] which is based on Continuous Time Markov Chains (CTMCs). An alternative semantics for Bio-PEPA is also given in [7,8] where Bio-PEPA models are mapped into sets of ordinary differential equations (ODEs) which allow for *fluid flow* approximation. As we have seen above, a Bio-PEPA model consists of a number of sequential components each of which represents a number of entities in a distinct state. The result of an action is to increase the number of some entities and decrease the number of others, these adjustments reflecting the stoichiometry with respect to the action. Thus we can represent the total state of the system at any point in time as a vector whose elements store the counts of each species component. This gives rise to a discrete state system which undergoes discrete events. Intuitively, the idea of fluid flow approximation is to *approximate* these discrete jumps by continuous flows between the states of the system. This approximation becomes good when entities are present in such high numbers as to make the frequency of actions high and the relative change from each single event small. In this case we can derive a set ODEs capturing the continuous approximation of system jumps, the solution of which is a vector of functions of time, which approximate the average behaviour of the CTMC; there is one such a function per each species and its value at time t gives the expected fraction, over the total population, of entities of that species at time t.

Bio-PEPA is supported by a suite of software tools which automatically process Bio-PEPA models and generate internal representations suitable for different types of analysis [8,5]. These tools include mappings from Bio-PEPA to ODEs, supporting fluid flow approximation [14], to stochastic simulation models [12], to CTMCs with levels [7] and to PRISM models [16,17] amenable to (statistical) model-checking. Consistency of the analyses is supported by a rich theory including process algebra, and the relationships between CTMCs and ODE.

4   A Bio-PEPA Model of Foraging Ants

To model the behaviour of foraging ants in Bio-PEPA [8,6] the following parameters are used:

- N denotes the total, and constant, number of worker ants in the ants colony.
- *move* denotes the constant rate at which ants leave site `nest` to look for food. The rate at which ants leave site `food` depends also on the number of ants present on site `food` and is modelled by a mass action law.
- *walk_long* (*walk_short*) is the rate related to the average time an ant needs to traverse a section of the long (short, respectively) branch of the bridge.

Both the long and the short branch are composed of the same number of sections, i.e. 2. The length of a branch is modelled by the average time it takes an ant to traverse a section on that branch. This time is longer for the long branch than for the short branch and is specified by the two parameters walk_long and walk_short. An alternative solution would be to vary the number of sections on the paths and keep the average walking time for each section the same.

The following compartments (locations) are introduced (apart from the default location 'top'):

- nest is the location of the ants' nest from which ants start initially.
- A is the location where they choose between the long and the short path when leaving the nest.
- S1 and S2 are the locations where ants lay pheromone after they selected the short branch. They do this every time they pass by these locations.
- L1 and L2 are the locations where ants lay pheromone after they selected the long branch. They do this every time they pass by these locations.
- food is the place where they collect food.
- B is the location where the ants decide which branch to take when returning from the food to the nest.

In Figure 1 the locations as well as the names of the transitions modelling the movement of individual ants are indicated. The direction of movement of the ants is modelled as part of the name of the species.

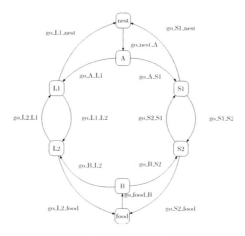

Fig. 1. Locations and transitions of ants in the model

In the following the behaviour of an *individual* ant is modelled. The focus is on how its behaviour effects the population of ants and the amount of pheromones in the relevant locations. It is assumed that all ants are in location nest initially. From there they move with a rate of one ant every 2 seconds towards the food. This rate is associated with the action go_nest_A labelling the transition of an ant moving from location nest to choice point A. In A ants choose between the long (go_A_L1) and the short (go_A_S1) branch. The total exit rate of an ant at a choice point is 1, i.e. the sum of the probabilities given by the choice function to choose a branch. In this paper, we assume that, initially, there is no pheromone in locations S1 and L1, so an ant chooses either way with approximately equal probability for $k = 20$. When there is significantly more pheromone in one of the locations, the rate with which that branch is chosen increases and the race condition between the rates for the long and the short branch model a probabilistic choice between them. So, the larger the difference between the amounts of pheromone at the beginning of a path, the higher the probability that an ant chooses the branch with the highest amount of pheromone. The Bio-PEPA fragment below models this initial behaviour of the ant:

$$Ant\_nest = go\_nest\_A{\downarrow}Ant\_nest@nest+$$
$$go\_S1\_nest{\uparrow}Ant\_nest@nest+$$
$$go\_L1\_nest{\uparrow}Ant\_nest@nest;$$

$$Ant\_A = go\_A\_S1{\downarrow}Ant\_A@A+$$
$$go\_A\_L1{\downarrow}Ant\_A@A+$$
$$go\_nest\_A{\uparrow}Ant\_A@A;$$

After an ant selects a branch, it lays some pheromone in the location at the beginning of a branch in S1 or L1 as a side-effect of the actions go_A_S1 and go_A_L1, respectively. This part of the behaviour is modelled as processes Ant_S1_NtoF and Ant_L1_NtoF, where the suffix 'NtoF' indicates that the ant's travelling direction is from nest to food. Pheromone is also left in the locations along the branch when ants pass by them on their way back. This part of the behaviour is modelled by the processes with suffix 'FtoN'. Below an excerpt from the model for an ant moving to and returning via $S1$ is shown. The behaviour involving $S2$, $L1$ and $L2$ is similar and not shown.

$$Ant\_S1\_NtoF = go\_A\_S1{\uparrow}Ant\_S1\_NtoF@S1+$$
$$go\_S1\_S2{\downarrow}Ant\_S1\_NtoF@S1;$$

$$Ant\_S1\_FtoN = go\_S2\_S1{\uparrow}Ant\_S1\_FtoN@S1+$$
$$go\_S1\_nest{\downarrow}Ant\_S1\_FtoN@S1;$$

After traversing the short or long branch, ants end up in location food. From there they go eventually back to the nest, passing by choice point B, as specified in the fragment below:

$$Ant\_food = go\_food\_B{\downarrow}Ant\_food@food+$$
$$go\_S2\_food{\uparrow}Ant\_food@food+$$
$$go\_L2\_food{\uparrow}Ant\_food@food;$$

$$Ant\_B = go\_B\_S2{\downarrow}Ant\_B@B+$$
$$go\_B\_L2{\downarrow}Ant\_B@B+$$
$$go\_food\_B{\uparrow}Ant\_B@B;$$

The increment in pheromone level takes place as a side-effect of an ant passing by a particular location on its path. This is modelled by the change in pheromone level at each of the locations and occurs when a go_X_Y action happens on which the pheromone process is synchronised, for example:

$$P\_S1 = go\_A\_S1{\uparrow}P\_S1@S1 + go\_S2\_S1{\uparrow}P\_S1@S1;$$

The system model below shows the initial number of ants in each location using cooperation with synchronisation on shared actions:

$Ant\_Nest@Nest[N]$ ⋈ $Ant\_A@A[0]$ ⋈
$Ant\_S1\_NtoF@S1[0]$ ⋈ $Ant\_S1\_FtoN@S1[0]$ ⋈ $P\_S1@S1[0]$ ⋈
$Ant\_S2\_NtoF@S2[0]$ ⋈ $Ant\_S2\_FtoN@S2[0]$ ⋈ $P\_S2@S2[0]$ ⋈
$Ant\_L1\_NtoF@L1[0]$ ⋈ $Ant\_L1\_FtoN@L1[0]$ ⋈ $P\_L1@L1[0]$ ⋈
$Ant\_L2\_NtoF@L2[0]$ ⋈ $Ant\_L2\_FtoN@L2[0]$ ⋈ $P\_L2@L2[0]$ ⋈
$Ant\_Food@Food[0]$ ⋈ $Ant\_B@B[0]$

The rates of the actions in the model reflect those found empirically by Goss et al. [13].

Ants leave the nest at a rate of one ant every 2 seconds. This is modelled by the constant rate *move*. To avoid that a reaction takes place when there are no ants present in the nest, the rate is multiplied with a factor that makes sure that there is a positive number of ants in the nest (H(Ant_nest@nest)). Ants returning to their nest from location food are assumed to leave that location with a rate depending on the number of ants present in that location.

$$kineticLawOf go\_nest\_A : move * H(Ant\_nest@nest);$$
$$kineticLawOf go\_food\_B : move * Ant\_food@food;$$

The rates at which ants choose a branch at a choice point are defined using the choice function of degree 2, for example for ants leaving choice point **A**:

$$kineticLawOf go\_A\_S1 : \frac{(k+P\_S1@S1)^2}{(k+P\_S1@S1)^2+(k+P\_L1@L1)^2} * Ant\_A@A;$$
$$kineticLawOf go\_A\_L1 : \frac{(k+P\_L1@L1)^2}{(k+P\_S1@S1)^2+(k+P\_L1@L1)^2} * Ant\_A@A;$$

It takes ants more time to traverse a section on the long branch than on the short branch. This is simply modelled by two different rates; **walk_long** and **walk_short**. For example:

$$kineticLawOf go\_L1\_L2 : walk\_long * Ant\_L1\_NtoF@L1;$$
$$kineticLawOf go\_S1\_S2 : walk\_short * Ant\_S1\_NtoF@S1;$$

5   Emerging Paths

Despite the simplicity of the model of foraging ants there are a number of interesting aspects to analyse. In the present paper we focus on whether or under what conditions stochastic simulation and fluid flow analysis confirm that the simple trail laying and selection mechanism indeed are enough to lead to the emergence of the shortest path in most cases. In other words, we want to know whether or under what conditions our model shows a similar emergent behaviour as has been observed in empirical research, so that we can validate it.

In order to be able to compare results obtained from the model with those from empirical research presented in Goss et al. [13] the model is analysed for the following values of the parameters taken from [13]:

- $N = 1000$: number of workers in the ant colony
- $move = 0.5$: one ant every two seconds leaves the nest
- $r = 2$: relation between length of long branch w.r.t. short branch
- $walk\_short = 0.05$: the short branch takes on average 20 seconds to be traversed
- $walk\_long = 0.05/r$: traversing the long branch takes r times much time as traversing the short branch
- $k = 20$: factor k in the choice function

One way to visualize the relative preference of ants for one branch w.r.t. the other is to show how the fraction of pheromone present on each branch changes over time. This is shown in Fig. 2(a) for a stochastic simulation with 10000 independent runs over a time period of 3000 seconds (50 min.), covering the duration of the experiments by Goss et al.. The figure shows that, after a brief initial time interval, on average, there is more pheromone on the short branch than on the long branch. Inspection of single simulation runs reveals that the behaviour tends to two different stable states: one in which all ants use the short branch (Fig. 3(a)) and one in which all ants use the long branch (Fig. 3(b)). Two such simulations are shown in Fig. 3. However, on average the short branch emerges more often than the long branch for the given parameter values, which explains the results in Fig. 2(a).

Fig. 2(b) shows the total number of ants in the colony and the number of ants that are in the nest over time, which are at least 942 at any time.

Let us now turn to a fluid flow analysis of the same model and same parameter values as shown in Fig. 5(a). It is immediately clear that the fluid results are

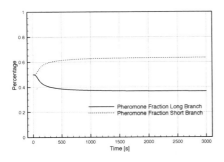
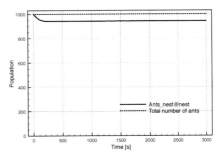

(a) Fraction of pheromone amounts at beginning of short (S1) and long (L1) branch over time

(b) Number of ants present in the nest

Fig. 2. Stochastic simulation, 10000 independent runs

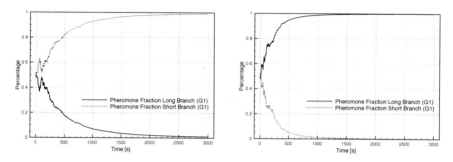

(a) Fraction of pheromone amounts in S1   (b) Fraction of pheromone amounts in S1
and L1   and L1

Fig. 3. Two different single simulation runs

quite different from the simulation results of Fig. 2(a). Fig. 5(a) seems to indicate
that the short branch emerges much earlier and more often than results from a
stochastic simulation of the same model with 10000 independent runs.

An important result by Kurtz [15] on continuous approximation of stochastic
processes says that the fluid approximation can be obtained as the limit of a
sequence of CTMC models for increasing population levels. In particular, it has
been shown that such approximation works well if the rates of the model can
be shown to be density dependent. But let us first consider what it would mean
to generate a sequence of models with increasing population levels for the ant
colony model. If a system has a total number of components that does not change
when the system evolves this total could be taken as the system size. However,
in the ant colony model the number of ants is constant, but the amount of
pheromone in the various locations grows unlimited over time. So, let us consider
as the system size the sum of the *initial* populations of ants and pheromone and
consider a sequence of systems where this populations are scaled with a factor
$E \in \mathbb{N}$, so $N = 1000 * E$. Unfortunately, this alone does not mean that there are
really more ants active (i.e. out of the nest) in our system. This is due to the
fact that ants leave the nest with a constant rate of one ant every two seconds.
We can work around this by scaling the exit rate as well by factor E, i.e. define
$move = 0.5 * E$. Fig. 4(a) shows the result of a single simulation of the model
scaled by a factor $E = 100000$ and renormalised afterwards. The shape of the
graph seems to get closer to the fluid flow results of Fig. 5(a). However, a second
simulation, shown in Fig. 4(b) of exactly the same model and parameters shows
that it is also possible that the *long* branch emerges, giving a simulation trace
that differs completely from that obtained by fluid flow analysis. In other words
the simulation results are very unstable despite the large population considered.

Let us consider the rate function of the actions go_A_S1 and go_A_L1 for
the choice between two branches. The factor k in that function could also be
interpreted as the initial amount of pheromone present at both branches. Viewed
that way, it would be interesting to consider a model in which also k is scaled

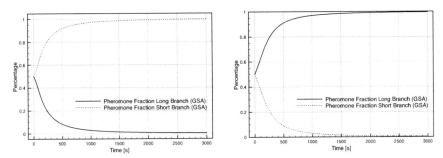

(a) Fraction of pheromone amounts in S1 (b) Fraction of pheromone amounts in S1
and L1   and L1

Fig. 4. Two different single simulation runs for model scaled by E=100000

in a similar way as N, i.e. $k = 20 * E$. We found that, in this case, single
simulation traces, such as the one shown in Fig. 5(b), give indeed results that
are very similar to the fluid flow results in Fig. 5(a); in the sequel we give
a formal justification to this intuitive interpretation. A closer inspection of the
rate function involving the choice between branches showed that it is indeed easy
to verify that it is density dependent when also k is scaled, thus the hypothesis
of Kurtz' theorem are fulfilled and the stochastic process associated with the
underlying CTMC—which the simulation is based on—*coincides*, in the limit,
when scaling the population to infinite, with the solution of the ODEs. If k is
not scaled, it is not immediate how a remaining dependency on the population
size in the formula could be dealt with.

More formally, consider the rate function for the transition go_A_S1 for the
choice of the short branch at choice point A:

$$f_{go\_A\_S1}(\bar{X}) = \frac{(k+P\_S1@S1)^2}{(k+P\_S1@S1)^2+(k+P\_L1@L1)^2} * Ant\_A@A;$$

where $\bar{X}$ denotes the population vector of the model containing the values for
$P\_S1@S1$, $P\_L1@L1$, $Ant\_A@A$ etc. To show that this rate function is density
dependent we need to find a function g such that:

$$E \cdot A_0 \cdot g(\frac{1}{E \cdot A_0}(\bar{X})) = f(\bar{X})$$

where A_0 is the initial value of ants in the nest and E is the multiplication factor.

Let us focus on transition go_A_S1. Consider a function g such that its component for transition go_A_S1, which we denote by $g_{go\_A\_S1}$, is defined as below,
assuming that also k is scaled and is part of the population vector $\bar{X}$. Let us
also assume that the arguments of $g_{go\_A\_S1}$ for the values related to $P\_S1@S1$,
$P\_L1@L1$, $Ant\_A@A$, k etc. are indicated by Y_{P_S1}, Y_{P_L1}, Y_{Ant_A}, Y_k etc., resp.:

$$g_{go\_A\_S1}(\bar{Y}) = \frac{(Y_k + Y_{P\_S1})^2}{((Y_k + Y_{P\_S1})^2 + (Y_k + Y_{P\_L1})^2)} \cdot Y_{Ant\_A}$$

Now we need to show that $E \cdot A_0 \cdot g(\frac{1}{E \cdot A_0}(\bar{X})) = f(\bar{X})$ for the transition from
A to the short branch:

$$E \cdot A_0 \cdot g_{go\_A\_S1}\left(\frac{1}{E \cdot A_0}(\bar{X})\right)$$

$$= E \cdot A_0 \cdot \frac{\left(\frac{k}{E \cdot A_0} + \frac{P\_S1@S1}{E \cdot A_0}\right)^2}{\left(\left(\frac{k}{E \cdot A_0} + \frac{P\_S1@S1}{E \cdot A_0}\right)^2 + \left(\frac{k}{E \cdot A_0} + \frac{P\_L1@L1}{E \cdot A_0}\right)^2\right)} \cdot \frac{Ant\_A@A}{E \cdot A_0}$$

$$= \frac{\left(\frac{k}{E \cdot A_0} + \frac{P\_S1@S1}{E \cdot A_0}\right)^2}{\left(\left(\frac{k}{E \cdot A_0} + \frac{P\_S1@S1}{E \cdot A_0}\right)^2 + \left(\frac{k}{E \cdot A_0} + \frac{P\_L1@L1}{E \cdot A_0}\right)^2\right)} \cdot Ant\_A@A$$

$$= \frac{\frac{1}{(E \cdot A_0)^2} \cdot (k + P\_S1@S1)^2}{\frac{1}{(E \cdot A_0)^2} \cdot (k + P\_S1@S1)^2 + \frac{1}{(E \cdot A_0)^2} \cdot (k + P\_L1@L1)^2} * Ant\_A@A$$

$$= \frac{(k + P\_S1@S1)^2}{(k + P\_S1@S1)^2 + (k + P\_L1@L1)^2} * Ant\_A@A$$

It is easy to see that g in this case is indeed the function we were looking for. Other rate functions in the model are simple mass action functions or similar to the one shown above. So, the model can be shown to be density dependent when scaling the ant population, the pheromones and the factor k. This explains the good correspondence found in that case between fluid flow results and renormalised stochastic simulation runs of a scaled model with $E = 100000$ as shown in Fig. 4.

6   Related Work

It is not the first time that formalisms of a process algebraic nature are used to model and analyse the social behaviour of insects. In the work by Tofts in the early nineties [20] the calculus Weighted Synchronous CCS (WSCCS), an extension of Milner's SCCS [18], was used to describe a probabilistic synchronisation algorithm assumed to underly the observed auto-synchronisation behaviour of ants. In that work the behaviour of individual ants has been modelled and the

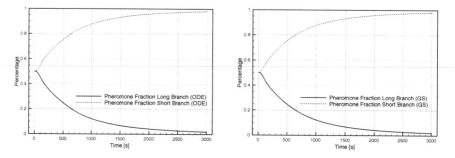

(a) Fraction of pheromone amounts in S1 and L1 (ODE)

(b) Fraction of pheromone amounts in S1 and L1 (G1 scaled)

Fig. 5. Fluid flow analysis and scaled simulation

global behaviour has been analysed by studying the related transition matrices and by performing model based simulation. Later work by Sumpter et al. [19] extends Tofts' work on modelling ant colony behaviour by further types of analyses of the WSCCS models, like Markov chain analysis and mean field methods. Mean field approximation is a technique which is similar to fluid flow analysis but it is usually applied to Discrete Time Markov Chains (DTMCs) rather than CTMCs. The use of CTMCs instead of DTMCs adds to the model the dimension of (continuous) *time*, still preserving the probabilistic behaviour. Consequently, it makes it natural to model issues like the fact that it takes *longer* to ants to traverse the long path.

7   Discussion and Further Work

The emergent effect of ants choosing the short branch can be explained by the positive feedback information that returning ants provide. The ants that choose the short branch arrive before those that chose the long branch and therefore more pheromone builds up at the beginning of the short branch. This only works if pioneer ants have time to return to the nest before many of their fellow ants start to look for food too. Choosing a constant rate for ants leaving the nest leads to a model that better reflects such experimental observations.

The small exploratory study of ants described in the present note illustrates some of the progress that has been made in recent years that facilitates considerably the analysis of process algebraic models of collective behaviour. Among such progress is the development of automated tools for the generation of stochastic simulations and *continuous* fluid flow approximations from process algebraic models of large collectives of interacting agents. The inclusion of explicit notions of locality and context dependent flexible definition of activity rates in the formalism may further broaden the kind of dynamical systems that can be modelled and analysed using a formal modelling approach. Such an approach has the additional advantage that it provides a mathematical underpinning of the collective behaviour under study and the related underlying distributed and stochastic algorithms. Furthermore, fluid flow methods exhibit a high degree of *scalability* in the numbers of individuals of each species or, more generally, in the number of processes in a certain state. In fact, such numbers are just the initial condition of the initial value problem for the associated ODEs. On the other hand, the approach is more sensitive to the number of different species, since the number of differential equations in the system grows (linearly) with it.

As we have seen, scaling k made it easy to prove density dependence. This fact brought us to the conjecture that if k is considered a constant of the model, then the scaling conditions of Kurtz' theorem might not be fulfilled. The full consequences of these findings are topic of further study.

There are several other issues which remain to be addressed and which we would like to study further, in the future. We have observed that which of the two branches emerges depends critically on the initial conditions of the model. Such effects can be studied by imposing artificially a larger initial amount of pheromone on the long branch than on the short branch and perform a fluid flow analysis. It would be interesting to study this phenomenon and establish a critical value for such a "phase shift" for different conditions of sensitivity of ants to pheromone differences and its relation to the value k, i.e. the sensitivity of ants to differences in relatively small amounts of pheromone. Another parameter to which sensitivity of the model could be studied is the ratio r between the long and the short path (set to 2 in this paper). It would also be interesting to investigate the effect of choice functions with higher or lower degrees and, of course, to investigate whether and how the model could be extended for more complicated topologies.

Finally, in this work we have used Bio-PEPA as modelling language and the related Bio-PEPA toolset for fluid flow analysis and simulation. However, a number of other interesting formal languages for stochastic modelling have been proposed, among which SCCP [2,3,4], a Stochastic Concurrent Constraint language, fluid flow PEPA [14] and StoKLAIM [9], a stochastic variant of a Linda-like language based on tuple spaces and with asynchronous coordination. These languages reflect different modelling concepts, while for all of them, analysis techniques such as stochastic simulation, e.g. in PRISM [16], and fluid flow approximation have been implemented or are under development. We plan to consider the various approaches taking variants of the foraging ant colony as a central modelling theme.

Acknowledgments. The authors would like to thank Stephen Gilmore, Allan Clark and Adam Duguid (University of Edinburgh) for their support with the Bio-PEPA plug-in and other features. We also would like to thank Jane Hillston (University of Edinburgh) for making us aware of the earlier work on modelling ant colony behaviour and Mirco Tribastone (LMU Munich), Luca Bortolussi (University of Trieste) and Michele Loreti (University of Florence) for taking up ant modelling as well in different formalisms and sharing with us their findings and results which contributed to improvements in the model and analysis presented in the present paper. This research has been partially funded by the EU-IP FET-Open project ASCENS (nr. 257414) and Project TRACE-IT - PAR FAS 2007-2013 - Regione Toscana.

References

1. Ascens Project, http://www.ascens-ist.eu/
2. Bortolussi, L.: Stochastic concurrent constraint programming. In: Proceedings of the 4th International Workshop on Quantitative Aspects of Programming Languages, QAPL 2006. ENTCS, vol. 164-3 (2006)
3. Bortolussi, L., Policriti, A.: Modeling biological systems in concurrent constraint programming. Constraints 13(1-2), 66–90 (2008)
4. Bortolussi, L., Policriti, A.: Dynamical Systems and Stochastic Programming: To Ordinary Differential Equations and Back. In: Priami, C., Back, R.-J., Petre, I. (eds.) Transactions on Computational Systems Biology XI. LNCS, vol. 5750, pp. 216–267. Springer, Heidelberg (2009)

5. Ciocchetta, F., Duguid, A., Gilmore, S., Guerriero, M.L., Hillston, J.: The Bio-PEPA Tool Suite. In: Proc. of the 6th Int. Conf. on Quantitative Evaluation of SysTems, QEST 2009, pp. 309–310 (2009)
6. Ciocchetta, F., Guerriero, M.L.: Modelling biological compartments in Bio-PEPA. ENTCS 227, 77–95 (2009)
7. Ciocchetta, F., Hillston, J.: Bio-PEPA: An extension of the process algebra PEPA for biochemical networks. ENTCS 194(3), 103–117 (2008)
8. Ciocchetta, F., Hillston, J.: Bio-PEPA: A framework for the modelling and analysis of biological systems. TCS 410(33-34), 3065–3084 (2009)
9. De Nicola, R., Katoen, J., Latella, D., Loreti, M.: StoKLAIM: A stochastic extension of KLAIM, CNR-ISTI Technical Report number ISTI-2006-TR-01 (2006)
10. Deneubourg, J.L., Aron, S., Goss, S., Pasteels, J.M.: The self-organizing exploratory pattern of the argentine ant. Journal of Insects Behaviour 3(2) (1990)
11. Dorigo, M., Stützle, T.: Ant Colony Optimization. The MIT Press (2004)
12. Gillepie, D.T.: Exact stochastic simulation of coupled chemical reactions. The Journal of Physical Chemistry 81(25), 2340–2361 (1977)
13. Goss, S., Aron, S., Deneubourg, J.L., Pasteels, J.M.: Self-organized shortcuts in the Argentine Ant. Naturwissenschaften 76, 579–581 (1989)
14. Hillston, J.: Fluid flow approximation of PEPA models. In: Proceedings of QEST 2005, pp. 33–43. IEEE Computer Society (2005)
15. Kurtz, T.G.: Solutions of ordinary differential equations as limits of pure Markov processes. Journal of Applied Probability 7(1), 49–58 (1970)
16. Kwiatkowska, M., Norman, G., Parker, D.: PRISM: Probabilistic model checking for performance and reliability analysis. ACM SIGMETRICS Performance Evaluation Review (2009)
17. Kwiatkowska, M., Norman, G., Parker, D.: PRISM 4.0: Verification of Probabilistic Real-Time Systems. In: Gopalakrishnan, G., Qadeer, S. (eds.) CAV 2011. LNCS, vol. 6806, pp. 585–591. Springer, Heidelberg (2011)
18. Milner, R.: Calculi for synchrony and asynchrony. Theoretical Computer Science 25(3), 267–310 (1983)
19. Sumpter, D.J.T., Blanchard, G.B., Broomhead, D.S.: Ants and agents: a process algebra approach to modelling ant colony behaviour. Bulletin of Mathematical Biology 63, 951–980 (2001), doi:10.1006/bulm.2001.0252
20. Tofts, C.: The autosynchronisation of *leptothorax acervorem* (fabricius) described in WSCCS. Tech. Rep. ECS-LFCS-90-128, LFCS, University of Edinburgh (1990)

Real-Time Coordination Patterns for Advanced Mechatronic Systems

Stefan Dziwok[1], Christian Heinzemann[1], and Matthias Tichy[2]

[1] Software Engineering Group, Heinz Nixdorf Institute,
University of Paderborn, Germany
{stefan.dziwok,christian.heinzemann}@uni-paderborn.de
[2] Software Engineering Division, Department of Computer Science and Engineering,
Chalmers University of Technology and University of Gothenburg, Sweden
tichy@chalmers.se

Abstract. Innovation in today's mechanical systems is often only possible due to the embedded software. Particularly, the software connects previously isolated systems resulting in, so-called, advanced mechatronic systems. Mechatronic systems are often employed in a safety-critical context, where hazards that are caused by faults in the software have to be prevented. Preferably, this is achieved by already avoiding these faults during development. A major source of faults is the complex coordination between the connected mechatronic systems. In this paper, we present Real-Time Coordination Patterns for advanced mechatronic systems. These patterns formalize proven communication protocols for the coordination between mechatronic systems as reusable entities. Furthermore, our approach exploits the patterns in the decomposition of the system to enable a scalable formal verification for the detection of faults. We illustrate the patterns with examples from different case studies.

Keywords: Advanced Mechatronic Systems, Patterns, Coordination, Communication, Real-Time, MechatronicUML.

1   Introduction

Mechanical engineering has a long tradition in sustained development of innovation, e.g., innovation in cars in the last century. However, in the last decades, software is the driving force for innovation in mechanical engineering as, e.g., in the automotive domain [17]. Modern mechanical systems are developed by experts from several engineering disciplines: mechanical engineering, electrical engineering, control engineering, and software engineering. These systems are called mechatronic systems. Mechatronic systems often operate in a safety-critical context where failures can lead to death or serious injury to people.

Furthermore, previously isolated systems increasingly form systems of systems where each autonomous part communicate with each other by means of complex message exchange protocols [16] in an ad-hoc manner. This results in very complex systems.

M. Sirjani (Ed.): COORDINATION 2012, LNCS 7274, pp. 166–180, 2012.

| (i) RailCabs building a convoy | (ii) BeBots exploring the area together | (iii) Robots playing ping-pong without using a camera |

Fig. 1. Examples for advanced mechatronic systems

These trends make the development of advanced mechatronic systems a big challenge. Thus, appropriate development approaches have to be utilized and rigorously followed. Particularly, the software has to be subject of rigorous verification and validation activities.

Figure 1 shows three advanced mechatronic systems developed at the University of Paderborn in the last couple of years. On the left, two autonomous shuttles of the RailCab systems are shown. RailCab shuttles are autonomous railway vehicles which combine the flexibility of individual transport with the energy efficiency of public transport systems. They save energy by forming convoys which reduce the air resistance. In the middle, two miniature robots called BeBots are shown. BeBots form ad-hoc networks in order to jointly execute tasks. The robots can collectively agree on taking different roles to achieve the common task. On the right, two cooperating robots are shown which play ping-pong. They do so without any external global camera system but instead rely on the timely exchange of position, velocity, and trajectory of the batted ball.

In all three advanced mechatronic systems, coordination plays an important role because they consist of independent, communicating actors (e.g., autonomous mechatronic systems), who join their efforts towards mutually defined goals (cf. [15]). For example, the communication actors decide on a common strategy (e.g., activating the convoy) or they decide on a master who delegates tasks to the slaves. These coordination aspects require sophisticated coordination protocols.

We developed the coordination protocols for these systems based on the patterns presented in [10,6,7,8] in order to exploit the vast amount of existing experience. The patterns listed in these approaches proved to be very helpful in developing our systems. However, they lack a formal description which may lead to the introduction of errors in the application to new systems. As we focus on safety-critical mechatronic systems, a pattern approach which avoids this introduction of errors in the first place is beneficial in order to guarantee the safety of the system.

Based on that experience, we developed Real-Time Coordination Patterns which formalize coordination protocols for mechatronic systems with a particular focus on safety properties and hard real-time constraints. Furthermore, protocols that are based on these patterns enable to decompose the mechatronic system in such a way that a scalable formal verification using model checking can be employed. This is possible because of our previous work on compositional verification [12]. In contrast to the pattern formalism of [12], we further abstract from application-specific details for a better reusability, define a description format for the patterns, and have build up a catalog of patterns.

In summary, the contribution of this paper is as follows: (1) we present Real-Time Coordination Patterns as formal representation of reusable coordination protocols, (2) we present formal refinement steps which define how these patterns are applied and refined, and (3) we report on a case study in which the approach was applied to the aforementioned cooperating robots example.

Section 2 presents MECHATRONICUML, which is the foundation for our approach. In Section 3, we introduce Real-Time Coordination Patterns that are patterns for Real-Time Coordination Protocols. We show how these patterns are applied to new systems in Section 4. Thereafter, we present the cooperating robots case study in Section 5. Next, we distinguish our results from related work in Section 6. Finally, we conclude with an outlook on future work in Section 7.

2 MechatronicUML

MECHATRONICUML [3] is a language for the model-driven design of software of advanced mechatronic systems. It follows the component-based approach where each component encapsulates a part of the software. In advanced mechatronic systems, the components that constitute the software do not work in isolation, but they have to coordinate their actions using communication for achieving the intended functionality of the system. Therefore, each component defines a set of external interaction points, which we call ports. Components can communicate via their ports if a connector connects them.

A connection between two components implies that they are able to communicate correctly. The protocol definition formally defines the message exchange and the timing constraints that the message exchange needs to adhere to. In MECHATRONICUML, a protocol is defined by a pair of communicating roles and a connector. We call it a Real-Time Coordination Protocol. We describe the behavior of each role with a Real-Time Statechart.

Real-Time Statecharts are an extension of UPPAAL timed automata [5] to support, e.g., modeling of worst-case execution times and deadlines for actions. Real-Time Statecharts especially support the specification of asynchronous messages as well as real-time constraints. In addition, Real-Time Statecharts may define variables and operations that are required for the communication. Their semantics is defined by a mapping to UPPAAL timed automata [11].

Figure 2 shows an example of a Real-Time Coordination Protocol named Convoy Coordination which is used for coordinating a convoy of RailCabs. The behavior is as follows: Initially, both Real-Time Statecharts are in the states NoConvoy/Default. Then, the rear RailCab, i.e., the RailCab driving behind, may switch to state Waiting by sending an asynchronous message convoyProposal to the front RailCab to initiate the convoy build-up. The front RailCab receives this message and switches to EvaluateProposal. In this state, the front RailCab decides

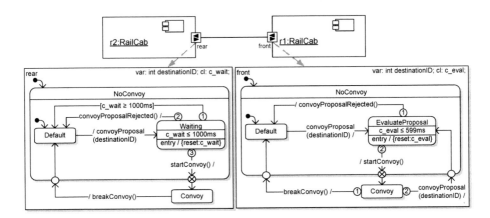

Fig. 2. Real-Time Statecharts of Real-Time Coordination Protocol *Convoy Coordination*

whether a convoy is useful or not. The decision depends, among others, on how long both RailCabs share the same route. For this reason, the rear RailCab sends the ID of its destination as a parameter of the convoyProposal. Within 599ms, either the front RailCab rejects the proposal by sending convoyProposalRejected or it accepts by sending startConvoy. In the first case, both Real-Time Statecharts return to the Default states. In the second case, both Real-Time Statecharts switch to state convoy. For avoiding a deadlock in the rear RailCab, it specifies a time out in state Waiting which causes it to return to Default after 1000ms. The transition, however, has lowest priority (indicated by 1) such that a message will be considered if it has been received. While being in state Convoy, the rear RailCab may propose to break the convoy by sending breakConvoy, which causes both to return to the NoConvoy/Default state. The transition from Convoy to EvaluateProposal is needed to prevent deadlocks in case of message loss.

The protocol definition in MECHATRONICUML explicitly considers that a transmission of a message from sender to receiver takes time. Therefore, the connectors may receive a transmission delay. In our example, we assume a transmission delay of up to 200ms.

In many cases, the communication of the components is safety-critical, i.e., a malfunctioning communication may cause severe damage to property or human lives. For example in case of the convoy coordination, RailCabs may collide if the RailCab driving behind assumes to be in convoy mode while the RailCab driving in front does not. In convoy mode, the RailCab driving in front must notify its follower before braking. If the RailCab driving in front is not in convoy mode, it will not send the notification. Thus, we must ensure that the RailCab driving behind, i.e., the rear role of the protocol, only enters the state Convoy if the front role is in state Convoy as well. We formalize such properties using the Timed Computation Tree Logic (TCTL) [1]. Thus, the aforementioned property is formalized as *AG rear.Convoy implies front.Convoy*.

The properties are formally verified using timed model checkers like UP-PAAL [4]. In our verification, we explicitly consider the delay of the connector as well as the case that messages may be lost, e.g., when using an unreliable transmission medium. In addition, we assume that messages are not reordered during the transmission and that they are stored in a FIFO-queue allowing only access to the first element. The protocol introduced in this section remains safe w.r.t. the specified property and free of deadlocks.

The behavior of a component constitutes from the Real-Time Statecharts of the ports. In addition, the component may provide additional internal behavior, e.g., for resolving conflicts between different ports or for providing additional operations as discussed in Section 4.

In most cases, the system under construction cannot be verified as a whole using model checking because of the state space explosion problem (the number of reachable states is often exponential in the size of the specification). To achieve a scalable formal verification, we use the compositional verification approach of [12]. Here, we verify each Real-Time Coordination Protocol separately before verifying each component. This is enabled by clearly separating component internal behavior and communication behavior using Real-Time Coordination Protocols.

3   Patterns for Real-Time Coordination Protocols

In MechatronicUML, connectors are first class entities. Therefore, the focus within the first process steps is to design the coordination and communication behavior. Based on given requirements, the developer has to specify one Real-Time Coordination Protocol per connector. While doing so, he has to ensure that it is free of faults despite hard real-time constraints, message delay and the possibility of message loss. Although the developer is able to identify faults regarding the behavior description using model checkers, removing the faults is a non trivial task. In general, specifying a Real-Time Coordination Protocol is very complex and thus, very time-consuming and error-prone. Moreover, the intention of an already existing protocol is often hard to grasp.

While modeling Real-Time Coordination Protocols for different advanced mechatronic systems, we identified that the coordination is based on recurring use-cases. This applies for the coordination between autonomous systems, but also for the coordination between components within one system. Therefore, we define general, reusable solutions for these recurring use cases (we call them Real-Time Coordination Patterns). These patterns support the developer by offering solutions that contain formal models and a comprehensive documentation. By doing so, our goal is to increase the quality of the resulting Real-Time Coordination Protocols as well as the efficiency of their development.

3.1   Real-Time Coordination Patterns

In general, a pattern within software design "provides a scheme for refining the subsystems or components of a software system, or the relationships between them. It describes a commonly recurring structure of communicating components that solves a general design problem within a particular context" [6].

A Real-Time Coordination Pattern describes a well-proven, reusable, and formal solution to a commonly occurring coordination problem within the domain of advanced mechatronic systems. These systems communicate under hard real-time constraints in a safety-critical environment. Hence, Real-Time Coordination Patterns are a special kind of software patterns and support inexperienced developers in specifying Real-Time Coordination Protocols. A Real-Time Coordination Pattern is defined such that it respects certain safety properties, which can be formally verified using model checkers. Moreover, if a developer defines coordination protocols based on our patterns, the system under construction can be fully verified based on our compositional verification approach [12].

A Real-Time Coordination Pattern abstracts from application-specific details to be reusable in different scenarios. For example, time parameters are defined instead of concrete time values. However, the correctness of a protocol depends on real-time constraints and properties of the connector (e.g., reliability) and is therefore not automatically correct for all possible time parameters and all connectors. Thus, we define the steps a developer has to execute for each pattern to get a correct protocol (see Section 4).

The Real-Time Coordination Patterns that we identified so far are collected and described within a pattern catalog [9]. Currently, the catalog consists of eight patterns. A briefly overview of those follows:

Synchronized Collaboration synchronizes the activation and deactivation of a collaboration of two roles. The pattern assumes that a safety-critical situation appears if the role, which initialized the activation, is in collaboration mode and the other role is not in collaboration mode. Therefore, the pattern ensures that this situation never happens.

Fail-Safe Delegation realizes a delegation of a task from a master role to a slave role. The slave executes the task in a certain time and answers regarding success or failure. If the execution fails, no other task may be delegated until the master ensures that the failure has been corrected. Moreover, only one delegation at a time is allowed.

Fail-Operational Delegation realizes a delegation of a task from a master role to a slave role. The slave executes the task in a certain time and answers regarding success or failure. The pattern assumes that a failure is not safety-critical, though only one delegation at a time is allowed.

Master-Slave-Assignment is used if two systems can dynamically change between one state in which they have equal rights and another state in which one is the master and the other one is the slave.

Periodic Transmission can be used to periodically transmit information from a sender to a receiver. If the receiver does not get the information within a certain time, a specified behavior must be activated to prevent a safety-critical situation.

Producer-Consumer is used when two roles shall access a safety-critical section alternately. For example, one produces goods, the other consumes them. The pattern guarantees that only one is in the critical section at the same time.

Block Execution coordinates a blocking of actions, e.g., due to safety-critical reasons.

Limit Observation is used to communicate if a certain value violates a defined limit or not.

3.2   Description Format of Our Patterns

For describing our patterns, we defined a uniform description format such that a developer can understand, compare, and use our patterns more easily.

Several popular description formats for software patterns already exist [6,10]. We analyzed how well they fit to our patterns and, hence, decided to choose the format of Buschmann et al. [6] and adapt it to our needs.

We use all attributes of their description format except of *implementation* and *example resolved* because we propose to use code generators and resolve our example already within the other attributes. Furthermore, we divide the attribute *see also* into the two attributes *alternative patterns* and *combinability* because these are two different contents, which are easier to find and understand for the developer if they are separated from each other. At last, we add the attribute *verification properties* to explain the verification properties that must hold for the pattern.

To conclude, Real-Time Coordination Patterns are described with the following attributes: *name* (including a short summary), *context, problem, solution, structure, behavior, verification properties, consequences, examples, variants, alternative patterns*, and *combinability*.

3.3   Example: Synchronized Collaboration

The Real-Time Coordination Protocol *Convoy Coordination* (Fig. 2) is a good solution when two communicating actors have to synchronize the (de-) activation of a concrete collaboration. Therefore, we abstracted it from all its application specific details and defined the Real-Time Coordination Pattern *Synchronized Collaboration* (Fig. 3). We will now give a short description for this pattern. We omitted the attributes *variants, alternative patterns*, and *combinability* because of the limited space of the paper. The full description can be found within our pattern catalog [9].

Name: Synchronized Collaboration (also known as: Strategy Coordination)

This pattern synchronizes the activation and deactivation of a collaboration of two systems. The pattern assumes that a safety-critical situation appears if the system that initialized the activation is in collaboration mode and the other system is not in collaboration mode. Therefore, the pattern ensures that this situation never happens.

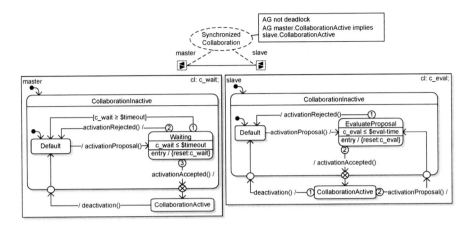

Fig. 3. Structure and behavior of Real-Time Coordination Pattern *Synchronized Collaboration*

Context: Two independent systems can dynamically collaborate in a safety-critical environment.

Problem: Switching between collaboration and no collaboration adds hazards. It may be the case that one system assumes they are working together while the other one does not think so. This must be avoided. The possibility for this problem occurrence increases, if the communication is asynchronous and the communication channel is unreliable. This patterns assumes that the safety-critical situation only occurs, if system s1 assumes they are working together and system s2 does not think so. The other way round is considered as not safety-critical.

Solution: Define a coordination protocol that enables to activate and deactivate the collaboration while it considers the given problems. The systems act with different roles: System s1 is the master and system s2 is the slave. The master initiates the activation and the deactivation. The activation is a proposal so that the slave can decide whether the collaboration is possible and useful. The deactivation is a direct command so that the master can deactivate the collaboration as soon as it is no longer useful.

Structure: The pattern consists of the two roles master and slave and a connector (Fig. 3). The master may send the messages activationProposal and deactivation to the slave. The slave may send the messages activationAccepted and activationRejected to the master. The time parameter of the master role is $timeout, the time parameter of slave role is $eval-time. The connector may lose messages. The delay for sending a message is defined by the time parameters $delay-min and $delay-max.

Behavior: The Real-Time Statecharts of both roles are shown in Fig. 3. A short description is as follows: First, the collaboration is in both roles inactive. The slave is passive and has to wait for the master to decide to send a proposal for activating the collaboration. In this case, the slave has a certain time to answer if he accepts or rejects the proposal. If the slave rejects, the collaboration will remain inactive. If the slave accepts, he activates the collaboration and informs the master so that he also activates the collaboration. If the master receives no answer in a certain time (e.g. because the answer of the slave got lost), he cancels its waiting and may send a new proposal. Only the master can decide to deactivate the collaboration. He informs the slave so that he also deactivates it.

Verification Properties: There will never be a deadlock within the protocol: AG not deadlock. If the master is in state CollaborationActive, then the slave must always be in state CollaborationActive:
AG master.CollaborationActive implies slave.CollaborationActive.

Consequences: Both roles must have a pre-defined behavior when the collaboration is active or inactive. At run-time, the behavior must be adapted accordingly, because master and slave decide on this defined behavior to activate or deactivate the collaboration. Moreover, the slave cannot deactivate the collaboration.

Examples: Two RailCabs are driving on the same track. The rear RailCab wants to create a convoy to take advantage of the slipstream. However, it has to drive with a small gap to the front RailCab. Therefore, the rear RailCab cannot avoid a collision, if the front RailCab brakes hard without informing the rear RailCab. *Synchronized Collaboration* enables to build a secure convoy if the rear RailCab acts as the master and the front RailCab acts as the slave and the rear RailCab only drives with a small gap as long as the convoy collaboration is active.

4 Developing Advanced Mechatronic Systems Using Real-Time Coordination Patterns

In this section, we illustrate how a developer may use the provided Real-Time Coordination Patterns during the development of a concrete system. The general process for each pattern is depicted in Fig. 4.

The developer starts with the requirements for the coordination protocol. Based on these requirements, the developer selects a Real-Time Coordination Pattern which suites the requirements in Step 1. In Step 2, the developer may adapt the Real-Time Coordination Pattern to the concrete domain of the system under development. We call this an *application-specific adaptation* which we describe in detail in Section 4.1. At the end of Step 2, we perform model checking to ensure that all verification properties are met. The result is a Real-Time Coordination Protocol. In Step 3, this protocol is applied to the components of the

Fig. 4. Process for Developing with Design Patterns

system to specify their communication. That requires an *implementation-specific refinement* which we introduce in Section 4.2. The correctness of the refinement is ensured by a refinement check. Finally, the result is a MECHATRONICUML model of the system under construction.

4.1 Application-Specific Adaptation

Real-Time Coordination Patterns are intended to be reused in different applications that operate in different domains. Consequently, they abstract from all application-specific details, e.g., concrete timing information, and use generic names for states and messages. The Real-Time Coordination Pattern *Synchronized Collaboration* in Fig. 3 gives an example.

When applying a Real-Time Coordination Pattern to an application of a specific domain, the developer needs to specify concrete values for all time parameters and the properties of the connector. That includes message delay, consideration of message loss, and the concrete implementation variant of a buffer.

Besides the mandatory steps described above, the developer may adapt the Real-Time Coordination Pattern to the application. This adaptation includes: (1) renaming elements (protocol, roles, states, messages, clocks, variables, operations) to concretize their application-specific meaning, (2) adding new message parameters, (3) changing the state hierarchy (increasing or flattening), (4) adding variables and clocks, and (5) splitting transitions into several transitions with intermediate states. Further adaptations, e.g., adding entirely new states, transitions, and messages, change the solution provided by the pattern significantly. Then, it cannot be assured that the verification properties are still meaningful and sufficient for guaranteeing the safety of the resulting protocol.

After executing all adaptation steps, we obtain a Real-Time Coordination Protocol for the specific application. Given the essential timing information, we can perform model checking on the Real-Time Coordination Protocol to ensure that it satisfies all verification properties specified in the pattern definition. The model checking task is carried out by a timed model checker, e.g., UPPAAL [4].

4.2 Implementation-Specific Refinement

In this step, we assign the resulting Real-Time Coordination Protocols to the components of the system under construction to define their communication. The assignment of a Real-Time Coordination Protocol to a component requires to integrate it with the internal behavior of the component and to resolve conflicts or dependencies between several protocols. As an example for such dependencies, consider the RailCab system. A RailCab may only enter the convoy mode if it is correctly registered at a track side control unit. The registration is performed by another Real-Time Coordination Protocol.

The assignment of a protocol to a concrete component might also require the implementation of component-specific operations. In our example, the front role of the convoy coordination protocol needs to be extended by an implementation that determines whether a convoy is useful or not. The changes which are applied to a Real-Time Coordination Protocol must not invalidate the verified safety and liveness properties which is achieved by a refinement.

The changes which we allow for the implementation-specific refinement are so-called lightweight changes only. The lightweight changes that we support are: (1) adding deadlines to transitions, (2) adding actions to states and transitions, (3) adding synchronizations, and (4) splitting transitions into a sequence of states and transitions. We allow to add invariants to the states and time guards to the transition that originate from splitting transitions.

After applying the lightweight changes, we need to verify that they have been applied correctly. Model checking the whole Real-Time Coordination Protocol, again, is costly and not necessary in this case. Instead, we only need to verify that each role of the Real-Time Coordination Protocol has been refined correctly. That requires the refined role to be checked against the role obtained after application-specific adaptation. If the refinement has been done correctly, the Real-Time Coordination Protocol with the refined role fulfills all verified properties. In [13], we have shown that checking for correct refinement of a single role is more efficient than a repetition of the verification of the whole Real-Time Coordination Protocol. Formal definitions for refinements of timed automata have been introduced in [19] and [13].

5   Case Study: Cooperating Robots

After we collected a set of eight Real-Time Coordination Patterns, we started a case study to answer the following questions: (1) Are our patterns reusable? (2) Is our pattern catalog including our pattern description format helpful? (3) Is our proposed process after selecting a pattern appropriate?

Our new case study were the cooperating robots (Fig. 1 (iii)) that have to play ping-pong using different squash balls without needing a camera to trace the ball. Instead, the two fully independent robots use contact sensors to trace the ball and use communication to inform each other. Among others, the following requirements were defined: (1) Initially, one of both robots receives the ball. (2) Balls with different properties should be supported. (3) The robot that initially receives the ball, first has to juggle it alone to identify the ball properties. (4) The game is restricted to a maximum of 30s. (5) The robot that initially receives the ball has to ensure that the other robot must be ready and knows the ball properties before the ball is hit to it. Otherwise, the other robot cannot hit the squash ball correctly or will not perform a hit at all. Both problems lead to an unwanted behavior.

A computer science student, who has basic knowledge regarding model-driven development, carried out the design of the MECHATRONICUML model and especially the modeling of the coordination and communication. We gave him a detailed introduction of MECHATRONICUML, our existing case studies including the documentation and our pattern catalog. Afterward, we defined the requirements of the application. The student worked primarily on his own except some questions of him regarding the given documents.

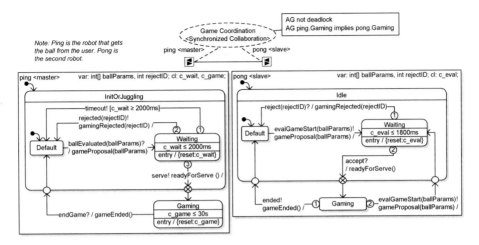

Fig. 5. Real-Time Coordination Protocol *Game Coordination* that is adapted and refined for the coordination of the cooperating robots

As a result, the student defined four Real-Time Coordination Protocols to realize the robot-to-robot communication. Two are based on Real-Time Coordination Patterns, namely: *Master-Slave-Assignment*, and *Synchronized Collaboration*. One of the two non pattern-based protocols is a good solution for an alternating transmission. Thus, we want to abstract it to a new pattern. Regarding the internal communication within each robot, the student used just three protocols to define all 13 internal connectors. Two of them were patterns and the third is a good candidate for a new pattern.

For example, the student selected the pattern Synchronized Collaboration to synchronize the start and the end of the game between the robots while ensuring that the robot that initially receives the ball may only start the game if the other robot is aware of that and does know the ball properties. He adapted the pattern to the Real-Time Coordination Protocol Game Coordination (Fig. 5), e.g., he defined the time variables, renamed some elements, and added a new invariant for state Gaming of statechart ping to restrict the length of the game. The model checker did not found any errors within the resulting protocol. Therefore, the student assigned the protocol to a connector and refined it by synchronization channels to integrate it with the internal behavior of the connected components.

Concluding, the student successfully reused our Real-Time Coordination Patterns, adapted them to Real-Time Coordination Protocols, and reused these protocols, but with different refinement-variants. Regarding the pattern catalog, the student found the description and its format fitting and on the correct level of abstraction. The student was able to carry out the steps of our proposed process, which defined the application-specific adaptation and the implementation-specific refinement, in an efficient manner.

6   Related Work

Patterns regarding the coordination and communication between classes, components, and systems already exist and were a great help for defining our own patterns. However, most of them only illustrate the communication informally using sequence diagrams. If at all, they only define simple timing behavior. Examples for these are the patterns *Chain of Responsibility*, *Command*, and *Observer* by Gamma et al. [10] and the patterns *Master-Slave*, *Forwarder-Receiver*, *Client-Dispatcher-Server*, and *Publisher-Subscriber* by Buschmann et al [6]. In contrast to these pattern systems, we formally specify the coordination using Real-Time Statecharts. Using them, the messages a communication participant may receive and send depend on its current state and on additional real-time constraints.

Real-Time Coordination Patterns are protocol patterns for the domain of advanced mechatronic systems. Other domains-specific languages also defined patterns for communication, e.g., in the domain of multi-agent-system. For example, AGENTUML is a modeling language to specify agent interaction protocols [2]. For such protocols the Foundation of Intelligent Physical Agents defined so-called protocol templates, e.g., the *Propose Interaction Protocol*, which proposes an interaction that can be accepted or rejected. Agent interaction protocols combine sequence diagrams with the notion of state diagrams, though they do not support real-time constraints that are mandatory in our domain of advanced mechatronic systems.

Douglass [7,8] defined real-time design patterns for the collaboration between components, e.g., *Watchdog*. The behavior is described by UML state machines including useful real-time constraints and message exchanges. However, our behavior is described using Real-Time Statecharts, which are more expressive (e.g., they can define how long a state may be active). Furthermore, Douglass does not define how a developer may adapt this pattern for his application.

We define our patterns in a formal way and describe the process of their subsequent adaptation and refinement. Taibi et al. [18] describe several approaches regarding the formalization of patterns and their subsequent refinement, but they do not focus on coordination protocols of advanced mechatronic systems.

In contrast to the mentioned related work, our patterns consider safety-critical situations (in the domain of advanced mechatronic systems) that must not happen. They offer a solution which ensures that these situations never appear. Furthermore, we define a process that preserves these characteristics during the application of the pattern.

7   Conclusions and Future Work

In this paper, we proposed patterns for Real-Time Coordination Protocols, which we call Real-Time Coordination Patterns. They describe safety-critical problems that appear when a developer designs the coordination through communication between advanced mechatronic systems. Furthermore, our patterns suggest a solution that is reusable in different applications and specifies the behavior in such a way that it can be proven regarding safety-critical requirements. We used a real application example to explain the need of our patterns. Moreover, we defined how developers should develop the coordination when they use our patterns. We identified eight patterns through several case studies and were able to reuse them in a new case study. We mainly differ from existing pattern systems, because we specify safety-critical requirements that our patterns ensure.

Our patterns may help developers to increase the quality of coordination protocols for advanced mechatronic systems and to improve the efficiency developing them.

Several topics require further investigations: (1) We have to carry out a comprehensive evaluation to confirm our results. (2) We want to examine more case studies for advanced mechatronic systems to identify additional Real-Time Coordination Patterns. (3) In this paper we only introduced patterns for a one-to-one communication. However, Real-Time Coordination Protocols for one-to-many and many-to-many communication also exist. Therefore, we want to extend our catalog with such patterns. (4) To enable a developer to improve the search for an appropriate pattern, we are currently designing an ontology to store our patterns within the Semantic Web as suggested in [14]. Afterward, we want to enable the developer to search after patterns within our MECHATRONICUML modeling tool Fujaba Real-Time Tool Suite. (5) Our patterns have many variants. Therefore, we want to define a feature model for each pattern so that a developer may select a feature configuration and the system automatically constructs the corresponding structure, behavior model, and verification properties.

Acknowledgment. We thank Marcel Sander for being the test person of our case study *cooperating robots*. This work was developed in the project "EN-TIME: Entwurfstechnik Intelligente Mechatronik" (Design Methods for Intelligent Mechatronic Systems). The project ENTIME is funded by the state of North Rhine-Westphalia (NRW), Germany and the EUROPEAN UNION, European Regional Development Fund, "Investing in your future". This work was developed in the course of the Special Research Initiative 614 - Self-optimizing Concepts and Structures in Mechanical Engineering - University of Paderborn, and was published on its behalf and funded by the Deutsche Forschungsgemeinschaft. Christian Heinzemann is supported by the International Graduate School Dynamic Intelligent Systems.

References

1. Alur, R., Courcoubetis, C., Dill, D.: Model-checking in dense real-time. Information and Computation 104, 2–34 (1993)
2. Bauer, B., Müller, J.P., Odell, J.: Agent UML: A Formalism for Specifying Multiagent Software Systems. In: Ciancarini, P., Wooldridge, M.J. (eds.) AOSE 2000. LNCS, vol. 1957, pp. 91–103. Springer, Heidelberg (2001)

3. Becker, S., Brenner, C., Dziwok, S., Gewering, T., Heinzemann, C., Pohlmann, U., Priesterjahn, C., Schäfer, W., Suck, J., Sudmann, O., Tichy, M.: The MechatronicUML method – process, syntax, and semantics. Tech. Rep. tr-ri-12-318, Software Engineering Group, University of Paderborn (February 2012)

4. Behrmann, G., David, A., Larsen, K.G.: A Tutorial on UPPAAL. In: Bernardo, M., Corradini, F. (eds.) SFM-RT 2004. LNCS, vol. 3185, pp. 200–236. Springer, Heidelberg (2004)

5. Bengtsson, J.E., Yi, W.: Timed Automata: Semantics, Algorithms and Tools. In: Desel, J., Reisig, W., Rozenberg, G. (eds.) ACPN 2003. LNCS, vol. 3098, pp. 87–124. Springer, Heidelberg (2004)

6. Buschmann, F., Meunier, R., Rohnert, H., Sommerlad, P., Stal, M.: Pattern-Oriented Software Architecture. A System of Patterns, vol. 1. Wiley (1996)

7. Douglass, B.P.: Doing hard time: developing real-time systems with UML, objects, frameworks, and patterns. Addison-Wesley, Boston (1999)

8. Douglass, B.P.: Real-Time Design Patterns: Robust Scalable Architecture for Real-Time Systems. Addison-Wesley, Boston (2002)

9. Dziwok, S., Bröker, K., Heinzemann, C., Tichy, M.: A catalog for Real-Time Coordination Patterns of advanced mechatronic systems. Tech. Rep. tr-ri-12-319, University of Paderborn (February 2012)

10. Gamma, E., Helm, R., Johnson, R.E., Vlissides, J.: Design Patterns: Elements of Reusable Object-Oriented Software. Addison-Wesley, Boston (1995)

11. Giese, H., Burmester, S.: Real-time statechart semantics. Tech. Rep. tr-ri-03-239, Software Engineering Group, University of Paderborn (June 2003)

12. Giese, H., Tichy, M., Burmester, S., Schäfer, W., Flake, S.: Towards the compositional verification of real-time UML designs. In: Proceedings of the 9th European Software Engineering Conference held Jointly with the 11th ACM SIGSOFT International Symposium on Foundations of Software Engineering, ESEC/FSE 2003, pp. 38–47. ACM Press (September 2003)

13. Heinzemann, C., Henkler, S.: Reusing dynamic communication protocols in self-adaptive embedded component architectures. In: Proceedings of the 14th International Symposium on Component Based Software Engineering, CBSE 2011, pp. 109–118. ACM (June 2011)

14. Henninger, S., Corrêa, V.: Software pattern communities: Current practices and challenges. In: Proceedings of the 14th Conference on Pattern Languages of Programs, PLoP 2007, Monticello, Illinois, USA, September 5-8 (2007)

15. National Science Foundation: A report by NSF-IRIS review panel for research on coordination theory and technology. Tech. rep., NSSF Forms and Publication Unit, National Science Foundation, Washington, D.C (1989)

16. Schäfer, W., Wehrheim, H.: The Challenges of Building Advanced Mechatronic Systems. In: FOSE 2007: 2007 Future of Software Engineering, pp. 72–84. IEEE Computer Society (2007)

17. Scharnhorst, T., Heinecke, H., Schnelle, K.P., Bortolazzi, J., Lundh, L., Heitkämper, P., Leflour, J., Maté, J.L., Nishikawa, K.: Autosar - challenges and achievements 2005. In: 12th International VDI Congress Electronic Systems for Vehicles 2005, Baden-Baden. VDI Berichte, vol. 1907. VDI (2005)

18. Taibi, T. (ed.): Design Patterns Formalization Techniques. IGI Publishing, Hershey (2007)

19. Tripakis, S., Yovine, S.: Analysis of timed systems using time-abstracting bisimulations. Formal Methods in System Design 18(1), 25–68 (2001)

Group Orchestration in a Mobile Environment

Eline Philips*, Jorge Vallejos,
Ragnhild Van Der Straeten, and Viviane Jonckers

Software Languages Lab, Vrije Universiteit Brussel, Belgium
{ephilips,jvallejo,rvdstrae}@vub.ac.be,
vejoncke@soft.vub.ac.be

Abstract. The increasing popularity of mobile devices fosters the omnipresence of services in mobile environments. Software systems in a mobile environment often want to manage a set of services that form a logical group and orchestrate the execution of a particular process for all its members. To orchestrate a group of services, abstractions are required which allow control over the execution in a way that transcends the individual process of a single member. Currently, existing languages do not offer adequate abstractions to perform said group orchestration in a reliable way. In this paper we present high-level abstractions for group orchestration as a new set of workflow patterns. We show how these patterns are integrated in an existing workflow language for nomadic networks, i.e. NOW. The workflow language NOW handles network and service failures at the core of the language. By extending this fault tolerance to the new group abstractions, we show how to conduct these in a reliable way.

1 Introduction

People everywhere are surrounded by a wide range of mobile and stationary devices that can perform all kinds of services. For instance, today's smartphones are able to determine the temperature, location, orientation, etc. Since devices and services are everywhere nowadays, there is a need to address several services or devices at the same time. For instance, to determine the current temperature at a certain location, one could retrieve that information from several temperature services in the neighbourhood and calculate the average.

Existing approaches that interact with a group of services can be either classified in the domain of group communication or group behaviour. *Group communication* [14] addresses technologies that can enable effective communication between various groups in the network, using for instance multicasting. *Group behaviour* [12] is the capability of services to coordinate with each other. In order to coordinate a group of services, the dependencies between the members of the group must be managed in order to let them collaborate.

These domains focus on communication and/or coordination, but have little support for orchestration. *Service orchestration* is defined by Peltz [15] as a

---

* Funded by a doctoral scholarship of the "Institute for the Promotion of Innovation through Science and Technology in Flanders" (IWT Vlaanderen).

M. Sirjani (Ed.): COORDINATION 2012, LNCS 7274, pp. 181–195, 2012.

business process that interacts with both internal and external Web services. We define *group orchestration* in a mobile environment as the management of a set of services that form a logical group where all its members execute a particular process. Moreover, there is a need to control the execution of the group members in a way that transcends the individual process. Group orchestration should be able to deal with both the voluntary and involuntary removal and addition of group members. It is also essential that there are ways to synchronise and streamline the execution process of several group members.

As group orchestration provides high-level abstractions to manage the execution of processes for the group members, it differs from group communication which is only concerned about the low-level protocols that can be used for the underlying communication. Group orchestration also differs from group behaviour. Even though group behaviour also needs to take the necessary precautions to handle unforeseen network failures, it focusses on the collaboration between the group members unlike group orchestration which aims at the management of the execution of a process by all the members of the group.

In this paper we present high-level abstractions for group orchestration and introduce these abstractions in the workflow language NOW. NOW is a workflow language that allows the orchestration of distributed services in a mobile network. This workflow language introduces high-level control flow patterns and abstractions which can deal with network failures that are inherent to a mobile environment. We extend this workflow language with novel abstractions to enable reliable group orchestration in a mobile environment.

The paper is organised as follows: in Section 2 we give a motivating example and an enumeration of the requirements the proposed abstractions need to fulfill. In Section 3 we give a short introduction to NOW as we extend this language with novel patterns for group orchestration. In Section 4 the novel abstractions for group orchestration with services are presented. Before concluding the paper, we describe related work.

2   Motivation

In this section we describe an example scenario which emphasises requirements for group orchestration in a mobile environment.

"The headliner of the Pukkelpop festival decides to surprise its fans with a special concert by letting them vote for the songs that will be played. In order to accomplish this they use the festival's infrastructure to communicate with the mobile phones of the fans who are present in the festival area. All fans who are interested in participating in this vote receive a list of the band's discography. They are able to vote until two hours before the band's concert is scheduled. All votes that are received afterwards are considered invalid. As a special bonus, the voters have the benefit of receiving the band's final playlist before the start of the concert."

We enumerate the requirements for group orchestration that can be distilled from this small example. These requirements for group orchestration in a mobile environment can be divided into three categories, namely "definition of group membership", "synchronisation mechanisms", and "failure handling".

1. **[C1] Definition of Group Membership**:
   - *Intensional definition [R1]*: Users should be able to define processes that will be executed by a set of services that form a logical group. This group can be either defined extensionally, by enumerating all its members, or intensionally by giving a description all members must fulfill.
     In the example scenario, a group is defined intensionally, namely all fans of the headliner who are located in the festival area.
   - *Plurality encapsulation [R2]*: First of all, users want to orchestrate a group of services as if they are one single unit. Moreover, as we are targeting mobile environments, this quantity of group members can fluctuate over time as new services join and disjoin the group. This requirement is known in existing literature as the need for encapsulating plurality [11] or arity decoupling [10].
     As we show in the scenario, the members of the group are not known a priori and can change over time. For instance, fans can arrive at the festival area at a later point in time then other fans who were there earlier and who have already received the request to vote.
   - *Dynamic modification [R3]*: During the execution of the group it must be possible to redefine the members of this group. It should be possible to restrict the members by filtering out members based on a certain condition and also to change the group's description causing the arity of the group to change.
     In the motivating example, the group initially consists of all fans of the headliner. Later on, only those fans who are interested in voting are being addressed.
2. **[C2] Synchronisation Mechanisms [R4]**: In order to streamline all execution processes of the group members, the fact which service can do which task at what time needs to be managed and controlled. Moreover, the number of times a specific task is executed and the data needed during this execution should be controllable. Synchronisation mechanisms can let processes wait, redirect and even abort in order to let given criteria persist. This way, synchronisation mechanisms influence the amount of members of the group.
   In the example scenario, all results need to be gathered two hours before the headliner's concert is going to start. This task should only be performed by a single service at a specific point in time. Therefore, all data needs to be collected before the execution of that task can start.
3. **[C3] Failure Handling [R5]**: As mobile environments are liable to volatile connections, ways to detect and handle failures must be available. First of all, it should be possible to react upon a failure that occurs during the individual process execution of a single member of the group. Moreover,

there must be mechanisms to detect and handle failures at the group level and even propagate individual failures to the group level.

In case a failure occurs within an individual process execution of a single fan, there should be a compensating action that tries to re-execute the process (for instance, resending the message). However, when something goes wrong when the votes of all fans are being gathered, the compensation should apply for all fans, hence the entire group's execution.

3   Small Introduction to NOW

In this section we give a brief introduction of the workflow language NOW, as this is the language we extended with novel abstractions to support group orchestration. NOW [5] is a workflow language sculpted for *nomadic networks* [1]. These networks consist of a fixed infrastructure and mobile devices that try to maintain a connection with that infrastructure. These kinds of networks are omnipresent, for instance, airports, shopping malls, hospitals, etc.

NOW is built as a library on top of AMBIENTTALK, a distributed scripting language targeting mobile ad hoc networks [3]. For both types of mobile networks, disconnections are considered the rule rather than the exception. Hence, in order to ensure that the workflow description cannot become unavailable during its execution, the workflow description resides on the fixed infrastructure of the network.

Failure Handling. NOW introduces control flow patterns and failure handling patterns. The control flow patterns that are supported by the language range from very basic ones, like sequence and parallel split, to more advanced ones, like multiple instances patterns. NOW's *failure* pattern wraps a subworkflow and specifies compensating actions for possible failures that can occur. The different kinds of failures that can be detected are: a service that cannot be found, a disconnection that occurred, a timeout that occurred while interacting with a specific service, or an exception raised by that service. For these failures, one can specify compensating actions like restart, retry, rediscover, skip, wait, or executing an alternative subworkflow. These compensating actions can be chained together, to support compensations like *wait 20 seconds, retry to invoke the same service twice, when this fails execute another subworkflow.* As volatile connections are inherent to the type of networks targeted by NOW, the language supports default compensating actions.

Data Flow. NOW also uses a dynamic data flow mechanism that passes data between the distributed services in the environment by employing a *data environment.* Such a data environment is a dictionary, containing variable bindings, that is passed between the activities of the workflow. Each activity can specify input and output variables used for its service invocation. The output variables (specified by the @Output annotation) cause (new) variable bindings to be added to the data environment. In case of fork patterns (like parallel split), this data environment is conceptually copied and when a join occurs (like a synchronization pattern), these incoming data environments are merged using a merging strategy (like choosing the one with a maximum value for a certain variable). For more detailed information we refer the interested reader to [5] and [6].

4   Abstractions for Group Orchestration

In this section we describe the novel abstractions we introduce in NOW in order to satisfy the requirements for group orchestration we presented in Section 2. The description of these abstractions adheres to the categories and requirements we presented in Section 2. The implementation of NOW is extended with these novel abstractions and is available at [13]. In the remainder of this section we use small excerpts from the motivating example to illustrate their use. The entire implementation of this example scenario can also be found at [13].

4.1   Definition of Group Membership

First of all, we need to introduce an abstraction for a group, namely a subworkflow that must be executed for a set of services. In order to do so, we extended NOW with the notion of a *group* pattern.

```
Group( <description>, <variable name>, <subworkflow> )
```

This pattern is instantiated with a description of the services, a variable name that can be used to refer to the member services individually, and the subworkflow that must be executed several times.

Intensional Definition [R1]. The description of the services can be either achieved by enumerating all of them (extensional description) or by describing all properties those services must fulfill (intensional description). Deciding which services to interact with in a dynamically changing environment is hard when reasoning extensionally about it, as the set of services can vary over time. In these kinds of environments it is opportune to provide intensional descriptions for those services. Intensional descriptions abstract away the precise number of services during interaction and let services maintain anonymity during this interaction. A group should be able to specify a description such that not only services of the same type, like temperature services, but also more sophisticated characterisation of members can be achieved. In particular, there is a need for intensional descriptions of services such as *"the service I last used"*, *"my favourite service"*, or *"all temperature services that are nearby and have an accuracy of more than 95%"*. In order to support such intensional descriptions, the logical coordination language CRIME [4] can be used.

The Fact Space Model [4] of CRIME provides a logic coordination language for reasoning about context information that is represented as facts in a federated fact space. Concretely, facts are locally published by applications and transparently shared between nearby devices as long as they are within communication range. Applications have the ability to react upon the appearance of facts, by making use of rules. This logic language uses the forward chaining strategy for deriving new conclusions as this data-driven technique is very suitable for the event-driven nature of CRIME. Therefore, we integrated CRIME in NOW which is targeted towards nomadic networks where lots of events (connections, disconnections, etc.) occur.

We support both types of group descriptions: extensional and intensional. First of all, it is possible to instantiate a group with an array of objects. These objects can be either references to the services (e.g. the fans of Pukkelpop's headliner), or just plain objects (for instance all ids of those fans). Additionally, we allow intensional description of the group members by either using a *type tag*[1] or by writing a logical expression in CRIME.

In our example scenario, all the fans of Pukkelpop's headliner need to be addressed. This can be expressed by writing a logical expression in CRIME[2]:

```
pp_visitor(?id), band_info(?band, "headliner"), fan_info(?id, ?band)
```

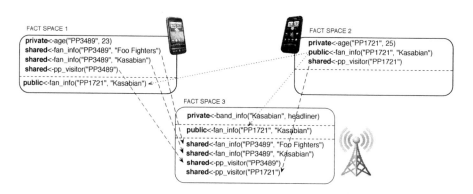

Fig. 1. Federated fact spaces of co-located devices

In Figure 1 we depict the federated fact spaces of two fans and the federated fact space residing on the festival's infrastructure who are connected in a mobile ad hoc network. Those fact spaces consist of *qualified facts* which denote the fact space the fact belongs to. The different kinds of fact spaces we support are "private", "public" and "shared".[3] Private facts are not exchanged between co-located devices, whereas public ones are. In order to limit the exchange of facts between co-located devices, we added a third type of fact space "shared". Facts that are published in this fact space are only exchanged to fact spaces who

---

[1] AMBIENTTALK's type tags, wrapped JAVA interfaces, represent service types.

[2] CRIME's syntax resembles the one of PROLOG, although CRIME is a forward chainer.

[3] The shared fact space was added when integrating CRIME in NOW.

have subscribed to that type of facts. In our example, the infrastructure of the festival is interested in a lot of information of the fans, for instance the facts of type pp_visitor and fan_info, whereas fans are, in general, not interested in those published facts of other fans. Therefore, the facts that are published in the shared fact space are only asserted in the federated fact space of the infrastructure (fact space 3 in Figure 1).

Plurality Encapsulation [R2]. A group pattern can be started by executing its start method with its incoming data environment, the same way it is done for other workflow patterns in NOW [6]. When the group pattern is started, first all services satisfying the group's description need to be retrieved. In case of an extensional description, there is no need to query the backbone, but for intensional descriptions the services satisfying the description need to be looked up. Once these services are retrieved, the incoming data environment is cloned for each of these services. This way, each member of the group has his own data environment where local changes can occur. In order to access the specific service (member) for which the subworkflow is executed, a reference to the service is added in the data environment used to start each individual instance. When an intensional description was used to define the group members, the variable name (<variable name>) is bound to an AMBIENTTALK *far reference*[4] to the particular member. Afterwards, the subworkflow that is wrapped by the group pattern, is started with each of these data environments, as can be seen in Figure 2.[5]

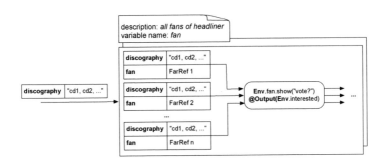

Fig. 2. Starting the execution of a group pattern

Once the group pattern is started, it is possible that the backbone discovers a new service that satisfies the group's description. In this case, a new member is added to the group and the subworkflow wrapped by the group is started once more. Note that this only applies when an intensional description (type tag or CRIME expression) was given. However, sometimes this behaviour is not wanted.

---

[4] A far reference is AMBIENTTALK's remote object reference.
[5] This diagram and the other diagrams in the remainder of the paper are used to help the reader follow the examples we present.

Therefore, NOW also allows the specification of a *snapshot group*, where the number of services communicated with is fixed.

```
SnapshotGroup( <description>, <variable name>, <subworkflow> )
```

Unlike a normal group, such a snapshot group does not allow new members to join the execution once started. Note however that once the snapshot group is made, members of the group can still disconnect. By using NOW's failure handling mechanisms, it is possible to react upon such a disconnection of a group member in an appropriate way. This is described in more detail in Section 4.3.

Dynamic Modification [R3]. As we already mentioned, it should be possible to redefine the members of a group when its execution is going on. For instance, it should be possible to restrict the members of the group by filtering out those members that do not satisfy a certain condition. Therefore, we introduce a *filter* pattern which only allows the instances who satisfy the given condition[6] to continue their execution.

```
Filter( <condition> )
```

In the motivating example of Section 2, the group is initially executed for all fans of Pukkelpop's headliner. However, after being asked if they are interested in participating, the members of the group are restricted to only those whom expressed their enthusiasm. This is depicted in Figure 3, where the condition of the filter will verify the value of the variable `interested` in the data environment, Env.

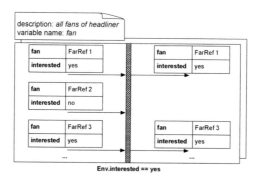

Fig. 3. Restricting the members of the group by using a filter

4.2   Synchronisation Mechanisms [R4]

The introduction of group orchestration gives rise to more advanced synchronisation patterns. The inherent volatile connections of the network cause communication partners to disconnect making full synchronisation not always possible.

---

[6] In Section 4.2 we give more details about the kinds of conditions that can be used to instantiate a filter with.

For instance, synchronisation should be able to succeed when only partial results are returned (after the first result, after a number of results, after some time, etc.). In this section we elaborate on the different synchronisation mechanisms needed to orchestrate a group in NOW. All of these synchronisation mechanisms do not only have an influence on the execution of the subworkflow by each of the group members, they are also reflected on the group itself. We present several types of synchronisation mechanisms that can be used to streamline the execution of the group's instances.

In this section we describe four patterns that enable group synchronisation, namely a *barrier*, *cancelling barrier*, *group join*, and *synchronised task*. Those patterns have some criteria in common:

- A condition is given to specify *when* the synchronisation may succeed. All individual instances whose execution was blocked, can continue their execution the moment the condition is satisfied.
- When the given condition is fulfilled, it is possible that next instances (i.e. instances that reach the synchronisation at a later point in time) should not continue their execution. Therefore, it should be possible to state whether or not a *cancellation* should take place.
- It is possible that when the condition is fulfilled, a specific task (subworkflow) needs to be executed *once*.
- When such a one-time task is specified, a merging strategy can be defined to specify which *data* must be available during the execution of that task.

In the remainder of this section, we first elaborate on the conditions that are used to instantiate group synchronisation patterns. Thereafter we describe four specific synchronisation patterns which use some of the criteria mentioned above.

Conditions Used by Group Synchronisation Patterns. All group synchronisation patterns are instantiated with a certain condition, such as *"after 10 seconds"*, *"when all instances have succeeded"*, or *"when 90% of the instances have succeeded"*. Such a condition can be either classified as a *time constraint*, a *quota constraint*, or a combination of both. NOW supports two different kinds of time constraints, namely a deadline (At) and a duration constraint (After). The *at* condition is fulfilled at a certain moment in time, whereas *after* succeeds a predefined time after the synchronisation pattern is reached for the first time. NOW also supports two kinds of quota constraints: Percentage and Amount. The *amount* and *percentage* condition take as argument a number and are satisfied when that number, or that given percentage of instances respectively, has reached the pattern. The above conditions can be combined using logical expressions and a *combiner* pattern. For instance the expression Combiner(or(Amount(1), After(60)) implements a condition that is satisfied *"when one instance has started the synchronisation pattern, or after 60 seconds"*. It is also possible to extend the quota constraints with a user-defined function.

Barrier and CancellingBarrier Pattern. We now present two novel patterns that allow synchronisation of individual instances of group members by blocking their execution until a specified condition is fulfilled.

```
Barrier( <condition> )
CancellingBarrier( <condition> )
```

When the execution of an individual instance of a group member reaches a *barrier*, the condition of the pattern is verified. When the condition is not yet fulfilled, the execution of that instance is blocked. At the moment the condition is fulfilled, all instances that were blocked resume their execution.

Figure 4(a) depicts the scenario where the individual instances of two group members are blocked as the barrier's condition is not yet satisfied. Once the condition is satisfied (e.g. time has passed 20:30 o'clock), the blocked instances can continue their execution. This is shown in Figure 4(b).

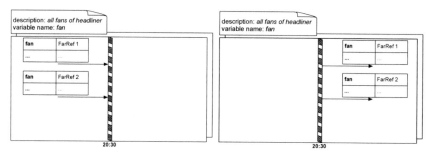

(a) Barrier of which the condition is not yet satisfied.   (b) Barrier with a fulfilled condition.

Fig. 4. Synchronisation: the barrier pattern

The difference between a (normal) barrier and a *cancelling barrier* is explained by the way they treat instances that arrive at a barrier whose condition is already fulfilled (i.e. the "cancellation" criteria mentioned earlier). Individual instances of a member that arrive later at a normal barrier continue their execution without waiting. On the other hand, when a *cancelling barrier* is used, only the blocked instances will execute the remainder of the workflow after the barrier. The execution of the next instances that reach the cancelling barrier pattern are cancelled.

Remark that a cancelling barrier, by definition, has an influence on the amount of members of the group. Once the condition of the cancelling barrier pattern is fulfilled, the blocked instances of the individual members continue their execution. From that moment on, the amount of members of the group is restricted to those that were able to continue their execution.

GroupJoin Pattern. In order to terminate the execution of the group pattern both control flow and data flow must be merged. The *group join* pattern allows managing how control flow and data flow are merged. The default merging strategy used to merge the data environments of all instances is "accumulating all values for each variable", one of the merging strategies proposed in [5]. However, it is often wanted to specify another merging strategy. Therefore, the fourth optional argument to instantiate a group can be instantiated with a specific GroupJoin pattern.

Group(<description>, <variable name>, <subworkflow>, [<group join>])

A group join pattern is instantiated with both a condition and a merging strategy. Once this condition is fulfilled, the control flow of all individual instances is merged such that the remainder of the workflow pattern after the group pattern is executed only once. Therefore, a group join pattern is, by definition, always cancelling, meaning that instances that reach the pattern after the condition is fulfilled, will not be able to continue their execution.

GroupJoin(<condition>, <merging strategy>)

In Figure 5 we show how both control flow and data flow are merged to terminate the execution of a group pattern. Note that we do not depict the group join pattern explicitly, as it is the only place the pattern is allowed.

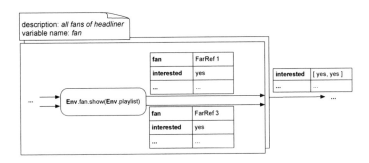

Fig. 5. Synchronisation: a group join pattern to terminate the group

Synchronised Task. In this section we present the notion of a synchronised task, a subworkflow that only needs to be executed once for the entire group at a specific moment. In essence, each member of the group executes its own instance, but there should be provisions to allow a single task to be executed *once* for several or all members of the group. Therefore, a *synchronised task* is, by definition, always cancelling, meaning that instances that reach the pattern after the condition is fulfilled, will not be able to continue their execution.

SynchronisedTask(<subworkflow>, <condition>, <merging strategy>)

A synchronised task starts the execution of its wrapped subworkflow once a given condition is fulfilled. In Figure 6 we show the functionality of the synchronised task, that is depicted as a gray box wrapping a subworkflow (in this example, one single activity). As can be seen in the figure, both control flow and data flow of the instances must be merged before the wrapped subworkflow can be started.

During the execution of the synchronised task's subworkflow, new variable bindings can be added to the merged data environment. In this concrete example, shown in Figure 6, a new binding is added for the variable `playlist`. At the end of the synchronised task pattern, the incoming data environments of all instances are restored, and extended with those new variable bindings.

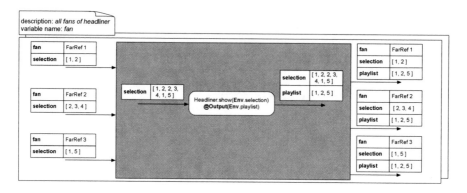

Fig. 6. Synchronised task: executing a single task synchronised

4.3   Failure Handling [R5]

As mobile environments are liable to volatile connections, ways to detect and handle failures must be available. NOW's failure handling mechanism, described in Section 3, allows the specification of compensating actions for specific kinds of failures. In this section we present the influence of this failure handling mechanism on the novel abstractions for group orchestration we presented above. First of all, we describe *individual failure handling*, meaning the handling of failures that occurred during the individual instance of a group member. Thereafter we elaborate on how failures can be detected for the entire group.

Individual Failure Handling. In order to specify compensating actions for a single individual instance of a group member, it is necessary to use the failure pattern wrapping a subworkflow *inside* the group pattern. When using the failure pattern outside the group pattern, compensating actions might (depending on the specific type) affect the group as a whole.

```
Group( <description>, <variable name>,
       Failure( <subworkflow>, <failure descriptions>) )
```

When a failure pattern is defined inside a group pattern and wraps (part of) its subworkflow, the compensating actions only have an effect on the individual instance of that subworkflow. For instance, suppose that during the execution of a single instance a disconnection failure occurs, whose compensating action is defined as "restart the wrapped subworkflow". In that particular case, the subworkflow is restarted for that single instance (i.e. one single group member). This is in contrast with the behaviour that is accomplished when this failure pattern is defined on the outside of the group pattern.

Failure Handling for Groups It is also possible to wrap the group pattern itself with a failure pattern.

```
Failure( Group( <description>, <variable name>, <subworkflow> ),
         <failure descriptions> )
```

When the failure pattern is defined outside the group pattern, the compensating actions have an effect on the execution of the entire group. Recall the example we used earlier. When a disconnection failure occurs now, the compensating action will restart the wrapped subworkflow, in this case the group pattern. This causes all instances of the group to be cancelled and to restart the execution of the entire group.

We extended the failure handling support of NOW in order to distinguish between a failure that occurred during the execution of a group member (service), or another service, such that all failures have a *participant* variant. For instance, we make the distinction between a normal disconnection and a participant-disconnection failure. In our example scenario, we would like to specify a different compensating action for when the mobile device of single fan disconnects (for instance, drop that fan from the group), in contrast to a disconnection of the headliner (where the compensation will send a message to the crew members backstage).

The compensating actions that were provided by NOW are extended with two group-specific ones, namely *drop* and *wait-and-resume*. Both compensating actions can only be used in combination with a participant-failure (a failure that affects a group member or the communication with that member). The *drop* compensating action drops the member from the group. The second compensating action, *wait-and-resume*, can be used in combination with a participant-disconnection or a participant-not-found failure. When such a failure occurs, the place (activity) where that failure occurs is stored, such that the execution can be resumed when that specific group member (re)connects.

5   Related Work

van der Aalst [2] describes *multiple instances patterns* which wrap part of a process that needs to be instantiated multiple times. These patterns are supported by YAWL [7]. Defining a group of services can be achieved in YAWL by writing queries to retrieve the data for which the multiple instances pattern must be executed, and defining a multiple instances variable that can be used during its execution. However, this multiple instance variable does not have a reference to the service as its value, but the data resulting from the query. In YAWL it is possible to add new instances during the execution of the "multiple instances without a priori run-time knowledge" pattern. However, the synchronisation mechanisms that are supported by YAWL are rather restricted. The only synchronisation mechanism YAWL supports, is used to terminate the execution of the multiple instances pattern. There are no mechanisms like the barriers we propose provided to synchronise the execution of all instances inside the multiple instances pattern. Moreover, there is no support for the synchronised task abstraction we presented. This behaviour can be modelled in YAWL by defining a multiple instances pattern, followed by an activity or subworkflow proceeding a second multiple instances pattern. The disadvantage of this approach is that contextual information, i.e. the data for which the first multiple instances pattern was started, is discarded. The last requirement, regarding failure handling, is also not supported by YAWL. The language only has built-in support for failure handling for atomic tasks (i.e. a single activity and no subworkflow). Hence, it is not trivial to express failure handling strategies over all the activities in a group.

In the web services community, the notion of a *service group* [8] is introduced to denote a heterogeneous collection of web services that satisfy a given constraint. Such a service group only consists of fixed web services that are known beforehand (by means of a URL). Plurality encapsulation is supported as services can be added or removed from the service group, causing the service group registration to notify requestors of modifications to that service group.

Ambient References [9] enable communication with a volatile group of proximate objects by means of asynchronous message sends. Ambient references are developed as a programming language abstraction for AMBIENTTALK [3]. Both definition by means of an intensional description and arity decoupling are support by this language construct. Ambient references provide synchronisation mechanisms by providing observers that are triggered either when the first service has answered or when all services have responded. However, as communication with the set of services is expressed by means of an atomic message send, redefinition of group members and synchronised task abstractions do not make sense. Moreover, there are no mechanisms provided to express failure handling on an ambient reference, for instance express the action that must be performed when a service disconnects.

6   Conclusion

In this paper, we have presented the design of group orchestration patterns on top of the workflow language NOW. We introduced a novel group pattern and explained the need for advanced group synchronisation patterns. We also showed how network and service failures can be detected and handled during the orchestration of a group of services. By providing these high-level abstractions we enable orchestration with a group of services in a mobile environment where volatile connections dominate.

References

1. Mascolo, C., Capra, L., Emmerich, W.: Mobile Computing Middleware. In: Gregori, E., Anastasi, G., Basagni, S. (eds.) NETWORKING 2002. LNCS, vol. 2497, pp. 20–58. Springer, Heidelberg (2002)
2. Russell, N., ter Hofstede, A.H.M., van der Aalst, W.M.P., Mulyar, N.: Workflow control-flow patterns: A revised view. Technical report, BPMcenter.org (2006)
3. Van Cutsem, T., Mostinckx, S., Gonzalez Boix, E., Dedecker, J., De Meuter, W.: AmbientTalk: object-oriented event-driven programming in mobile ad hoc networks. In: Proceedings of SCCC 2007, pp. 3–12 (2007)
4. Mostinckx, S., Scholliers, C., Philips, E., Herzeel, C., De Meuter, W.: Fact Spaces: Coordination in the Face of Disconnection. In: Murphy, A.L., Ryan, M. (eds.) COORDINATION 2007. LNCS, vol. 4467, pp. 268–285. Springer, Heidelberg (2007)
5. Philips, E., Van Der Straeten, R., Jonckers, V.: NOW: A Workflow Language for Orchestration in Nomadic Networks. In: Clarke, D., Agha, G. (eds.) COORDINATION 2010. LNCS, vol. 6116, pp. 31–45. Springer, Heidelberg (2010)
6. Philips, E., Van Der Straeten, R., Jonckers, V.: NOW: Orchestrating Services in a Nomadic Network using a dedicated Workflow Language. Science of Computer Programming (2011), http://dx.doi.org/10.1016/j.scico.2011.10.012
7. ter Hofstede, A.H.M.: YAWL: yet another workflow language. Information Systems 30, 245–275 (2005)
8. Graham, S., Maguire, T., Frey, J., Nagaratnam, N., Sedukhin, I., Snelling, D., Czajkowski, K., Tuecke, S., Vambenepe, W.: Web Services Service Group - Specification (WS-Service Group), Version 1.2,
   http://docs.oasis-open.org/wsrf/
   wsrf-ws_service_group-1.2-spec-os.pdf
9. Van Cutsem, T., Dedecker, J., Mostinckx, S., Gonzalez Boix, E., D'Hondt, T., De Meuter, W.: Ambient references: addressing objects in mobile networks. In: OOPSLA Companion, pp. 986–997 (2006)
10. Van Cutsem, T., Dedecker, J., De Meuter, W.: Object-Oriented Coordination in Mobile Ad Hoc Networks. In: Murphy, A.L., Ryan, M. (eds.) COORDINATION 2007. LNCS, vol. 4467, pp. 231–248. Springer, Heidelberg (2007)
11. Black, A.P., Immel, M.P.: Encapsulating Plurality. In: Nierstrasz, O.M. (ed.) ECOOP 1993. LNCS, vol. 707, pp. 57–79. Springer, Heidelberg (1993)
12. Guerraoui, R., Rodrigues, L.: Introduction to Reliable Distributed Programming. Springer-Verlag New York, Inc., Secaucus (2006)
13. Philips, E.: Website NOW (2012), http://soft.vub.ac.be/~ephilips/NOW
14. Luo, J., Eugster, P.T., Hubaux, J.-P.: PILOT: ProbabilistIc Lightweight grOup communication sysTem for Mobile Ad Hoc Networks. IEEE Transactions on Mobile Computing, 164–179 (2004)
15. Peltz, C.: Web services orchestration and choreography. IEEE Computer 36(10), 46–52 (2003)

Node Coordination in Peer-to-Peer Networks

Luigia Petre[1], Petter Sandvik[1,2], and Kaisa Sere[1]

[1] Department of Information Technologies, Åbo Akademi University
[2] Turku Centre for Computer Science (TUCS)
Turku, Finland

Abstract. Peer-to-peer networks and other many-to-many relations have become popular especially for content transfer. To better understand and trust these types of networks, we need formally derived and verified models for them. Due to the large scale and heterogeneity of these networks, it may be difficult and cumbersome to create and analyse complete models. In this paper, we employ the modularisation approach of the Event-B formalism to model the separation of the functionality of each peer in a peer-to-peer network from the network structure itself, thereby working towards a distributed, formally derived and verified model of a peer-to-peer network. As coordination aspects are fundamental in the network structure, we focus our formalisation effort in this paper especially on these. The resulted approach demonstrates considerable expressivity in modelling coordination aspects in peer-to-peer networks.

1 Introduction

In recent years, there has been a trend of moving away from the traditional client-server model in network software towards peer-to-peer networks and other many-to-many relations. Especially when it comes to large scale content transfer, peer-to-peer applications and protocols such as BitTorrent [8] have become popular [24], and even found their way into electronic appliances such as network routers [6] and television sets [26]. In short, the paradigm switch from client-server communication models to BitTorrent-supporting networks amounts to enabling "clients" that are already downloading e.g., video streams, to also become "servers" for other potential clients that may download the same content. The participation of every peer in content communication provides a tremendous increase in the communication efficiency, in the communication model flexibility, and in the content availability. It is therefore highly beneficial to have a thorough understanding of this communication paradigm, to uncover its potential weaknesses and recognise how to avoid them.

Peer-to-peer networking proposes a mixed coordination model among peers. At first sight, it resembles data-based coordination, such as distributed tuple spaces, in that one peer enumerates in a webpage its downloadable material and another peer starts downloading the material of interest, found via the webpage or via a special server called tracker. However, even during downloading,

M. Sirjani (Ed.): COORDINATION 2012, LNCS 7274, pp. 196–211, 2012.

the second peer also becomes a data provider of that material, solely due to its downloading and without any enumeration of downloadable material in a webpage. This resembles event-based coordination where communication between processes (peers) is enabled by events generated when certain state changes appear. This is also reminiscent of the publisher-subscriber model of coordination. This partial adherence of peer-to-peer networking to several coordination models is currently not singular. In [18], the authors propose the separation of the coarse grained (coordination) control flow into several event handlers that coordinate (via events) the mobile applications. In their turns, the event handlers need to communicate with each other, typically implicitly, via shared data. Coordination and concurrency are studied in the context of Prolog [25] by decoupling logic engines and multithreads for efficiency; cooperative constructs are then illustrated for both Linda [7] blackboards and publish/subscribe models. Real-time coordination in dataflow networks is typically asynchronous, but in [16], coordination patterns are proposed which combine synchrony and asynchrony. All these models simply try to address the ever-increasing complexity of contemporary software-intensive systems from various viewpoints. However, due to combining several aspects of several coordination models, peer-to-peer networking is a rather complicated model to analyse. In this paper we focus on this analysis problem.

In order to gain a thorough understanding of peer-to-peer networking, we develop and analyse models of a peer-to-peer media distribution system. In particular, in this paper we focus on modelling how peers in a such a system could discover and interact with each other, i.e., we model inter-peer relations as the basis of the peer-to-peer coordination model. In swarm-like peer-to-peer systems, where peers interact only when interested in the same content, a peer that is unable to receive incoming connections, for instance when it is behind a firewall, is at a serious disadvantage compared to other peers [10]. Extensions to the original BitTorrent protocol such as peer exchange (PEX) and distributed hash tables (DHT) [17] have been developed to alleviate this problem, and we need a reusable, extendable model of peer discovery and connectivity to be able to model these. Peer-to-peer systems and other distributed architectures have been formally modelled before [15,28,29], but our focus here is on creating a reusable formal model of inter-peer relations using BitTorrent as our model protocol.

Based on the formal modelling of peer-to-peer relations, we make the following contributions:

- We propose a formal model for analysing properties of peer-to-peer relations and networking.
- We distribute this model and the proven properties as a correct development from the initial model.
- We put forward the dual coordination nature of the distributed model (both data-driven and control-oriented) and the further applicability of our employed formal methodology.

We develop our models based on the Event-B formal method [2], which offers excellent tool support in form of the Rodin platform [3,11]. When developing models in Event-B, the primary concept is that of abstraction [2], as *models* are created from abstract specifications and then refined stepwise towards concrete implementations. We prove the correctness of each step of the development using the Rodin platform, which automatically generates *proof obligations*. These are mathematical formulas to prove in order to ensure correctness; the proving can be done automatically or interactively using the Rodin platform tool. The immediate feedback from the provers makes it possible to adapt our model to better suit automatic proving, and this ability to interleave modelling and proving is a big advantage of development in Event-B using the Rodin platform. Event-B is currently extending to also incorporate *modularisation methodology* [13]. This essentially amounts to proposing distributed versions for various models and proving the correctness of the distribution via refinement. Consider the example of a peer connection operation involving two nodes. We can specify this feature in Event-B typically within one module (called *machine*) that has data and operations on the data; we can also model various properties of the module and prove their correctness. However, at the implementation phase, the peer connection operation typically involves two modules, corresponding to the two connecting peers that synchronise with each other, so that each peer adds the required reference to the other. The modularisation methodology allows the transformation of the modelled peer connection operation into a distributed addition of links among the two peers.

We proceed as follows. In Section 2 we describe the Event-B formalism and its modularisation extension. In Section 3 we introduce our inter-peer relation modelling and in Section 4 we present our modular approach to this. We elaborate on our contribution in Section 5. We conclude this paper in Section 6 with discussion of our findings as well as future work.

2   Event-B and Its Modularisation Approach

In this section we overview Event-B and its modularisation approach to the extent needed in this paper.

2.1   Event-B

Event-B [2] is a state-based formal method focused on the stepwise development of correct systems. This formalism is based on Action Systems [5,27] and the B-Method [1]. In Event-B, the development of a model is carried out step by step from an abstract specification to more concrete specifications. The general form of an Event-B model is illustrated in Fig. 1. Models in Event-B consist of *contexts* and *machines*. A context describes the static part of a model, containing sets and constants, together with axioms about these. A machine describes the dynamic part of a model, containing variables, invariants (boolean predicates on the variables), and events, that evaluate (via event *guards*) and modify (via event *actions*) the variables. The guard of an event is an associated boolean predicate on the variables, that determines if the event can execute or not. The action of an event is a parallel composition of either deterministic or non-deterministic assignments. Computation proceeds by a repeated, non-deterministic choice and execution of an enabled event (an event whose guard holds). If none of the events is enabled then the system deadlocks. The relationship *Sees* between a machine and its accompanying context denotes a structuring technique that allows the machine access to the contents of the context.

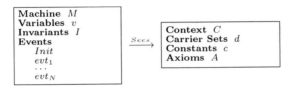

Fig. 1. A machine M and a context C in Event-B

The semantics of Event-B actions is defined using *before-after (BA) predicates* [2,3]. A before-after predicate describes a relationship between the system states before and after the execution of an event. The semantics of a whole Event-B model is formulated as a number of *proof obligations*, expressed in the form of logical sequents. The full list of proof obligations can be found in [2].

System Development. Event-B employs a top-down refinement-based approach to the formal system development. The development starts from an abstract system specification that models some essential functional requirements. While capturing more detailed requirements, each refinement step typically introduces new events and variables into an abstract specification. These new events correspond to stuttering steps that are not visible in the abstract specification. This type of refinement is called *superposition refinement*. Moreover, Event-B formal development supports *data refinement*, allowing us to replace some abstract variables with their concrete counterparts. In that case, the invariant of a refined model formally defines the relationship between the abstract and concrete variables; this type of invariants are called *gluing invariants*.

In order to prove the correctness of each step of the development, a set of proof obligations needs to be discharged. Thus, in each development step we have mathematical proof that our model is correct. The model verification effort and, in particular, the automatic generation and proving of the required proof obligations, are significantly facilitated by the provided tool support – the Rodin platform [3,4].

2.2 The Event-B Modularisation Approach

Recently the Event-B language and tool support have been extended with a possibility to define *modules* [13,12,21] – i.e., components containing groups of callable atomic operations. Modules can have their own external (i.e., global) and internal (i.e., local) state and invariant properties. An important characteristic of modules is that they can be developed separately and, when needed, composed with the main system.

A module description consists of two parts – a *module interface* and a *module body*, the latter being an Event-B machine. Let M be a module. A module interface MI is a separate Event-B component. It allows the user of the module M to invoke its operations and observe the external variables without having to inspect the module implementation details. MI consists of external module variables w, constants c, sets s, the external module invariant $M\_Inv(c, s, w)$, and a collection of module operations O_i, characterised by their pre- and post-conditions, as shown in Fig. 2.

Interface MI
  Sees $MI\_Context$
  Variables w
  Invariants $M\_Inv(c, s, w)$
  Initialisation $\cdots$
  Process
      $PE_1 = $ **any** vl **where** $g(c, s, vl, w)$ **then** $S(c, s, vl, w, w')$ **end**
      $\cdots$
  Operations
      $O_1 = $ **any** p **pre** $PRE(c, s, vl, w)$ **post** $POST(c, s, vl, w, w')$ **end**
      $\cdots$

Fig. 2. Interface Component

In addition, a module interface description may contain a group of standard Event-B events under the **Process** clause. These events model the autonomous module thread of control, expressed in terms of their effect on the external module variables. In other words, the module process describes how the module external variables may change between operation calls.

A formal module development starts with the design of an interface. Once an interface is defined, it is not further developed. This ensures that a module body may be constructed independently from a model relying on the module interface. A module body is an Event-B machine that implements the interface by providing a concrete behaviour for each of the interface operations. A set of additional proof obligations are generated to guarantee that each interface operation has a suitable implementation.

When the module M is imported into another Event-B machine (which is specified by a special clause **USES**), the importing machine can invoke the operations of M and read the external variables of M. To make a module specification generic, in $MI\_Context$ we can define some constants and sets (types) as parameters. The properties over these sets and constants define the constraints to be verified when the module is instantiated. The concrete values or constraints needed for module instantiation are supplied in the **USES** clause of the importing machine.

Module instantiation allows us to create several instances of the same module; we distinguish among these instances using a certain *prefix*. Different instances of a module operate on disjoint state spaces. Via different instantiation of generic parameters the designers can easily accommodate the required variations when developing components with similar functionality. Hence module instantiation provides us with a powerful mechanism for reuse.

The latest developments of the modularisation extension also allow the developer to import a module with a given concrete set as its parameter. This parameter becomes the index set of module instances. In other words, for each value from the given set, the corresponding module instance is created. Since each module instance operates on a disjoint state space, parallel calls to operations of distinct instances are possible in the same event.

3   Modelling Inter-peer Relations

We illustrate the first three steps of our development of a formal model for inter-peer relations in Fig. 3. In this section we shortly describe this Event-B model in order to facilitate an easier understanding of the modularised model described in the next section. More details can be found in our technical report [20].

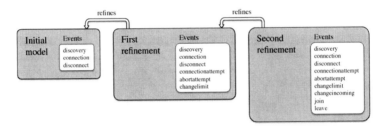

Fig. 3. Model Development

Our initial model is very abstract, with only two major functions. The first concerns one peer becoming aware of other peers. In a peer-to-peer network such as BitTorrent, this would correspond to receiving a list of other peers from a tracker, i.e., a server that keeps track of which peers are involved in sharing a particular content. However, at this stage we are not interested in the specifics of how this subset of all peers is retrieved, only that there is a way of peers to discover other peers. We also note that the tracker is an instantiation of the publish/subscribe coordination model. The second major function is to create a connection between a peer and another peer, where the first peer must be aware of the second but not necessarily vice versa. To model these functions, we define relations between peers, assuming peers are represented by natural numbers for simplicity. An "awareness" relation from 1 to 2 thereby means that peer 1 is aware of peer 2, which is different from a relation from 2 to 1. For the "connection" relation, we note that in practice we only have one connection between two peers, because in peer-to-peer networks such as those based on BitTorrent, connections are symmetrical and traffic can flow in both directions [9]. For that reason, we allow only one connection per peer pair here, e.g., if a "connection" relation exists from 1 to 2 we do not allow one from 2 to 1.

Our initial model is therefore composed of the following events, besides the obligatory *initialisation* event: *discovery*, which creates "awareness" relations from a peer to a subset of other peers, *connection*, which creates a "connection" relation between a peer and another if there is an "awareness" relation from the first to the second, and *disconnect*, which removes an existing "connection" relation between two peers. This disconnection could occur because of network issues or because the peer has decided to no longer participate in the swarm. However, peers also close connections that have had no traffic for a while; Iliofotou et al claim that the differences in download speed between BitTorrent clients can be partly attributed to differences in when they decide to close connections [14]. For this reason it is important for us to model a *disconnect* event that later can be refined into different types of disconnection events. The situation in which peers become unaware of each other does not exist in the actual peer-to-peer networks we are interested in, and therefore there is no need for an event that models such a situation.

For our first refinement step, we limit the amount of connections a peer can have, because otherwise every peer would eventually end up being connected to all the other peers. While this would be possible when the number of peers is low, it would be unrealistic for a large system, and we therefore introduce a connection limit specific to each peer. This means that a connection between two peers may not always be possible, and therefore we also need to modify our connection functionality. Because peers do not know whether another peer can accept their connection or not, we replace our single connection event with two events. The *connectionattempt* event takes a peer whose connection limit has not been reached and another peer that the first peer is aware of but not connected to, and adds a "connection attempt" relation from the first peer to the second one. The *connection* event here takes a peer whose connection limit has not been reached and another peer such that there is a "connection attempt" relation from the second to the first, and creates a "connection" relation from the second to the first while removing the corresponding "connection attempt" relation. We also add another event, *abortattempt*, for aborting a connection attempt, which in practice would happen after a time limit. Because the connection limit is not necessarily constant and can vary between peers, we also add the abstract *changelimit* event describing how the limit may change. The total amount of connections for a peer, specified by the variable *connections*, is here taken to be the sum of the amount of "connection" relations to and from the peer, and the amount of "connection attempt" relations originating from the peer. This means that the limit on connections is a limit on the amount of simultaneous active successful connections and unsuccessful connection attempts.

In the second refinement step we introduce the concept of peers not being able to accept incoming connections, i.e., not being able to have "connection" relations from another peer to itself. First we achieve this in an abstract way, by simply having a boolean variable for each peer and checking the value of that variable before allowing the connection to be created. We add the abstract event *changeincoming* to be able to change the value of this boolean variable for each peer. Later we can refine this situation by specifying a set of more complex relations, such as in the real-life situation where two peers are behind the same firewall and thereby able to accept incoming connections from each other but not from other peers. Furthermore, we refine our model to include *join* and *leave* events for when peers join and leave the swarm, respectively. To reduce the complexity of our model, we specify that all the connections to and from a peer, as well as all connection attempts made by the peer, must be removed before the peer can leave. This can be seen in the following Event-B code:

EVENT *leave* $\hat{=}$
    any
        peer
    where
        grd1 : $peer \in peers \land peer \in onlinepeers$
        grd2 : $\forall p, r \cdot (\{p \mapsto r\} \in connection) \Rightarrow (p \neq peer \land r \neq peer)$
        grd3 : $\forall p, r \cdot (\{p \mapsto r\} \in connectionattempt) \Rightarrow (p \neq peer)$
    then
        act1 : $onlinepeers := onlinepeers \setminus \{peer\}$
    end

So far, we have described a monolithic model of inter-peer relations in a peer-to-peer network. Our next step is to use the modularisation approach described in Section 2.2 to separate the internal functionality of a peer from the coordinating functionality of the network structure.

4   Modularising Inter-peer Relations

Our intent with modularising our model of inter-peer relations is to separate the internal functionality of each peer from the functionality of the network itself; this makes the peers, in a sense, independent of other peers. As we specify the interface that a peer presents to the coordinating network, we can continue to refine and implement the peer separately from the network coordination structure. Therefore, we need to consider which events from our previous model should be implemented in the peer module and which in the Event-B machine specifying the network coordination.

We note that the events *changelimit* and *changeincoming* affect only one peer at a time, and thus should be modelled as processes internal to the peer. Likewise, the *discovery* event only adds to one peer's view, and although it could be argued that this is an event concerning network coordination, nothing specifies that this event needs to invoke the network at all. In BitTorrent, for instance, peer discovery never depends on how peers connect to each other, and therefore it should be seen as a process internal to the peer in this context. The *join* and *leave* events also only affect one peer's status, because we require that the *leave* event is enabled only when the peer has no connections and no connection attempts. This is also reflected in the identically named process in the peer interface, which can be compared to the *leave* event shown in Section 3.

PROCESS *leave* $\hat{=}$
    when
        grd1 : $isonline = TRUE$
        grd2 : $connection = \varnothing \land connectionattempt = \varnothing$

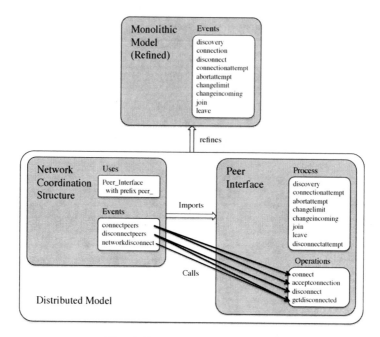

Fig. 4. Decomposition refinement

then
    act1 : *isonline* := *FALSE*
end

Regarding the *connectionattempt* and *abortattempt* events, we note that these events model the intent of one peer, and thus should be modelled as an event internal to the peer, although the variables modified will be read by the network coordination structure. The remaining events *connection* and *disconnect* require coordination between peers, and thus we will describe in more detail how the equivalent functionality is implemented in the distributed model. The overall structure of this decomposition refinement can be seen in Fig. 4.

As mentioned in Section 2.2, we use the **USES** clause to import an interface into an Event-B machine, specifying the name of the interface, the indexing set, and the prefix used to access varibles and operations from the interface.

USES   *Peer_Interface* (peers) with prefix *peer_*

We previously added a guard specifying that a *connectionattempt* must be done before a *connection*. Here, the *connectionattempt* is internal to the peer, and the network coordination structure has an event *connectpeers*. Given two different online peers *s* and *t*, who are not connected to each other, and where *s* has made a connection attempt to *t* and *t* can accept an incoming connection, the operation *acceptconnection* of peer *t* is called with the argument *s*, and likewise the operation *connect* of peer *s* is called with the argument *t*.

EVENT *connectpeers* $\widehat{=}$
  any
     s t
  where
     grd1 : $s \in peers \land t \in peers \land s \neq t$
     grd2 : $t \in peer\_connectionattempt(s) \land peer\_acceptincoming(t) = TRUE$
     grd3 : $t \notin peer\_connection(s) \land s \notin peer\_connection(t)$
     grd4 : $peer\_isonline(s) = TRUE \land peer\_isonline(t) = TRUE$
     grd5 : $peer\_connections(t) < peer\_connectionlimit(t)$
  then
     act1 : $void1 := peer\_acceptconnection(t)(s)$
     act2 : $void2 := peer\_connect(s)(t)$
  end

The variables *void1* and *void2* used here are of the type *VOID*, which is used when an operation call has no return value.

There is a difference between the *acceptconnection* and *connect* operations of the peer interface, in that the former is to be called on a peer that has not made a connection attempt, while the latter is to be called on a peer who has made one. This means that among the preconditions for the *acceptconnection* operation is that the peer must accept incoming connections and must not have reached its connection limit.

OPERATION *acceptconnection* $\widehat{=}$
  any
     dest
  pre
     pre1 : $dest \in peers \land dest \notin connection \land dest \notin connectionattempt$
     pre2 : $connections < connectionlimit$
     pre3 : $acceptincoming = TRUE \land isonline = TRUE$
  return
     void
  post
     post1 : $connection' = connection \cup \{dest\}$
     post2 : $connections' = connections + 1$
     post3 : $void' :\in VOID$
  end

For the peer receiving the *connect* operation call the amount of connections was already increased when making the connection attempt, and therefore should not be increased here. However, as a peer is added to the set of connections, it must also be removed from the set of connection attempts.

OPERATION *connect* $\widehat{=}$
  any
     dest
  pre
     pre1 : $dest \in peers \land dest \notin connection \land dest \in connectionattempt$
     pre2 : $isonline = TRUE$
  return
     void
  post
     post1 : $connection' = connection \cup \{dest\}$
     post2 : $connectionattempt' = connectionattempt \setminus \{dest\}$
     post3 : $void' :\in VOID$
  end

In our monolithic model, the *disconnect* event simply disconnected two peers that were connected. However, we note that in this refinement we need to separate disconnection into two cases; the first of which concerns a peer actively wanting to disconnect from another peer, and another case when the disconnection happens without the intent of any of the peers involved. In the first case, we will handle it similarly to the connection process. In the peer interface, we specify a new process, *disconnectattempt*, which modifies a variable that will be read by the network coordination machine. When the prerequisites are fulfilled, i.e., when two distinct peers are connected and one of them has made a disconnection attempt concerning the other, the event *disconnectpeers* in the machine then calls the *disconnect* operation on the originating peer and *getdisconnected* on the other.

EVENT *disconnectpeers* $\widehat{=}$
    any
        p r
    where
        grd1 : $p \in peers \wedge r \in peers \wedge p \neq r$
        grd2 : $r \in peer\_connection(p) \wedge p \in peer\_connection(r)$
        grd3 : $r \in peer\_disconnectionattempt(p)$
    then
        act1 : $void1 := peer\_getdisconnected(r)(p)$
        act2 : $void2 := peer\_disconnect(p)(r)$
    end

In the peer interface, the two operations *getdisconnected* and *disconnect* are very similar. In the first, the peer must remove the connection to a specific peer for which no "disconnection attempt" has been created, and decrease the number of total connections.

OPERATION *getdisconnected* $\widehat{=}$
    any
        dest
    pre
        pre1 : $dest \in peers \wedge dest \in connection \wedge dest \notin disconnectionattempt$
        pre2 : $connections > 0$
    return
        void
    post
        post1 : $connection' = connection \setminus \{dest\}$
        post2 : $connections' = connections - 1$
        post3 : $void' :\in VOID$
    end

For the *disconnect* operation to be enabled, there must be a "disconnection attempt", but otherwise the preconditions are the same as in the *getdisconnected* operation. The postconditions are also identical to the previously described operation, with the addition that the "disconnection attempt" must also be removed.

OPERATION *disconnect* $\widehat{=}$
    any
        dest
    pre
        pre1 : $dest \in peers \wedge dest \in connection \wedge dest \in disconnectionattempt$
        pre2 : $connections > 0$
    return
        void
    post
        post1 : $connection' = connection \setminus \{dest\}$
        post2 : $connections' = connections - 1$
        post3 : $void' :\in VOID$
        post4 : $disconnectionattempt' = disconnectionattempt \setminus \{dest\}$
    end

As we mentioned, two peers can get disconnected not only by their own intent but also because of external factors. We model this in the network structure machine with the event *networkdisconnect*. This event simply calls the operation *getdisconnected* on each of the two peers, with the other peer as argument, with the prerequisite that the peers must be connected to each other but not have tried to disconnect of their own intent.

EVENT *networkdisconnect* $\widehat{=}$
    any
        u v
    where
        grd1 : $u \in peers \wedge v \in peers \wedge u \neq v$
        grd2 : $v \in peer\_connection(u) \wedge u \in peer\_connection(v)$
        grd3 : $v \notin peer\_disconnectattempt(u) \wedge u \notin peer\_disconnectattempt(v)$
    then
        act1 : $void1 := peer\_getdisconnected(u)(v)$
        act2 : $void2 := peer\_getdisconnected(v)(u)$
    end

The intended goal when creating any formal model such as ours is to be able to prove various properties in the system being modelled. For our monolithic model, all generated proof obligations can be easily discharged using the proving environment of the Rodin platform tool [11]. As the Modularisation plugin includes proof generation and proving support for its extensions to the Event-B language [13], many of the properties that we can prove in the original monolithic model we can also prove in the distributed model. We put forward an example of the transformation of a property to prove from the monolithic to the distributed model in the following section.

Using this modularisation technique to do decomposition refinement increases the complexity of the model, which makes proving more difficult. This applies equally to the automatic proof obligation discharging and interactive proving in the Rodin platform tool. As the tool and the Modularisation plugin evolves, we hope that it will enable us to develop our models further than what is currently possible.

5   Discussion

In this section we summarise the contributions of this paper.

First, we propose a (stepwise developed) monolithic model for inter-peer relations in a peer-to-peer network. This model has a (simple) state consisting of the values of the variables and a set of events that can all access and modify the state. Due to the high level of abstraction, we can formulate and prove various properties about our model. For instance, we have an invariant stating that any peer that is connected to another peer, i.e., has a "connection" relation to it, cannot have a "connection attempt" relation to the same peer, put forward below. Coordination between peers is centralised and endogenous, for instance the event *connectionattempt* coordinates the establishment of a "pre-connection" relation and the event *connection* coordinates the establishment of a real "connection" when the proper conditions for it are met.

$$\forall p, r \cdot (\{p \mapsto r\} \in connection) \Rightarrow (\{p \mapsto r\} \notin connectionattempt) \qquad (1)$$

Second, we refine the monolithic model into a distributed one, in which we separate the coordination between peers from the internal actions (computation) of the peers. Coordination is now exogenous, modelled by the events *connectpeers*, *disconnectpeers*, and *networkdisconnect*. The properties proven in the monolithic model evolve as well, as exemplified in the following. In the peer interface of the distributed model, we are modelling the interface of one peer, and therefore that peer does not need to be included. Thus, the corresponding invariant in the peer interface states that each peer that we have a connection to must not be in the set of connection attempts.

$$\forall p \cdot p \in peers \land p \in connection \Rightarrow p \notin connectionattempt \qquad (2)$$

In both cases, it is of course also trivial to prove the inverse implication, i.e., that a connection attempt between two peers implies that there is no existing connection between the two.

We note that the coordination in the distributed model is rather sophisticated. The coordinator (the network coordination structure) only reads the value of the coordinated peer state (via external variables such as *peer_connection(u)* in event *networkdisconnect*). The peer state is only modified via the nodes' own actions, as described in the operation *getdisconnected*. We can also argue for the coordination paradigm displayed by our modelling to be of a mixed nature. On one hand, the external variables of the peers model a distributed (tuple) space; the coordinator only acts based on reading this space, hence a data-driven coordination. On the other hand, the execution of the coordination actions is not performed directly on the data, but via procedure calls mechanisms, hence, a control-oriented coordination model.

6   Conclusions

Using the *refinement* approach, a system can be described at different levels of abstraction, and the consistency in and between levels can be proved mathematically. With the aim of modelling and analysing a whole, fully featured peer-to-peer media distribution system, we have used Event-B to model inter-peer relations in a BitTorrent-like peer-to-peer network. We have started from an abstract specification and stepwise introduced functionality so that the proving effort remains reasonable. For instance, we could have introduced the *join* and *leave* events already in the first model; however, this would have generated unnecessary proving at an abstract level.

Our focus has been on creating a model of a peer-to-peer system in a way that allows it to be reused and extended for different protocol additions, while keeping the reliability of the system intact. This gives us a foundation from which we can develop a well behaving and scalable peer-to-peer media distribution system. Our goal is to have all the parts, from the network structure up to the content playback, formally modelled and verified. We have previously modelled different parts of such a system, including algorithms for acquiring pieces of media content [22,23] and parts of a video decoding process [19].

A general strategy of a distributed system development in Event-B is to start from an abstract centralised specification and incrementally augment it with design-specific details. When a suitable level of details is achieved, certain events of the specification are replaced by the calls of interface operations and variables are distributed across modules [12]. As a result, a monolithic specification is decomposed into separate modules. Since decomposition is a special kind of refinement, such a model transformation is also correctness-preserving. Therefore, refinement allows us to efficiently cope with complexity of distributed systems verification and gradually derive an implementation with the desired properties and behaviour [2].

With respect to proving properties about models, our strategy is very useful: we formulate and prove properties for the monolithic model and then we develop the distributed model from the monolithic one so that the properties remain valid. This is however not new, as it has been proposed in a number of earlier works, for instance in [5]. With respect to the coordination paradigm, we consider that modularisation in Event-B provides a very interesting methodology for emphasising the separation of the coordination features from the computation ones. This is especially useful in the context of the Rodin tool platform [11] that can significantly improve the property proving effort and thus puts forward our approach to coordination as a practical one.

As future work, we plan to develop the peer-to-peer networking models into an Event-B theory. This means that we can then model specific peer-to-peer networks simply by instantiating them from the theory, much like declaring data types. Hence, we envision a language construct for modern network architectures. With this, we stress once more the reuse potential of our proposal.

Acknowledgements. We would like to thank Alexei Iliasov for helping us to better understand the Modularisation plugin.

References

1. Abrial, J.R.: The B-Book: Assigning Programs to Meanings. Cambridge University Press (1996)
2. Abrial, J.R.: Modeling in Event-B: System and Software Engineering. Cambridge University Press (2010)
3. Abrial, J.R., Butler, M., Hallerstede, S., Hoang, T.S., Mehta, F., Voisin, L.: Rodin: An Open Toolset for Modelling and Reasoning in Event-B. International Journal on Software Tools for Technology Transfer (STTT) 12(6), 447–466 (2010)
4. Abrial, J.R., Butler, M., Hallerstede, S., Voisin, L.: An Open Extensible Tool Environment for Event-B. In: Liu, Z., Kleinberg, R.D. (eds.) ICFEM 2006. LNCS, vol. 4260, pp. 588–605. Springer, Heidelberg (2006)
5. Back, R., Kurki-Suonio, R.: Decentralization of Process Nets with Centralized Control. In: Proceedings of the 2nd ACM SIGACT-SIGOPS Symposium on Principles of Distributed Computing, pp. 131–142 (1983)
6. Belkin Play N600 HD Wireless Dual-Band N+ Router F7D8301, http://www.belkin.com/IWCatProductPage.process?Product_Id=522112 (accessed April 2012)

7. Carriero, N., Gelernter, D.: Data Parallelism and Linda. In: Banerjee, U., Gelernter, D., Nicolau, A., Padua, D.A. (eds.) LCPC 1992. LNCS, vol. 757, pp. 145–159. Springer, Heidelberg (1993)
8. Cohen, B.: Incentives Build Robustness in BitTorrent. In: 1st Workshop on Economics of Peer-to-Peer Systems (June 2003)
9. Cohen, B.: The BitTorrent Protocol Specification (January 2008), http://www.bittorrent.org/beps/bep_0003.html (accessed April 2012)
10. D'Acunto, L., Meulpolder, M., Rahman, R., Pouwelse, J., Sips, H.: Modeling and Analyzing the Effects of Firewalls and NATs in P2P Swarming Systems. In: IEEE International Symposium on Parallel & Distributed Processing, Workshops and PhD Forum, IPDPSW (2010)
11. Event-B and the Rodin Platform, http://www.event-b.org/ (accessed April 2012)
12. Iliasov, A., Laibinis, L., Troubitsyna, E., Romanovsky, A.: Formal Derivation of a Distributed Program in Event B. In: Qin, S., Qiu, Z. (eds.) ICFEM 2011. LNCS, vol. 6991, pp. 420–436. Springer, Heidelberg (2011)
13. Iliasov, A., Troubitsyna, E., Laibinis, L., Romanovsky, A., Varpaaniemi, K., Ilic, D., Latvala, T.: Supporting Reuse in Event B Development: Modularisation Approach. In: Frappier, M., Glässer, U., Khurshid, S., Laleau, R., Reeves, S. (eds.) ABZ 2010. LNCS, vol. 5977, pp. 174–188. Springer, Heidelberg (2010)
14. Iliofotou, M., Siganos, G., Yang, X., Rodriguez, P.: Comparing BitTorrent Clients in the Wild: The Case of Download Speed. In: Freedman, M.J., Krishnamurthy, A. (eds.) Proceedings of the 9th International Workshop on Peer-to-Peer Systems, IPTPS 2010. USENIX (April 2010)
15. Kamali, M., Laibinis, L., Petre, L., Sere, K.: Self-Recovering Sensor-Actor Networks. In: Mousavi, M., Salan, G. (eds.) Proceedings of the Ninth International Workshop on the Foundations of Coordination Languages and Software Architectures, FOCLASA 2010, vol. 30, pp. 47–61. EPTCS (2010)
16. Kemper, S.: Compositional Construction of Real-Time Dataflow Networks. In: Clarke, D., Agha, G. (eds.) COORDINATION 2010. LNCS, vol. 6116, pp. 92–106. Springer, Heidelberg (2010)
17. Loewenstern, A.: DHT Protocol (2008), http://www.bittorrent.org/beps/bep_0005.html (accessed April 2012)
18. Lombide Carreton, A., D'Hondt, T.: A Hybrid Visual Dataflow Language for Coordination in Mobile Ad Hoc Networks. In: Clarke, D., Agha, G. (eds.) COORDINATION 2010. LNCS, vol. 6116, pp. 76–91. Springer, Heidelberg (2010)
19. Lumme, K., Petre, L., Sandvik, P., Sere, K.: Towards Dependable H.264 Decoding. In: Ahmed, N., Quercia, D., Jensen, C.D. (eds.) Workshop Proceedings of the Fifth IFIP WG 11.11 International Conference on Trust Management (IFIPTM 2011), pp. 325–337. Technical University of Denmark (June 2011)
20. Petre, L., Sandvik, P., Sere, K.: A Modular Approach to Formal Modelling of Peer-to-Peer Networks. Tech. Rep. 1039, Turku Centre for Computer Science (TUCS) (2012)
21. RODIN Modularisation Plug-in, http://wiki.event-b.org/index.php/Modularisation_Plug-in (accessed April 2012)
22. Sandvik, P., Neovius, M.: The Distance-Availability Weighted Piece Selection Method for BitTorrent: A BitTorrent Piece Selection Method for On-Demand Streaming. In: Liotta, A., Antonopoulos, N., Exarchakos, G., Hara, T. (eds.) Proceedings of The First International Conference on Advances in P2P Systems, AP2PS 2009, pp. 198–202. IEEE Computer Society (October 2009)

23. Sandvik, P., Sere, K.: Formal Analysis and Verification of Peer-to-Peer Node Behaviour. In: Liotta, A., Antonopoulos, N., Di Fatta, G., Hara, T., Vu, Q.H. (eds.) The Third International Conference on Advances in P2P Systems, AP2PS 2011, pp. 47–52. IARIA (November 2011)

24. Schulze, H., Mochalski, K.: Ipoque Internet Study (2008/2009),
    `http://www.ipoque.com/en/resources/internet-studies`
    (accessed April 2012)

25. Tarau, P.: Coordination and Concurrency in Multi-Engine Prolog. In: De Meuter, W., Roman, G.-C. (eds.) COORDINATION 2011. LNCS, vol. 6721, pp. 157–171. Springer, Heidelberg (2011)

26. Vestel to Launch the First Bittorrent Certified Smart TV,
    `http://www.bittorrent.com/company/about/vestel_to_`
    `launch_the_first_bittorrent_certified_smart_tv` (accessed April 2012)

27. Waldén, M., Sere, K.: Reasoning About Action Systems Using the B-Method. Formal Methods in Systems Design 13, 5–35 (1998)

28. Yan, L.: A Formal Architectural Model for Peer-to-Peer Systems. In: Shen, X., Yu, H., Buford, J., Akon, M. (eds.) Handbook of Peer-to-Peer Networking, Part 12, pp. 1295–1314. Springer, US (2010)

29. Yan, L., Ni, J.: Building a Formal Framework for Mobile Ad Hoc Computing. In: Bubak, M., van Albada, G.D., Sloot, P.M.A., Dongarra, J. (eds.) ICCS 2004, Part I. LNCS, vol. 3036, pp. 619–622. Springer, Heidelberg (2004)

Linda in Space-Time:
An Adaptive Coordination Model
for Mobile Ad-Hoc Environments

Mirko Viroli[1], Danilo Pianini[1], and Jacob Beal[2]

[1] Alma Mater Studiorum – Università di Bologna, Italy
{mirko.viroli,danilo.pianini}@unibo.it
[2] Raytheon BBN Technologies, USA
jakebeal@bbn.com

Abstract. We present a vision of distributed system coordination as a
set of activities affecting the space-time fabric of interaction events. In
the tuple space setting that we consider, coordination amounts to control of the spatial and temporal configuration of tuples spread across
the network, which in turn drives the behaviour of situated agents. We
therefore draw on prior work in spatial computing and distributed systems coordination, to define a new coordination language that adds to
the basic Linda primitives a small set of space-time constructs for link-
ing coordination processes with their environment. We show how this
framework supports the global-level emergence of adaptive coordination
policies, applying it to two example cases: crowd steering in a pervasive computing scenario and a gradient-based implementation of Linda
primitives for mobile ad-hoc networks.

1 Introduction

A common viewpoint in developing coordination models on top of Linda [16] is
that tuples are a mechanism to reify and exchange events/data/knowledge that
are important to system coordination, and to synchronise the activities of coordinated components in a parallel and/or distributed system. A tuple is, however,
a very point-wise abstraction, and applications often need to express relationships articulated across the physical environment through which the computational system is distributed. There is thus a need for coordination models and
languages that raise the level of abstraction from the single tuple to a spatial
structure of tuples, without forgetting the possibility that such a structure, as
well as being distributed, may also be highly dynamic and mobile.

Such spatial coordination models have been developed in a number of previous papers [29,17,18,24]. These span multiple application contexts, such as
pervasive computing, where mobility, large system scale, and/or situatedness in-
vite the coordination space to be interpreted as a distributed substrate for spatial
data structures. These models enhance the standard tuple-space settings with
primitives for spreading tuples from nodes to their neighbors, and letting them

M. Sirjani (Ed.): COORDINATION 2012, LNCS 7274, pp. 212–229, 2012.

affect (or be affected by) the context of neighbors. Iterative spreading can then lead to the stabilisation of given tuple structures, which find applications such as retrieval of items of interest in mobile environments, as in the TOTA middleware [17] or the pervasive ecosystems model [30]. These prior models, however, tend to be either ad hoc (e.g., [24]) or tightly tied to a particular metaphor (e.g., [29]).

These approaches may also be viewed through the research lens of spatial or amorphous computing [6], which argues that computation in a dense and mobile system is best understood and designed in terms of spatial abstractions (e.g., regions, partitions, gradients, trails, paths) and temporal abstractions (e.g., fading, growth, movement, perturbation). The Proto language [4] is an archetype of this approach, presenting a model in which these abstraction—intrinsically discrete because of the nature of computing devices—would actually tend toward their continuum version as the density of the network, which we are continuing to experience with current ICT technologies. As this research program links geometric continuum abstractions and individual computing devices, it thus has the potential of addressing the crucial issue of designing distributed systems where adaptiveness globally emerges out of local interactions in a predictable and controllable way.

Based on the above works, and on an existing trend of studies of concurrency "in space" [12,11], we introduce a new coordination model and language aiming at further bridging the gap between coordination and the continuum ideas of spatial computing. In our model, we make situated agents interact by injecting into the coordination substrate so-called *space-time activities*, namely, processes that manipulate the space-time configuration of tuples in the network. Such activities are expressed in terms of a process-algebra like language, composing atomic coordination primitives in the style of Linda with additional Proto-derived constructs that deal with spatial and temporal aspects: *(i)* spreading of an activity in a node's neighbourhood depending on its relative orientation; *(ii)* scheduling an activity at the next computation round of a node; and *(iii)* accessing space-time contextual information to link the configuration of tuples with the actual physical space.

Contribution: The main contribution of this work is hence the definition of a spatial computing coordination language, which we call $\sigma\tau$-Linda, extending Linda to flexibly enact coordinated activities tightly linked in space-time with their environment. It provides more advanced mechanisms for controlling space-time behaviour of coordination activities than those of existing coordination middlewares such as TOTA [17], and overcomes the restrictions of Proto [4] that make it unsuitable as an open coordination framework (as will be detailed in Section 5).

The proposed model can be used to design coordination mechanisms that emergently adapt to environment stimuli, such as agent interactions or changes due to mobility and faults. We describe two applications for this model: first we develop an adaptive crowd steering coordination service by which people in a structured environment can be guided (by signs appearing in their personal smartphone or public devices) towards a point of interest through the shortest path that circumvents dynamically-formed crowded areas. Second, we provide a space-time extension of standard Linda coordination primitives (out, in and rd) working in a distributed mobile environment, and relying on the self-organisation pattern known as a computational gradient [2].

The remainder of this paper is organised as follows. Section 2 illustrates the proposed model and language, Section 3 describes a formalisation expressed as a core calculus, Section 4 presents application cases, Section 5 relates our model with prior work, and finally Section 6 concludes with final remarks.

2   Linda in Space-Time

2.1   Basic Model

Our coordination infrastructure runs on a (possibly very dense and mobile) set of situated computational devices, e.g., located in specific points (i.e. nodes) of the physical environment. Each node hosts software agents (the coordinated components) and a tuple space, and has ability of interaction with nodes in the neighbourhood—where proximity can be seen as a physical or virtual property. Differently from Linda, in which agents interact by atomic actions (inserting, removing and reading tuples in the local tuple space), in $\sigma\tau$-Linda, agents interact by injecting *space-time activities* (activities for short). These activities are processes composing atomic Linda-like actions with additional constructs allowing the activity to diffuse in space (i.e. to other nodes) and in time (i.e. to be delayed). The net effect of an activity is hence to evolve the population of tuples in the network, thereby affecting the distributed structures of tuples that agents use to for global coordination.

In our model, each node undergoes the following *computation round*: (i) it sleeps, remaining frozen; (ii) it wakes up, gathers all incoming activities (contained in messages received either from neighbour nodes or from local agents) and executes them; (iii) it executes the continuation of the activity executed in previous computation round; (iv) spreads asynchronous messages to neighbourhood; and (v) schedules an activity continuation for next round. The node then sleeps again, returning to the beginning of the cycle. The duration of the computation round is dictated by the underlying infrastructure, and could possibly change over time or from device to device (as in [1]). We only assume that it is long enough for executing steps (ii-iii-iv) above. This particular computational model for a tuple space has many similarities with the platform assumptions of the Proto language [4,27], which we adopt for its facility of situating computations in space-time—a thorough comparison is reported in Section 5.

2.2   The Coordination Language

A key role in the proposed coordination model is played by the concept of space-time activities. We here incrementally describe their features by presenting a surface language for their specification.

Primitive Actions. We being with three basic Linda actions for manipulating the tuple space: "out *tuple*", "in *tuple*", "rd *tuple*". These respectively insert, remove and read a tuple from the local tuple space. A tuple is a ground first-order term in our model—similarly to [22]. Read and removal specify a template (a term with variables, denoted as literals starting with an upper-case letter) that should be syntactically matched with the retrieved tuple. Read and removal are predicative: they are non-blocking and yield a negative result if no matching tuple is found. To these, we add a fourth primitive, "eval *pred*", which evaluates the predicate expression *pred*.

When such actions are defined for an activity injected by an agent, and are executed in the tuple space where the agent is situated in, then a notification result is shipped to the agent—although, following the spirit of [8], we shall not discuss internal aspects of agent interactions in this paper.

Protocols. Primitive actions can be sequentially composed in a protocol-like manner. Other standard operators of parallel composition and choice could be orthogonally added, but are not discussed in this paper for brevity. Additionally, in, rd and eval define branches leading to two different continuations, one for positive and one for negative outcome of the predicative action. Three examples of activities are:

```
out t(1,2,3); out t(a,1+2,b)
in r(X,2,3) ? out r(X,2,3) : out r(0,2,3)
(in r(X,2,3) ? (eval X=1 ? out r(X,2,3) : 0) : 0); out ok
```

The first expression inserts tuple t(1,2,3) and then t(a,3,b). Note that tuples are evaluated before being used in actions: evaluation amounts to computing the result of (mathematical) expressions used in a tuple's arguments.

The second expression removes any tuple matching r(X,2,3) (variable X is bound to the value of first argument, and this substitution propagates through the remainder of the activity). If it succeeds (? branch) the tuple is inserted back, otherwise (: branch) a new tuple r(0,2,3) is inserted.

The third example attempts to remove any tuple matching r(X,2,3). If it succeeds and X = 1 then it inserts it back, otherwise it does nothing (0). Independently of the outcome of such a removal, tuple ok is then inserted. We may also omit the denotation of a ":" branch when it leads to the execution of empty process 0, writing e.g. "(in r(X,2,3) ? eval X=1 ? out r(X,2,3)); out ok" in place of the third example above.

Definitions. When desired, one can equip the specification of an activity with *definitions* (which can possibly be recursive), in the style of agent definition in π-calculus. These have the form "$N(x_1, \ldots, x_n)$ is *activity*", which define *activity* as having name N and arguments $x_1, \ldots, x_n$. For instance, after declaration

```
in-out(T) is (in T; out T)
```

we have for instance that activity "in-out(r(1,2,3))" behaves just like "in r(1,2,3); out r(1,2,3)", namely, the tuple is added if it is not already there. Note that since no branches are used for the removal operation, this in turn is equivalent to "(in r(1,2,3)?0:0); out r(1,2,3)", or, similarly, to "in r(1,2,3)?out r(1,2,3):out r(1,2,3)".

Time. The language provided so far is still point-wise in space and time. We now expand it, beginning by adding construct **next** to situate activities in time. Executing action "**next** P" (where P is the protocol – also called process – defining an activity), amounts to scheduling P for execution at the next computation round of the current node. Special variable $delay can be used in P and evaluates to the amount of time passed in between the current computation round and the previous one. Similarly, variable $this can be used to denote the identifier of the node on which it is evaluated. Useful examples of definitions (along with a brief descriptions of them) are then the following ones:

```
% When a tuple matching T is found, it is removed and replaced with T2
chg(T,T2) is (in T ? out T2 : next chg(T,T2) )

% Inserts a tuple time(T,X), updated as time X passes
rep(T)  is (out time(T,0); next rep2(T))
rep2(T) is (in time(T,Y); out time(T,Y+$delay); next rep2(T))

% Inserts tuple T that is removed after X time units elapse
outt(T,X) is (in-out(T); eval X<=0 ? in T : next outt(T,X-$delay))
```

Note that by the use of **next** in conjunction with a recursive definition, **chg** actually declares an activity with a duration in time, which will be stopped only when a tuple matching T is eventually found. Concerning the use of $delay, we then observe that – in the spirit of a Proto-style space-time computing model – as the average duration of computation rounds tends to zero, activity **rep** tends to define a continuous update of tuple time(T,X) as time X passes, and similarly, outt(T,X) tends to remove tuple T precisely as time X passed.

Space. To situate activities in space we introduce construct **neigh**. Executing action "**neigh** P" amounts to sending a broadcast message containing P to all neighbours, which will then execute P at their next computation round. Special variable $distance is also introduced, which evaluates to the estimated distance between the node that sent the message and the one that received it. Similarly, variable $orientation can be used to denote the relative direction from the receiver to the sender (e.g., as a vector of coordinates [11]). Some examples are as follows:

```
% Broadcasts tuple T in the neighbourhood
bcast(T) is (neigh out T)

% Broadcasts tuple T in the neighbourood but only within range R
```

```
bcastr(T,R) is (neigh (eval $distance<R ? out T))

% Gossips tuple T in the whole network within range R
goss(T,R) is (eval R>=0 ? (in-out(T); neigh goss(T,R-$distance)))
```

Of particular interest is the last definition, which spreads one copy of T to all
the nodes whose hop-by-hop distance from the source is smaller than R. As in
the case of time, as devices become increasingly dense, and their distance tends
to zero, the set of devices holding tuple T will actually form a continuous sphere
with radius R around the origin of goss.

Note that it is an easy exercise to define processes dealing with both space and
time—as will be developed in Section 4. For instance, one can define a process
gosst that adds temporal aspects to the goss example, such as to make the
sphere of tuples created by goss all disappear following a timeout. In the sense
of spatial computing interpretation [4], the definition of gosst(T,R,TO) would
be the definition of a geometric space-time activity called "sphere of tuple T
with radius R and timeout TO"—useful to limit the spatial and temporal extent
of some advertised information.

Finally. We conclude by introducing a construct named finally, used to simplify the task of structuring the activities executed at a given round. Executing
action "finally P" makes activity P executed in the current round, but only
when all the others actually completed. A typical use of this construct is to start
an aggregation activity for incoming messages only when all of them have been
processed, as in the following equivalent specification of gossiping:

```
gossf(T,R) is (eval R>=0 ? (out T; neigh gossf(T,R-$distance);
                           finally clean(T)))
% Cleans multiple copies of T, leaving just one of them
clean(T) is (in T ? (in-out(T); clean(T)))
```

Messages spread by gossiping cause the receiver to execute the gossf activity, which inserts tuple T, further spreads messages, and finally schedules the
clean(T) process for a later time. Only when all such messages have been processed in a round (and there are typically more than one) will the set of all clean
activities be executed . The result of their execution is that only one tuple T will
remain in the tuple space. The finally construct can thus, e.g., serve a similar
aggregation and simplification role to the *-hood constructs in Proto.

3   Core Calculus

In this section we introduce a formalisation of the proposed framework similar
in spirit to those of [8,18,28], namely, by a core calculus taking the shape of a
process algebra.

3.1 Syntax

Let meta-variable σ range over tuple space (or node) identifiers, x over logic variables, τ over real numbers used to model continuous time, and f over function names (each with a given arity, and used either in infix of prefix notation)—as usual we refer to functions with arity 0 as constants. Meta-variable t ranges over terms built applying functions to variables, numbers, identifiers, and constants, and will be written in typetext font. For simplicity, we shorten special variable $orientation to ω, and neglect $distance since it can be "compiled away" to term $length(\omega)$ where $length$ is a function. We let ϵ range over evaluations (functions) for terms, write t^ϵ for application of ϵ to term t, and denote $\epsilon(\sigma, \tau)$ the evaluation that (other than computing mathematical functions) maps $this to σ and $delay to τ. For instance, we have $a(\$this,1+\$delay)^{\epsilon(\mathrm{id}23,5.1)} = a(\mathrm{id}23,6.1)$. A substitution θ of variables $x_1, \ldots, x_n$ to terms $t_1, \ldots, t_n$ is expressed by notation $\{t_1/x_1, \ldots, t_n/x_n\}$, and is applied to a term t by syntax $t\theta$, e.g., $a(x,1)\{x/2\}$ means $a(2,1)$. We write $mgs(t,t')$ for the most general substitution θ such that $t'\theta = t$—such a notation makes no sense (as in partial functions) if $mgs(t,t') = \perp$, i.e., when t is not an instance of t'.

Given these premises, the core syntax of the model is expressed by the grammar in Figure 1 (a). P defines the syntax of a process (or activity): it includes empty process 0, action prefix, predicative actions with branches, and call of a definition. Note we skipped from this syntax the composition operator ";", which can be basically compiled away once we have action prefix "." and branching "? :"—by straightforward equivalences like $0; P \equiv P$, $(\pi?P : Q); R \equiv \pi?(P; R) : (Q; R)$ and $(\alpha.P); R \equiv \alpha.(P; R)$. A space S is a composition, by operator " | ", of processes and tuple sets. The topology of a network is modelled by a composition L of connections of kind $\sigma \overset{t}{\rightsquigarrow} \sigma'$, representing proximity of node σ' to σ with orientation vector t—e.g., expressed as term $coord(x,y,z)$ or the like. Finally, a system configuration C is a composition, by operator $\otimes$, of nodes $[S]_\sigma^{\tau,\tau'}$ (with id σ, space S, current round at time τ and previous one at τ'), topology L, and messages $P \triangleright \sigma$ (with content P and recipient σ).

Figure 1 (b) introduces a congruence relation "$\equiv$", stating when two configurations are to be considered syntactically equal, and hence can be used one in place of the other. First line introduces standard multiset-like properties of operators " | " and "$\otimes$". Second line states that scheduling operators can be lifted out of action prefix placed in parallel with the continuation, and can also distribute in parallel processes. Last line states that when a finally and next actions are in parallel composition, the latter can enter the former: this will in fact leave scheduling policy for Q unchanged.

3.2 Operational Semantics

We define operational semantics by transitions $C \overset{\lambda}{\rightarrow} C'$, where labels λ can have the syntax described in Figure 1 (a). Label "$\cdot$" means a silent action internal

$$t ::= x \mid \sigma \mid \tau \mid f \mid f(t_1, \ldots, t_n) \qquad \text{Terms}$$
$$P, Q, R ::= 0 \mid \alpha.P \mid \pi?P : Q \mid D(t_1, \ldots, t_n) \qquad \text{Process}$$
$$\alpha ::= out\ t \mid \square P \qquad \text{Action}$$
$$\square ::= next \mid neigh \mid finally \qquad \text{Scheduling operator}$$
$$\pi ::= rd\ t \mid in\ t \mid eval\ t \qquad \text{Predicative action}$$
$$T ::= 0 \mid t \mid (T \mid T) \qquad \text{Tuple set}$$
$$S ::= 0 \mid T \mid P \mid (S \mid S) \qquad \text{Space}$$
$$L ::= 0 \mid \sigma \overset{t}{\rightsquigarrow} \sigma \mid (L \mid L) \qquad \text{Topology}$$
$$C, D ::= 0 \mid [S]_\sigma^{\tau,\tau'} \mid P \triangleright \sigma \mid L \mid (C \otimes C) \qquad \text{Configuration}$$
$$\lambda ::= \cdot \mid \sigma!P \mid \sigma\tau?P \mid P \triangleright \sigma \mid L : L \qquad \text{Labels}$$

"$\mid$" and "$\otimes$" are commutative, associative, and absorb 0
$$(\square P).Q \equiv Q \mid \square P \qquad \square(P \mid Q) \equiv (\square P) \mid (\square Q) \qquad \square 0 \equiv 0$$
$$finally\ P \mid next\ Q \equiv finally\ (P \mid next\ Q)$$

(STR)
$$\frac{C \equiv C' \qquad C' \overset{\lambda}{\to} D' \qquad D' \equiv D}{C \overset{\lambda}{\to} D}$$

(SND)
$$\frac{C \xrightarrow{\sigma!P} C'}{(\sigma \overset{t}{\rightsquigarrow} \sigma') \otimes C \xrightarrow{\sigma!P} C' \otimes (P\{t/\omega\} \triangleright \sigma') \otimes (\sigma \overset{t}{\rightsquigarrow} \sigma')}$$

(BRO)
$$\frac{(\sigma \overset{t}{\rightsquigarrow} \sigma') \notin C \qquad P \not\equiv 0}{[S \mid neigh\ P]_\sigma^{\tau,\tau'} \otimes C \xrightarrow{\sigma!P} C \otimes [S]_\sigma^{\tau,\tau'}}$$

(REC)
$$\frac{C \xrightarrow{\sigma\tau?P \mid Q} C'}{(P \triangleright \sigma) \otimes C \xrightarrow{\sigma\tau?Q} C'}$$

(NEW)
$$\frac{P \triangleright \sigma \notin C \qquad \tau_2 > \tau_1}{[T \mid next\ Q]_\sigma^{\tau_1,\tau_0} \otimes C \xrightarrow{\sigma\tau_2?P} C \otimes [T \mid P \mid finally\ Q]_\sigma^{\tau_2,\tau_1}}$$

(FIN)
$$\frac{-}{[T \mid finally\ P]_\sigma^{\tau,\tau'} \otimes C \dashrightarrow C \otimes [T \mid P]_\sigma^{\tau,\tau'}}$$

(RUN)
$$\frac{S\langle P \rangle \xrightarrow{\epsilon(\sigma,\tau-\tau')} S'\langle P' \rangle}{[S \mid P]_\sigma^{\tau,\tau'} \otimes C \dashrightarrow C \otimes [S' \mid P']_\sigma^{\tau,\tau'}}$$

(MOV)
$$\frac{-}{L \otimes C \xrightarrow{L:L'} C \otimes L'}$$
(AGN)
$$\frac{-}{C \xrightarrow{P \triangleright \sigma} C \otimes (P \triangleright \sigma)}$$

(OUT)	$S\langle out\ t.P \rangle \overset{\epsilon}{\hookrightarrow} (S \mid t^\epsilon)\langle P \rangle$	
(IN1)	$(S \mid t')\langle in\ t?P : Q \rangle \overset{\epsilon}{\hookrightarrow} S\langle P\theta \rangle$	if $\theta = mgs(t', t^\epsilon)$
(IN2)	$S\langle in\ t?P : Q \rangle \overset{\epsilon}{\hookrightarrow} S\langle Q \rangle$	if $\nexists t' \in S$ and $mgs(t', t) \neq\, \bot$
(RD1)	$(S \mid t')\langle rd\ t?P : Q \rangle \overset{\epsilon}{\hookrightarrow} (S \mid t')\langle P\theta \rangle$	if $\theta = mgs(t', t^\epsilon)$
(RD2)	$S\langle rd\ t?P : Q \rangle \overset{\epsilon}{\hookrightarrow} S\langle Q \rangle$	if $\nexists t' \in S$ and $mgs(t', t) \neq\, \bot$
(EV1)	$S\langle eval\ t?P : Q \rangle \overset{\epsilon}{\hookrightarrow} S\langle P \rangle$	if $t^\epsilon = \textbf{true}$
(EV2)	$S\langle eval\ t?P : Q \rangle \overset{\epsilon}{\hookrightarrow} S\langle Q \rangle$	if $t^\epsilon \neq \textbf{true}$
(D)	$S\langle D(t_1, \ldots, t_n) \rangle \overset{\epsilon}{\hookrightarrow} S\langle P\{t_1^\epsilon/x_1, \ldots, t_n^\epsilon/x_n\} \rangle$	if $D(x_1, \ldots, x_n)$ is P

Fig. 1. (a) Grammar, (b) Congruence, (c) Global semantics and (d) Local semantics

to a node σ; "$\sigma!P$" means device σ is broadcasting a message with content P; "$\sigma\tau?P$" means device σ starts a new computation round at (its local) time τ and still needs to gather messages with content P (at the top level it will take the form $\sigma\tau?0$); "$P \triangleright \sigma$" means an agent is injecting process P in the tuple space σ; and "$L : L'$" means (sub)topology L changes to L' to reflect some mobility or failure in the system. Semantic rules are shown in Figure 1 (c).

Rule (STR) defines classical structural congruence. Rules (BRO) and (SND) recursively handle broadcasting (mostly in line with [26]), namely, create messages for all neighbours as soon as a process P is scheduled for broadcasting. Rule (SND) recursively selects a neighbour σ' at orientation t, and creates a message for it in which orientation variable ω is substituted with t. Rule (BRO) is the fixpoint: when all neighbours have been handled, scheduling action $neigh\ P$ is removed. Note we do not send empty messages.

Similarly, rules (REC) and (NEW) recursively handle the reception of all messages when a new computation round starts. Rule (NEW) states that, given node σ in which Q is the process to execute at the next round, when a new round starts at time τ_2 and with overall incoming messages P, then the new process to start with is "$P|finally\ Q$", since we prescribe messages to be handled before Q as already described in previous section. Also note that this rule updates round times τ_1, τ_0 to τ_2, τ_1, and that it activates only when all incoming messages have been actually handled. Rule (REC) recursively gathers all incoming messages: it takes one with content P and proceeds recursively adding P to the set Q of messages considered so far.

Rule (FIN) handles semantics of $finally\ P$ construct, by simply stating that when this is the only activity in a node, we can simply execute P—note all "finally-scheduled" processes can be gathered together (along with "next-scheduled" ones) because of congruence. Rule (RUN) handles one-step execution of a process, by simply deferring the task to transition relation $\overset{\epsilon}{\hookrightarrow}$, defined in Figure 1 (d)—its rules are quite straightforward, as they correspond to the standard semantics of Linda primitives in their predicative version [8]. Note that $\overset{\epsilon}{\hookrightarrow}$ takes the evaluation function to use, initialised in rule (RUN) with the proper value of $this and $delay. Finally, rule (MOV) addresses topological changes due to mobility or failures, and rule (AGN) models the injection of a process by an agent in the local node.

We conclude stating isolation and progress properties. First property allows one to reason about the execution of an activity into a node without considering its environment. Namely, we have that nodes get affected by the external environment only at the time a new computation round starts (because of reception of messages), otherwise they proceed in isolation possibly just spawning new messages.

Property 1. If $C \otimes [S]_\sigma^{\tau_0, \tau_0'} \overset{\lambda}{\to} C' \otimes [S']_\sigma^{\tau, \tau'}$ with $S \not\equiv S'$ then λ is either $\cdot$, $\sigma!P$, or $\sigma\tau?P$. In the former two cases (namely, unless we change computation round), $\tau_0 = \tau$, $\tau_0' = \tau'$, and $C' \equiv C \otimes C_m$ (where C_m is either 0 or a broadcast), and moreover, for each D we have also $D \otimes [S]_\sigma^{\tau_0, \tau_0'} \overset{\lambda}{\to} D \otimes [S']_\sigma^{\tau_0, \tau_0'} \otimes C_m$, i.e., computation is independent of the environment.

The progress property states instead that when a computation round is completed it is necessarily composed of a next scheduling: at that point (NEW) can surely fire for that node, starting a new computation round. This ensures that our computations never get stuck.

Property 2. $C \otimes [S]_{\sigma}^{\tau,\tau'} \nrightarrow$ and $C \otimes [S]_{\sigma}^{\tau,\tau'} \overset{\sigma!P}{\nrightarrow}$ iff $S \equiv (T \mid next\ P)$. In that case, we have $C \otimes [S]_{\sigma}^{\tau,\tau'} \xrightarrow{\sigma\tau_0?0} C' \otimes [S']_{\sigma}^{\tau_0,\tau}$ for any $\tau_0 > \tau$.

4   Case Studies

4.1   Adaptive Crowd Steering

As a first example we study a specification able to support the case study presented in [30,25], with the goal of showing how $\sigma\tau$-Linda can provide support to easily define complex, distributed and adaptive data structures, and how they can be used in practice in a pervasive computing scenario.

```
―――――――――――― Crowd-aware gradient ――――――――――
% creating a gradient spreading tuple T
source(T) is (in-out(source(T)); grad(T,0,$this))
% gradient process for tuple T, at distance D, coming from node S
grad(T,D,S) is grad(T,D,S,$this)
grad(T,D,S,This) is (
   rd source(T)
     ? in-out(pre(T,0))
     : in pre(T,N) ? (eval N<D
                    ? out pre(T,N)
                    : (in target(T,M); out target(T,S); out pre(T,D)))
); finally (in pre(T,N)? (in field(T,M);
   (rd crowd(C)
     ? out field(T,N-1.2*C)
     : out field(T,N)); rd field(T,V); neigh grad(T,V+$distance,This)))
```

Fig. 2. Definitions for the crowd-aware computational gradient. At each site, if this is the source we consolidate pre(T,0). Otherwise, we replace the pre tuple if a smaller distance D is found, and target tuple is inserted as well. Finally, we take the remaining pre tuple, and apply the crowd factor: the resulting distance N goes into the field tuple.

Our reference environment is a bidimensional continuous space made of various rooms connected by strict corridors. Inside rooms and corridors, a dense grid of computational devices (nodes) is set up. Each node hosts its own tuple space, receives coordination activities (programmed using our spatial language) by software agents running in it, interacts with nodes in its proximity, and has a sensor locally injecting a tuple crowd(CrowdLevel) where CrowdLevel is an estimation of the number of people sensed around. People want to reach a point

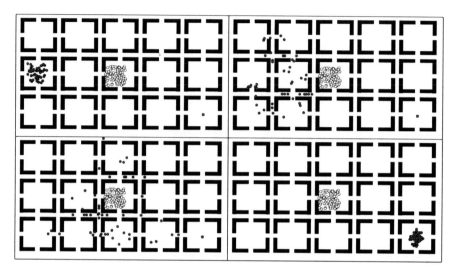

Fig. 3. Simulation snapshots: the coloured visitors reach its POI avoiding crowd

of interest (POI) by the fastest path, and receives directions suggested by their handheld device and/or by public displays on the walls. It is worth noting that the fastest path does not correspond to the shortest: if everybody followed the same way, in fact, corridors would become crowded. We want the system to be able, relying only on local interactions, to avoid crowded paths, dynamically adapting to any emerging and unforeseen situation. However, we will not implement algorithms to predict future situations, but rather make information about a crowded area spread around such that it becomes a less attractive transiting place to reach a POI.

Our strategy is to build a computational gradient injected by an agent located in the POI. A computational gradient holds in any node the estimated distance to the source by the shortest path [4], computed by further spreading and then aggregating at the destination the local estimation of distance. This distributed data structure must take into account also the crowding level, increasing estimated distance where a crowd is forming, and thus deflecting people towards longer but less crowded paths. This strategy can be encoded as in Figure 2, where the goal is achieved by maintaining a tuple `target(Poi,Id)` containing the `Id` of the neighbour node where to steer people to following a certain `Poi`. The crowding level influences the local field generation, and is weighted using a constant $K_{crowd} = 1.2$. Values between 1 and 1.5 have been established as good ones after running several simulations: more generally, the higher K_{crowd}, the more sensitive is path computation to the presence of crowd.

We implemented and ran simulations using Alchemist simulator [25], assuming that computation rounds are fired at the same rate for all nodes, and modelling such a rate following the Continuous-Time Markov Chain model. Four screenshots of a simulation run are provided in Figure 3, in which we built an environment of fifteen rooms with an underlying grid-like network of infrastructure nodes, an initial configuration with two groups of people, and a POI of interest for the first group which is reachable by a path crossing a crowded area. Note that not only every visitor reached the POI, but they all bypassed the crowded room (even if it is part of the shortest path, the large amount of people inside makes the whole area rather disadvantageous to walk); additionally, the visitors group is subject to "self-crowding", in that when a group is following a path it forms crowded areas itself (e.g. near doors), hence people behind the group tend to follow different paths. Further simulations we do not describe here for the sake of space show that the above properties hold for a large set of situations, including presence of crowds in different locations and dynamic formation and movement of such crowds during simulation[1].

4.2   Linda in a Mobile Ad-Hoc Environment

As a second case study we show a possible extension for Linda standard primitives taking into account both time and spatiality. In particular, our aim is to show how would it be possible in a mobile ad-hoc environment to specify, along with an operation over a tuple, a spatial and temporal horizon of validity: only retrieval operations whose horizon embraces the respective target tuple will actually succeed. We will show an implementation for the spatio-temporal out (stout) and the spatio-temporal in (stin) primitives—the easier case of strd being a simple variant of stin.

The key idea is to make primitive Linda actions actually generate waveform-like space-time data structures, with limited extent in space and dissolving as a timeout expires. Those structures will be responsible to determine the pertinence in space and time of each operation. An example of such a structure is realised by the code shown in Figure 4 (top). A wave works similarly to the gradient in Figure 2, maintaining a target tuple reifying the shortest past through a similar specification. A main difference – other than the obvious absence of any crowd management – is the evaluation of the age and distance, which makes the wave disappear whenever and wherever the horizon is reached.

When a stin operation requiring retrieval of a tuple template T is triggered, it will spawn a messenger activity called hermes (with Op set to in) which will propagate to a matching tuple T' following the corresponding wave it generated. As soon as the tuple is found, a new hermes (with Op set to in_back) is spawned which will follow the stin gradient back. This behaviour can be coded as shown in Figure 4 (middle).

Given these two basic bricks, the stout and stin primitives would be encoded as in Figure 4 (bottom). For each, a tuple template, a spatial range and a validity time must be specified. stout implementation is concise, because it just needs to manifest itself trough a wave and make the tuple available; stin, instead, needs also to spawn a hermes, whose goal is to retrieve a tuple and move it to the tuple space where the operation was spawned.

---

[1] The interested reader can download an example clip at:
http://apice.unibo.it/xwiki/bin/download/Publications/
Coord2012/museum-small.avi

```
────────────────── Wave-form: a space-time gradient ──────────────────
wave(T,Range,Ttl) is wawe(T,Range,0,$this,$this,Ttl, 0)
wave(T,Range,D,Source,Ttl,Age) is wave(T,Range,D,Source,$this,Ttl,Age)
wave(T, Range, D, Dest, This, Ttl, Age) is (
  eval (Age>Ttl or D>Range)
    ? (in pre(T,D); in field(T,N))      % disappearing
    : rd source(T)
        ? (in-out(pre(T,0)))            % default behaviour in a source
        : in pre(T,N) ? (eval N<D        % choosing minimum distance
                    ? out pre(T,N)
                    : ( in target(T,_); out target(T,Dest);
                        out pre(T,D))))
); finally (in pre(T,N) ? (             % consolidating target
      in field(T,M); out field(T,N);
      rd target(T, Dest); next wave(T,Range,D,Dest,This,Ttl,$delay);
      eval Age = 0 ? neigh wave(T,Range,N+$distance,This,Ttl,0)))
```

```
────────────────────────── Tuple retrieval ──────────────────────────
hermes(Op, T, This) is
  eval This = $this
    ? (eval Op = in ? ( in T
        ? (rd target(op_in(T), Dest); neigh hermes(in_back, T, Dest))
        : (rd target(op_out(T), Dest); neigh hermes(in, T, Dest))))
    : (eval Op = in_back ? (in in_request(T)
        ? out(T)
        : (rd target(op_in(T), Dest); neigh hermes(in_back, T, Dest))))
```

```
───────────────────── Space-time Linda operations ─────────────────────
stout(T,Range,Ttl) is out(T); wave(op_out(T), Range, Ttl)
stin(T, Range, Ttl) is out in_request(T);
                    wave(op_in(T), Range, Ttl);
                    hermes(in, T, $this)
```

Fig. 4. Definitions of Linda space-time operations

These new primitives allow agents to publish/retrieve information flexibly tuning the space-time horizons, relying on lower-level gradients (and routing paths) which adapt to the mobility of the network [2].

5   Related Work

Spatial Computing. The coordination model presented in this paper is very much in line with the motivations and basic mechanisms proposed in spatial computing research [6,5], and in particular by Proto [4]. Proto is a functional language used to specify the aggregate behaviour of all nodes in a space-filling network. It introduces specific space-time operators to situate computation in the physical world, and these operators form the inspiration for the space-time operators introduced in $\sigma\tau$-Linda. For example, there is a neighbourhood primitive **nbr** by which one can atomically compute an expression locally, spread the result to neighbours, gather neighbours' messages previously sent, and return their collection. In Proto, the function computing a gradient data structure could be specified as:

```
(def distance-to (source)        % defining a unary function distance-to
  (rep d inf                     % d starts with value infinity
    (mux source 0                % d becomes 0 in the source, otherwise..
      (fold-hood* min inf        % d is the minimum value taken from
        (+ (nbr d) (nbr-range))) % neighbour's d plus neighbour's range
) ) ) )
```

As previously noted, the underlying execution on a node follows a cycle roughly similar to the one we use in Section 2 [27]. To achieve a similar expressiveness to Proto, we introduced the **next** and **neigh** constructs (playing a role similar to Proto's constructs **rep** and **nbr**), along with the space-time variables **#distance** and **#delay** (similar to Proto's constructs **nbr-range** and **dt**), and **finally**, which plays a role similar to Proto's *-hood constructs.

The main differences with respect to Proto are as follows: *(i)* in our model a node stores a tuple space, whereas in Proto only a fixed tuple of values is maintained, hence specific constructs to perform generative communication are lacking in Proto; *(ii)* being purely functional, Proto cannot easily deal with state transitions as typically required when programming coordination activities; and *(iii)* in Proto all nodes run the same program, which is assumed to be installed everywhere before computation starts (this is because the information to be exchanged and the structure of programs has to be known at design-time for construct **nbr** to properly work), whereas we assume nodes are initially empty, and computation starts from the run-time injection of activities by agents.

On the other hand, Proto provides functionalities that we neglected at this stage, though they are interesting for future works: Proto nodes can be programmed to move, a feature that could be interesting as a coordination metaphor for pervasive scenarios featuring physically-mobile devices; and Proto functions can be seen as operators applying to whole spatial structures and their behavior can be modified by changing the region of space on which they execute, a very important property for modularly building complex spatial computations.

It is also interesting to mention a trend in formal calculi for distribution converging to spatial computing. 3π was developed as an extension of π-calculus with the idea of modelling the space where processes execute as a 3-dimensional geometric space [11]. In 3π, each process has a position and an orientation in space (a *basis*), encoded in a so-called geometric data. Other than accessing it (symbolically), a process can also send or receive geometric data through channels and can evolve to new processes located elsewhere (i.e., movement). From 3π we inherited the idea of letting orientation vector of a node being accessible from a neighbour. An even more abstract approach is taken in the Ambient calculus [12] and its derivatives – like Brane Calculi [10] and P-systems [23] – in which processes execute in a spatial system of hierarchically nested compartments, which could be of interest as soon as one wants to considered the hierarchical structure of complex environments.

Traditional Coordination Models. Our approach relates to the idea of engineering the coordination space of a distributed system by some policy "inside" the tuple spaces, following e.g. the pioneer work of programmable tuple spaces like TuCSoN [22] or Mars [9]—and subsequent coordination frameworks such as those of *coordination artifacts* [20,19]. Though our coordination activities can be mapped to a certain extent on top of those fully-expressive programming models, we believe they are different in spirit in at least two ways: first, we foster the idea that agents inject the desired behaviour (which is not to be seen as a program for the space), and second, we push forward the idea of space-time computations which the above works typically neglect.

The KLAIM language and core calculus [18] extend the tuple-space concept with several notions that are related to our approach. KLAIM has a networked tuple-space model very similar to ours, since nodes host a tuple space, processes, and has interaction ability with a (virtual) neighbourhood; it also supports the idea of executing processes in a remote location, with a mechanism by which a process explicitly mentions the location of the action to be executed. Our approach differs in the use of broadcasts for node-to-node communication, in its ability of controlling temporal evolution and spatial location of a process continuation, and in the use of computation rounds for tuple spaces. It is an interesting future work to see to which extent KLAIM can be seen as a lower level model to describe our space-time activities, or vice versa.

The application example shown in Section 4.2 is also related to Geo-Linda [24], another example of spatial coordination approach combining the tuple manipulation of LINDA with the geometric addressing concepts of SPREAD [13]. In Geo-Linda, tuples are read and published over an assortment of geometric primitives, such as boxes, spheres, cylinders, and cones, all defined relative to a device. The language also introduces primitives to detect coarse movement of devices through the appearance or disappearance of tuples.

Self-organisation in Tuple Spaces. As described in [21], applications of coordination models and languages – and especially space-based ones – are inevitably entering the realm of self-organisation, where complexity of interactions becomes the key to make desired properties appear by emergence. Given the intrinsic difficulty of *designing emergence*, most approaches mimic nature-inspired techniques to organise and evolve tuples according to specified rules.

Among the many existing approaches, one that is very related to ours is TOTA (Tuples On The Air) [17], a tuple-based middleware supporting field-based coordination for pervasive-computing applications. In TOTA each tuple, when inserted into a node of the network, is equipped with a content (the tuple data), a diffusion rule (the policy by which the tuple has to be cloned and diffused around) and a maintenance rule (the policy whereby the tuple should evolve due to events or time elapsing). Compared with the language proposed here, and although TOTA was an evident inspiration to the idea of building dynamic and distributed structures of tuples, we observe a number of differences: *(i)* TOTA is a middleware and defines no true language or primitives to program spatial structures (content and maintenance rule are programmed directly in Java and can access and manipulate the whole tuple space); *(ii)* TOTA has no specific mechanisms to keep track of physical space and time, for it only has a concept of "spreading to the neighbourhood", which allows to estimate distance in terms of number of hops to the source. TOTA could be possibly used as an underlying framework for implementing our language, provided additional ability to perceive the physical world are added.

A chemical-inspired self-organisation model is instead studied in [28,29]. There, tuples are associated with an *activity level*, which resembles chemical concentration and measures the extent to which the tuple can influence the state of system coordination—e.g., a tuple with low activity level would be rather inert, hence taking part in coordination with very low frequency. Chemical-like reactions following the CTMC model, properly installed into the tuple space, evolve activity level of tuples over time in the same way chemical concentration is evolved in chemical systems, and provide a diffusion mechanism that is shown to provide spatial notions like gradients as well. The SAPERE approach in [30] adds to this model the notion of semantic matching and tailors it to the pervasive computing context. We believe that, as density and speed of nodes grows, our language can be used to approximate the behaviour of those chemical rules.

6   Conclusions and Future Work

The current trend in ICT will shortly bring us distributed systems of huge size, density, mobility and openness. Following the direction of a good deal of recent works – including [17,6,11] and many others – we claim that this will require to elect the notion of "spatial coordination" as first-class abstraction in coordination models and languages, and distributed systems in general. The present paper is a first exploration in the direction of filling the gap between Linda-based and spatial computing models, obtained by a coordination model incorporating – though in an innovative guise – mechanisms for the space-time situation of processes [4], used to realise adaptive coordination mechanisms. We argue that the proposed language can be rather easily implemented on top of those existing coordination middleware providing basic features of space-to-space interaction and space programmability, such as TuCSoN [22], Klava [7] and TOTA [17]. We also plan to implementation further case studies of self-organisation, according e.g. to the pattern-based approaches in [15,14].

Another interesting thread of future research activities will be devoted to clarify what would be a good notion of expressiveness, and what would be a minimal set of primitives for fully-expressive space-time computation—a problem already stated in [3] for the spatial computing settings. Accordingly, we plan to use the presented language to define basic calculi in the style of the one presented here, which would be able to model higher-level languages like, e.g., the eco-law language for pervasive service ecosystems [30], and paving the way towards formal methods for the predictability and control of emergent adaptation in collective systems.

Acknowledgments. This work has been supported by the EU FP7 project "SAPERE - Self-aware Pervasive Service Ecosystems" under contract No. 256873.

References

1. Bachrach, J., Beal, J., Fujiwara, T.: Continuous space-time semantics allow adaptive program execution. In: IEEE SASO 2007, New York, pp. 315–319. IEEE (July 2007)
2. Beal, J.: Flexible self-healing gradients. In: Proceedings of the 2009 ACM Symposium on Applied Computing, SAC, pp. 1197–1201. ACM (2009)
3. Beal, J.: A basis set of operators for space-time computations. In: Self-Adaptive and Self-Organizing Systems Workshop (SASOW 2010), pp. 91–97 (September 2010)
4. Beal, J., Bachrach, J.: Infrastructure for engineered emergence on sensor/actuator networks. IEEE Intelligent Systems 21(2), 10–19 (2006)
5. Beal, J., Dulman, S., Usbeck, K., Viroli, M., Correll, N.: Organizing the aggregate: Languages for spatial computing. CoRR, abs/1202.5509 (2012)
6. Beal, J., Michel, O., Schultz, U.P.: Spatial computing: Distributed systems that take advantage of our geometric world. ACM Transactions on Autonomous and Adaptive Systems 6, 11:1–11:3 (2011)
7. Bettini, L., Nicola, R.D., Pugliese, R.: Klava: a java package for distributed and mobile applications. Softw., Pract. Exper. 32(14), 1365–1394 (2002)
8. Busi, N., Gorrieri, R., Zavattaro, G.: On the expressiveness of Linda coordination primitives. Inf. Comput. 156(1-2), 90–121 (2000)
9. Cabri, G., Leonardi, L., Zambonelli, F.: MARS: A programmable coordination architecture for mobile agents. IEEE Internet Computing 4(4), 26–35 (2000)
10. Cardelli, L.: Brane Calculi. Interactions of Biological Membranes. In: Danos, V., Schachter, V. (eds.) CMSB 2004. LNCS (LNBI), vol. 3082, pp. 257–278. Springer, Heidelberg (2005)
11. Cardelli, L., Gardner, P.: Processes in Space. In: Ferreira, F., Löwe, B., Mayordomo, E., Mendes Gomes, L. (eds.) CiE 2010. LNCS, vol. 6158, pp. 78–87. Springer, Heidelberg (2010)
12. Cardelli, L., Gordon, A.D.: Mobile ambients. Theoretical Computer Science 240(1), 177–213 (2000)
13. Couderc, P., Banatre, M.: Ambient computing applications: an experience with the spread approach. Hawaii International Conference on System Sciences, HICSS 2003 (January 2003)
14. Fernandez-Marquez, J.L., Di Marzo Serugendo, G., Montagna, S., Viroli, M., Arcos, J.L.: Self-organising design patterns. Natural Computing (to appear, 2012)
15. Gardelli, L., Viroli, M., Omicini, A.: Design Patterns for Self-organising Systems. In: Burkhard, H.-D., Lindemann, G., Verbrugge, R., Varga, L.Z. (eds.) CEEMAS 2007. LNCS (LNAI), vol. 4696, pp. 123–132. Springer, Heidelberg (2007)
16. Gelernter, D.: Generative communication in Linda. ACM Trans. Program. Lang. Syst. 7(1), 80–112 (1985)
17. Mamei, M., Zambonelli, F.: Programming pervasive and mobile computing applications: The tota approach. ACM Trans. Softw. Eng. Methodol. 18(4), 1–56 (2009)
18. Nicola, R.D., Ferrari, G.L., Pugliese, R.: Klaim: A kernel language for agents interaction and mobility. IEEE Trans. Software Eng. 24(5), 315–330 (1998)

19. Omicini, A., Ricci, A., Viroli, M.: An algebraic approach for modelling organisation, roles and contexts in MAS. Applicable Algebra in Engineering, Communication and Computing 16(2-3), 151–178 (2005)
20. Omicini, A., Ricci, A., Viroli, M.: Coordination Artifacts as First-Class Abstractions for MAS Engineering: State of the Research. In: Garcia, A., Choren, R., Lucena, C., Giorgini, P., Holvoet, T., Romanovsky, A. (eds.) SELMAS 2005. LNCS(LNAI), vol. 3914, pp. 71–90. Springer, Heidelberg (2006)
21. Omicini, A., Viroli, M.: Coordination models and languages: From parallel computing to self-organisation. The Knowledge Engineering Review 26(1), 53–59 (2011); Special Issue 01 (25th Anniversary Issue).
22. Omicini, A., Zambonelli, F.: Coordination for Internet application development. Autonomous Agents and Multi-Agent Systems 2(3), 251–269 (1999)
23. Paun, G.: Membrane Computing: An Introduction. Springer-Verlag New York, Inc., New York (2002)
24. Pauty, J., Couderc, P., Banatre, M., Berbers, Y.: Geo-linda: a geometry aware distributed tuple space. In: IEEE 21st International Conference on Advanced Networking and Applications (AINA 2007), pp. 370–377 (May 2007)
25. Pianini, D., Montagna, S., Viroli, M.: A chemical inspired simulation framework for pervasive services ecosystems. In: Proceedings of the Federated Conference on Computer Science and Information Systems, pp. 667–674. IEEE Computer Society Press (2011)
26. Singh, A., Ramakrishnan, C.R., Smolka, S.A.: A process calculus for mobile ad hoc networks. Sci. Comput. Program. 75(6), 440–469 (2010)
27. Viroli, M., Beal, J., Casadei, M.: Core operational semantics of Proto. In: 26th Annual ACM Symposium on Applied Computing, SAC 2011, Tunghai University, TaiChung, Taiwan, March 21-25. ACM (2011)
28. Viroli, M., Casadei, M.: Biochemical Tuple Spaces for Self-organising Coordination. In: Field, J., Vasconcelos, V.T. (eds.) COORDINATION 2009. LNCS, vol. 5521, pp. 143–162. Springer, Heidelberg (2009)
29. Viroli, M., Casadei, M., Montagna, S., Zambonelli, F.: Spatial coordination of pervasive services through chemical-inspired tuple spaces. ACM Transactions on Autonomous and Adaptive Systems 6(2), 14:1–14:24 (2011)
30. Viroli, M., Pianini, D., Montagna, S., Stevenson, G.: Pervasive ecosystems: a coordination model based on semantic chemistry. In: Ossowski, S., Lecca, P., Hung, C.-C., Hong, J. (eds.) 27th Annual ACM Symposium on Applied Computing, SAC 2012, Riva del Garda, TN, Italy, March 26-30. ACM (2012)

A Space-Based Generic Pattern
for Self-Initiative Load Clustering Agents

Eva Kühn, Alexander Marek, Thomas Scheller, Vesna Sesum-Cavic,
Michael Vögler, and Stefan Craß

Vienna University of Technology, Institute of Computer Languages
Argentinierstr. 8, Vienna, Austria
{eva,amarek,ts,vesna,mvoegler,sc}@complang.tuwien.ac.at

Abstract. Load clustering is an important problem in distributed systems, which proper solution can lead to a significant performance improvement. It differs from load balancing as it considers a collection of loads, instead of normal data items, where a single load can be described as a task. Current approaches that treat load clustering mainly lack of provisioning a general framework and autonomy. They are neither agent-based nor configurable for many topologies. In this paper we propose a generic framework for self-initiative load clustering agents (SILCA) that is based on autonomous agents and decentralized control. SILCA is a generic architectural pattern for load clustering. The SILCA framework is the corresponding implementation and thus supports exchangeable policies and allows for the plugging of different algorithms for load clustering. It is problem independent, so the best algorithm or combination of algorithms can be found for each specific problem. The pattern has been implemented on two levels: In its basic version different algorithms can be plugged, and in the extended version different algorithms can be combined. The flexibility is proven by means of nine algorithms. Further contributions are the benchmarking of the algorithms, and the working out of their best combinations for different topologies.

Keywords: Agents, Load Clustering, Load Balancing, Coordination, Tuple Space.

1   Introduction

Clustering or *cluster analysis* is a method of unsupervised learning and a technique for the analysis of statistical data. It is used in many fields, including data mining, machine learning and information retrieval. Clustering deals with the problem of grouping a collection of observations into smaller subsets, so called clusters. A cluster therefore consists of elements which are similar in some way and dissimilar to elements that belong to other clusters. The greater the similarity within a cluster and the greater the difference between the clusters, the better or more distinct is the clustering.

Load clustering, as the name already states, deals with the clustering of work loads in a computer system. It is strongly related to *load balancing*, which is a

M. Sirjani (Ed.): COORDINATION 2012, LNCS 7274, pp. 230–244, 2012.

methodology to distribute load among multiple computers to achieve an optimal utilization of resources. The difference between the two is that load clustering tries to make further optimizations of the load distribution based on the content of the load items: A single load item can be described as a task that consists of several attributes (e.g. a certain priority), has a payload, a dynamic life cycle and is handled by a computer or processor. The goal of load clustering is to cluster loads not only on the basis of simple attributes but also take into consideration the payload, as well as the dynamic and therefore changing status of the system load. Load clustering is a derived form of simple data clustering. Its main goal is to increase performance, by allowing a worker in a computer system to process not only a single load at once but a cluster of loads which are similar and therefore easier and faster to process.

Since load clustering systems are complex and need to react to various factors, it is important that they are self-organizing and adaptive, so that they can flexibly adapt to dynamically changing loads and resources. Different algorithms and configurations are needed to satisfy different kinds of load clustering scenarios, so a framework is needed that allows the comparison of algorithms and fine-tuning of their behavior to achieve optimal performance results. There are currently no frameworks with the needed degree of flexibility to satisfy these requirements. Existing frameworks are specialized for data clustering, not load clustering. Moreover they follow no agent based approach, hence need a central coordinator. This makes the system more prone to errors since that coordinator is a single point of failure.

In this paper we present a load clustering framework, that provides the possibility for plugging and benchmarking different clustering algorithms. It is based on autonomous agents with decentralized control and a blackboard based communication mechanism.

According to this specification the framework is called *Self-Initiative Load Clustering Agents* (in short SILCA). The design of SILCA is based on [18], which is a generic architectural pattern for load balancing that consists of several sub-patterns that can be composed to solve different problem scenarios.

In section 2 we review existing work about clustering in general and load clustering in particular. In section 3 we present our load clustering approach and explain the different patterns that are part of it. To show the validity of our approach we evaluate it with several different load clustering algorithms which are presented in section 4. The results of this evaluation are shown in section 5, where we present benchmarks for each load clustering algorithm.

2   Related Work

Until today, a lot of research has been done on the subject of clustering and a broad range of solutions around that problem has evolved spanning different problem domains.

An interesting problem domain is search clustering. Carrot2 [30] is an open source search clustering engine allowing for automatically clustering collections of search results or document abstracts into thematic categories. Hence it supports data clustering, not load clustering. Furthermore, Carrot2 does not allow for plugging in different clustering algorithms.

Other popular domains are data mining and analysis. There exists a broad range of open source and proprietary solutions: KNIME (Konstanz Information Miner) [3] is an open source data analysis, reporting and integration platform mainly used in pharmaceutical research. Proprietary products are STATISTICA[1] by Statsoft, SPSS Modeler[2] by SPSS Inc. and SAS[3] by SAS Institute Inc.

Another domain is machine learning. WEKA [14] (Waikato Environment for Knowledge Analysis) for example is an open source software for machine learning and supports several standard data-mining tasks like data preprocessing, clustering and classification. RapidMiner, formerly YALE (Yet Another Learning Environment) [21], is another open source machine learning environment with data-mining and clustering capabilities. Shogun [27] is an open source software toolbox focusing on kernel machines such as support vector machines for regression and classification problems. It was designed for bioinformatics applications and is therefore capable of processing datasets with up to 10 million samples. Orange [8] is another machine learning software suite designed for bioinformatics, coming with a visual front-end allowing for performing data analysis, -mining and visualization.

However, none of the mentioned software solutions supports all features we require: SPSS Modeler and SAS do not allow for the plugging of other algorithms, and the others are specialized on data clustering whereas SILCA aims to provide a framework for load clustering. Additionally, while most of these tools support extensibility through scripts, none of them follows a framework approach.

Frameworks in the area of data mining and analysis are jHepWork [6] and ELKI (Environment for DeveLoping KDD-Applications Supported by Index-Structures) [1]. jHepWork is a free data-analysis framework designed for scientists, engineers and students aiming to create a data-analysis environment based on open-source packages to create a tool that is competitive to commercial programs. However, it does not allow for benchmarking algorithms. ELKI is written in Java and allows for combining arbitrary algorithms, distance functions and indexes in order to evaluate and benchmark these combinations.

ELKI offers framework abstraction, the pluggability of algorithms and ability to benchmark those, but it does not follow a decentralized, agent-based approach, which is one of the main aims of SILCA. Moreover, to obtain the best performance results, it must be possible to fine-tune algorithms by changing related parameters and swapping similarity functions, which is not supported by ELKI.

SILCA follows a similar approach as introduced in [18] where a generic pattern for a load balancing framework is proposed, allowing for plugging and benchmarking different load balancing algorithms in different configurable settings and therefore easing the selection of the best algorithm for a specific problem scenario.

---

[1] http://www.statsoft.com/

[2] http://www-01.ibm.com/software/analytics/spss/

[3] http://www.sas.com/

3   Load Clustering Pattern

The objective of SILCA is the design of general patterns that abstract the problem of load clustering. Patterns are re-usable building blocks that can be composed towards solutions for certain problems like in our case the load clustering scenario. The SILCA *framework* is built according to these patterns to provide the needed flexibility.

The main requirement on the SILCA design is support of decentralized control so that the system can flexibly react on dynamically changing loads and resources, which is a basic condition for a self-organized, adaptive system. Moreover, a peer-to-peer system is less vulnerable. This means the avoidance of a central coordinator and leads to a software architecture design based on autonomous agents. Such an agent is an autonomic software component [10] that is self-responsible to be up and running, implements a reactive and continuous behavior, and can dynamically join and leave.

The blackboard based architectural style supports very well communication and synchronization between many independent, distributed software components, especially if they carry out computations where a complex task must be divided into smaller ones [2]. Therefore the SILCA design is based on a secure tuple space based middleware [7] that has proven useful in agent based use cases [17]. We assume the possibility to add reactive behavior [9] which especially enables notifications in near time as well as dynamic policies that are triggered by the arising of events, and the support of transactions with specifiable timeouts.

A second requirement on SILCA is the flexible exchange of different algorithms (see section 4) simply through "plugging" in order to gain a testbed for the comparison and evaluation of best solutions for certain problem scenarios. This is achieved by means of a component based design of the agents.

In all patterns, shared spaces hold the information produced by agents, as well as all events on which agents react. Pattern composition is carried out in that several agents access the same space and agree about its entries' structures, semantics and coordination principles.

The sub-patterns of SILCA and their implementation and composition towards a load clustering framework that can be configured for many different network topologies are explained in the following.

3.1   Local Node Pattern

The local node pattern has many similarities with local load balancing [25] as on one single computer site there is no load to be distributed or clustered, yet. Its main purpose is to model the autonomous agents as independent workers that actively compete for work. Worker agents register themselves at a load space. Clients write work into the load space which triggers the workers by means of aspects to take the load in chunks, process it and write the result into a result space (Figure 1) where the clients will pick them up eventually. If a worker fails, another one takes over its work. This is achieved by using the same transaction to take the load and write the result back. This transaction possesses a timeout and if it expires, the entire action of the worker is rolled back, the locks on the taken entries are released and another worker can proceed.

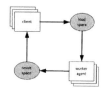

Fig. 1. Local node pattern

3.2   Arbiter Pattern

The arbiter pattern implements the clustering activation policy which determines whether load shall be shifted from the local node to a cluster. This can e.g. be configured by a parameter that specifies a certain threshold for loads: If this amount is exceeded and if not enough workers are available, load is taken from the load space and written to a clustering space (Figure 2). Comparable to worker agents, the arbiter agents are also implemented as space aspects that are activated every time when new load arrives, and in addition also when load is removed, or a new worker is de/registered. The arbiter also reacts on clustered loads that it receives via the clustering space and moves it from there to the local load space.

Fig. 2. Arbiter pattern

3.3   Clustering Pattern

The clustering pattern consists of clustering agents that execute a clustering strategy to distribute the load in the network. They access clustering spaces and clustering agent spaces. Figure 3 shows this pattern with one clustering space and one clustering agent space. The latter space holds information like neighbor nodes, pheromones etc. that the clustering agents need to collaborate with each other by executing a particular algorithm (see section 4).

3.4   Pattern Composition

The three described patterns can now be used to build up arbitrary load clustering patterns. The composition of the local node, arbiter and clustering pattern

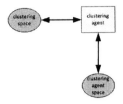

Fig. 3. Clustering pattern

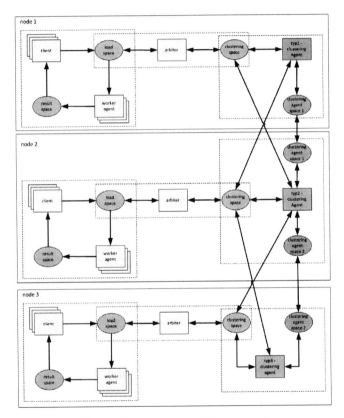

Fig. 4. Pattern composition example

forms the Basic SILCA pattern. The Extended SILCA pattern is the composition of several Basic SILCA patterns. A load clustering agent may interact with many arbiters and other load clustering agents in that it accesses multiple clustering and clustering agent spaces. Depending on the compositions of the arbiter and load clustering patterns via their shared spaces, different logical network overlay topologies arise. Figure 4 shows e.g. three single nodes that form a chain topology. Moreover, the load clustering agents might execute different algorithms within the same framework setting.

The space-based pattern approach leads to highly flexible agent coordination and an agile software architecture that is resistant against changing requirements concerning new policies and algorithms. Its advantages are a loose coupling of the collaborating agents through asynchronous communication, general abstraction of the load clustering problem, and modularization into re-usable sub-patterns.

4   Algorithms

Since many different algorithms cope with the clustering problem, we chose some of the well known and widely used clustering algorithms: Hierarchical, K-Means, Fuzzy C-Means, Genetic K-Means and Ant K-means.

As classification or statistical classification can also be seen as a supervised form of clustering, where observations get assigned into classes according to a given training set, we will also use some algorithms which cope with the classification problem, to demonstrate the agility of SILCA: K-Nearest Neighbor, Decision Tree, Ant-Miner, cAnt-Miner.

These 9 algorithms are implemented and benchmarked with SILCA, since they are well documented and implementations of them are already tested and available. The focus here is not the choice of the algorithms, but to prove the concept of SILCA with the help of them.

Hierarchical clustering is used to build a hierarchy of clusters. There are two types to build a hierarchy. The first one is the **Agglomerative** [12] approach (bottom up) where each data point is assigned to one cluster and pairs of clusters get merged to build the hierarchy. The second one is the **Divisive** [13] approach (top down), where all data points are captured in one cluster and this cluster is recursively split to build the hierarchy.

K-Means [15,28] is one of the simplest clustering algorithms. K-Means uses k centriods (one for each cluster), which get placed far away from each other. According to the location of the centriods each data point from the given data set is associated to the cluster which has the nearest centriod. In the next step k new centriods get calculated in the barycenters of the previously generated groupage. Now the data points get reassigned according to new centroids. The step of the recalculation of centriods and the reassignment of data points is performed in a loop. As a result of this loop the centriods change their location as long the centriods don't move anymore.

Fuzzy C-Means [11,4] is an adapted version of the K-Means algorithm, that allows data items to belong to more than one cluster. The Fuzzy C-Means algorithm almost works the same way as the K-Means algorithm, but with the small difference that each data item has some kind of parameter that indicates the degree of membership to a certain cluster. For each recalculation of the k centroids, the degree of membership of each data item is updated. At the end of the algorithm the degree of membership parameter can be used to place the data item in the best cluster.

The **Genetic K-Means** [16] algorithm is a mixture of the classical K-Means algorithm and an algorithm that follows Darwin's theory of evolution. The algorithm uses an initial population of clusters, where data items get placed randomly, and the clustering gets evolved over several generations. At each generation phase, every cluster gets evaluated and fresh clusters get generated with two genetic operations: crossover and mutation. The crossover operation randomly selects a location at a cluster and concatenates two clusters at this crossover point with each other to generate new clusters. The mutation operation brings disturbance in the crossover operation by inverting some elements during the regeneration process. This operation provides diversity and prevents stagnation.

Ant K-Means [26,19,29] combines the classical K-Means algorithm with an ant colony optimization. The principle of ant colony optimization is a pheromone trail which is used by real ants to communicate with each other. When an ant follows a certain trail it leaves a specific amount of pheromones. The more ants follow this trail, the more pheromones are placed and therefore this trail becomes more attractive for other ants, which also obtains the shortest route. Now this behaviour is used in the clustering domain to produce an optimal assignment of a set of observations to several clusters. The algorithm uses R agents (ants) to build the solution. To represent the pheromone trail a so called pheromone matrix τ is used, where a pheromone value τ_{ij} stands for the pheromone concentration of observation i associated to cluster j. At any iteration of the algorithm, each agent develops a trail solution by using the pheromone matrix to produce an optimal clustering. After this step R trail solutions are produced, a local search is performed to improve the solutions and the pheromone matrix gets updated. According to the updated pheromone matrix the previous steps are repeated for a specified number of iterations to improve the solution.

The **K-Nearest Neighbor** [20,24] algorithm is one of the simplest classification algorithms. K-Nearest Neighbor classifies an object according to its k nearest neighbors, where k is a positive (small) number. These neighbors are taken from the given training set where the correct classification of the objects is already known.

Decision Tree [5] learning is a commonly used method in data mining. This algorithm uses a tree structure that consists of leaves which represent the classifications and branches which describe the conjunctions of the observations' attributes that lead to the classification. To construct the tree the algorithm chooses an attribute of the data set that efficiently splits the set into two subsets which are classified by one class or the other. This step gets recursively repeated for the sub-sets as long as there is a split of the sub-set possible.

Ant-Miner [23] and **cAnt-Miner** [22] are classification methods that use an ant colony optimization approach. These algorithms follow a sequential approach to construct a list of rules (so called classification-rules) to classify objects. The algorithms are executed several times in a loop, each time against a reduced test data set. During one cycle of the loop the ants sequentially start their rule generation phase with an empty rule set and add one term, which represents the attribute of an object, at time. The choice of adding a term depends on both a heuristic value (based on the entropy of the term) and the current pheromone level of each term. When an ant produced a rule the pheromone levels get updated and another ant starts its run. If all possible cases of the training set are covered the loop stops and each data item of the data set is classified according to the previously retrieved classification rules.

5   Benchmarks and Evaluation

We performed benchmarks in several settings in order to demonstrate the agility of the SILCA pattern and prove that nature/swarm based enhanced algorithms can outperform several well-known algorithms. For this purpose we implemented the algorithms mentioned in Section 4.

Each test-run for one of the nine algorithms consisted of five cycles and the average was taken as result which guarantees their validity. The load tuples had the form "[taskID:12345, clientID:client1, priority:high, param:Prog1, description:'compile prog1', answerURL:url, workerType:compiler, timeout:200]" where "param" refers to a real and compilable Java class file. Each load tuple had a size of 5 to 10 kB. The comparison was done based on the given attributes and the similarities among the source code of the Java class file. All tests were executed on a cluster of four machines with 2*Quad AMD 2.0 GHz CPUs and three GB of RAM. Additionally we used three test settings for Basic SILCA and one for Extended SILCA.

5.1   Basic SILCA Benchmarks

The **first basic test setting** (Figure 5) uses only one worker to investigate how good a particular clustering-algorithm can find similarities among the load and how fast one worker can process that load.

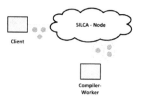

Fig. 5. Setting with 1 worker

In the **second and third basic test setting** (Figures 6 and 7), we added additional workers to investigate how the clustering results change if the worker-type is also taken into consideration and how the number of workers affect the clustering performance.

For each of the three basic test settings, each algorithm was benchmarked with 10, 20 and 50 loads. The results are shown in the figures 8, 9 and 10. Note that increasing the number of workers does not decrease execution time, because

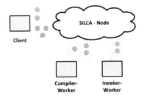

Fig. 6. Setting with 2 workers

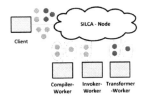

Fig. 7. Setting with 3 workers

each worker is responsible for a separate load type. In essence, increasing the number of workers also increases clustering complexity and thus execution time.

Using the absolute execution time as metric for the benchmarks, the Hierarchical algorithm shows the best results for all test-settings. Not only is it fast in constructing clusters, but also performs distinct and therefore good clustering. Additionally, its execution time is nearly constant in all three test-settings. More surprisingly is the fact that the biological enhanced Ant K-Means algorithm performs better than K-Means and quite equal to Fuzzy C-Means. The worst performing algorithm is Genetic K-Means, because of the algorithmic complexity of the genetic approach. According to the results, the classification algorithms also perform well on the given test settings. All of them deliver a good grouping of the loads and are able to keep up with the clustering algorithms. The best of them is the Ant-Miner algorithm due to the result of the fast rule generation phase and a good and distinct classification. Ant-Miner performs 2% faster than Decision Tree, 5% faster than cAnt-Miner and 14% faster than K-Nearest Neighbour. Decision Tree is not as good as Ant-Miner, since the generation of the tree is not as fast as the rule generation phase of Ant-Miner. The biologically enhanced cAnt-Miner does not outperform the well-known Decision Tree algorithm due to the fact that it has a pretty slow rule generation phase. The K-Nearest Neighbour algorithm performed worst during the benchmarks, since this algorithm strongly depends on the amount of neighbours to choose the correct class and therefore produced a worse classification for some test-settings. Nevertheless we have to mention that the training step of the classification algorithms was not included into the absolute execution time.

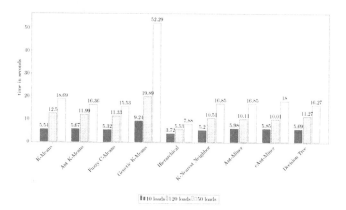

Fig. 8. Comparison of algorithm results for one worker

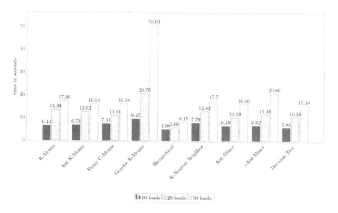

Fig. 9. Comparison of algorithm results for two workers

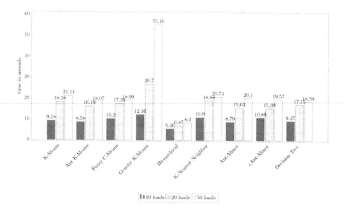

Fig. 10. Comparison of algorithm results for three workers

5.2   Extended SILCA Benchmarks

The extended SILCA pattern makes use of SILCAs composability and hence allows for combining different algorithms within one collaborative clustering approach. To prove this we created a test setting that allows for combining two algorithms at a time (Figure 11).

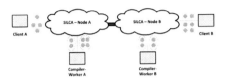

Fig. 11. Test Setting for extended SILCA benchmarks

In each benchmark, two clients assign 20 loads each, so in total 40. The metric used in these benchmarks is the absolute execution time. According to the obtained results (Figure 12), it can be seen that the combination of the Hierarchical algorithm with any other, except the Genetic K-Means algorithm, leads to a good execution time. The best result is delivered by the combination of the Hierarchical and Fuzzy C-Means algorithm, which is obvious since both perform well in the basic benchmarks. Also the combination of Ant K-Means with Hierarchical and Fuzzy C-Means with Ant K-Means produces pretty good results. Any combination with Genetic K-Means, compared to the other combinations, is extremely slow (taking up to 295% more time than the fastest combination), which is also foreseeable since the genetic aspect leads to a big performance lack in these test settings.

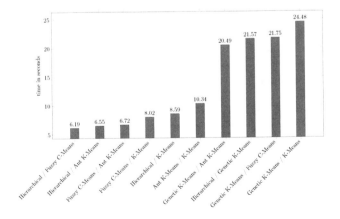

Fig. 12. Comparison of algorithm combinations in extended SILCA

The aforementioned benchmark settings are clearly kept simple and are not meant to be representative for real-world scenarios. Yet we claim that they are sufficient as a proof of concept and to demonstrate that increasing workers and worker types can increase execution time, and mixing different clustering algorithms can lead to better performance

6   Conclusions

In this paper, we presented a generic framework for self-initiative load clustering agents (SILCA), which is based on autonomous agents that communicate and operate in a peer-to-peer manner, and decentralized control. SILCA is a composable and agile software architecture pattern for load clustering that has been implemented on two levels: basic and extended. SILCA is problem independent and allows for plugging different clustering and classification algorithms (both intelligent and unintelligent). Basic SILCA consists of several sub-patterns, implemented in a space-based architectural style, which allows decoupling of the agents and guarantees their autonomic behavior. This allows finding the best algorithm for each specific problem. In extended SILCA several Basic SILCA nodes are connected via shared spaces towards arbitrary network topologies, which supports the plugging of combinations of different algorithms. Further contributions include benchmarking of the algorithms, and finding their best combinations for different topologies. The following clustering and classifying algorithms have been implemented and benchmarked on a cluster of 4 machines through 4 different test settings: K-Means, Ant K-Means, Fuzzy C-Means, Genetic K-Means, Hierarchical Clustering, K-Nearest Neighbor, Ant-Miner, cAnt-Miner, and Decision Tree. The absolute execution time was used as metric for the benchmarks. The preliminary results show the following: From the group of clustering algorithms, Hierarchical Clustering obtained the best results, whereas from the group of classification algorithms the Ant-Miner algorithm was the best which is the result of the fast rule generation phase and a good and distinct classification. In the extended SILCA, several combinations were benchmarked. The combination of the Hierarchical algorithm with any other, except the Genetic K-Means algorithm, leads to a good execution time. The best result was delivered by the combination of the Hierarchical and Fuzzy C-Means algorithm (both performed well in the Basic SILCA benchmarks, too). The unintelligent Hierarchical Clustering showed the best results in a small network with only one client that supplies load. For large and more complex networks, an intelligent approach with an appropriate similarity function will help. The similarity function is a crucial issue on which the quality of obtained clusters depends, so an intelligent approach should provide an improvement in results: both quantitatively - the absolute execution time, and qualitatively – the quality of obtained clusters. Future work will include the following issues: Plugging of new intelligent clustering algorithms based on bee intelligence and slime mold behavior, composition of load clustering and load balancing, and benchmarking on networks with other topologies and of larger dimensions.

Acknowledgments. The work is partly funded by the Austrian Government under the program BRIDGE (Brückenschlagprogramm der FFG), project 827571 AgiLog – Komplexitätsreduzierende Middleware-Technologien für Agile Logistik and under the program FFG FIT-IT (Forschung, Innovation und Technologie für Informationstechnologien), project 825750 Secure Space – A Secure Space for Collaborative Security Services.

References

1. Achtert, E., Kriegel, H.-P., Zimek, A.: ELKI: A Software System for Evaluation of Subspace Clustering Algorithms. In: Ludäscher, B., Mamoulis, N. (eds.) SSDBM 2008. LNCS, vol. 5069, pp. 580–585. Springer, Heidelberg (2008)
2. Avgeriou, P., Zdun, U.: Architectural patterns in practice. In: Longshaw, A., Zdun, U. (eds.) EuroPLoP, pp. 731–734. UVK - Universitaetsverlag Konstanz (2005)
3. Berthold, M.R., Cebron, N., Dill, F., Gabriel, T.R., Kötter, T., Meinl, T., Ohl, P., Sieb, C., Thiel, K., Wiswedel, B.: KNIME: The konstanz information miner. In: Preisach, C., Burkhardt, H., Schmidt-Thieme, L., Decker, R. (eds.) Data Analysis, Machine Learning and Applications. Studies in Classification, Data Analysis, and Knowledge Organization, pp. 319–326. Springer, Heidelberg (2008)
4. Bezdek, J.C.: Pattern Recognition with Fuzzy Objective Function Algorithms. Kluwer Academic Publishers, Norwell (1981)
5. Breiman, L., Friedman, J., Stone, C.J., Olshen, R.A.: Classification and Regression Trees, 1st edn. Chapman and Hall/CRC (January 1984)
6. Chekanov, S.: Hep data analysis using jhepwork and java. In: Proceedings of the Workshop HERA and the LHC, 2nd Workshop on the Implications of HERA for LHC Physics (2008)
7. Craß, S., Kühn, E.: Coordination-based access control model for space-based computing. In: 27th Annual ACM Symposium on Applied Computing (2012)
8. Demšar, J., Zupan, B., Leban, G., Curk, T.: Orange: From Experimental Machine Learning to Interactive Data Mining. In: Boulicaut, J.-F., Esposito, F., Giannotti, F., Pedreschi, D. (eds.) PKDD 2004. LNCS (LNAI), vol. 3202, pp. 537–539. Springer, Heidelberg (2004)
9. Denti, E., Omicini, A.: An architecture for tuple-based coordination of multi-agent systems. Softw. Pract. Exper. 29, 1103–1121 (1999)
10. Dobson, S., Denazis, S., Fernández, A., Gaïti, D., Gelenbe, E., Massacci, F., Nixon, P., Saffre, F., Schmidt, N., Zambonelli, F.: A survey of autonomic communications. ACM Trans. Auton. Adapt. Syst. 1, 223–259 (2006)
11. Dunn, J.C.: A Fuzzy Relative of the ISODATA Process and Its Use in Detecting Compact Well-Separated Clusters. Journal of Cybernetics 3(3), 32–57 (1973)
12. Gowda, K.C., Krishna, G.: Agglomerative clustering using the concept of mutual nearest neighbourhood. Pattern Recognition 10(2), 105–112 (1978)
13. Gowda, K.C., Ravi, T.V.: Divisive clustering of symbolic objects using the concepts of both similarity and dissimilarity. Pattern Recognition 28(8), 1277–1282 (1995)
14. Hall, M., Frank, E., Holmes, G., Pfahringer, B., Reutemann, P., Witten, I.H.: The weka data mining software: an update. SIGKDD Explor. Newsl. 11, 10–18 (2009)
15. Jain, A.K., Murty, M.N., Flynn, P.J.: Data clustering: a review. ACM Comput. Surv. 31, 264–323 (1999)
16. Krishna, K., Narasimha-Murty, M.: Genetic K-means algorithm. IEEE Transactions on Systems, Man and Cybernetics, Part B (Cybernetics) 29(3), 433–439 (1999)

17. Kühn, E., Mordinyi, R., Keszthelyi, L., Schreiber, C.: Introducing the concept of customizable structured spaces for agent coordination in the production automation domain. In: The Eighth International Conference on Autonomous Agents and Multiagent Systems, AAMAS, May 10-15, pp. 625–632 (2009)

18. Kühn, E., Sesum-Cavic, V.: A Space-Based Generic Pattern for Self-Initiative Load Balancing Agents. In: Aldewereld, H., Dignum, V., Picard, G. (eds.) ESAW 2009. LNCS, vol. 5881, pp. 17–32. Springer, Heidelberg (2009)

19. Kuo, R.J., Wang, H.S., Hu, T.L., Chou, S.H.: Application of ant k-means on clustering analysis. Comput. Math. Appl. 50, 1709–1724 (2005)

20. Mhamdi, F., Elloumi, M.: A new survey on knowledge discovery and data mining. In: RCIS, pp. 427–432 (2008)

21. Mierswa, I., Wurst, M., Klinkenberg, R., Scholz, M., Euler, T.: YALE: rapid prototyping for complex data mining tasks. In: KDD 2006: Proceedings of the 12th ACM SIGKDD International Conference on Knowledge Discovery and Data Mining, pp. 935–940. ACM, New York (2006)

22. Otero, F.E.B., Freitas, A.A., Johnson, C.G.: Handling continuous attributes in ant colony classification algorithms. In: CIDM, pp. 225–231. IEEE (2009)

23. Parpinelli, R., Lopes, H., Freitas, A.: Data Mining with an Ant Colony Optimization Algorithm. IEEE Trans. on Evolutionary Computation, Special Issue on Ant Colony Algorithms 6(4), 321–332 (2002)

24. Phyu, T.N.: Survey of classification techniques in data mining. In: Proceedings of the International Multi Conference of Engineers and Computer Scientists 2009, IMECS 2009, Hong Kong, March 18-20. Lecture Notes in Engineering and Computer Science, vol. I, pp. 727–731. International Association of Engineers, Newswood Limited (2009)

25. Šešum-Čavić, V., Kühn, E.: Chapter 8 Self-Organized Load Balancing through Swarm Intelligence. In: Bessis, N., Xhafa, F. (eds.) Next Generation Data Technologies for Collective Computational Intelligence. SCI, vol. 352, pp. 195–224. Springer, Heidelberg (2011)

26. Shelokar, P.S., Jayaraman, V.K., Kulkarni, B.D.: An ant colony approach for clustering. Analytica Chimica Acta 509(1) (2004)

27. Sonnenburg, S., Rätsch, G., Henschel, S., Widmer, C., Behr, J., Zien, A., de Bona, F., Binder, A., Gehl, C., Franc, V.: The SHOGUN Machine Learning Toolbox. Journal of Machine Learning Research (2010)

28. Tan, P.N., Steinbach, M., Kumar, V.: Introduction to Data Mining, 1st edn., ch. 8. Addison-Wesley Longman Publishing Co., Inc., Boston (2005)

29. Tiwari, R., Husain, M., Gupta, S., Srivastava, A.: Improving ant colony optimization algorithm for data clustering. In: Proceedings of the International Conference and Workshop on Emerging Trends in Technology, ICWET 2010, pp. 529–534. ACM, New York (2010)

30. Weiss, D.: A Clustering Interface For Web Search Results In Polish And English. Master's thesis, Poznan University of Technology, Poland (2001)

On the Realizability of Contracts in Dishonest Systems

Massimo Bartoletti[1], Emilio Tuosto[2], and Roberto Zunino[3]

[1] Dipartimento di Matematica e Informatica, Università degli Studi di Cagliari, Italy
[2] Department of Computer Science, University of Leicester, UK
[3] DISI, Università di Trento and COSBI, Italy

Abstract. We develop a theory of contracting systems, where behavioural contracts may be violated by dishonest participants after they have been agreed upon — unlike in traditional approaches based on behavioural types. We consider the contracts of [10], and we embed them in a calculus that allows distributed participants to advertise contracts, reach agreements, query the fulfilment of contracts, and realise them (or choose not to). Our contract theory makes explicit who is culpable at each step of a computation. A participant is honest in a given context S when she is not culpable in each possible interaction with S. Our main result is a sufficient criterion for classifying a participant as honest in all possible contexts.

1 Introduction

Contracts are abstract descriptions of the behaviour of services. They are used to compose services which are *compliant* according to some semantic property, e.g. the absence of deadlocks [6,9,10], the satisfacion of a set of constraints [8], or of some logical formula [1,4,15]. Most of the existing approaches tacitly assume that, once a set of compliant contracts has been found, then the services that advertised such contracts will behave accordingly. In other words, services are assumed to be *honest*, in that they always respect the promises made.

In open and dynamic systems, the assumption that all services are honest is not quite realistic. In fact, services have different individual goals, are made available by different providers, and possibly do not trust each other. What happens is that services agree upon some contracts, but may then violate them, either intentionally or not. Since this situation may repeatedly occur in practice, it should not be dealt with as the failure of the whole system. Instead, contract violations should be automatically detected and sanctioned by the service infrastructure.

The fact that violations may be sanctioned gives rise to a new kind of attacks, that exploit possible discrepancies between the promised and the runtime behaviour of services. If a service does not accurately behave as promised, an attacker can induce it to a situation where the service is sanctioned, while the attacker is reckoned honest. A crucial problem is then how to avoid that a service results *culpable* of a contract violation, despite of the honest intentions of its developer. More formally, the problem is that of deciding if a process *realizes* a contract: when this holds, the process is guaranteed to never be culpable w.r.t. the contract in all the possible execution contexts.

In this paper we develop a formal theory of contract-oriented systems that enjoys a sound criterion for establishing if a process always realizes its contracts. Our theory

M. Sirjani (Ed.): COORDINATION 2012, LNCS 7274, pp. 245–260, 2012.

combines two basic ingredients: a calculus of contracts, and a calculus of processes that use contracts to interact. Contracts are used by distributed participants to reach agreements; once stipulated, participants can inspect them and decide what to do next.

Ideally, a honest participant is supposed to harmoniously evolve with her contracts; more realistically, our theory also encompasses computations of *dishonest* participants, which may violate at run-time some contracts they have stipulated. A remarkable result (Theorem 2) is that it is always possible to detect who is culpable of a contract violation at each state of a computation. Also, a participant can always exculpate herself by performing the needed actions (Theorems 1 and 3).

Notably, instead of defining an ad-hoc model, we have embedded the contract calculus in [10] within the process calculus CO_2 [2]. To do that, the contracts of [10] have been slightly adapted to define culpability, and CO_2 has been specialized to use these contracts. We have formalised when a participant realizes a contract in a given context, i.e. when she is never (irreparably) culpable in computations with that context, and when she is *honest*, i.e. when she realizes *all* her contracts, in *all* possible contexts. We have proved that the problem of deciding whether a participant is honest or not is undecidable (Theorem 4). Our main contribution (Theorem 6) is a sound criterion for detecting when a participant is honest. Technically this is achieved through a semantics of participants that abstracts away the behaviour of the context. Such semantics allows us to define when a participant always fulfills her contracts, even in the presence of dishonest participants.

Because of space constraints, we include the proofs of all our statements in a separated Technical Report [3].

2   A Calculus of Contracts

We assume a finite set of *participant names* (ranged over by $A, B, \ldots$) and a denumerable set of *atoms* (ranged over by $a, b, \ldots$). We postulate an involution $co(a)$, also written as $\bar{a}$, extended to sets of atoms in the natural way.

Def. 1 introduces the syntax of contracts, taking inspiration from [10]. We distinguish between (*unilateral*) contracts c, which model the promised behaviour of a single participant, and *bilateral* contracts γ, which combine the contracts of two participants.

Definition 1. Unilateral contracts *are defined by the following grammar:*

$$c, d ::= \bigoplus_{i \in I} a_i ; c_i \quad \Big| \quad \sum_{i \in I} a_i . c_i \quad \Big| \quad ready\ a.c \quad \Big| \quad rec\ X . c \quad \Big| \quad X$$

where (i) the index set I is finite; (ii) the atoms in $\{a_i\}_{i \in I}$ are pairwise distinct; (iii) the ready prefix may appear at the top-level, only; (iv) recursion is guarded.

Let e be a distinguished atom such that $e = \bar{e}$, and with continuation $E = rec\ X . e ; X$. We say that c succeeds iff either $c = e ; E \oplus d$, or $c = e . E + d$, or $c = ready\ e. E$. We will omit trailing occurrences of E in contracts.

Bilateral contracts are terms of the form $A\ says\ c \mid B\ says\ d$, where $A \neq B$ and at most one occurrence of ready is present.

$$\text{A } says \text{ } (\text{a}; c \oplus c') \mid \text{B } says \text{ } (\bar{\text{a}}.d + d') \xrightarrow{\text{A } says \text{ a}} \text{A } says \text{ } c \mid \text{B } says \text{ } ready \text{ } \bar{\text{a}}.d \qquad [\text{INTEXT}]$$

$$\text{A } says \text{ } (\text{a}; c \oplus c') \mid \text{B } says \text{ } \bar{\text{a}}; d \xrightarrow{\text{A } says \text{ a}} \text{A } says \text{ } c \mid \text{B } says \text{ } ready \text{ } \bar{\text{a}}.d \qquad [\text{INTINT}]$$

$$\text{A } says \text{ } (\text{a}.c + c') \mid \text{B } says \text{ } (\bar{\text{a}}.d + d') \xrightarrow{\text{A } says \text{ a}} \text{A } says \text{ } c \mid \text{B } says \text{ } ready \text{ } \bar{\text{a}}.d \qquad [\text{EXTEXT}]$$

$$\text{A } says \text{ } ready \text{ } \text{a}. \text{ } c \mid \text{B } says \text{ } d \xrightarrow{\text{A } says \text{ a}} \text{A } says \text{ } c \mid \text{B } says \text{ } d \qquad [\text{RDY}]$$

$$\frac{\text{a} \notin co(\{\text{b}_i\}_{i \in I})}{\text{A } says \text{ a}; c \oplus c' \mid \text{B } says \text{ } \sum_{i \in I} \text{b}_i.d_i \xrightarrow{\text{A } says \text{ a}} \text{A } says \text{ } E \mid \text{B } says \text{ } 0} \qquad [\text{INTEXTFAIL}]$$

$$\frac{\{\text{a}\} \neq co(\{\text{b}_i\}_{i \in I})}{\text{A } says \text{ a}; c \oplus c' \mid \text{B } says \text{ } \bigoplus_{i \in I} \text{b}_i; d_i \xrightarrow{\text{A } says \text{ a}} \text{A } says \text{ } E \mid \text{B } says \text{ } 0} \qquad [\text{INTINTFAIL}]$$

$$\frac{(\{\text{a}\} \cup \{\text{a}_i\}_{i \in I}) \cap co(\{\text{b}_i\}_{i \in J}) = \emptyset}{\text{A } says \text{ } (\text{a}.c + \sum_{i \in I} \text{a}_i.c_i) \mid \text{B } says \text{ } \sum_{i \in J} \text{b}_i.d_i \xrightarrow{\text{A } says \text{ a}} \text{A } says \text{ } E \mid \text{B } says \text{ } 0} \qquad [\text{EXTEXTFAIL}]$$

Fig. 1. Semantics of contracts (symmetric rules for B actions omitted)

Intuitively, the internal sum $\bigoplus_{i \in I} \text{a}_i; c_i$ allows to choose one of the branches $\text{a}_i; c_i$, to perform the action a_i, and then behave according to c_i. Dually, the external sum $\sum_{i \in I} \text{a}_i.c_i$ constrains to wait for the other participant to choose one of the branches $\text{a}_i.c_i$, then to perform the corresponding a_i and finally behave according to c_i. Separators ; and . allow us to distinguish singleton *internal* sums (e.g., $\text{a}; c$) from singleton *external* sums (e.g., $\text{a}.c$). The atom e (for "end") enables a participant to successfully terminate, similarly to [10]. This will be reflected in Def. 4. Hereafter, we shall always consider contracts with no free occurrences of recursion variables X. We shall use the binary operators to isolate a branch in a sum: e.g. $(\text{a}; c) \oplus c'$ where c' is an internal sum. We let ; and . have higher precedence than $\oplus$ and $+$, e.g., $\text{a}; c \oplus \text{b}; c' = (\text{a}; c) \oplus (\text{b}; c')$.

The evolution of bilateral contracts is modelled by a labelled transition relation $\xrightarrow{\mu}$ (Def. 2), where labels $\mu = \text{A } says \text{ a}$ model a participant A performing the action a.

Definition 2. *The relation $\xrightarrow{\mu}$ on bilateral contracts is the smallest relation closed under the rules in Fig. 1 and under the structural congruence relation $\equiv$, defined as the least congruence which includes α-conversion of recursion variables, and satisfies $rec \text{ } X. \text{ } c \equiv c\{rec \text{ } X. c/X\}$ and $\bigoplus_{i \in \emptyset} \text{a}_i; c_i \equiv \sum_{i \in \emptyset} \text{a}_i.c_i$. Accordingly, empty sums (either internal or external) will be denoted with 0. We will not omit trailing occurrences of 0. Hereafter we shall consider contracts up to $\equiv$.*

In the first three rules in Fig. 1, A and B expose complementary actions $\text{a}, \bar{\text{a}}$. In rule [IN-TEXT], participant A selects the branch a in an internal sum. Participant B is then forced to commit to the corresponding branch $\bar{\text{a}}$ in his external sum: this is done by marking that branch with *ready* $\bar{\text{a}}$ while discarding all the other branches. Participant B will then perform his action in the subsequent step, by rule [RDY]. In rule [INTINT], both participants make an internal choice; a reaction is possible only if one of the two is a singleton — B in the rule — namely he can only commit to his unique branch. Were B exposing multiple branches, the transition would not be allowed, to account for the fact that B could pick a conflicting internal choice w.r.t. that of A. In rule [EXTEXT], both participants expose external sums with complementary actions, and each of the two can choose a branch (unlike in the case [INTEXT], where the internal choice has to move first). In the [*FAIL] rules, the action chosen by A is not supported by B. Then, A will reach the success state E, while B will fall into the failure state 0.

Example 1. Let $\gamma = A\ says\ (a; c_1 \oplus b; c_2) \mid B\ says\ (\bar{a}.d_1 + \bar{c}.d_2)$. If the participant A internally chooses to perform a, then γ will take a transition to A *says* c_1 | B *says ready* $\bar{a}.d_1$. Suppose instead that A chooses for perform b, which is not offered by B in his external choice. In this case, γ will take a transition to A *says* E | B *says* 0, where 0 indicates that B cannot proceed with the interaction. Coherently with [10], below we will characterise this behaviour by saying that the contracts of A and B are *not* compliant.

The following lemma states that bilateral contracts are never stuck unless both participants have contract 0. Actually, if none of the first four rules in Fig. 1 can be applied, the contract can make a transition with one of the [*FAIL] rules.

Lemma 1. *A bilateral contract* A *says* c | B *says* d *is stuck iff* $c = d = 0$.

Below we establish that contracts are deterministic. This is guaranteed by the requirement (ii) of Def. 1. Determinism is a very desirable property indeed, because it ensures that the duties of a participant at any given time are uniquely determined by the past actions. Note that the contracts in [10] satisfy distributivity laws like $(a; c) \oplus (a; d) = a; (c \oplus d)$, which allow for rewriting them so that (ii) in Def. 1 holds. Therefore, (ii) is not a real restriction w.r.t. [10].

Lemma 2 (Determinism). *For all* γ, *if* $\gamma \xrightarrow{\mu} \gamma'$ *and* $\gamma \xrightarrow{\mu} \gamma''$, *then* $\gamma' = \gamma''$.

Compliance. Below we define when two contracts are *compliant*, in a similar fashion to [10]. Intuitively, two contracts are compliant if whatever sets of choices they offer, there is at least one common option that can make the contracts progress. Differently from [10], our notion of compliance is symmetric, in that we do not discriminate between the participant roles as client and server. Consequently, we do not consider compliant two contracts where only one of the parties is willing to terminate. For example, the buyer contract ship; E is not compliant with the seller contract $\overline{ship}$.pay; E, because the buyer should not be allowed to terminate if the seller still requires to be paid.

Similarly to [10], given two contracts we observe their *ready sets* (Def. 3) to detect when the enabled actions allow them to synchronise correctly.

Definition 3 (Compliance). *For all contracts* c, *we define the set of sets* $RS(c)$ *as:*

$$RS(0) = \{\emptyset\} \qquad RS(ready\ a.c) = \{\{ready\}\} \qquad RS(rec\ X.c) = RS(c)$$

$$RS(\bigoplus_{i \in I} a_i; c_i) = \{\{a_i\} \mid i \in I\}\ if\ I \neq \emptyset \qquad RS(\Sigma_{i \in I} a_i.c_i) = \{\{a_i\} \mid i \in I\}\ if\ I \neq \emptyset$$

The relation $\bowtie$ *between contracts is the largest relation such that, whenever* $c \bowtie d$:

(1) $\forall X \in RS(c), \mathcal{Y} \in RS(d).\ co(X) \cap \mathcal{Y} \neq \emptyset\ or\ ready \in (X \cup \mathcal{Y}) \setminus (X \cap \mathcal{Y})$

(2) A *says* c | B *says* $d \xrightarrow{\mu}$ A *says* c' | B *says* $d' \implies c' \bowtie d'$

When $c \bowtie d$, *we say that the contracts* c *and* d *are* compliant.

Example 2. Recall from Ex. 1 the contracts $c = \mathsf{a}; c_1 \oplus \mathsf{b}; c_2$ and $d = \bar{\mathsf{a}}.d_1 + \bar{\mathsf{c}}.d_2$. We have that $RS(c) = \{\{\mathsf{a}\}, \{\mathsf{b}\}\}$, and $RS(d) = \{\{\bar{\mathsf{a}}, \bar{\mathsf{c}}\}\}$, which do not respect item (1) of Def. 3 (take $X = \{\mathsf{b}\}$ and $\mathcal{Y} = \{\bar{\mathsf{a}}, \bar{\mathsf{c}}\}$). Therefore, c and d are *not* compliant.

The following lemma provides an alternative characterization of compliance. Two contracts are compliant iff, when combined into a bilateral contract γ, no computation of γ reaches a state where one of the contracts is 0. Together with Lemma 1, we have that such γ will never get stuck. (Below, the Kleene * denotes reflexive transitive closure.)

Lemma 3. *For all bilateral contracts* $\gamma =$ A *says* c | B *says* d:

$$c \bowtie d \iff \left(\forall c', d'. \gamma \rightarrow^* \text{A } says \text{ } c' \mid \text{B } says \text{ } d' \implies c' \neq 0 \text{ and } d' \neq 0 \right)$$

The following lemma guarantees, for all c not containing 0, the existence of a contract d compliant with c. Intuitively, we can construct d from c by turning internal choices into external ones (and *viceversa*), and by turning actions into co-actions.

Lemma 4. *For all* 0-*free contracts* c, *there exists* d *such that* $c \bowtie d$.

Culpability. We now tackle the problem of determining who is expected to make the next step for the fulfilment of a bilateral contract. We call a participant A *culpable* in γ if she is expected to perform some action so to make γ progress. Also, we consider A culpable when she is advertising the "failure" contract 0. This agrees with our [*FAIL] rules, which set A's contract to 0 when the other participant legitimately chooses an action not supported by A. Note that we do not consider A culpable when her contract has enabled e actions.

Definition 4. *A participant* A *is culpable in* $\gamma =$ A *says* c | B *says* d, *written* A $\overset{\frown}{\sim} \gamma$, *iff*:

$$c = 0 \quad \lor \quad \left(\gamma \overset{\text{A } says \text{ } e}{\nrightarrow} \quad \land \quad \exists \mathsf{a}. \; \gamma \overset{\text{A } says \text{ } a}{\nrightarrow} \right)$$

When A *is not* culpable *in* γ *we write* A $\overset{\smile}{} \gamma$.

The following result states that a participant A is always able to recover from culpability by performing some of her duties. Furthermore, this requires at most two steps in an "A-solo" trace where no other participant intervenes.

Definition 5. *Let* $\rightarrow$ *be an LTS with labels of the form* A_i *says* $(\cdots)$, *for* A_i *ranging over participants names. For all* A, *we say that a* $\rightarrow$-*trace* η *is* A-*solo iff* η *only contains labels of the form* A *says* $(\cdots)$. *If* $\eta = (\mu_i)_{i \in 0..n}$, *we will write* $\overset{\eta}{\rightarrow}$ *for* $\overset{\mu_0}{\longrightarrow} \cdots \overset{\mu_n}{\longrightarrow}$.

Theorem 1 (Contractual exculpation). *For all* $\gamma =$ A *says* c | B *says* d *with* 0-*free* c, *there exists* γ' *and* A-*solo* η *with* $|\eta| \leq 2$ *such that* $\gamma \overset{\eta}{\twoheadrightarrow} \gamma'$ *and* A $\overset{\smile}{} \gamma'$.

commutative monoidal laws for | on processes and systems

$$u[(v)P] \equiv (v)u[P] \text{ if } u \neq v \quad Z \mid (u)Z' \equiv (u)(Z \mid Z') \text{ if } u \notin \mathrm{fv}(Z) \cup \mathrm{fn}(Z) \quad (u)(v)Z \equiv (v)(u)Z$$

$$(u)Z \equiv Z \text{ if } u \notin \mathrm{fv}(Z) \cup \mathrm{fn}(Z) \qquad \mathsf{A}[K] \mid \mathsf{A}[P] \equiv \mathsf{A}[K \mid P] \qquad \downarrow_s c \equiv \mathbf{0} \equiv \mathrm{fuse}_s . P$$

Fig. 2. Structural equivalence for CO_2 (Z, Z' range over systems or processes)

A crucial property of culpability is to ensure that either two participants are both succeeding, or it is possible to single out who has to make the next step. An external judge is therefore always able to detect who is violating the contracts agreed upon.

Theorem 2. *For all c, d if $c \bowtie d$ and A says $c \mid \mathsf{B}$ says $d \twoheadrightarrow^* \gamma = \mathsf{A}$ says $c' \mid \mathsf{B}$ says d', then either c' and d' succeed, or $\mathsf{A} \overset{\frown}{\sim} \gamma$, or $\mathsf{B} \overset{\frown}{\sim} \gamma$.*

Example 3. A participant might be culpable even though her contract succeeds. For instance, let $\gamma = \mathsf{A}$ *says* $c \mid \mathsf{B}$ *says* d, where $c = \mathsf{e} + \bar{\mathsf{a}}$ and $d = \mathsf{a} + \mathsf{b}$. By Def. 1 we have that c succeeds, but A is culpable in γ because she cannot fire e, while she can fire $\bar{\mathsf{a}}$ by rule [EXTEXT]. This makes quite sense, because A is saying that she is either willing to terminate or to perform $\bar{\mathsf{a}}$, but the other participant is not allowing A to terminate. Note that also B is culpable, because he can fire a.

3 A Calculus of Contracting Processes

We now embed the contracts introduced in § 2 in a specialization of the parametric process calculus CO_2 [2]. Let $\mathcal{V}$ and $\mathcal{N}$ be two disjoint countably infinite sets of *session variables* (ranged over by $x, y, \ldots$) and *session names* (ranged over by $s, t, \ldots$). Let $u, v, \ldots$ range over $\mathcal{V} \cup \mathcal{N}$.

Definition 6. *The abstract syntax of* CO_2 *is given by the following productions:*

Systems	$S ::=$	$\mathbf{0}$	$\mid \quad \mathsf{A}[P]$	$\mid \quad s[\gamma]$	$\mid \quad S \mid S$	$\mid \quad (u)S$
Processes	$P ::=$	$\downarrow_u \mathsf{A}$ *says* c	$\mid \quad \sum_i \pi_i . P_i$	$\mid \quad P \mid P$	$\mid \quad (u)P$	$\mid \quad X(\vec{u})$
Prefixes	$\pi ::=$	τ	$\mid \quad \mathrm{tell}_{\mathsf{A}} \downarrow_u c$	$\mid \quad \mathrm{fuse}_u$	$\mid \quad \mathrm{do}_u \, \mathsf{a}$	$\mid \quad \mathrm{ask}_u \, \phi$

The only binder for session variables and names is the delimitation $(\vec{u})$, both in systems and processes. Free variables/names are defined accordingly, and they are denoted by $\mathrm{fv}(\_)$ and $\mathrm{fn}(\_)$. A system or a process is *closed* when it has no free variables.

Systems are the parallel composition of *participants* $\mathsf{A}[P]$ and *sessions* $s[\gamma]$.

A *latent contract* $\downarrow_x \mathsf{A}$ *says* c represents a contract c (advertised by A) which has not been stipulated yet; upon stipulation, x will be instantiated to a fresh session name. We impose that in a system $\mathsf{A}[P] \mid \mathsf{A}[Q] \mid S$, either P or Q is a parallel composition of latent contracts. Hereafter, $K, K', \ldots$ are meta-variables for compositions of latent contracts. We allow prefix-guarded finite sums of processes, and write $\pi_1 . P_1 + \pi_2 . P_2$ for $\sum_{i=1,2} \pi_i . P_i$, and $\mathbf{0}$ for $\sum_{\emptyset} P$. Recursion is allowed only for processes; for this we stipulate that each process identifier X has a unique defining equation $X(u_1, \ldots, u_j) \overset{\mathrm{def}}{=} P$

$$A[\tau.P + P' \mid Q] \to A[P \mid Q] \qquad\qquad [\text{Tau}]$$

$$A[\text{tell}_B \downarrow_x c.P + P' \mid Q] \to A[P \mid Q] \mid B[\downarrow_x A \; says \; c] \qquad [\text{Tell}]$$

$$\frac{K \rhd^\sigma_x \gamma \qquad \vec{u} = \text{dom} \, \sigma \qquad s = \sigma(x) \; \text{fresh}}{(\vec{u})(A[\text{fuse}_x.P + P' \mid K \mid Q] \mid S) \to (s)(A[P \mid Q]\sigma \mid s[\gamma] \mid S\sigma)} \qquad [\text{Fuse}]$$

$$\frac{\gamma \xrightarrow{A \; says \; a} \gamma'}{s[\gamma] \mid A[\text{do}_s a.P + P' \mid Q] \to s[\gamma'] \mid A[P \mid Q]} \qquad [\text{Do}]$$

$$\frac{\gamma \vdash \phi}{A[\text{ask}_s \phi.P + P' \mid Q] \mid s[\gamma] \to A[P \mid Q] \mid s[\gamma]} \qquad [\text{Ask}]$$

$$\frac{X(\vec{u}) \stackrel{\text{def}}{=} P \qquad P\{\vec{v}/\vec{u}\} \to P'}{X(\vec{v}) \to P'} \; [\text{Def}] \qquad \frac{S \to S'}{S \mid S'' \to S' \mid S''} \; [\text{Par}] \qquad \frac{S \to S'}{(u)S \to (u)S'} \; [\text{Del}]$$

Fig. 3. Reduction semantics of CO_2

such that $fv(P) \subseteq \{u_1, \ldots, u_j\} \subseteq \mathcal{V}$ and each occurrence of process identifiers in P is prefix-guarded. We shall take the liberty of omitting the arguments of $X(\vec{u})$ when they are clear from the context.

Prefixes include silent action τ, contract advertisement $\text{tell}_A \downarrow_u c$, contract stipulation fuse_u, action execution $\text{do}_u a$, and contract query $\text{ask}_u \phi$. In each prefix $\pi \neq \tau$, u refers to the target session involved in the execution of π. We omit trailing occurrences of $\mathbf{0}$.

Note that participants can only contain latent contracts, while sessions can only contain bilateral contracts, constructed from latent contracts upon reaching agreements.

The semantics of CO_2 is formalised by a reduction relation $\to$ on systems that relies on the structural congruence defined in Fig. 2, where the last law allows for collecting garbage terms possibly arising from variable substitutions.

Definition 7. *The relation* $\to$ *is the smallest relation closed under the rules of Fig. 3, defined over systems up to structural equivalence, as defined in Fig. 2. The relation* $K \rhd^\sigma_x \gamma$ *holds iff (i)* K *has the form* $\downarrow_y A \; says \; c \mid\downarrow_z B \; says \; d$*, (ii)* $c \bowtie d$*, (iii)* $\gamma = A \; says \; c \mid B \; says \; d$*, and (iv)* $\sigma = \{s/x,y,z\}$ *maps all* $x, y, z \in \mathcal{V}$ *to* $s \in \mathcal{N}$*.*

Rule [Tau] simply fires a τ prefix as expected. Rule [Tell] advertises a latent contract $\downarrow_x A \; says \; c$, by putting it in parallel with the existing participants and sessions (the structural congruence laws in Fig. 2 allow for latent contracts to float in a system and, by the second last law, to move across the boxes of participants as appropriate). Rule [Fuse] finds agreements among the latent contracts K of A; an agreement is reached when K contains a bilateral contract γ whose unilater contracs are compliant (cf. Def. 7). Note that, once the agreement is reached, the compliant contracts start a fresh session containing γ. Rule [Do] allows a participant A to fulfill her contract γ, by performing the needed actions in the session containing γ (which, accordingly, evolves to γ'). Rule [Ask] checks if a condition ϕ holds in a session. The actual nature of ϕ is almost immaterial in this paper: the reader may assume that ϕ is a formula in an LTL logic [13]. For closed γ and ϕ, $\gamma \vdash \phi$ holds iff $\gamma \models_{LTL} \phi$ according to the standard LTL semantics where, for a $\twoheadrightarrow$-trace $\eta = (\gamma_i \xrightarrow{\mu_i} \gamma_{i+1})_i$ from $\gamma_0 = \gamma$, we define $\eta \models a \iff \exists A. \mu_0 = A \text{ says } a$. The last three rules are standard.

Hereafter it will be sometimes useful to record the prefix π fired by A by implicitly decorating the corresponding reduction step, as in $\xrightarrow{A : \pi}$.

The rest of this section is devoted to a few examples that highlight how bilateral contracts can be used in CO_2.

Example 4. Consider an online store A with the following contract c_A: buyers can add items to the shopping cart, and then either leave the store or pay with a credit card. Assume the store modelled as the CO_2 process $P_A = (x)(\text{tell}_A \downarrow_x c_A.X \mid \text{fuse}_x)$, where:

$$c_A = rec\ Z.\ \mathsf{addToCart}.Z + \mathsf{creditCard}.(\overline{\mathsf{ok}} \oplus \overline{\mathsf{no}}) + e$$

$$X \stackrel{\text{def}}{=} \mathsf{do}_x\ \mathsf{addToCart}.X + \mathsf{do}_x\ \mathsf{creditCard}.(\tau.\mathsf{do}_x\ \overline{\mathsf{ok}} + \tau.\mathsf{do}_x\ \overline{\mathsf{no}})$$

Let B be a buyer with contract $c_B = \overline{\mathsf{addToCart}}; \overline{\mathsf{creditCard}}; (\mathsf{ok} + \mathsf{no})$, and let:

$$P_B = (y)\,\mathsf{tell}_A \downarrow_y c_B.Y \qquad\qquad Y \stackrel{\text{def}}{=} \mathsf{do}_y\ \overline{\mathsf{addToCart}}.\,\mathsf{do}_y\ \overline{\mathsf{creditCard}}.\,\mathsf{do}_y\ \mathsf{ok}$$

A possible, successful, computation of the system $S = A[P_A] \mid B[P_B]$ is the following:

$$
\begin{aligned}
S \to^* &(x,y)\ \big(A[\downarrow_x A \text{ says } c_A \mid \downarrow_y B \text{ says } c_B \mid \mathsf{fuse}_x \mid X] \mid B[Y]\big) \\
\to\ &(s)\ \big(A[X\{^s/_x\}] \mid B[Y\{^s/_y\}] \mid s[A \text{ says } c_A \mid B \text{ says } c_B]\big) \\
\to^* &(s)\ \big(A[X\{^s/_x\}] \mid B[\!]\mathsf{do}_y\ \overline{\mathsf{creditCard}}.\,\mathsf{do}_y\ \mathsf{ok} \mid s[A \text{ says } c_A \mid B \text{ says } \overline{\mathsf{creditCard}}; (\mathsf{ok}+\mathsf{no})]\big) \\
\to^* &(s)\ \big(A[\tau.\mathsf{do}_x\ \overline{\mathsf{ok}} + \tau.\mathsf{do}_x\ \overline{\mathsf{no}}] \mid B[\mathsf{do}_y\ \mathsf{ok}] \mid s[A \text{ says } \overline{\mathsf{ok}} \oplus \overline{\mathsf{no}} \mid B \text{ says } \mathsf{ok}+\mathsf{no}]\big) \\
\to\ &(s)\ \big(A[\mathsf{do}_x\ \overline{\mathsf{ok}}] \mid B[\mathsf{do}_y\ \mathsf{ok}] \mid s[A \text{ says } \overline{\mathsf{ok}} \oplus \overline{\mathsf{no}} \mid B \text{ says } \mathsf{ok}+\mathsf{no}]\big) \\
\to^* &(s)\ \big(A[0] \mid B[0] \mid s[A \text{ says } E \mid B \text{ says } E]\big)
\end{aligned}
$$

Example 5. An on-line store A offers buyers two options: clickPay or clickVoucher. If a buyer B chooses clickPay, A accepts the payment (pay) otherwise A checks the validity of the voucher with V, an electronic voucher distribution and management system. If V validates the voucher, B can use it (voucher), otherwise he will pay.

The contracts $c_A = \mathsf{clickPay}.\mathsf{pay} + \mathsf{clickVoucher}.(\overline{\mathsf{reject}};\mathsf{pay} \oplus \overline{\mathsf{accept}};\mathsf{voucher})$ and $c'_A = \mathsf{ok} + \mathsf{no}$ model the scenario above. A CO_2 process for A can be the following

$$P_A = (x)(\mathsf{tell}_A \downarrow_x c_A.(\mathsf{do}_x\ \mathsf{clickPay}.\mathsf{do}_x\ \mathsf{pay} + \mathsf{do}_x\ \mathsf{clickVoucher}.((y)\mathsf{tell}_V \downarrow_y c'_A.X)))$$
$$X = \mathsf{do}_y\ \mathsf{ok}.\mathsf{do}_x\ \overline{\mathsf{accept}}.\mathsf{do}_x\ \mathsf{voucher} + \mathsf{do}_y\ \mathsf{no}.\mathsf{do}_x\ \overline{\mathsf{reject}}.\mathsf{do}_x\ \mathsf{pay} + \tau.\mathsf{do}_x\ \overline{\mathsf{reject}}.\mathsf{do}_x\ \mathsf{pay}$$

Contract c_A (resp. c'_A) is stipulated when (i) B (resp. V) advertises to A (resp. V) a contract d with $c_A \bowtie d$ (resp. $c'_A \bowtie d$) and (ii) a fuse_z is executed in A (resp. V).

Variables x and y in P_A correspond to two separate sessions, where A respectively interacts with B and V. The semantics of CO_2 ensures that x and y will be instantiated to different session names (if at all).

The advertisement of c'_A causally depends on the stipulation of the contracts of A and B, otherwise A cannot fire do_x clickVoucher. Instead, A and B can interact regardless the presence of V since $\mathsf{tell}_V \downarrow_y c'_A$ is non blocking and the τ-branch of A in X is enabled (letting A to autonomously reject the voucher, e.g. because B is not entitled to use it).

Example 6. Consider a travel agency A which queries in parallel an airline ticket broker F and a hotel reservation service H in order to complete the organization of a trip. The travel agency service $A[P]$ can be defined as follows:

$$P = (x,y)(\text{tell}_F \downarrow_x \text{ ticket}; (\text{commitF} \oplus \text{abortF}).X \mid \text{tell}_H \downarrow_y \text{ hotel}; (\text{commitH} \oplus \text{abortH}).Y)$$

$$X \stackrel{\text{def}}{=} \text{do}_x \text{ ticket}. ((\text{ask}_y \textit{ true}. \text{do}_x \text{ commitF}) + \tau.\text{do}_x \text{ abortF})$$

$$Y \stackrel{\text{def}}{=} \text{do}_y \text{ hotel}. ((\text{ask}_x \textit{ true}. \text{do}_y \text{ commitH}) + \tau.\text{do}_y \text{ abortH})$$

where the τ actions model timeouts used to ensure progress. The travel agency in process X starts buying a ticket, and commits to it only when the hotel reservation session y is started. Similarly for process Y.

The next example shows a peculiar use of ask whereby a participant inspects a stipulated contract to decide its future behaviour.

Example 7. An online store A can choose whether to abort a transaction ($\overline{\text{abort}}$) or to commit to the payment ($\overline{\text{commit}}$). In the latter case, the buyer has two options, either he pays by credit card (creditCard) or by bank transfer (bankTransfer). The contract of A is modelled as $c = \overline{\text{abort}} \oplus \overline{\text{commit}}; (\text{creditCard} + \text{bankTransfer})$. Consider the process

$$P_A = (x)(\text{tell}_A \downarrow_x c. (\text{ask}_x \phi. \text{do}_x \overline{\text{commit}}. \text{do}_x \text{creditCard} + \text{do}_x \overline{\text{abort}}))$$

where $\phi = \Box(\overline{\text{commit}} \rightarrow \neg\Diamond\text{bankTransfer})$. The process P_A first advertises c. Once a session $s[\gamma]$ is initiated with $\gamma = A \textit{ says } c \mid B \textit{ says } d$, A tests γ through $\text{ask}_x \phi$ before committing to the payment. If $\text{ask}_x \phi$ detects that B has promised not to use the bank transfer option, then A commits to the payment, and then never offers B to perform a bank transfer. Otherwise, if d does not rule out the bank transfer, even if B might actually pay by credit card, A aborts the session. Note that in both cases A realizes her own contract, even if she is never performing the bank transfer. This notion of "realization of a contract" will be formalized in Def. 11.

4   On Honesty

In this section we set out when a participant A is honest (Def. 11). Intuitively, we consider all the possible runs of all possible systems, and require that in every session A is not definitely culpable. To this aim, we first provide CO2 with the counterpart of the (non)culpability relation introduced in Def. 4. Intuitively, we write $A \smile_s S$ when, in the system S, if the participant A is involved in the session s, then she is not culpable w.r.t. the contract stipulated therein.

Definition 8. *We write* $A \smile_s S$ *whenever* $\forall \vec{u}, \gamma, S'. (S \equiv (\vec{u})(s[\gamma] \mid S') \implies A \smile \gamma)$. *We write* $A \smile S$ *whenever* $A \smile_s S$ *for all session names* s.

A technical issue is that a participant may not get a chance to act in all the traces. For instance, let $S = A[\text{do}_s \text{pay}] \mid B[X] \mid S'$, where S' enables A's action and $X \stackrel{\text{def}}{=} \tau.X$; note that S generates the infinite trace $S \rightarrow S \rightarrow S \rightarrow \cdots$ in which A never pays, despite her honest intention. To account for this fact, we will check the honesty of a participant in *fair* traces, only, i.e. those where persistent transitions are eventually followed.

Definition 9. *Given an LTS* $\xrightarrow{\mu}$*, we say that a (finite or infinite) trace* $\eta = (P_i \xrightarrow{\mu_i} P_{i+1})_i$ *having length* $|\eta| \in \mathbb{N} \cup \{\infty\}$ *is* fair *w.r.t. a set of labels* $\mathcal{L}$ *if and only if*

$$\forall i \in \mathbb{N}, \mu \in \mathcal{L}. \left(i \le |\eta| \wedge (\forall j \in \mathbb{N}. \, i \le j \le |\eta| \implies P_j \xrightarrow{\mu}) \implies \exists j \ge i. \, \mu_j = \mu \right)$$

A fair trace *is a trace which is fair w.r.t. all the labels in the LTS.*

Note that, by Def. 9, a fair trace is also a maximal one (w.r.t. $\mathcal{L}$). Indeed, if a fair trace is finite, the condition above guarantees that its final state has no $\mathcal{L}$ transitions enabled.

Finally, when checking the fairness of a trace, we shall implicitly assume that the labels μ in our LTSs of contracts and processes always distinguish between different occurrences of the same prefix. E.g., a $\rightarrow$-fair trace of $A[X \mid X]$ where $X \stackrel{\text{def}}{=} \tau.X$ is not allowed to only perform the τ's of the first X. Technically, labels μ always implicitly carry the syntactic *address* of the prefix which is being fired, in the spirit of the Enhanced Structured Operational Semantics [12].

It is often useful to reason about how a specific session s evolves in a given trace. Technically, α-conversion allows the name s to be renamed at every step, making it hard to trace the identity of names. More concretely, α-conversion is only needed to make delimitations fresh when unfolding recursive processes. Accordingly, w.l.o.g. hereafter we shall often restrict α-conversion by considering *stable* traces, only, defined below. In this way, we ensure that s represents the same session throughout the whole trace.

Definition 10. *A* stable $\rightarrow$-trace *is a trace* $(\vec{u}_0)S_0 \rightarrow (\vec{u}_1)S_1 \rightarrow (\vec{u}_2)S_2 \rightarrow \cdots$ *in which* (1) *all delimitations carry distinct names and variables,* (2) *delimitations have been brought to the top-level as much as possible (using* $\equiv$*), and* (3) *no* α*-conversion is performed in the trace except when unfolding recursive processes.*

Below, we define several notions of contract faithfulness for participants. We start by clarifying when a participant A *realizes* a contract (inside a session s) within a specific context. This happens when from any reachable system state S_0, participant A will eventually perform actions to exculpate herself (in s). In this phase, A is protected from interference with other participants. Then, we say A *honest in a system* if she realizes every contract in that system. When $A[P]$ is honest independently of the system, we simply say that $A[P]$ is *honest*. In this last case, we rule out those systems carrying stipulated or latent contracts of A outside of $A[P]$; otherwise the system can trivially make A culpable: e.g., we disallow $A[P] \mid B[\downarrow_x A \text{ says } \overline{pay} \mid \cdots]$.

Definition 11 (Honesty). *We say that:*

- *A realizes c at s in S iff whenever $S = (\vec{u})(s[A \text{ says } c \mid B \text{ says } d] \mid S')$, $S \rightarrow^* S_0$, and $(S_i)_i$ is a $\{A : \pi\}$-fair A-solo stable $\rightarrow$-trace then $A \smile_s S_j$ for some $j \ge 0$;*
- *A is honest in S iff for all c and s, A realizes c at s in S;*
- *$A[P]$ is honest iff for all S with no $A \text{ says } \cdots$ nor $A[\cdots]$, A is honest in $A[P] \mid S$.*

Example 8. A computation of the store-buyer system $S = A[P_A] \mid B[P_B]$ from Ex. 4 is:

$$S \rightarrow^* (s) \left(A[\tau.\text{do}_x \, \overline{\text{ok}} + \tau.\text{do}_x \, \overline{\text{no}}] \mid B[\text{do}_y \, \text{ok}] \mid s[A \text{ says } \overline{\text{ok}} \oplus \overline{\text{no}} \mid B \text{ says } \text{ok} + \text{no}] \right)$$
$$\rightarrow (s) \left(A[\text{do}_x \, \overline{\text{no}}] \mid B[\text{do}_y \, \text{ok}] \mid s[A \text{ says } \overline{\text{ok}} \oplus \overline{\text{no}} \mid B \text{ says } \text{ok} + \text{no}] \right)$$
$$\rightarrow (s) \left(A[\mathbf{0}] \mid B[\text{do}_y \, \text{ok}] \mid s[\gamma] \right)$$

where $\gamma = $ A *says* E | B *says ready* no. The system is then stuck, because γ is not allowing the [DO] step. By Def. 4 we have A $\smile$ γ, B $\not\frown$ γ, so A is honest in S while B is not. Actually, B has violated the contract agreed upon, because he is waiting for a positive answer from the store, while in c_B he also promised to accept a $\overline{no}$. By Def. 11, B is not honest, while we will show in § 5 that A is honest (see Ex. 10).

Example 9. Consider the system $A[(x,y) (P_A | \text{fuse}_x | \text{fuse}_y)] | B[P_B] | C[P_C]$, where:

$$P_A \overset{\text{def}}{=} \text{tell}_A (\downarrow_x \text{a}.E).\text{tell}_A (\downarrow_y \text{b}; E).\text{do}_x \text{a}.\text{do}_y \text{b}$$

$$P_B \overset{\text{def}}{=} (z) (\text{tell}_A (\downarrow_z \bar{\text{b}}.E).\text{do}_z \text{b})$$

$$P_C \overset{\text{def}}{=} (w) (\text{tell}_A (\downarrow_w \bar{\text{a}}; E).\mathbf{0})$$

Even though A might apparently look honest, she is not. Indeed, A cannot fulfill her contract with B, because the do_x a is blocked due to the fact that C (dishonestly) does not perform his internal choice. Note that, if we considered honest a participant whose culpability only depends on the culpability of someone else, then a participant could cunningly have one of her contracts violated, so to avoid fulfilling another contract (e.g., to avoid paying one million euros to B, A stipulates a dummy contract "I ship one candy if you pay 1 cent", which is then violated by a colluding participant C).

We now define when a process enables a contract transition, independently from the context. To do that, first we define the set $RD_s(P)$ (after "ready do"), which collects all the atoms with an unguarded action do_s in P.

Definition 12. *For all P and all s, we define the set of atoms $RD_s(P)$ as:*

$$RD_s(P) = \{\text{a} \mid \exists \vec{u}, P', Q, R . P \equiv (\vec{u}) (\text{do}_s \text{a}.P' + Q \mid R) \text{ and } s \notin \vec{u}\}$$

Next, we check when a contract "unblocks" a set of atoms X: e.g., if X accounts for at least one branch of an internal choice, or for all the branches of an external choice.

Definition 13. *For all sets of atoms X and for all $c \neq 0$, we say that c unblocks X iff:*

$$\exists Y \in RS(c).Y \subseteq X \cup \{\text{e}\} \qquad or \qquad c = ready \text{ a}.c' \wedge \text{a} \in X \cup \{\text{e}\}$$

Lemma 5. *For all P and for all $\gamma = $ A says c | B says d, if c unblocks $RD_s(P)$ and $S = (\vec{u})(A[P] | s[\gamma] | S')$, then either $A \smile \gamma$ or $S \xrightarrow{A : \text{do}_s \text{a}}$.*

The following theorem is the CO_2 counterpart of Theorem 1. It states that, when a session s is established between two participants A and B, A can always exculpate herself by performing (at most) two actions A : do $-$. Note that when the contracts used to establish s are compliant, then we deduce the stronger thesis $A \smile_s S_j$.

Theorem 3 (Factual exculpation). *Let $(S_i)_i$ be the following A-solo stable $\rightarrow$-trace, with $S_i = (\vec{u}_i) (A[Q_i] | s[A \text{ says } c_i | B \text{ says } d_i] | S'_i)$, and:*

$$S_0 \xrightarrow{\mu_0} \cdots \xrightarrow{\mu_{i-2}} S_{i-1} \xrightarrow{A : \text{do}_s \text{a}} S_i \xrightarrow{\mu_i} \cdots \xrightarrow{\mu_{j-2}} S_{j-1} \xrightarrow{A : \text{do}_s \text{b}} S_j \xrightarrow{\mu_j} \cdots$$

where $\mu_h \neq $ A : $\text{do}_s -$ for all $h \in [i, j-2]$. Then, either $c_j = 0$ or $A \smile_s S_j$.

$$a;c \oplus c' \xrightarrow{a}_{\sharp} c \qquad a.c + c' \xrightarrow{a}_{\sharp} c \qquad ready\ a.c \xrightarrow{a}_{\sharp} c \qquad a;c \oplus c' \xrightarrow{a}_{\sharp} E \qquad a.c + c' \xrightarrow{a}_{\sharp} E$$

$$\oplus a_i;c_i \xrightarrow{0}_{\sharp} 0 \qquad \Sigma\, a_i.c_i \xrightarrow{0}_{\sharp} 0 \qquad \Sigma\, a_i.c_i \xrightarrow{ctx}_{\sharp} ready\ a_n.c_n \qquad a;c \xrightarrow{ctx}_{\sharp} ready\ a.c \qquad c \xrightarrow{ctx}_{\sharp} c$$

$$\pi.P + Q \mid R \xrightarrow{\pi}_{\sharp} \begin{cases} open(\downarrow_x A\ says\ c \mid P \mid R) & \text{if } \pi = tell_A \downarrow_x c \qquad P \xrightarrow{ctx}_{\sharp} \downarrow_x B\ says\ c \mid P \text{ if } B \neq A \\ open(P \mid R)\sigma & \text{otherwise} \qquad\qquad\quad P \xrightarrow{ctx}_{\sharp} P\sigma \end{cases}$$

$$open(P) = P' \text{ where } P \equiv (\vec{u}_i)P' \text{ and no delimitation of } P' \text{ can be brought to the top level}$$

Fig. 4. Abstract LTSs for contracts and processes ($\sigma : \mathcal{V} \to \mathcal{N}$, name A in $\to^A_{\sharp}$ is omitted)

The following theorem states the undecidability of honesty. Our proof reduces the halting problem to checking dishonesty.

Theorem 4. *The problem of deciding whether a participant* A[P] *is dishonest is recursively enumerable, but not recursive.*

5   A Criterion for Honesty

In this section we devise a sufficient criterion for honesty. Actually, checking honesty is a challenging task: indeed, by Th. 4, it is not even decidable. We will then provide a semantics of contracts and processes, that focusses on the actions performed by a single participant A, while abstracting from those made by the context. Note that our abstract semantics assumes processes without top-level delimitations, in accordance with Def. 10 which lifts such delimitations outside participants. Further, we sometimes perform this lifting explicitly through the $open(-)$ operator.

Definition 14. *For all participant names* A, *the abstract LTSs* $\twoheadrightarrow_{\sharp}$ *and* $\to^A_{\sharp}$ *on contracts and on processes, respectively, are defined by the rules in Fig. 4, where* $\sigma : \mathcal{V} \to \mathcal{N}$.

The intuition behind the abstract rules is provided by Lemma 6 and Lemma 7 below, which establish the soundness of the abstractions.

Lemma 6. *For all bilateral contracts* $\gamma = $ A *says* c | B *says* d:

1. $\gamma \xrightarrow{A\ says\ a} $ A *says* c' | B *says* d' $\qquad \implies c \xrightarrow{a}_{\sharp} c' \wedge (d \xrightarrow{ctx}_{\sharp} d' \vee d \xrightarrow{0}_{\sharp} d')$
2. $\gamma \xrightarrow{A\ says\ a} $ A *says* c' | B *says* d' $\wedge c \bowtie d \implies c \xrightarrow{a}_{\sharp} c' \wedge d \xrightarrow{ctx}_{\sharp} d'$

Intuitively, a move of γ is caused by an action performed by one of its components c and d. If c moves, the $\xrightarrow{a}_{\sharp}$ rules account for its continuation. This might make d commit to one of the branches of a sum, as shown in the $\xrightarrow{ctx}_{\sharp}$ rules. Further, c can perform an action not supported by d, by using a [*FAIL] rule: accordingly, $\xrightarrow{0}_{\sharp}$ transforms d into 0. The compliance between c and d ensures the absence of such failure moves.

Lemma 7. *For each (finite or infinite) stable $\rightarrow$-trace $(S_i)_i$, with $S_i = (\vec{u}_i)(A[Q_i] \mid S'_i)$, there exists a $\rightarrow_\sharp$-trace $Q_0 \xrightarrow{\mu_0}_\sharp Q_1 \xrightarrow{\mu_1}_\sharp Q_2 \xrightarrow{\mu_2}_\sharp \cdots$ where $\mu_i = \pi$ if $S_i \xrightarrow{A:\pi} S_{i+1}$, and $\mu_i = ctx$ otherwise. Moreover, if $(S_i)_i$ is fair, then $(Q_i)_i$ is $\{\tau, \text{tell}\}$-fair.*

In the above lemma, each step of the whole system might be due to either the process Q_i or its context. If Q_i fires a prefix π, then it changes according to the $\xrightarrow{\pi}_\sharp$ rule in Fig. 4. In particular, that accounts for tell_A — adding further latent contracts to Q_i, as well as fuse possibly instantiating variables. Newly exposed delimitations are removed using $open(-)$: indeed, they already appear in $\vec{u}_i$, since the trace is stable.

We now define when a process P "$\sharp$-realizes" a contract c in a session s (written $P \models_s c$), without making any assumptions about its context. Intuitively, $P \models_s c$ holds when (1) P eventually enables the do_s actions mandated by c, and (2) in the abstract LTS $\rightarrow_\sharp$, the continuation of P after firing some do_s must realize the continuation of c (under $\rightarrow_\sharp$). Note that P is not required to actually perform the relevant do_s, because the context might prevent P from doing so. For instance, in the system $A[P] \mid s[A \text{ says } c \mid B \text{ says ready } a.d]$ the process P can not fire any do_s.

Definition 15. *Given a session s and a participant A, we define the relation $\models^A_s$ ("$\sharp$-realizes") between processes and contracts as the largest relation such that, whenever $P_0 \models^A_s c$, then for each $\{\tau, \text{tell}\}$-fair $\rightarrow^A_\sharp$-trace $(P_i)_i$ without labels $do_s -$, we have:*

1. *$\exists k. \forall i \geq k. \, c$ unblocks $RD_s(P_i)$*
2. *$\forall i, a, P', c'. \, (P_i \xrightarrow{do_s a}_\sharp P' \wedge c \xrightarrow{a}_\sharp c' \implies P' \models^A_s c')$*

Example 10. Recall the online store A from Ex. 4. We show that $X\{s/x\} \models_s c_A$. First note that transitions in $\{\tau, \text{tell}\}$-fair $\rightarrow_\sharp$-traces without do_s from $X\{s/x\}$ can only be labelled with ctx. Thus, each P_i on such traces has the form $X\{s/x\} \mid K_i$, for some K_i. We have $RD_s(P_i) = RD_s(X\{s/x\}) = \{\text{addToCart}, \text{creditCard}\}$. Also, c_A unblocks $RD_s(X\{s/x\})$ hence condition (1) of Def. 15 holds. For condition (2), if $c_A \xrightarrow{\text{creditCard}}_\sharp c' = \overline{\text{accept}} \oplus \overline{\text{reject}}$ and $P_i \xrightarrow{do_s \, \text{creditCard}}_\sharp P' = \tau.do_s \overline{\text{accept}} + \tau.do_s \overline{\text{reject}} \mid K_i$ then $P' \models_s c'$. Actually, all processes on a $\{\tau, \text{tell}\}$-fair $\rightarrow_\sharp$-traces without do_s from P' have either the form $do_s \overline{\text{accept}} \mid K$ or the form $do_s \overline{\text{reject}} \mid K$. For the recursive case, $c_A \xrightarrow{\text{addToCart}}_\sharp c_A$ and $P_i \xrightarrow{do_s \, \text{addToCart}}_\sharp X\{s/x\}$, hence $X\{s/x\} \models_s c_A$ by coinduction. Note that the case $c_A \xrightarrow{e}_\sharp$ did not apply, because P_i cannot take $\rightarrow_\sharp$-transitions labelled $do_s e$.

Theorem 5 below establishes an invariant of system transitions. If a participant $A[Q_0]$ $\sharp$-realizes a stipulated contract c_0, then in each evolution of the system the descendant of $A[Q_0]$ still $\sharp$-realizes the related descendant of c_0. The theorem only assumes that c_0 is in a session with a compliant contract, as it is the case after firing a fuse.

Theorem 5. *Let $(S_i)_i$ be a stable $\rightarrow$-trace with $S_i = (\vec{u}_i)(A[Q_i] \mid s[A \text{ says } c_i \mid B \text{ says } d_i] \mid S'_i)$ for all i. If $c_0 \bowtie d_0$ and $Q_0 \models^A_s c_0$, then $Q_i \models^A_s c_i$ for all i.*

We now define when a participant is $\sharp$-*honest*. Intuitively, we classify as such a participant $A[P]$ when, for all prefixes $\text{tell} \downarrow_x c$ contained in P, the continuation Q of the prefix $\sharp$-realizes c. We also require that the session variable x cannot be used by any process in parallel with Q, because such processes could potentially compromise the ability of Q to realise c (see Ex. 11).

Definition 16 ($\sharp$-honest participant). *A participant* A$[P]$ *is $\sharp$-honest iff P does not contain* $\downarrow_y$ A *says c, and for all linear contexts* $C(\bullet)$, *x, c, Q, R, and s fresh in P*

$$P = C(\text{tell} \downarrow_x c.Q + R) \implies open(Q\{s/x\}) \models_s^A c \ \wedge \ C \text{ is } x\text{-safe}$$

where $C(\bullet)$ *is x-safe iff* $\exists C'. \ C(\bullet) = C'((x)\bullet)$ *or C is free from* $\text{do}_x -$.

Example 11. Substitute $Q = \text{fuse}_x.\text{do}_x \text{creditCard}$ for fuse_x in the process P_A from Ex. 4. Then A$[P_A]$ is not honest, because A cannot complete her contract if the do_x within Q is performed. However, the modified A$[P_A]$ violates x-safety, hence it is not $\sharp$-honest.

The following lemma relates $\sharp$-honesty with the abstract semantics of processes. If a $\sharp$-honest process P abstractly fires a tell$\downarrow_x c$, then the continuation of P realises c (item 1). Also, $\sharp$-honesty is preserved under abstract transitions (item 2).

Lemma 8. *For all $\sharp$-honest participants* A$[P]$, *such that* $P = open(P)$:

1. *if* $P \xrightarrow{\text{tell}_B \downarrow_x c}_\sharp P'$, *then* $P'\{s/x\} \models_s^A c$, *for all s fresh in P.*
2. *if* $P \to_\sharp P'$, *then* A$[P']$ *is $\sharp$-honest.*

Our main result states that $\sharp$-honesty suffices to ensure honesty. Note that while honesty, by Def. 11, considers all the (infinite) possible contexts, $\sharp$-honesty does not. Hence, while verifying honesty can be unfeasible in the general case, it can also be ensured by establishing $\sharp$-honesty, which is more amenable to verification. For instance, for finite control processes [11] it is possible to decide $\sharp$-honesty e.g. through model-checking. In fact, in these processes parallel composition cannot appear under recursion, hence their behaviour can be represented with finitely many states.

Theorem 6. *All $\sharp$-honest participants are honest.*

Noteworthily, by Theorem 6 we can establish that all the participants named A in Examples 4, 5, and 6 are honest. This is obtained by reasoning as in Example 10. Instead, participant A in Example 7 is honest but not $\sharp$-honest.

6   Related Work and Conclusions

We have developed a formal model for reasoning about contract-oriented systems. Our approach departs from the common principle that contracts are always respected after they are agreed upon. We represent instead the more realistic situation where promises are not always kept. The process calculus CO_2 [2] allows participants to advertise contracts, to establish sessions with other participants with compliant contracts, and to fulfill them (or choose not to). Remarkably, instead of defining an ad-hoc contract model, we have embedded the contract theory of [10] within CO_2. To do that, we have slightly adapted the contracts of [10] in order to define culpability, and we have specialized CO_2 accordingly at the system-level. The main technical contribution of this paper is a criterion for deciding when a participant is honest, i.e., always respects the advertised contracts in all possible contexts. This is not a trivial task, especially when multiple sessions are needed for realizing a contract (see e.g. Ex. 5 and 6) or when participants want to inspect the state of a contract to decide how to proceed next (see e.g. Ex. 7).

At the best of our knowledge, this is the first paper that addresses the problem of establishing when a participant is honest in a contract-based system populated by dishonest participants. Several papers investigated the use of contracts in concurrent systems; however, they typically focus on coupling processes which statically guarantee conformance to their contracts. This is achieved e.g. by typing [5,9,10], by contract-based process synthesis [7], or by approaches based on behavioural preorders [6]. As future work, it may also be interesting to study weaker notions of honesty, e.g., by requiring participants to respect contracts in *honest* contexts, only.

The process calculus CO_2 has been introduced in [2] as a generic framework for relating different contract models; the variant in this paper has been obtained by instantiating it with the contracts of [10]. Some primitives, e.g. multiparty fuse, have been consequently simplified. In [2], a participant A is honest when A becomes not culpable from a certain execution step; here, we only require that, whenever A is culpable, then she can exculpate herself by performing some actions. This change reflects the fact that bilateral contracts à la [10] can describe endless interactions.

The notion of compliance in [10] is asymmetric. Namely, if c is the client contract and d is the server contract, then c and d are compliant if c always reaches a success state or engages d in an endless interaction. In our model instead compliance is symmetric: the server contract, too, has to agree on when a state is successful. The LTS semantics of unilateral contracts in [10] yields identical synchronization trees for internal and external choice; to differentiate them, one has to consider their ready sets. We instead give semantics to *bilateral* contracts, and distinguish between choices at the LTS level. Note that we do not allow for unguarded sums, unlike [10]. Were these be allowed, we would have to deal e.g. with a participant A with a contract of the form $a; c_0 \oplus (b. c_1 + c. c_2)$. According to our intuition A should be culpable, because of the internal choice. If A legitimately chooses not to perform a, to exculpate herself she would have to wait for the other participant to choose (internally) between b and c. Therefore, A can exculpate herself only if the other participant permits her to. By contrast, by restricting to guarded sums our theory enjoys the nice feature that a culpable participant can always exculpate herself by performing some actions, which pass the buck to the other participant (Theorems 1 and 3).

Design-by-contract is transferred in [5] to distributed interactions modelled as (multiparty) asserted global types [14]. The projection of asserted global types on local ones allows for the automatic generation of monitors whereby incoming messages are checked against the local contract. Such monitors have a "local" view of the computation, i.e. they can detect a violation but cannot, in general, single out the culpable component. In fact, a monitor cannot know if an expected message is not delivered because the partner is violating his contract, or because he is blocked on interactions with other participants. Conversely, in our approach we compose participants in a "bottom-up" fashion: a participant declares its contract independently of the others and then advertises it; the fuse primitive tries then to harmonise contracts by searching for a suitable agreement. Our notion of *honesty* singles out culpable components during the computation. An interesting problem would be to investigate how our notion of culpability could be attained within the approach in [5]. In fact, this seems to be a non trivial problem, even if forbidding communication channels shared among more than two participants.

Contracts are rendered in [8,7] as soft constraints (values in a c-semiring) that allow for different levels of agreement between contracts. When matching a client with a service, the constraints are composed. This restricts the possible interactions to those acceptable (if any) to both parties. A technique is proposed in [7] for compiling clients and services so that, after matching, both actually behave according to the mutually acceptable interactions, and reach success without getting stuck. Our framework is focused instead on blaming participants, and on checking when a participant is honest, i.e. always able to avoid blame in all possible contexts. The use of soft constraints in a context where participants can be dishonest seems viable, e.g. by instantiating the abstract contract model of CO_2 with the contracts in [7]. A challenging task would be that of defining culpability in such setting.

Acknowledgments. This work has been partially supported by the Aut. Region of Sardinia under grants L.R.7/2007 CRP2-120 (Project TESLA) and CRP-17285 (Project TRICS), and by the Leverhulme Trust Programme Award "Tracing Networks".

References

1. Artikis, A., Sergot, M.J., Pitt, J.V.: Specifying norm-governed computational societies. ACM Trans. Comput. Log. 10(1) (2009)
2. Bartoletti, M., Tuosto, E., Zunino, R.: Contracts in distributed systems. In: ICE (2011)
3. Bartoletti, M., Tuosto, E., Zunino, R.: On the Realizability of Contracts in Dishonest Systems. In: COORDINATION 2012. LNCS, vol. 7274, pp. 245–260. Springer, Heidelberg (2012)
4. Bartoletti, M., Zunino, R.: A calculus of contracting processes. In: LICS (2010)
5. Bocchi, L., Honda, K., Tuosto, E., Yoshida, N.: A Theory of Design-by-Contract for Distributed Multiparty Interactions. In: Gastin, P., Laroussinie, F. (eds.) CONCUR 2010. LNCS, vol. 6269, pp. 162–176. Springer, Heidelberg (2010)
6. Bravetti, M., Zavattaro, G.: Towards a Unifying Theory for Choreography Conformance and Contract Compliance. In: Lumpe, M., Vanderperren, W. (eds.) SC 2007. LNCS, vol. 4829, pp. 34–50. Springer, Heidelberg (2007)
7. Buscemi, M.G., Coppo, M., Dezani-Ciancaglini, M., Montanari, U.: Constraints for service contracts. In: TGC (2011) (to appear)
8. Buscemi, M.G., Montanari, U.: CC-Pi: A Constraint-Based Language for Specifying Service Level Agreements. In: De Nicola, R. (ed.) ESOP 2007. LNCS, vol. 4421, pp. 18–32. Springer, Heidelberg (2007)
9. Carpineti, S., Laneve, C.: A Basic Contract Language for Web Services. In: Sestoft, P. (ed.) ESOP 2006. LNCS, vol. 3924, pp. 197–213. Springer, Heidelberg (2006)
10. Castagna, G., Gesbert, N., Padovani, L.: A theory of contracts for web services. ACM Transactions on Programming Languages and Systems 31(5) (2009)
11. Dam, M.: On the Decidability of Process Equivalences for the π-calculus. Theoretical Computer Science 183(2), 215–228 (1997)
12. Degano, P., Priami, C.: Enhanced operational semantics. ACM Comput. Surv. 33(2), 135–176 (2001)
13. Emerson, E.A.: Temporal and modal logic. In: Handbook of Theoretical Computer Science, Volume B: Formal Models and Sematics (B). North-Holland Pub. Co./MIT Press (1990)
14. Honda, K., Yoshida, N., Carbone, M.: Multiparty asynchronous session types. In: POPL (2008)
15. Prisacariu, C., Schneider, G.: A Formal Language for Electronic Contracts. In: Bonsangue, M.M., Johnsen, E.B. (eds.) FMOODS 2007. LNCS, vol. 4468, pp. 174–189. Springer, Heidelberg (2007)

Types for Coordinating Secure Behavioural Variations*

Pierpaolo Degano, Gian-Luigi Ferrari, Letterio Galletta, and Gianluca Mezzetti

Dipartimento di Informatica
Università di Pisa
{degano,giangi,galletta,mezzetti}@di.unipi.it

Abstract. Context-Oriented programming languages provide us with primitive constructs to adapt program behaviour depending on the evolution of their operational environment. We are interested here in software components, the behaviour of which depend on the following: their actual operating context; the security policies that control accesses to their resources and the potential interactions with the external environment. For that, we extend a core functional language with mechanisms to program behavioural variations, to manipulate resources and to enforce security policies over both variations and resource usages. Additionally, there are message passing primitives to interact with the environment, also subject to a simple policy. Changes of the operational context are triggered both by the program and by the exchanged messages. Besides a definition of the dynamic semantics, we introduce a static analysis for guaranteeing programs to safely operate in any admissible context, and to correctly interact with the environment they comply with.

1 Introduction

A major concern of current software engineering is the development of adaptive software components, capable of dynamically modifying their behaviour depending on changes in their execution environment and in response to the interactions with other components. The problem of developing adaptive components has been investigated from different perspectives (control theory, artificial intelligence, programming languages) and some solutions have been proposed. We refer to [1,2,3] for a more comprehensive discussion. In this paper, we adopt a programming languages approach, that allows us to describe fine-grain adaptability mechanisms.

We consider the Context-Oriented Programming (COP)[4] paradigm, that extends standard programming languages with suitable constructs to express context-dependent behaviour in a modular fashion. The design and development of ubiquitous and autonomic systems would greatly benefit from such languages [5]. The fundamental concept in COP is that of *behavioural variation*. A behavioural variation is a chunk of behaviour that can be activated depending on the current working environment so to dynamically modify the execution. The current working environment is represented by the notion of *context*. The context is a stack of layers, i.e. properties identifying the actual structure of the environment. In this setting a programmer can (de)activate layers to represent

*This work has been partially supported by IST-FP7-FET open-IP project ASCENS and Regione Autonoma Sardegna, L.R. 7/2007, project TESLA.

M. Sirjani (Ed.): COORDINATION 2012, LNCS 7274, pp. 261–276, 2012.

changes in the environment. This (de)activation mechanism is the engine of context evolution. Usually, behavioural variations are bound to layers: the (de)activation of a layer correspond to the (de)activation of a behavioural variation.

The development of complex adaptive systems presents issues that cannot be tackled only by COP primitives. Indeed, a complex adaptive system is made up of a massive number of interacting components. Each component is able to modify its behaviour, it can access a private set of resources and it has security constraints (security policies). Policies govern behaviour adaptation, access to resources, interaction with other components. A system behaves correctly when each component respects its own security policies and interacts with others by respecting the communication protocol.

We aim at contributing to the design of language-based methods and techniques that support the development of complex adaptive components. An adaptive component has (*i*) mechanisms to manipulate the context, (*ii*) security policies governing behaviour and resource usages, (*iii*) an abstract, declarative representation of the operational environment. We adopt a *top-down* approach [1] to describe the interactions with other components, because we do not want to wire a component to a specific communication infrastructure. Our communication model is based on a bus through which messages are exchanged.

The main contribution of this paper is the introduction of a method to program adaptive components. This proposal suitably extends and integrates together techniques from COP, type theory and model-checking. In particular, it consists of a static technique ensuring that a component (*i*) adequately reacts to context changes, (*ii*) accesses resources in accordance with security policies, (*iii*) exchanges messages on the bus, complying with a specific communication protocol provided by the operating environment.

Our proposal requires several stages.

I First, we extend the COP functional language ContextML [6] with constructs for resource manipulation, following [7]. Also, our extension of ContextML has mechanisms to declare and enforce security policies by adopting the local sandbox approach of [7]. Finally, another novel feature is the introduction of message passing constructs for the communication with external parties (Section 3).

II Next, we design a type and effect system for ContextML (Section 5). We exploit it for ensuring that programs adequately react to context changes and for computing as effect an abstract representation of the overall behaviour. This representation, in the form of *History Expressions* (Section 4), describes the sequences of resource manipulation and communication with external parties in a succinct form.

III Finally, we model check effects to verify that the component behaviour is correct, i.e. that the behavioural variations can always take place, that resources are manipulated in accordance with the given security policies and that the communication protocol is respected. The model checking is performed in two phases. The first determines whether security policies are obeyed, the second one verifies compliance with the protocol (Section 6).

In Section 2 we introduce a motivating example, that is also instrumental in displaying our methodology at a glance.

2   A Motivating Example: An e-Library App

Consider a simple scenario consisting of a smartphone app that uses some service supplied by a cloud infrastructure. The cloud offers a repository to store and synchronize a library of ebooks and computational resources to execute customised applications (among which full-text search).

A user buys ebooks online and reads them locally through the app. The purchased ebooks are stored into the remote user library and some books are kept locally in the smartphone. The two libraries may not be synchronized. The synchronization is triggered on demand and depends on several factors: the actual bandwidth available for connection, the free space on the device, etc. We specify below the fragment of the app that implements the full-text search over the user's library.

Consider now the context dependent behaviour emerging because of the different energy profiles of the smartphone. We assume that there are two: one is active when the device is plugged in, the other is active when it is using its battery. These profiles are represented by two *layers*: ACMode and BatMode. The function getBatteryProfile returns the layer describing the current active profile depending on the value of the sensor (plugged):

$$\textbf{fun } \texttt{getBatteryProfile } x = \textbf{if } (\texttt{plugged}) \textbf{ then } \texttt{ACMode} \textbf{ else } \texttt{BatMode}$$

Layers can be activated, so modifying the context. The expression

$$\textbf{with}(\texttt{getBatteryProfile}()) \textbf{ in } exp_1 \tag{1}$$

activates the layer obtained by calling getBatteryProfile. The scope of this activation is the expression exp_1 in Fig. 1(a). In lines 2-10, there is the following *layered expression*:

$$\texttt{ACMode. } \langle \text{DO SEARCH} \rangle,$$
$$\texttt{BatMode. } \langle \text{DO SOMETHING ELSE} \rangle$$

This is the way context-dependent *behavioural variations* are declared. Roughly, a layered expression is an expression defined by cases. The cases are the different layers that may be active in the context, here BatMode and ACMode. Each layer has an associated expression. A *dispatching mechanism* inspects at runtime the context and selects an expression to be reduced. If the device is plugged in, then the search is performed, abstracted by $\langle$DO SEARCH$\rangle$. Otherwise, something else gets done, abstracted by $\langle$DO SOMETHING ELSE$\rangle$. Note that if the programmer neglects a case, then the program throws a runtime error being unable to adapt to the actual context.

In the code of exp_1 (Fig. 1(a)), the function g consists of nested layered expressions describing the behavioural variations matching the different configurations of the execution environment. The code exploits context dependency to take into account also the actual location of the execution engine (remote in the cloud at line -3- or local on the device -4-), the synchronization state of the library -5,6- and the active energy profile -2,10-. The smartphone communicates with the cloud system over the bus through message passing primitives -7-9-.

The search is performed locally only if the library is fully synchronized and the smartphone is plugged in. If the device is plugged in but the library is not fully synchronized, then the code of function g is sent to the cloud and executed remotely by a suitable server.

In Fig. 1(b) we show a fragment of the environment provided by the cloud infrastructure. The service considered is offering generic computational resources to the devices connected on the bus by continuously running function f. The function f listens to the bus for incoming code (a function) and an incoming layer. Then, it executes the received function in a context extended with the received layer.

In the code of the cloud it appears a security policy φ to be enforced before running the received function. This is expressed by the security framing $\varphi[\dots]$ that causes a sandboxing of the enclosed expression, to be executed under the strict monitoring of φ. Take φ to be a policy expressing that writing on the library write(library) is forbidden (so only reading is allowed). The framing guarantees that the execution of foreign code does not alter the remote library. In this example, we simply state that φ only concerns actions on resources, e.g. the library. Our approach also allows us to enforce security policies governing behaviour adaptation and communication.

The cloud system constraints communications on the bus by also declaring a protocol P, prescribing the viable interactions. Additionally, the cloud infrastructure will make sure that the protocol P is indeed an abstraction of the behaviour of the various services of it involved in the interactions. We do not address here how protocols are defined by the environment and we only check whether a user respect the given protocol.

The actual protocol guaranteed by the environment is

$$P = (send_\tau send_{\tau'} receive_{\tau''})^*$$

It expresses that the client must send a value of type τ then a value of type τ' and then must receive back a value of type τ''. These actions can be repeated a certain number of times. We will discuss later on the actual types τ, τ', τ''.

Function getBatteryProfile returns a value of type $ly_{\{ACMode.BatMode\}}$. This type means that the returned layer is one between ACMode and BatMode.

The type of function g is $\tau' = \text{unit} \xrightarrow{\mathbb{P}|H} \tau''$, assuming that the value returned by the search function has type τ''. The type τ' is annotated by a set of preconditions $\mathbb{P}$ (see below) and a latent effect H (discussed later on).

$$\mathbb{P} = \{\{ACMode, IsLocal, LibrarySynced\}, \{ACMode, IsCloud\}, \dots\}$$

Each precondition in $\mathbb{P}$ is a set of layers. To apply g, the context of the application must contains all the layers in υ, for a precondition $\upsilon \in \mathbb{P}$.

As we will see later on, our type system guarantees that the dispatching mechanism always succeeds at runtime. In our example, the expression (1) will be well-typed whenever the context in which it will be evaluated contains IsLocal or IsCloud and LibraryUnsynced or LibrarySynced. The requirements about ACMode and BatMode coming from exp_1 are ensured in (1). This is because the type of getBatteryProfile guarantees that one among them will be activated in the context by the **with**.

An effect H (history expression) represents (an over-approximation of) the sequences of events, i.e. of resource manipulation or layer activations or communication actions.

```
1   fun g x =                                    1  fun f x =

2      ACMode.                                    2     let lyr = receiveτ in

3         IsCloud.search(),                       3     let g = receiveτ' in

4         IsLocal.                                4     φ[with(lyr) in

5            LibrarySynced.search(y),             5        let res = g() in

6            LibraryUnsynced.                     6        sendτ''(res)

7               sendτ(ACMode);                    7     ];f()

8               sendτ'(g);                        8  f()

9               receiveτ''

10     BatMode. ⟨DO SOMETHING ELSE⟩

11  g()
```

(a) The definition of exp_1	(b) The code for a service

Fig. 1. Fragments of an App and of a service in the cloud

The effect H in τ' is the latent effect of g, over-approximating the set of histories, i.e. the sequences of events, possibly generated by running g.

Effects are then used to check whether a client complies with the policy and the interaction protocol provided by the environment. Verifying that the code of g obeys the policy φ is done by standard model-checking the effect of g (a context-free language) against the policy φ (a regular language). Obviously, the app never writes, so the policy φ is satisfied, assuming that the code for the BatMode case has empty effect.

To check compliance with the protocol, we only considering communications. Thus, the effect of exp_1 becomes:

$$H_{sr} = send_\tau \cdot send_{\tau'} \cdot receive_{\tau''}$$

Verifying whether the program correctly interacts with the cloud system consists of checking that the histories generated by H_{sr} are a subset of those allowed by the protocol P. In our scenario this is indeed the case.

3   ContextML: A Context-Oriented ML Core

ContextML [6] is a fragment of ML designed to deal with adaptation, providing us with mechanisms to change the context and to define behavioural variations in a functional style. We extend it by introducing resources manipulation, enforcement of security properties and communication.

Resources available in the system are represented by identifiers and can be manipulated by a fixed set of actions. For simplicity, we do not provide ContextML with constructs for dynamically creating resources, but these can be added following [7,8].

We enforce security properties by protecting expressions with policies: $\varphi[e]$. This mechanism is known in the literature as *policy framing* [8]. Roughly, it means that during the evaluation of e the computation must respect φ. Our policies turn out to be regular properties of computation histories; more details in Section 6.

The communication model is based on a bus which allows programs to interact with the environment by message passing. The operations of writing and reading values over this bus can be seen as a simple form of asynchronous I/O. We will not specify this bus in detail, but we will consider it as an abstract entity representing the whole external environment and its interactions with programs. Therefore, ContextML programs operate in an open-ended environment.

The syntax and the structural operational semantics of ContextML follow.

Syntax Let $\mathbb{N}$ be the naturals, Ide a set of identifiers, LayerNames a finite set of layer names, Policies a set of security policies, Res a finite set of resources identifiers and Act a finite set of actions for manipulating resources. Then, the syntax of ContextML is:

$$n \in \mathbb{N} \qquad x, f \in \mathsf{Ide} \qquad L \in \mathsf{LayerNames}$$
$$\varphi \in \mathsf{Policies} \qquad r \in \mathsf{Res} \qquad \alpha, \beta \in \mathsf{Act}$$

$$v, v_1, v' ::= n \mid L \mid () \mid \lambda_f\, x \Rightarrow e$$
$$e, e_1, e' ::= \varphi[e] \mid v \mid x \mid e_1 e_2 \mid \mathbf{let}\ x = e_1\ \mathbf{in}\ e_2 \mid e_1\ \mathbf{op}\ e_2 \mid$$
$$\qquad \mathbf{if}\ e_0\ \mathbf{then}\ e_1\ \mathbf{else}\ e_2 \mid \mathbf{with}(e_1)\ \mathbf{in}\ e_2 \mid \mathbf{unwith}(e_1)\ \mathbf{in}\ e_2 \mid lexp$$
$$\qquad \mathbf{send}_\tau(e) \mid \mathbf{receive}_\tau \mid \alpha(r)$$
$$lexp ::= L.e \mid L.e, lexp$$

Additionally, we assume the syntactic sugar $e_1; e_2 \triangleq (\lambda_f x \Rightarrow e_2) e_1$ where x and f are not free in e_2.

The novelties of ContextML with respect to ML are primitives for handling resources, policy framing and communication and some features borrowed from COP languages (for their description we refer the reader to the seminal paper [4]). Usually, COP paradigm have layers as expressible values; the (**unwith**) **with** construct for manipulating the context by (de)activating layers; layered expressions (*lexp*), defined by cases each specifying a context-dependent behaviour. The expression $\alpha(r)$ indicates that we access the resource r through the action α, possibly causing side effects. The security properties are enforced by policy framing $\varphi[e]$ guaranteeing that the computation satisfies the policy φ. Of course, policy framings can be nested. The communication is performed by **send**$_\tau$ and **receive**$_\tau$. They allow us to interact with the external environment by writing/reading values of type τ (see Section 5) to/from the bus.

Dynamic Semantics. We endow ContextML with a small-step operational semantics, only defined for closed expressions as usual. Note that, since ContextML programs can read values from the bus, a closed expression can be open with respect to the external environment. For example, **let** $x =$ **receive**$_\tau$ **in** $x + 1$ is closed but it reads an unknown value v from the bus. To give meaning to such programs, we have an early input similar to that of the π-calculus [9].

Our semantics is history dependent. Program histories are sequences of events, namely *histories*, occurring during program execution. Events *ev* indicate (de)activation layers, selection of behavioural variations and program actions, be they resource accesses, entering/exiting policy framing and communication. The syntax of events *ev* and programs histories η is the following:

$$ev ::= (\![_L \mid)\!]_L \mid \{_L \mid \}_L \mid \mathsf{Disp}(L) \mid \alpha(r) \mid send_\tau \mid receive_\tau \mid [\![_\varphi \mid]\!]_\varphi \tag{2}$$

$$\eta ::= \varepsilon \mid ev \mid \eta\eta \tag{3}$$

The event $(\!]_L)$ $(\![_L$ marks that we (end) begin the evaluation of a **with** body in a context where the layer L is (de)activated; symmetrically, the event $(\}_L)$ $\{_L$ signals that we (end) begin the evaluation of a **unwith** body in a context where the layer L is (un)masked; the event $\mathsf{Disp}(L)$ signals that layer L has been selected by the dispatch mechanism; the event $\alpha(r)$ marks that the action α has been performed over the resource r; the event $send_\tau/receive_\tau$ indicates that we have sent/read a value of type τ over/from the bus; the event $(\!]_\varphi)$ $[\![_\varphi$ marks that we (end) begin the enforcement of the policy φ.

A context C is a stack of active layers with two operations. The first $C - L$ remove a layer L from the context C if present, the second $L :: C$ pushes L over $C - L$. Formally:

Definition 1. *We denote the empty context by* $[\,]$ *and a context with n elements with top* L_1 *by* $[L_1, \ldots, L_n]$.
Let $C = [L_1, \ldots, L_{i-1}, L_i, L_{i+1}, \ldots, L_n], 1 \le i \le n$ *then*

$$C - L = \begin{cases} [L_1, \ldots, L_{i-1}, L_{i+1}, \ldots L_n] & \textit{if } L = L_i \\ C & \textit{otherwise} \end{cases}$$

Also, let $L :: C = [L, L_1, \ldots, L_n]$ *where* $[L_1, \ldots, L_n] = C - L$.

The transitions have the form $C \vdash \eta, e \to \eta', e'$, meaning that in the context C, starting from a program history η, the expression e may evolve to e' and the history η to η' in one evaluation step.

Most of semantic rules are inherited from ML. Fig. 2 shows the ones for new constructs. We briefly comment on them.

The rules for (**unwith**(e_1) **in** e_2) **with**(e_1) **in** e_2 evaluate e_2 in a context where the layer obtained evaluating e_1 is (de)activated. Additionally, we store in the history the events $(\![_L$ and $)\!]_L$ ($\{_L$ and $\}_L$) marking the beginning and the end of the evaluation of e_2 (note that being within the scope of layer L activation is recorded by using $\overline{L}$).

When a layered expression $e = L_1.e_1, \ldots, L_n.e_n$ has to be evaluated (rule lexp), the current context is inspected top-down to select the expression e_i to which e reduces. This dispatching mechanism is implemented by the partial function Dsp, defined as

$$Dsp([L'_0, L'_1, \ldots, L'_m], A) = \begin{cases} L'_0 & \text{if } L'_0 \in A \\ Dsp([L'_1, \ldots, L'_m], A) & \text{otherwise} \end{cases}$$

that returns the first layer in the context $[L'_0, L'_1, \ldots, L'_m]$ which matches one of the layers in the set A. If no layer matches, then the computation gets stuck.

The rule (action) establishes that performing an action α over a resource r yields the unit value () and extends η with $\alpha(r)$.

The rules governing communications reflect our notion of protocol, that abstractly represents the behaviour of the environment, showing the sequence of direction/type of messages. Accordingly, our primitives carry types as tags, rather than dynamically

$$\text{with}_1 \; \frac{C \vdash \eta, e_1 \to \eta', e_1'}{C \vdash \eta, \textbf{with}(e_1) \textbf{ in } e_2 \to \eta', \textbf{with}(e_1') \textbf{ in } e_2}$$

$$\text{with}_2 \; \frac{}{C \vdash \eta, \textbf{with}(L) \textbf{ in } e \to \eta \, (\!\!\!(_L, \textbf{with}(\bar{L}) \textbf{ in } e}$$

$$\text{with}_3 \; \frac{L :: C \vdash \eta, e \to \eta', e'}{C \vdash \eta, \textbf{with}(\bar{L}) \textbf{ in } e \to \eta', \textbf{with}(\bar{L}) \textbf{ in } e'} \qquad \text{with}_4 \; \frac{}{C \vdash \eta, \textbf{with}(\bar{L}) \textbf{ in } v \to \eta \,)\!\!\!)_L, v}$$

$$\text{unwith}_1 \; \frac{C \vdash \eta, e_1 \to \eta', e_1'}{C \vdash \eta, \textbf{unwith}(e_1) \textbf{ in } e_2 \to \eta', \textbf{unwith}(e_1') \textbf{ in } e_2}$$

$$\text{unwith}_2 \; \frac{}{C \vdash \eta, \textbf{unwith}(L) \textbf{ in } e \to \eta \, \{_L, \textbf{unwith}(\bar{L}) \textbf{ in } e}$$

$$\text{unwith}_3 \; \frac{C - L \vdash \eta, e \to \eta', e'}{C \vdash \eta, \textbf{unwith}(\bar{L}) \textbf{ in } e \to \eta', \textbf{unwith}(\bar{L}) \textbf{ in } e'}$$

$$\text{unwith}_4 \; \frac{}{C \vdash \eta, \textbf{unwith}(\bar{L}) \textbf{ in } v \to \eta \, \}_L, v}$$

$$\text{lexp} \; \frac{L_i = Dsp(C, \{L_1, \ldots, L_n\})}{C \vdash \eta, L_1.e_1, \ldots, L_n.e_n \to \eta \, \text{Disp}(L_i), e_i} \qquad \text{action} \; \frac{}{C \vdash \eta, \alpha(r) \to \eta \, \alpha(r), ()}$$

$$\text{send}_1 \; \frac{C \vdash \eta, e \to \eta', e'}{C \vdash \eta, \textbf{send}_\tau(e) \to \eta', \textbf{send}_\tau(e')} \qquad \text{send}_2 \; \frac{}{C \vdash \eta, \textbf{send}_\tau(v) \to \eta \, send_\tau, ()}$$

$$\text{receive} \; \frac{}{C \vdash \eta, \textbf{receive}_\tau \to \eta \, receive_\tau, v} \qquad \text{framing}_1 \; \frac{\eta^{-[]} \models \varphi}{C \vdash \eta, \varphi[e] \to \eta[_\varphi, \overline{\varphi}[e]}$$

$$\text{framing}_2 \; \frac{C \vdash \eta, e \to \eta', e' \quad \eta'^{-[]} \models \varphi}{C \vdash \eta, \overline{\varphi}[e] \to \eta', \overline{\varphi}[e']} \qquad \text{framing}_3 \; \frac{\eta^{-[]} \models \varphi}{C \vdash \eta, \overline{\varphi}[v] \to \eta]_\varphi, v}$$

Fig. 2. Semantic rules for new constructs

checking the exchanged values. In particular, there is no check that the type of the received value matches the annotation of the receive primitive. Our static analysis will guarantee the correctness of this operation.

In detail, $\textbf{send}_\tau(e)$ evaluates e and sends the obtained value over the bus. Additionally, the history is extended with the event $send_\tau$. A $\textbf{receive}_\tau$ reduces to the value v read from the bus and appends the corresponding event to the current history. This rule is similar to that used in the early semantics of the π-calculus, where we guess a name transmitted over the channel [9].

The rules for framing say that an expression $\varphi[e]$ can reduce to $\varphi[e']$, provided that the resulting history η' obeys the policy φ, in symbols $\eta'^{-[]} \models \varphi$ (see Section 4 and Section 6 for a precise definition). Also here, placing a bar over φ records that the policy is active. If η' does not obey φ, then the computation gets stuck. Of course, we store in the history through $[_\varphi/]_\varphi$ the point where we begin/end the enforcement of φ.

$$\varepsilon \cdot H \xrightarrow{\varepsilon} H \qquad\qquad \alpha(r) \xrightarrow{\alpha(r)} \varepsilon \qquad\qquad \mu h.H \xrightarrow{\varepsilon} H\{\mu h.H/h\}$$

$$\dfrac{H_1 \xrightarrow{\alpha(r)} H_1'}{H_1 \cdot H_2 \xrightarrow{\alpha(r)} H_1' \cdot H_2} \qquad\qquad \dfrac{H \xrightarrow{\alpha(r)} H'}{H_1 + H_2 \xrightarrow{\alpha(r)} H_1'} \qquad\qquad \dfrac{H_2 \xrightarrow{\alpha(r)} H_2'}{H_1 + H_2 \xrightarrow{\alpha(r)} H_2'}$$

Fig. 3. Transition system of History Expressions

4   History Expressions

History Expressions [10,7,8] are a simple process algebra providing an abstraction over the set of histories that a program may generate. We recall here the definitions and the properties of [8] but we consider histories with a different set of events ev, also endowing communication, layer activation and dispatching.

Definition 2 (History Expressions). *History Expressions are defined as follows:*

$H, H_1 ::=$	ε	*empty*	$H_1 + H_2$	*sum*
	ev	*events in (2)*	$H_1 \cdot H_2$	*sequence*
	h	*recursion variable*	$\mu h.H$	*recursion*
	$\varphi[H]$	*safety framing, abbrev. for* $[_\varphi \cdot H \cdot]_\varphi$		

The signature defines sequentialization, sum and recursion operations over sets of histories containing events; μh is a binder for the recursion variable h.

The following definition exploits the labelled transition system in Fig. 3.

Definition 3 (Semantics of History Expressions). *Given a closed H (i.e. without free variables), we define its semantics $[\![H]\!]$ to be the set of histories $\eta = w_1 \ldots w_n$ ($w_i \in ev \cup \{\varepsilon\}, 0 \le i \le n$) such that $\exists H'. H \xrightarrow{w_1} \cdots \xrightarrow{w_n} H'$.*

We remark that the semantics of a history expression is a prefix closed set of histories.

Back to the example in Section 2, assume that H is the history expression over-approximating the behaviour of function g. Then, the history expression of the fragment of the cloud service (Fig. 1(b)) is $\mu h.receive_\tau \cdot receive_{\tau'} \cdot \varphi[(\text{ACMode} \cdot H \cdot send_{\tau''})\text{ACMode}] \cdot h$ assuming $\tau = ly_{\text{ACMode}}$.

Closed history expressions are partially ordered: $H \sqsubseteq H'$ means that the abstraction represented by H' is less precise than the one by H. The structural ordering $\sqsubseteq$ is defined over the quotient induced by the (semantic preserving) equational theory presented in [7] as the least relation such that $H \sqsubseteq H$ and $H \sqsubseteq H + H'$. Clearly, $H \sqsubseteq H'$ implies $[\![H]\!] \subseteq [\![H']\!]$.

Validity of History Expressions Given a history η we denote with $\eta^{-[]}$ the history purged of all framings events $[_\varphi,]_\varphi$. For details and examples, see [7].

The multiset $ap(\eta)$ of the *active policies* of a history η is defined as follows:

$$ap(\varepsilon) = \{\} \qquad\qquad ap(\eta[_\varphi) = ap(\eta) \cup \{\varphi\}$$

$$ap(\eta\gamma) = ap(\eta) \quad \gamma \in ev \setminus \{[_\varphi,]_\varphi\} \qquad\qquad ap(\eta]_\varphi) = ap(\eta) \setminus \{\varphi\}$$

The validity of a history η ($\models \eta$ in symbols) is inductively defined as follows, assuming the notion of policy compliance $\eta \models \varphi$ of Section 6.

$$\models \varepsilon \quad \text{and} \quad \models \eta'w \qquad w \in ev \quad \text{if} \quad \models \eta' \text{ and } (\eta'w)^{-[]} \models \varphi \text{ for all } \varphi \in ap(\eta'w)$$

A history expression H is *valid* when $\models \eta$ for all $\eta \in [\![H]\!]$.

The following lemma states that validity is a prefix-closed property.

Property 1. If a history η is valid, then each prefix of its is valid.

The semantics of ContextML (in particular the rules for framing) ensure that the histories generated at runtime are all valid.

Property 2. If $C \vdash \varepsilon, e \rightarrow \eta', e'$, then η' is valid.

5 ContextML Types

We provide here ContextML with a type and effect system. We use it for over-approximating the programs behaviour and for ensuring that the dispatch mechanism always succeeds at runtime. The associated effect is a history expression representing all the histories that a program may generate. Here, we only give a logical presentation of our type and effect system, and we are confident that an inference algorithm can be developed, along the lines of [10].

Our typing judgements have the form $\langle \Gamma; C \rangle \vdash e : \tau \triangleright H$. This means that in "in the type environment Γ and in the context C the expression e has type τ and effect H".

Types are integers, unit, layers and functions:

$$\sigma \in \wp(\mathsf{LayerNames}) \qquad \mathbb{P} \in \wp(\wp(\mathsf{LayerNames}))$$

$$\tau, \tau_1, \tau' ::= \mathtt{int} \mid \mathtt{unit} \mid ly_\sigma \mid \tau_1 \xrightarrow{\mathbb{P}|H} \tau_2$$

We annotate types with sets of layer names σ for analysis reason. In ly_σ, σ over-approximates the set of layers that an expression can be reduced to at runtime. In $\tau_1 \xrightarrow{\mathbb{P}|H} \tau_2$, $\mathbb{P}$ is a set of *preconditions* υ. Each $\upsilon \in \mathbb{P}$ over-approximates the set of layers that must occur in the context to apply the function. The history expression H is the latent effect, i.e. the sequence of events generated while evaluating the function.

Fig. 4 introduces the rules for subeffecting ($H \sqsubseteq H'$) and for subtyping ($\tau_1 \leq \tau_2$). The rule (Sref) states that the subtyping relation is reflexive. The rule (Sly) says that a layer type ly_σ is a subtype of $ly_{\sigma'}$ whenever the annotation σ is a subset of σ'. The rule (Sfun) defines subtyping for functional types. As usual, it is contravariant in τ_1 but covariant in $\mathbb{P}, \tau_2$ and H. The ordering on the set of preconditions is defined as follows $\mathbb{P} \sqsubseteq \mathbb{P}'$ iff $\forall \upsilon \in \mathbb{P} . \exists \upsilon' \in \mathbb{P}' . \upsilon' \subseteq \upsilon$. By the (Tsub) rule, we can always enlarge types and effects.

Fig. 5 shows the rules of our type and effect system. Most of them are inhered from that of ML, so we only comment in detail on the rules for the new constructs. The rule (Talpha) gives expression $\alpha(r)$ type $\mathtt{unit}$ and effect $\alpha(r)$. The rule (Tly) asserts that the type of a layer L is ly annotated with the singleton set $\{L\}$ and its effect is empty. In the rule (Tfun) we guess a set of preconditions $\mathbb{P}$, a type for the bound variable x and for the function f. For all precondition $\upsilon \in \mathbb{P}$ we also guess a context C' satisfying υ. A

$$(\text{Sref}) \frac{}{\tau \leq \tau} \qquad (\text{Sfun}) \frac{\tau'_1 \leq \tau_1 \quad \tau_2 \leq \tau'_2 \quad \mathbb{P} \sqsubseteq \mathbb{P}' \quad H \sqsubseteq H'}{\tau_1 \xrightarrow{\mathbb{P}|H} \tau_2 \leq \tau'_1 \xrightarrow{\mathbb{P}'|H'} \tau'_2}$$

$$(\text{Sly}) \frac{\sigma \subseteq \sigma'}{ly_\sigma \leq ly_{\sigma'}} \qquad (\text{Tsub}) \frac{\langle \Gamma;C \rangle \vdash e : \tau' \triangleright H' \quad \tau' \leq \tau \quad H' \sqsubseteq H}{\langle \Gamma;C \rangle \vdash e : \tau \triangleright H}$$

Fig. 4. Subtyping rules

context satisfies the precondition υ whenever it contains all the layers in υ, in symbols $|C'| \subseteq \upsilon$, where $|C'|$ denotes the set of layers active in the context C'. We determine the type of the body e under these additional assumptions. Implicitly, we require that the guessed type for f, as well as its latent effect H, match that of the resulting function. Additionally, we require that the resulting type is annotated with $\mathbb{P}$.

The rule (Tapp) is almost standard and reveals the mechanism of function precondition. The application gets a type if there exists a precondition $\upsilon \in \mathbb{P}$ such that it is satisfied in the current context C. The effect is obtained by concatenating the ones of e_2 and e_1 and the latent effect H. To better explain how preconditions work, consider the technical example in Fig. 6. There, the function $\lambda_f\, x \Rightarrow L_1.0$ is shown having type $int \xrightarrow{\{L_1\}} int$ (for the sake of simplicity we ignore the effects). This means that L_1 must be in the context in order to apply the function.

The rule (Twith) establishes that the expression $\mathbf{with}(e_1)$ $\mathbf{in}$ e_2 has type τ, provided that the type for e_1 is ly_σ (recall that σ is a set of layers) and e_2 has type τ in the context C extended by the layers in σ. The effect is the union of the possible effects resulting from evaluating the body. This evaluation is carried on the different contexts obtained by extending C with one of the layers in σ. The special events $(\!|_L$ and $|\!)_L$ express the scope of this layer activation. The rule (Tunwith) is similar to (Twith), but instead removes the layers in σ and use $\{_L$ and $\}_L$ to delimit layer hiding.

By (Tlexp) the type of a layered expression is τ, provided that each sub-expression e_i has type τ and that at least one among the layers $L_1, \ldots L_n$ occurs in C. When evaluating a layered expression one of the mentioned layers will be active in the current context so guaranteeing that layered expressions will correctly evaluate. The whole effect is the sum of sub-expressions effects H_i preceded by $Disp(L_i)$.

The expression $\mathbf{send}_\tau(e)$ has type $\mathtt{unit}$ and its effect is that of e extended with event $send_\tau$. The expression $\mathbf{receive}_\tau$ has type τ and its effect is the event $receive_\tau$. Note that the rules establish the correspondence between the type declared in the syntax and the checked type of the value sent/received. An additional check is however needed and will be carried on also taking care of the interaction protocol (Section 6).

For technical reasons, we need the following rules dealing with the auxiliary syntactic constructs.

$$(\text{Tbphi}) \frac{\langle \Gamma;C \rangle \vdash e : \tau \triangleright H}{\langle \Gamma;C \rangle \vdash \overline{\varphi}[e] : \tau \triangleright H \cdot]_\varphi} \qquad (\text{Tbwith}) \frac{\langle \Gamma;L::C \rangle \vdash e_2 : \tau \triangleright H}{\langle \Gamma;C \rangle \vdash \mathbf{with}(\overline{L})\ \mathbf{in}\ e_2 : \tau \triangleright H \cdot |\!)_L}$$

$$(\text{Tbunwith}) \frac{\langle \Gamma;C - L \rangle \vdash e_2 : \tau \triangleright H}{\langle \Gamma;C \rangle \vdash \mathbf{unwith}(\overline{L})\ \mathbf{in}\ e_2 : \tau \triangleright H \cdot \}_L}$$

Our type system enjoys the following soundness results.

$$(\text{TVar})\frac{\Gamma(x)=\tau}{\langle\Gamma;C\rangle\vdash x:\tau\triangleright\epsilon}\quad(\text{Tint})\frac{}{\langle\Gamma;C\rangle\vdash n:\text{int}\triangleright\epsilon}\quad(\text{Tunit})\frac{}{\langle\Gamma;C\rangle\vdash():\text{unit}\triangleright\epsilon}$$

$$(\text{Tly})\frac{}{\langle\Gamma;C\rangle\vdash L:ly\{L\}\triangleright\epsilon}\quad(\text{Talpha})\frac{}{\langle\Gamma;C\rangle\vdash\alpha(a):\text{unit}\triangleright\alpha(a)}$$

$$(\text{Tfun})\frac{\forall\upsilon\in\mathbb{P}.\quad\langle\Gamma,x:\tau_1,f:\tau_1\xrightarrow{\mathbb{P}|H}\tau_2;C'\rangle\vdash e:\tau_2\triangleright H\quad|C'|\subseteq\upsilon}{\langle\Gamma;C\rangle\vdash\lambda_f x\Rightarrow e:\tau_1\xrightarrow{\mathbb{P}|H}\tau_2\triangleright\epsilon}$$

$$(\text{Tlet})\frac{\langle\Gamma;C\rangle\vdash e_1:\tau_1\triangleright H\quad\langle\Gamma,x:\tau_1,C\rangle\vdash e_2:\tau_2\triangleright H'}{\langle\Gamma;C\rangle\vdash\textbf{let }x=e_1\textbf{ in }e_2:\tau_2\triangleright H\cdot H'}$$

$$(\text{Tif})\frac{\langle\Gamma;C\rangle\vdash e_0:int\triangleright H\quad\langle\Gamma;C\rangle\vdash e_1:\tau\triangleright H_1\quad\langle\Gamma;C\rangle\vdash e_2:\tau\triangleright H_2}{\langle\Gamma;C\rangle\vdash\textbf{if }e_0\textbf{ then }e_1\textbf{ else }e_2:\tau\triangleright H\cdot(H_1+H_2)}$$

$$(\text{Twith})\frac{\langle\Gamma;C\rangle\vdash e_1:ly_{\{L_1,\ldots,L_n\}}\triangleright H'\quad\forall L_i\in\{L_1,\ldots,L_n\}.\langle\Gamma;L_i::C\rangle\vdash e_2:\tau\triangleright H_i}{\langle\Gamma;C\rangle\vdash\textbf{with}(e_1)\textbf{ in }e_2:\tau\triangleright H'\cdot\sum_{L_i}(\!|L_i\cdot H_i\cdot|\!)_{L_i}}$$

$$(\text{Tunwith})\frac{\langle\Gamma;C\rangle\vdash e_1:ly_{\{L_1,\ldots,L_n\}}\triangleright H'\quad\forall L_i\in\{L_1,\ldots,L_n\}.\langle\Gamma;C-L_i\rangle\vdash e_2:\tau\triangleright H_i}{\langle\Gamma;C\rangle\vdash\textbf{unwith}(e_1)\textbf{ in }e_2:\tau\triangleright H'\cdot\sum_{L_i}\{L_i\cdot H_i\cdot\}_{L_i}}$$

$$(\text{Tlexp})\frac{\forall i.\langle\Gamma;C\rangle\vdash e_i:\tau\triangleright H_i\quad L_1\in|C|\vee\cdots\vee L_n\in|C|}{\langle\Gamma;C\rangle\vdash L_1.e_1,\ldots,L_n.e_n:\tau\triangleright\displaystyle\sum_{L_i\in\{L_1,\ldots,L_n\}}\text{Disp}(L_i)\cdot H_i}$$

$$(\text{Tapp})\frac{\langle\Gamma;C\rangle\vdash e_1:\tau_1\xrightarrow{\mathbb{P}|H}\tau_2\triangleright H_1\quad\langle\Gamma;C\rangle\vdash e_2:\tau_1\triangleright H_2\quad\exists\upsilon\in\mathbb{P}.\upsilon\subseteq|C|}{\langle\Gamma;C\rangle\vdash e_1e_2:\tau_2\triangleright H_2\cdot H_1\cdot H}$$

$$(\text{Top})\frac{\langle\Gamma;C\rangle\vdash e_1:\text{int}\triangleright H_1\quad\langle\Gamma;C\rangle\vdash e_2:\text{int}\triangleright H_2}{\langle\Gamma;C\rangle\vdash e_1\textbf{ op }e_2:\text{int}\triangleright H_1\cdot H_2}\quad(\text{Tphi})\frac{\langle\Gamma;C\rangle\vdash e:\tau\triangleright H}{\langle\Gamma;C\rangle\vdash\varphi[e]:\tau\triangleright[_\varphi\cdot H\cdot]_\varphi}$$

$$(\text{Trec})\frac{}{\langle\Gamma;C\rangle\vdash\textbf{receive}_\tau:\tau\triangleright receive_\tau}\quad(\text{Tsend})\frac{\langle\Gamma;C\rangle\vdash e:\tau\triangleright H\quad H'=H\cdot send_\tau}{\langle\Gamma;C\rangle\vdash\textbf{send}_\tau(e):\text{unit}\triangleright H'}$$

Fig. 5. Typing rules

Theorem 1 (Subject reduction). *Let e be a closed expression, if* $\langle\Gamma;C\rangle\vdash e:\tau\triangleright H$ *and* $C\vdash\eta,e\to\eta',e'$, *then* $\langle\Gamma;C\rangle\vdash e':\tau\triangleright H'$ *with* $\eta H\sqsupseteq\eta'H'$

As a corollary we get that the history expression obtained as effect of an expression *e* over-approximates the set of histories that may actually be generated during the execution of *e*.

Corollary 1 (Over-approximation). *If* $\langle\Gamma;C\rangle\vdash e:\tau\triangleright H$ *and* $C\vdash\epsilon,e\to^*\eta,e'$, *then* $\eta\in[\![H]\!]$.

We also have the following result, where $C\vdash\eta,e\nrightarrow$ means that *e* is stuck.

Theorem 2 (Progress). *Let e be a closed expression such that* $\langle\Gamma;C\rangle\vdash e:\tau\triangleright H$. *If* $C\vdash\eta,e\nrightarrow$ *and* ηH *is valid and with balanced policy framings, then e is a value.*

Subject reduction and progress prove the soundness of our type system.

Corollary 2. *If $\langle \emptyset; C \rangle \vdash e.\tau \rhd H$ and H is valid and with balanced policy framings, then $C \vdash \varepsilon, e \to^* \eta', v$.*

This corollary guarantees that a well-typed expression will eventually be reduced to a value, provided that its H is valid and that it complies with the communication protocol.

6 Model Checking

In this section we introduce a model-checking machinery for verifying whether a history expression is compliant with respect to a policy φ and a protocol P. The idea is that the environment specifies P, and only accepts a user to join that follows P during the communication.

Policy checking A policy φ will be actually a safety property [11], expressing that nothing bad will occur during a computation. Policies are expressed through standard Finite State Automata (FSA). We take a default-accept paradigm, i.e. only the unwanted behaviour is explicitly mentioned. Consequently, the language of φ is the set of *unwanted traces*, hence an accepting state is considered as offending. Let $L(\varphi)$ denote the language of φ.

We depict in the left part of Fig. 7 a simple policy φ_2 that prevents the occurrence of two consecutive actions α on the resource r at the beginning of the computation.

We now define the meaning of $\eta \models \varphi$, completing the definition of validity presented in Section 4.

Definition 4 (Policy compliance). *Let η be a history without framing events, then $\eta \models \varphi$ iff $\eta \notin L(\varphi)$.*

The semantics of a history expression may contain histories with redundant framings, i.e. nesting of the same policy framing. For instance, $\mu h. (\varphi[\alpha(r)h] + \varepsilon)$ generates $[_\varphi \alpha(r)[_\varphi \alpha(r)]]$. Formally, a history η has *redundant framing* whenever the active policies $ap(\eta')$ contain a duplicate φ for some prefix η' of η.

Redundant framing can be eliminated without affecting validity of a history [7]. This is because the expressions monitored by the inner-framings are already under the scope of the outermost one and the definition of validity in Section 4 uses $\eta^{-\sqcup}$. Actually, given H there is a *regularisation* algorithm returning his regularized version $H \downarrow$ such that *(i)* each history in $[\![H \downarrow]\!]$ has no redundant framing, *(ii)* $H \downarrow$ is valid if and only if H

$$\dfrac{\dfrac{\langle \Gamma, x : \tau, f : \tau \xrightarrow{\{|C'|\}} \tau; C' \rangle \vdash 0 : \tau \quad L_1 \in C'}{\langle \Gamma, x : \tau, f : \tau \xrightarrow{\{|C'|\}} \tau; C' \rangle \vdash L_1.0 : \tau}}{\langle \Gamma; C \rangle \vdash \lambda_f \, x \Rightarrow L_1.0 : \tau \xrightarrow{\{|C'|\}} \tau} \qquad \dfrac{\dfrac{\langle \Gamma, g : \tau \xrightarrow{\{|C'|\}} \tau; C \rangle \vdash g : \tau \to \tau}{\langle \Gamma, g : \tau \xrightarrow{\{|C'|\}} \tau; C \rangle \vdash 3 : \tau \quad |C'| \subseteq |C|}}{\langle \Gamma, g : \tau \xrightarrow{\{|C'|\}} \tau; C \rangle \vdash g3 : \tau}$$

$$\langle \Gamma; C \rangle \vdash \mathbf{let} \, g = \lambda_f \, x \Rightarrow L_1.0 \, \mathbf{in} \, g\,3 : \tau$$

Fig. 6. Derivation of a function with precondition. We assume that $C' = [L_1]$, L_1 is active in C, LayerNames $= \{L_1\}$ and, for typesetting convenience, we also denote $\tau = int$ and we ignore effects.

is valid [7]. Hence, checking validity of a history expression H can be reduced to the problem of checking validity of a history expression $H\downarrow$ without redundant framings.

Our approach fits into the standard *automata based* model checking [12]. Indeed, there is an efficient and fully automata based method for checking the $\models$ relation for a regularized history expression H.

Let $\{\phi_i\}$ be the set of all policies ϕ_i occurring in H. From each ϕ_i it is possible to obtain a *framed automata* $\phi_i^{[]}$ such that η is valid iff $\eta \notin L(\bigcup \phi_i^{[]})$. The detailed construction of framed automata is in [7]. Roughly the framed automaton for the policy ϕ has two copies of ϕ. The first copy has no offending states, the second has the same offending states of ϕ. Intuitively, one uses the first copy when the actions are made while the policy is not active. The second copy is reached when the policy is activated by a framing event. Indeed, there are edges labelled with $[_\phi$ from the first copy to the second and $]_\phi$ in the opposite direction. So when a framing gets activated we can also reach an offending state. Fig. 7 shows the framed automaton used to model check the policy ϕ_2.

Validating a regularized history expression H amounts to verifying $[\![H]\!] \cap \bigcup L(\phi_i^{[]})$ is empty. Using the fact that for any history expression H there exists a pushdown automaton $B(H)$ (see [8]) that recognizes the semantics of H, we can state the following:

Theorem 3 (Model checking policies). *A given history expression H is valid if and only if $L(B(H\downarrow)) \cap \bigcup L(\phi_i^{[]}) = \emptyset$.*

Since regular languages are closed by union, context-free languages are closed by intersection with a regular language and the emptiness of context-free languages is decidable [13] the above is decidable.

Protocol compliance We are now ready to check whether a program will well-behave when interacting with other parties through the bus. We take a protocol P to be sequence S of $send_\tau$ and $receive_\tau$ actions designating the coordination interactions, possibly repeated (in symbols S^*), as defined below:

$$P ::= S \mid S^* \qquad\qquad S ::= \varepsilon \mid send_\tau.S \mid receive_\tau.S$$

A protocol P specifies the regular set of allowed interaction histories. We require a program to interact with the bus following the protocol, but we do not force the program to do the whole interaction specified. For this motivation the language $L(P)$ of P is a prefix

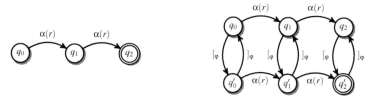

Fig. 7. On the left: a policy ϕ_2 expressing that two consecutive actions α on r at the beginning of the computation are forbidden. On the right: the framed automaton obtained from ϕ_2.

closed set of histories, obtained by considering all the prefixes of the sequences defined by P. Then we only require that all the histories generated by a program (projected so that only $send_\tau$ and $receive_\tau$ appear) belong to $L(P)$.

Let H^{sr} be a projected history expression where all non $send_\tau, receive_\tau$ events have been removed. Then we define compliance to be:

Definition 5 (Protocol compliance). *Let e be an expression such that $\langle \Gamma, C \rangle \vdash e : \tau \triangleright H$, then e is compliant with P if $[\![H^{sr}]\!] \subseteq L(P)$.*

This theorem provides us with a decidable model checking procedure to establish protocol compliance. In its statement we write $\overline{L(P)}$ for the complement of $L(P)$. Note that the types annotating $send_\tau/receive_\tau$ can be kept finite in both $L(P)$ and $\overline{L(P)}$, because we only take the types occurring in the effect H under checking.

Theorem 4 (Model checking protocols). *Let e be an expression such that $\langle \Gamma, C \rangle \vdash e : \tau \triangleright H$, then e is compliant with P iff*

$$L(B(H^{sr})) \cap L(P) \neq \emptyset \wedge L(B(H^{sr})) \cap \overline{L(P)} = \emptyset$$

We remark that, in our model, protocol compliance cannot be expressed only through security policies introduced above. As a matter of fact, $L(B(H^{sr})) \cap \overline{L(P)} = \emptyset$ expresses that H has no forbidden communication patterns, and this is a requirement much similar to a default-accept policy. However $L(B(H^{sr})) \cap L(P) \neq \emptyset$ requires that some communication pattern in compliance with P *must* be done. This highlights the different nature of security policies and protocols in our framework.

7 Conclusions

This paper is an initial step in defining language-based methods for the development of complex adaptive systems. We introduce static techniques for ensuring that a component developed in ContextML language (i) adequately reacts to context changes, (ii) securely manipulates its resources and (iii) correctly interacts with other parties.

This work crosses the boundaries of several research fields. Space limitation prevents us to make a comprehensive discussion of related works. Therefore we only point the reader to some papers — we apologise for our omissions. On the foundational aspects of COP, we only cite to [14,15,6], [16,4] that focus on implementation issues, while [5] is on the methodological side. The ContextML primitives for resources usage control are borrowed from [17,7]. Here we additionally deal with layer activation and dispatching, and with a restricted form of communication. Indeed, our communication model can be read as a minimal coordination paradigm, as it only requires the knowledge of the flow of the exchanged messages and their types. Other work in the literature presents richer coordination models; among others, see [18,19].

Our types are a simple form of dependent types, while effects and protocols may be seen as a form of *behavioural types* [20].

We plan to extend the present work by dealing with a more powerful coordination model including concurrency, distribution and asynchrony. It would be also interesting to investigate the relationships between our notion of protocol and *session types* [21].

Acknowledgments. We would like to thank the anonymous referees for their comments that pointed us inaccuracies and guided us to improve the quality of our paper.

References

1. Cheng, B.H.C., et al.: Software Engineering for Self-Adaptive Systems: A Research Roadmap. In: Cheng, B.H.C., de Lemos, R., Giese, H., Inverardi, P., Magee, J. (eds.) Software Engineering for Self-Adaptive Systems. LNCS, vol. 5525, pp. 1–26. Springer, Heidelberg (2009)
2. Bruni, R., Corradini, A., Gadducci, F., Lluch Lafuente, A., Vandin, A.: A Conceptual Framework for Adaptation. In: de Lara, J., Zisman, A. (eds.) FASE 2010. LNCS, vol. 7212, pp. 240–254. Springer, Heidelberg (2012)
3. Salehie, M., Tahvildari, L.: Self-adaptive software: Landscape and research challenges. TAAS 4(2) (2009)
4. Hirschfeld, R., Costanza, P., Nierstrasz, O.: Context-oriented programming. Journal of Object Technology 7(3), 125–151 (2008)
5. Salvaneschi, G., Ghezzi, C., Pradella, M.: Context-oriented programming: A programming paradigm for autonomic systems. CoRR abs/1105.0069 (2011)
6. Degano, P., Ferrari, G.L., Galletta, L., Mezzetti, G.: Typing context-dependent behavioural variations. In: PLACES 2012. EPTCS (to appear, 2012)
7. Bartoletti, M., Degano, P., Ferrari, G.L., Zunino, R.: Local policies for resource usage analysis. ACM Trans. Program. Lang. Syst. 31(6) (2009)
8. Bartoletti, M., Degano, P., Ferrari, G.L.: Planning and verifying service composition. Journal of Computer Security 17(5), 799–837 (2009)
9. Sangiorgi, D., Walker, D.: The Pi-Calculus - a theory of mobile processes. Cambridge University Press (2001)
10. Skalka, C., Smith, S., Horn, D.V.: Types and trace effects of higher order programs. Journal of Functional Programming 18(2), 179–249 (2008)
11. Hamlen, K.W., Morrisett, J.G., Schneider, F.B.: Computability classes for enforcement mechanisms. ACM Trans. on Programming Languages and Systems 28(1), 175–205 (2006)
12. Vardi, M.Y., Wolper, P.: An automata-theoretic approach to automatic program verification (preliminary report). In: LICS, pp. 332–344. IEEE Computer Society (1986)
13. Hopcroft, J., Motwani, R., Ullman, J.: Introduction to automata theory, languages, and computation, vol. 2. Addison-wesley, Reading (1979)
14. Clarke, D., Sergey, I.: A semantics for context-oriented programming with layers. In: International Workshop on Context-Oriented Programming, COP 2009, pp. 10:1–10:6. ACM, New York (2009)
15. Hirschfeld, R., Igarashi, A., Masuhara, H.: Context FJ: a minimal core calculus for context-oriented programming. In: Proceedings of the 10th International Workshop on Foundations of Aspect-Oriented Languages, pp. 19–23. ACM (2011)
16. Costanza, P.: Language constructs for context-oriented programming. In: Proceedings of the Dynamic Languages Symposium, pp. 1–10. ACM Press (2005)
17. Igarashi, A., Kobayashi, N.: Resource usage analysis. In: POPL, pp. 331–342 (2002)
18. Proença, J., Clarke, D., de Vink, E.P., Arbab, F.: Decoupled execution of synchronous coordination models via behavioural automata. In: Mousavi, M.R., Ravara, A. (eds.) FOCLASA. EPTCS, vol. 58, pp. 65–79 (2011)
19. Bonsangue, M., Clarke, D., Silva, A.: Automata for Context-Dependent Connectors. In: Field, J., Vasconcelos, V.T. (eds.) COORDINATION 2009. LNCS, vol. 5521, pp. 184–203. Springer, Heidelberg (2009)
20. Nielson, H.R., Nielson, F.: Higher-order concurrent programs with finite communication topology (extended abstract). In: Proceedings of the 21st ACM SIGPLAN-SIGACT Symposium on Principles of Programming Languages, POPL 1994, pp. 84–97. ACM, New York (1994)
21. Honda, K., Vasconcelos, V.T., Kubo, M.: Language Primitives and Type Discipline for Structured Communication-Based Programming. In: Hankin, C. (ed.) ESOP 1998. LNCS, vol. 1381, pp. 122–138. Springer, Heidelberg (1998)

Author Index